Working in Canada

A Sociological Exploration

Tracey Adams

OXFORD
UNIVERSITY PRESS

OXFORD
UNIVERSITY PRESS

Oxford University Press is a department of the University of Oxford.
It furthers the University's objective of excellence in research, scholarship,
and education by publishing worldwide. Oxford is a registered trade mark of
Oxford University Press in the UK and in certain other countries.

Published in Canada by
Oxford University Press
8 Sampson Mews, Suite 204,
Don Mills, Ontario M3C 0H5 Canada

www.oupcanada.com

Library and Archives Canada Cataloguing in Publication

Title: Working in Canada : a sociological exploration / Tracey Adams.
Names: Adams, Tracey Lynn, 1966- author.
Description: Includes bibliographical references and index.
Identifiers: Canadiana (print) 20210191821 | Canadiana (ebook) 20210191953 | ISBN 9780199037919
(spiral bound) | ISBN 9780199037872 (softcover) | ISBN 9780199037902 (EPUB)

Subjects: LCSH: Work—Social aspects—Canada.
Classification: LCC HD6957.C3 A33 2021 | DDC 306.3/60971—dc23

Cover image: Sherill Chapman

Cover design: Sherill Chapman

Interior design: Laurie McGregor

Oxford University Press is committed to our environment.
Wherever possible, our books are printed on paper which comes from responsible sources.

Paperback printed by Marquis, Canada

FSC www.fsc.org MIX Paper from responsible sources FSC® C103567

Table of Contents

Preface

Work dominates our days and shapes our lives. Between school work, housework, and paid work, many of us spend long hours each day working. Even when we are not *technically* working, we may be working—working out, updating our social media, honing our gaming skills, pursuing a hobby. We work, in part, because we have to do so—work activities are essential to our daily survival—but also, quite often, because we want to. Either way, we may not think too much about our work. This book takes an in-depth look at work through a sociological lens. Since we spend so much of our days, years, and lives working, some critical reflection is warranted.

Our personal experiences of work and working are interconnected with others' experiences. Those of us who work in Canada have common experiences shaped by legislative frameworks, our capitalist economy, and shared norms and practices. As a discipline, sociology helps us to see these commonalities and makes us aware of patterns that can provide new insights into our experiences. Still, our experiences differ too. What province we are based in, whether we live (and work) in rural or urban areas, and our personal characteristics—our gender identity, race and ethnicity, sexual orientation, disability status, and social class, among others—shape our experiences profoundly. Our experiences of working are impacted by structured social inequalities that can determine our opportunities and outcomes. This book is different from most other textbooks in the field because it homes in on these differences and explores how multiple dimensions of inequality (like race, gender, and class) intersect to shape our experiences.

Through this approach, hopefully, you as readers will see yourselves on the page and begin to think about how sociological theory and research connect to your experiences of working in Canada (or elsewhere). The opening sections of the book provide an overview of key theories and concepts, as well as historical and current trends in work. These chapters provide background information that helps us to understand the nature and organization of work in Canada. Then we look at different types of work in detail. The remaining chapters look at work thematically, touching on key issues of interest to Canadian workers, like health and well-being, skills, discrimination, and harassment, to name only a few. Throughout, the book examines how multiple dimensions of social inequality intersect to structure experiences and opportunities at work. The sociological literature is richer in some areas (gender and racial inequalities) than in others (Indigenous, transgender inequalities at work), but the book builds on existing research to enhance understanding of inequalities at work to the extent possible. Some of this book was written under quarantine during the COVID-19 pandemic of 2020. Hence, the book also incorporates existing data and research on the pandemic's impact on work; however, that literature was limited at the time of writing.

Many people assisted in the preparation of this book, and I would like to take this opportunity to thank them. First, I'd like to thank the team at Oxford University Press. Ian Nussbaum as acquisitions editor provided early encouragement and ensured the project would move forward. Brian Witzel was also very supportive of the project. Editor Emily Kring was a wonderful help guiding the project early on, and Mariah Fleetham saw the book (and me) through the writing and publication process. Thanks are also extended to Patricia Berube, project manager; Dorothy Turnbull, copyeditor, and the many others at Oxford University Press who saw the manuscript through the production process.

I also owe a big thanks to research assistant Awish Aslam, who helped me to locate recent literature on work and employment and assisted with the references. Moreover, I would like to thank the many reviewers who took time to review (in some cases multiple) early drafts of the book chapters and provided excellent advice for revision. Any errors and omission are my own responsibility.

Finally, I want to thank my husband for his patience, support, and encouragement every step of the way and my children for their continuing support of my work.

PART I

Introduction to the Sociology of Work

1 Introduction

Learning Objectives

After reading this chapter, readers will:

- Understand the complexities surrounding defining work.
- Understand the impact of work on people in Canadian society.
- Be able to describe key areas of interest in the sociology of work.

Introduction

Think back to work you have done, whether that means a job you have now or held previously, some volunteer experience you have had, or even a project you worked on. What, if anything, made that work *meaningful* for you? Was there some service you provided or something you made that had meaning for you and/or others? What stands out as being particularly important to you about that work, if anything? Perhaps the relationships you formed or skills you learned? Did having a job make you feel special in any way?

Now, thinking about that same job or work, was there anything about it you particularly *liked*? The actual activities you completed? Or the relationships with your coworkers, clients, or supervisors? The paycheque? An opportunity to be creative and/or learn something new? Was there anything you *did not* like about your job? These could include aspects mentioned above (pay, colleagues, bosses, nature of the work) or something else. Was the work pace reasonable? Did doing the work ever make you feel unsafe? Did you feel as though there was always someone looking over your shoulder, monitoring what you did? Were you treated fairly?

Through this thought-exercise, we can start to think about how the content and organization of work affect our experiences of it. When sociologists study work, we focus on many of these issues: the organization of work, the content of work, skills and knowledge related to work, health, safety and well-being, pay and related inequalities. Sociologists also look at the meanings workers attach to their work. In this respect, we can consider whether there are intrinsic or extrinsic rewards associated with work. **Intrinsic rewards** are found in the characteristics of work that make it rewarding or meaningful:

intrinsic rewards Characteristics inherent in a job that make it rewarding or meaningful for example, a chance to exercise your skills, forge relationships, or help others. **Extrinsic rewards** might make a job seem worthwhile, even if we do not like what we are doing—like a good income, extended health benefits, or prestige.

extrinsic rewards Benefits that accompany a job (like income, status) that make it rewarding

Most of us will spend large portions of our lives working. Work structures our days and shapes our lives. It provides us with income and affects our social relationships; it influences our well-being and health. Because working can impact so many different aspects of our lives, we may have high hopes when looking for full-time work. We hope to find work that has many positives—work that is both intrinsically and extrinsically rewarding—and few negatives. Finding those jobs seems to be harder than ever. There are more skilled and educated workers seeking good jobs than there are good jobs available. By **good jobs** sociologists typically mean work that pays well, provides benefits, offers job security and reasonable and stable working hours, and potentially offers opportunities for promotion (Glenday, 1997). In contrast, **bad jobs** are those that are low-paying, **precarious**, and/or have unpredictable or undesirable working hours. Among other characteristics, precarious jobs offer no guarantee of continued employment.

good jobs Employment that pays well, provides benefits, job security, and reasonable and stable working hours, and potentially offers opportunities for promotion

bad jobs Those that pay little, provide few benefits, are precarious, and/or have unpredictable or undesirable working hours

precarious There is no guarantee that employment will continue, and wages may be uneven and discontinuous

This book provides an overview of sociological research, theory, and documented trends respecting work and working in Canada. While workers have much in common across national boundaries, historical developments, laws, policies, and cultures vary cross-nationally such that national context significantly shapes lived experiences. Although this book explores work within the Canadian context, it is important to highlight international similarities and differences and acknowledge global influences on work in Canada. The focus is on both workers' experiences of working and the work structures they navigate. Although the book provides a general overview of research and trends, it is organized thematically to provide an in-depth exploration of key issues and challenges relevant to workers in the Canadian labour market. Importantly, the book proceeds from the understanding that while many of us will share experiences of work, those experiences also vary, not only by the kind of work we do and where we do it but by structural social inequalities such as gender, race/ethnicity, class, age, Indigeneity, sexual orientation, and immigration status.

To begin, this chapter lays the conceptual groundwork—defining work, discussing why the sociological study of work is important, and outlining the book's subject matter. Then it describes where we go from here.

Source: © Louis.Roth/Shutterstock

Pay can be a major factor that sociologists use to distinguish "good" jobs from "bad" jobs, fuelling the campaign for a $15/hour federal minimum wage. As you read this text, consider what other factors can be used to assess experiences of work and the factors contributing to workplace change in Canada.

Defining Work

"Work" is a term we use often to describe what we do, but we seldom define it. Most of us would use the term to describe our paid job, but sometimes we also use it to describe other activities—we might talk, for instance, about doing "schoolwork" or "housework." Moreover, there are some activities that we might not be really clear on whether they count as work or not. When you shop for groceries or cook dinner, is that work? When you write a blog or record and upload something on YouTube, are you working? How about when you look after your younger siblings, cousins, or neighbours—does that count?

work
"Human effort adding use value to goods and services" (Tilly & Tilly, 1998, p. 22)

The dictionary defines **work** as "action or activity involving physical or mental effort" that is "undertaken in order to achieve a result" (*Oxford English Dictionary*, 2020e). This is a very broad definition—indeed it is too broad for sociologists, since it seems to include almost any purposeful activity. Tilly and Tilly (1998, p. 22) define work as "human effort adding use value to goods and services." The idea of "use value" stems from early political economists, including Karl Marx, who distinguished between the "use value" and "exchange value" of goods and services. A use value satisfies a human need or want (Marx, 1967; Tilly & Tilly, 1998). Exchange value, by contrast, refers to value in the marketplace. Thus, for sociologists, work is not simply effort directed towards achieving something but rather achieving or accomplishing something *useful*. This definition encompasses paid work providing goods and services as well as unpaid work that produces or achieves useful things (including preparing meals, babysitting, writing essays, creating content for posting online, and so on).

labour
Paid work done under the direction of a boss or supervisor

Some distinguish between work and labour. Although dictionary definitions of the two are virtually identical, a distinction can be made between **labour**—paid work done under the direction of a boss or supervisor—and "work," which can encompass paid and unpaid work and includes that which you direct and determine yourself. For economists and many policy-makers, only "labour" counts as "real work" deserving of recognition and remuneration. Sociologists generally adopt the broader definition of work. Nevertheless, most sociological research also focuses on paid work because of its implications for income, life chances, class, status, and other dimensions of social inequality. Since this textbook provides an overview of existing research on work, it too emphasizes paid work. Still, it is important to remember that unpaid activities that contribute value are a form of work and that these activities too have implications for not only social inequality but for paid work as well. Indeed, as we will see later on, the lines between paid work and unpaid work, and between work and leisure, appear to be blurring.

The Importance of Work and Working

productive leisure
Engaging in hobbies that involve work (whether paid or unpaid)

When work is defined in this broad sense, as human effort generating useful products and services, it should be evident that most adults spend most of our days—most of our lives—working. When we are not engaged in paid labour, we are doing housework, schoolwork, yard-work, volunteer work, childcare work, or even what some call **productive leisure**—that screenplay or game or quilt or website you work on in your spare time. We structure our days around work so that even when we are not working, we are influenced by our work commitments. We watch something on television or online, or we game, work out, or spend time on social media in part so that we can decompress after work, and re-energize ourselves to work again. Our eating and sleeping schedule is also often shaped around our work schedule. We may spend some of our time commuting to and from work. In this manner, a lot of our time is spent working, thinking about work, going to or returning from work, and even engaging in leisure as a deliberate strategy to avoid thinking about work. The impact of work on our lives is substantial.

Work affects us in other ways as well. Work provides us with an income that allows us to support ourselves (we hope) and sometimes to support others. The kind of job we do and how well that job is rewarded might determine where we live, how well we live, what we buy, and what we eat and wear. Our life chances and opportunities, our social class, and our economic stability are largely determined through our work.

Our health and well-being are also impacted by our work. Some work is dangerous, exposing us to risks of physical harm. Jobs may be physically demanding, leading to fatigue, strains, and injuries; even sedentary work is associated with strains and health problems. Work can expose us to viruses and other disease, as the COVID-19 pandemic illustrated so devastatingly. Work is often stressful, straining our mental health. In this manner, our work can shape our physical and mental well-being.

Work affects our social relationships. Some of us have jobs in which we meet and interact with many people. We may form friendships with our coworkers and socialize with them outside of work. What we do might also influence the nature and tone of our social interactions, since people make judgments about us based on what we do. It is not unusual for adults to ask one another what they do for a living upon meeting someone new. New acquaintances may even try to infer what kind of person we are based on the kind of work that we do, and this could influence how they interact with us.

Work can be a source of **prestige** and/or **stigma**. Prestigious work is socially valued and hence confers **social rewards**, such as recognition, appreciation, praise, or being held in high regard. Social rewards may result in economic rewards—for instance, we might get a raise if our work is highly appreciated. Sometimes, however, social rewards might substitute for economic rewards: for instance, we may simply get a pat on the back for a job well done, or workers might actually take a pay cut in order to work at a prestigious firm or in a high-status job. In contrast, some jobs are socially discredited and regarded as either unimportant or quite often important but undesirable in some way (for example, people who clean up after others). Stigmas attached to work can be widely held or operate within local communities or family groups. The lone automotive mechanic in a family of medical doctors, for example, might experience stigma within their family, even though they possess important skills. Working hard at a job that those close to us deem unimportant, or which leads some in society to look down on us, can have a negative effect on our well-being.

Work is often an important component of **identity**—who we think we are, or how others perceive us. Some of us define who we are through what we do. Identity can be wrapped up with work rewards. If work is prestigious and brings economic rewards and we find it personally meaningful, we are more likely to derive a positive sense of self from doing it. If extrinsic and intrinsic rewards are fewer, we may be more likely to locate our identity outside of our paid work. Even in these instances, however, our identity might be tied with other work-related activities—child-rearing, schooling, volunteering, or a side job that is meaningful to us. Studies suggest that work can also shape our **attitudes** and

prestige
Respect or admiration. Linked with status

stigma
An attribute that at least some members of society associate with disgrace or dishonour

social rewards
Recognition, appreciation, praise (as opposed to economic rewards like money)

identity
Who we think we are and how we believe others perceive us

attitudes
The ways we think or feel about people, places, and things

outlook—the ways we think or feel about people, places, and things. That is, people in different occupations and those at different levels of organizational hierarchies express different attitudes concerning material success and achievements, politics, and social rights (Lamont, 1992; Livingstone, 2019a). For example, employees are more likely than managers and owners to express attitudes favourable towards workers' rights (Livingstone, 2019a). The significance of work for us as human beings is immense, making it an excellent topic for sociological investigation.

The Sociology of Work

social action
Behaviour to which an actor attaches meaning that takes into account (and/or is directed towards) the behaviour of others (Weber, 1968)

As you may know, sociology is the study of human society. To understand society, sociologists pay particular attention to **social action** (activity that is oriented towards others and/or takes others into account), social interaction, social institutions, and social inequalities. Work is an important area of sociological investigation because it is a core activity within society that contributes to societal functioning and well-being. Work contributes goods and services people need to live. Work is also a common form of social action—as noted, we spend much of our time working, and our work activity routinely takes others into account. Work often brings social interaction. Work is intimately bound up with social inequalities. Furthermore, it takes place within social institutions, and even when it occurs outside institutional contexts, it is shaped by them. For example, self-employed web designers working from home must still contend with the organizations that contract them to do a job, and their work is likely shaped by other organizations within their industry, the companies that produce the software they work with, the future users of their sites, and the financial institutions providing capital to support their work, among others. Thus, work is an important social activity with many implications for society. As such, it is an important area of sociological investigation.

When sociologists study work, we are strongly interested in all of these areas and others. Among the core areas of research are the following:

primary sector
The primary sector of the economy is concerned with the extraction and use of raw materials and natural resources (including agriculture, forestry, fishing)

secondary sector
The secondary sector of the economy entails the production and processing of goods as well as construction

1) *The organization and content of work*: Sociologists examine what people do at work, how work is organized and managed, and how social institutions structure work. Sector of employment is also of interest: How does work in the **primary** (agriculture, forestry, fishing), **secondary** (manufacturing, utilities), and **tertiary** (services) sectors differ? Does work based in the **private** (for-profit) **sector** differ from that in the **public** or **non-profit** sectors? The inter-relationship between different kinds of work (paid work and family work done in the home, for example) is also an area of interest.
2) *Workers' experiences*: We are also interested in how people feel about their work, the meanings they attach to it, and whether work is fulfilling or not. The implications of work for health and well-being, identity and attitudes, and social interactions at work are also areas of key concern.
3) *Opportunities and barriers*: Sociologists study the rewards (or lack of rewards) generated from work, including income, employment and promotion

opportunities, prestige, and autonomy. People's opportunities for obtaining jobs, as well as discrimination and bias that might limit opportunities, are common areas of research within the sociology of work.

4) *Social inequalities within and outside the workplace*: Linked with all of the above, we are interested in examining how work opportunities, income, and other rewards (health benefits, well-being, prestige) are distributed and how these inequalities may be patterned across various structural dimensions, including class, race, gender identity, sexual orientation, and/or disability status.
5) *Trends in work and working*: Sociologists also study social change in all of the above respects. The structure of work, and opportunities and inequalities surrounding work, change over time. People are the primary drivers of change: owners and managers seek to reorganize work to make the work process more efficient, and workers fight for better working conditions or wages. State actors alter laws regulating work. Economic, environmental, and technological changes, globalization, and many other trends also affect experiences of working. Sociologists not only map trends in work, but they document how these changes are brought about through human agency and what impact these changes have on workers.

This list is not exhaustive, but it does capture the majority of research in the field.

tertiary sector
The services or tertiary sector of the economy encompasses the provision of services

private sector
The part of the economy that is under private ownership

public sector
The part of the economy that is under government ownership or is funded by governments (such as public education, public health care)

non-profit sector
This sector includes organizations that are not profit-focused (charities, social services, community organizations)

Issues at Work

1.1 | Work-Life Balance

People spend large portions of their days and weeks working, but most workers hope to achieve some measure of **work-life balance**. That is, we hope to balance our work time with time for leisure, friends, and family. Having this balance contributes to our health and well-being. The International Labour Organization (Boulin et al., 2006, pp. v-vi) has argued that the dimensions of "decent working time" include the following: work time expectations should be healthy, family-friendly; they should support gender equity, facilitate worker choice, and advance productivity. Currently, many workplaces do not allow their workers "decent" working time in this sense. However, challenges vary across workplace, field, and type of work (Zeytinoglu & Cooke, 2006; Messenger, 2004). Some workers have overly rigid working hours with no flexibility: Workers in a variety of fields may be expected to clock in and clock out at fixed times, with little allowance for exceptions. Others may have overly flexible hours—for instance, the part-time retail workers who may be given few guaranteed hours but are expected to be on stand-by—ready to come to work at a moment's notice. For some, overtime is considered standard, if often unpaid. In short, work hours are unevenly distributed, with some workers having too much work and others less work than is optimal. Both have significant implications for health, well-being, and economic stability. Still, it is not only the total *amount* of work that has implications for workers' lives but precisely *which* hours people are asked to work. Working evenings and weekends if one's family and friends work more standard hours can bring additional stress and less time for relationships and leisure time. Those with children may also struggle to find daycare.

work-life balance
A healthy balance between our work commitments and other aspects of our lives

Work in Canada

This book explores the organization and experience of work in Canada by reviewing research and available data. The rest of this book is organized into two main sections. The next section, *Foundations of Work*, outlines key background information for understanding the current nature of work in Canada and provides an overview of the labour market, occupations, and various kinds of work. Chapter 2 reviews theoretical perspectives to help us understand the ways in which work is structured and experienced. Because knowing about the past helps us to understand the present, Chapter 3 discusses historical trends in work. Chapter 4 provides an overview of the contexts surrounding work, first through a discussion of the Canadian labour market and second through a look at the organizational structures in which work typically occurs. Chapters 5 and 6 round out this section by taking a closer look at different kinds of work, focusing on the content of work and workers' experiences of it. Chapter 5 explores common occupations, while Chapter 6 broadens the focus by looking at unpaid work (domestic labour, volunteering), non-standard and discredited work (including illegal activity), and productive leisure.

The final section, *Dimensions of Work*, examines work thematically, focusing on several issues that sociological research has highlighted as being important. Chapter 7 looks at education, skill, and expertise at work, exploring changes in these areas over time and the controversies that have surrounded them. Chapter 8 explores health at work, taking into consideration both aspects that encourage job satisfaction and well-being and those that foster stress and may lead to injury, illness, or death. Chapter 8 also touches on workers' strategies to resist unpleasant work. Chapter 9 addresses the structure of work and resulting social inequalities through a look at the causes and consequences of **occupational segregation**—the uneven distribution of people across jobs based on race, gender, and other characteristics. Chapter 10 looks at inequalities at work further by reviewing the literature on discrimination and harassment in the workplace, highlighting dimensions, causes, and consequences. Chapter 11 takes an intersectional life course approach to explore how class, gender, race, and age intersect to shape young workers' transition to employment, work-family conflict, and older workers' transition to retirement. Finally, Chapter 12 considers the future of work through an examination of the impact of technology on work, especially artificial intelligence, gig work, and telework.

occupational segregation
This occurs when people who differ by some marker (gender, race, disability status, sexual orientation) work in different occupations

A few common themes appear across all chapters. First, the book aims to provide both an overview of research on the sociology of work and opportunities for in-depth exploration of several prevalent themes, including health and well-being, expertise and knowledge, discrimination and harassment. Second, the book combines research using a variety of methodologies and provides an overview of the social structures shaping work as well as a consideration of how workers experience that structure. Third, the book links the organization and structure of work to broader social inequalities by gender, class, and race and, where possible, other dimensions, including gender identity and expression, sexual orientation, age, Indigeneity, citizenship, disability, and so on. These dimensions of inequality are produced, reproduced, and restructured on the job. By exploring these connections and considering the ways in which different dimensions of inequality intersect, we can obtain a clearer picture of the organization and experience of work. Finally, the book encourages readers to reflect on how sociological research on work is relevant to them as workers navigating labour markets in Canadian society.

Reviewing the Learning Objectives

After reading this chapter, you should:

- Understand the complexities surrounding defining work
- Understand the impact of work on people in Canada.
- Be able to describe key areas of interest in the sociology of work.

Questions for Critical Thought

1. Given the centrality of work for people's lives, think about the implications of not working. What impact would you expect unemployment to have?
2. In light of sociologists' broad definition of work, think about how many hours a day or week you spend working. How many hours do you engage in paid work? What about unpaid work such as schoolwork, cooking, or cleaning?
3. What aspects of work are core to your identity, health, relationships? Why are some types of work more meaningful than others?

Annotated Additional Readings

Bonstead-Bruns, M. (2007). Work, sociology of. In G. Ritzer (Ed.), *The Blackwell encyclopedia of sociology*. doi:10.1002/9781405165518.wbeosw025.

This entry provides an introduction to the sociology of work. The encyclopedia has several other related entries as well.

Pupo, N., Duffy, A., & Glenday, D. (2017). *Crises in Canadian work*. Toronto, ON: Oxford University Press.

This book provides an overview of challenges and crises related to work in Canada using a critical sociology and feminist political economy lens.

Tilly, C., & Tilly, C. (1998). *Work under capitalism*. Boulder, CO: Westview Press.

This book reviews the nature of work using a Marxist lens.

Related Websites

Canadian Mental Health Association (CMHA), resources and information on mental health at work:

https://cmha.ca/resources/mental-illness-in-the-workplace

Victoria State, Australia's website on worker health and wellbeing:

https://www.betterhealth.vic.gov.au/health/healthyliving/work-and-your-health

Government of Canada job bank. Search for information on occupations and jobs in Canada:

https://www.jobbank.gc.ca/trend-analysis/search-job-outlooks

Government of Canada website with information on job opportunities in government and private companies:

https://www.canada.ca/en/services/jobs/opportunities.html

2 Theoretical Perspectives on Work

Learning Objectives

After reading this chapter, readers will:

- Understand that there are many different sociological theories that provide explanations for the organization and experience of work.
- Have a sense of the key arguments and important concepts advanced in different sociological theories.
- Understand that work has been tied to broader social trends and social inequalities.

Introduction

sociological theories Systematic explanations of the social world and people's experiences of their social environments

Sociological theories provide systematic explanations of the social world and people's experiences of their environments. Theorists differ on what aspects of social experience are deemed most important and meaningful and how social experience is understood. Sociological theory provides a lens (or multiple lenses) through which we can re-examine our experiences, often revealing new dimensions and considerations that were not initially apparent to us. It can also allow us to make clearer connections between experiences or enable us to see that our individual experiences of working may be part of broader patterns and trends. This chapter reviews a variety of sociological theories, focusing on aspects most relevant to work and working. In doing so, it provides an important foundation not only for the remaining chapters in this book but also for our understanding of working in Canada generally.

We begin with classical theorists like Marx and Weber, follow up with 20th-century theorists like Bourdieu and Foucault and major approaches, including symbolic interactionism, feminist theory, and critical race theory, before finishing with intersectionality theory.

Marx and Neo-Marxian Theories

Karl Marx (1864–1920) was a 19th-century, Prussian-born philosopher whose accounts of the social world, especially under capitalism, have been highly influential within sociology. Best known popularly as a supporter of communism, Marx advanced sophisticated theories of social life and social change and critiques of the status quo that have influenced generations of scholars. Within the sociology of work, it is Marx's account of the distinct nature of work under capitalism that has been particularly influential. Marx's contributions built upon, and contested, popular accounts of the economy and social change prevalent during his lifetime. The power of his ideas and writing has given his work a lasting influence.

Marx and those influenced by his ideas (many of whom can be labelled neo-Marxists—a term used to describe people whose theories are strongly influenced by Marx's ideas but are nonetheless distinct) argue that work under capitalism, as a **mode of production** (or method of producing life necessities), is different from work under other production systems (for instance, feudalism). It is more closely managed and more focused on productivity and profit. Some of Marx's predecessors and contemporaries held that a free-market capitalist economy brought many benefits. For example, Adam Smith (2000) documented the advantages of capital accumulation and explained how capitalism provided new opportunities for skill enhancement and societal benefit through advanced divisions of labour. Marx acknowledged productivity gains but critiqued this optimistic picture, arguing that rather than "freeing" workers, capitalism reproduced inequalities by compelling the disadvantaged to work under unfavourable conditions to generate profit for capitalists. Workers' freedom was a compromised freedom: Because they were "free" of any other means of support, they were forced to sell their labour to survive (Marx, 1967, p. 166).

mode of production
A way of organizing production, which varies across economic systems. The mode of production under capitalism is distinct from other modes of production

To understand Marx's argument, it is first necessary to review two assumptions that underlie his theories. These assumptions were not Marx's alone—they have been shared by many other thinkers past and present—but they are the starting point for his theories relating to work under capitalism. The first assumption is the **Labour Theory of Value**. Simply stated, this belief holds that nothing has value unless labour is expended on it (Marx, 1967). All goods and services, anything that we use that has some value to us, require some human labour to ready it for our use. The beds we sleep in are manufactured, as are the plates and utensils we use to eat. The room we sit in has been constructed, and someone (perhaps ourselves) has provided the services required to set it up and keep it relatively tidy. Even apples that grow on trees and carrots that grow in the ground must be picked and washed before we can eat them. Every object and service we use and consume is a product of labour (Marx, 1967). Nevertheless, this assumption goes one step further to assert that the value of an object or service is equivalent to the sum total of labour expended on it. Therefore, the true value of the chair on which you sit is equal to the value of the labour to obtain the raw materials, to form and shape them as needed to manufacture the chair, and to assemble the pieces to make the chair, and even to market and sell that chair to the purchaser. This is the Labour Theory of Value.

Labour Theory of Value
The belief that labour is the source of all value in goods and services

The other assumption that underlies Marx's core theories pertaining to work is the idea that the manner in which human beings work is what distinguishes us from animals and other living beings. Animals, Marx asserts, work hard: beavers build lodges, bees construct hives, and spiders spin webs. However, Marx believes that in doing so, they are largely driven by instinct. In contrast, when human beings build structures, we first plan what we will do and how we will do it and then we proceed with the build. To quote Marx's (1967, p. 174) own lively phrasing,

> A spider conducts operations that resemble those of the weaver, and a bee puts to shame many an architect in the construction of her cells. But what distinguishes the worst architect from the best of bees is this, that the architect raises his structure in imagination before he erects it in reality. At the end of every labour process, we get a result that already existed in the imagination of the labourer at its commencement.

Moreover, the act of working often requires people to "subordinate their own wills" and purposely focus their attention on the task at hand. For humans, working requires both physical and mental capacities. Work is not simply something that we do but something we think about doing. It involves both conception and execution (Marx, 1967; Braverman, 1974).

You might personally agree or disagree with both of Marx's assumptions. Regardless, it is easier to understand Marx's concerns about work under capitalism and its potentially detrimental impacts on workers if you understand the ideas underlying his philosophy. In *Capital*, Marx (1967) offers a meticulous account of the nature of labour markets, the labour process, and the organization of work under capitalism. The first volume of *Capital* runs over 1000 pages in length, but of greatest interest to us here is Marx's account of how workers under capitalism are taken advantage of, or exploited. This **exploitation** entails a process that Marx calls "the extraction of surplus value." If we accept the labour theory of value, then the value of any product is equivalent to the total of the labour that went into its production. The key problem, for Marx and others, is that workers are never paid for the full value of their labour. Workers expend physical and mental effort to produce goods and services for their employers, but the amounts they earn never match the full value of what they produce. Rather, our wages are determined by other factors related to the cost of living, the amount of skill and education we have, market trends, and laws related to minimum wages, among other factors. During an hour of work, we may generate hundreds of dollars for our employers but only earn minimum wage or a little more. The rest is surplus value taken by our employers in profit at our expense. Looked at another way, it may take us only three hours of working to produce the value for our employers that is equivalent to our wage for eight hours' worth of work. In essence, Marx would argue, we spend part of our working day labouring for free.

exploitation
For Marxists, exploitation occurs when capitalists extract surplus value from workers during the process of production

The extraction of surplus value is a process essentially hidden from workers. We do work and in exchange are paid a wage. On the surface, this wage may seem fair, consistent with market value and local laws. We are not aware that at some point during our work shift we are working, or producing value, for free. Nevertheless, many workers in the private sector are aware of when their employers are profiting and do understand that they have contributed to that profit. This can lead to conflict between workers and employers and/or the managers who represent them. Marx contended that workers and owners—which he termed the **proletariat** and **bourgeoisie**—had interests that were diametrically opposed. Owners possessed the **means of production** (tools, instruments, and resources required for production), while workers (or the proletariat) possessed nothing but their own capacity to labour. Owners were constantly seeking to organize work in a manner that increased the surplus value (and profit) they acquired, while workers sought to earn wages that were more in proportion to the value they produced. For Marx, the **social relations of production**—the conflictive relationship between the owners of the means

proletariat
Marx's term for workers who do not have access to the means of production

bourgeoisie
Marx's term for owners who own the means of production

means of production
tools, instruments, and resources required for production

social relations of production
The conflictive relationship between those who own the means of production and those who do not. According to Marx, these relations are a driver of history

of production and others—was a driver of historical change. He predicted that conflicts between workers and owners would increase until the former decided to overthrow the latter and establish a fairer society with shared ownership.

These conflicts often play out at work, not only in disagreements over pay but also over how work is done. The main way in which employers (and managers) seek to expand surplus value is through achieving gains in productivity (Marx, 1967). Technological innovations, reorganization of work processes, and even replacing skilled workers with less-skilled workers are all strategies pursued in the drive for surplus value and profit. These practices are now viewed as standard, and hence we see them in the public sector too. Workers contest these changes, especially when they lead to job loss and **work intensification**, whereby workers are producing more value and possibly working harder for the same pay or a minor increase. However, when there is a pool of unemployed and underemployed workers available for employment—**a reserve army of labour** willing, out of necessity, to work for low wages in precarious and temporary jobs—then even skilled workers may be replaced, and capitalists have the upper hand in their dealings with workers.

work intensification
Processes whereby workers are asked to do more work, to work harder, and to produce more value

reserve army of labour
A pool of workers who are unemployed or underemployed and ready to fill the jobs of the employed should they be needed. The presence of a reserve army of labour helps to keep wages low

Marx's discussion of worker exploitation through the extraction of surplus value has been influential because it reveals processes that are largely hidden from view. Marx's theories have remained relevant to the organization of work in our society despite dramatic shifts in our economy, away from the agricultural and manufacturing production of Marx's lifetime towards a service economy. His accounts of conflict, the pursuit of innovation in the name of profit, and worker disadvantage have remained pertinent, even in contexts where workers earn a **living wage** (i.e., a wage sufficient to sustain a reasonable standard of living). Marx's linking of social class to work and the labour process has also been influential, if contested.

living wage
A wage sufficient to sustain a reasonable standard of living

Another influential concept from Marx is that of **alienation**. As you may recall, Marx believed that the nature of human beings' work distinguished us from animals: we think about our work before (and while) we do it. We do not simply act on instinct. The problem, for Marx, was that the organization of work under capitalism threatens to reduce us to mindless drones, or animals, by stifling our creativity and reducing our control over what we do. Marx believed that the organization of work under capitalism had psychological implications for workers, reducing our enjoyment, making us feel less fulfilled, and undermining our social relationships with others as well as our sense of self.

alienation
Workers' estrangement under capitalism from the products of their labour, the labour process, their true nature/humanity, and others

Marx (1975) identified four sources of alienation, or estrangement (as it is sometimes called). These are forms of separation that, while structural in nature, have psychological consequences. First, workers are separated (alienated) from the products they produce. When we work, we put a little of ourselves—our effort, our creativity, our labour—into what we do. However, under capitalism, what we produce does not belong to us but to our employer. Second, workers are separated from the **labour process** (loosely defined as our work and the objects, instruments, and organization of our work [Marx, 1975, p. 284]). Decisions about how we work, what we do, how we do it, the equipment and tools we use to perform that work, when it is scheduled, and so on are rarely made by us but by our employers and their managers. Our opportunities to plan our own work may also be minimized; many workers are tasked with following the orders and instructions set by others. This leads to the third form of alienation: separation from ourselves, nature, and humanity. For Marx, this meant that many workers could not truly be themselves at work and found little self-fulfillment there.

labour process
In Marxian theory, the labour process consists of the objects, instruments, and organization of our work as well as what we do

> Labour [under capitalism] is external to the worker, i.e. does not belong to his [*sic*] essential being; . . . he therefore does not confirm himself in his work, but denies himself, feels miserable, and not happy, does not develop free mental and physical energy, but mortifies his flesh and ruins his mind. Hence the worker feels himself only when he is not working; when he is working he does not feel himself (Marx, 1975, p. 326).

Fourth, Marx felt that work under capitalism separated workers from each other—their fellow workers as well as managers, capitalists, and others in society. Workers must compete with others for jobs, opportunities, and rewards and are divided from employers and managers by their diametrical interests. Work is too often not a collective process that brings people together but a process that physically and emotionally isolates workers from one another.

Thus, for Marx, alienation was a structural condition—one of physical separation from products, processes, and people—that had psychological impacts, including loss of creativity and social isolation, leaving workers unsatisfied and vulnerable. Later writers have expanded on the concept of alienation (see, for example, Blauner, 1964; Rinehart, 2001). They have tended to argue that alienation must be seen along a continuum: some workers are clearly more alienated than others, both structurally and emotionally. Moreover, because structural aspects of alienation have become the norm, some workers may not experience the psychological impacts noted by Marx, finding other sources for creativity and emotional connection away from work. The reduction in the length of the working day since Marx's time has facilitated this.

Labour Process Theory A theoretical approach influenced by Marx that focuses on the labour process and conflicts between managers and workers over the conduct of work

In the 1970s and 1980s, Marx's ideas enjoyed a resurgence in the sociology of work, and they gave rise to a neo-Marxist theory, known as **Labour Process Theory**. Researchers working under this approach focused on the conflict between managers and workers at the point of production, since this conflict was both central to class inequality in society and profoundly shaped the organization and experience of work. Harry Braverman's (1974) seminal book, *Labour and Monopoly Capital*, spurred subsequent developments in Labour Process Theory. Braverman (1974), building on Marx, argued that managers and owners were constantly seeking to expand productivity at the point of production. To achieve their ends, they needed to seize control of the labour process and limit workers' autonomy and control in

Source: THE CANADIAN PRESS IMAGES/Rachel Verbin

A protester at a one-day strike against the Ontario government's cuts to OSAP encourages unity between students and workers, reflecting Marx's ideas that capitalism is used to divide workers from each other in order to keep them vulnerable to exploitation, as well as the theorist's lasting influence on the world of work.

the conduct of their work. Moreover, the labour process was changed so that jobs were distilled down to smaller segments that could be performed by workers with less skill and training; worker **deskilling** could result. Braverman (1974) argued that these trends were not only evident in manufacturing but in all other sectors of the economy as well.

Later contributors adopting a neo-Marxist theoretical lens broadened the focus, arguing that there were several other techniques through which managers sought to control workers (Edwards, 1979). Scholars explored workers' resistance to this control, as well as the conditions under which they consented to it (Burawoy, 1979). Finally, researchers have also argued that skill trends and processes are more complex than labour process theory originally implied (Sawchuk, 2013). Nonetheless, scholars using this theoretical lens still tend to focus on the organization of the labour process, changes to job content, skill, and autonomy, as well as tensions between managers and workers at the point of production.

deskilling
Process of job degradation through which workers are denied the opportunity to use skills (and autonomy) formerly exercised on the job

Weber and Neo-Weberian Theory

Max Weber (1864–1920) was a Prussian-born intellectual who wrote widely on sociological phenomena, from religion and sociological methods to politics, the state, and social change. It is his work on organizations, social change, and social inequality that has been most influential to the study of work. Weber (1968, p. 24) argued that the study of social action (in its broadest meaning) should be the "central subject matter" for sociology. He defined social action as behaviour to which an actor attaches meaning that takes into account (and/or is directed towards) the behaviour of others. Weber (1968) also studied social organizations and institutions, but he viewed these entities largely as collections of individuals pursuing social action to obtain their interests and goals. Weber was particularly interested in social action that was goal-oriented—what he called **rational action**. Not all action is rational or aimed at achieving a specific goal: sometimes we act according to our emotions, custom, or habit, without any specific goal in mind. Weber focused on two types of rational action: **instrumentally rational action** and **value-rational action**. First, instrumentally rational action is pursued to achieve "calculated ends" (Weber, 1968, p. 24). When we seek a job so that we can pay our rent and meet our other expenses, we are engaging in instrumentally rational action. Second, value-rational action is "determined by a conscious belief in the value for its own sake of some ethical, aesthetic, religious, or other form of behaviour, independent of its prospects of success" (Weber, 1968, pp. 24–25). When we spend our free time volunteering at the local pet shelter because we care about animals, we are engaging in value-rational action.

For Weber, rational action is shaped by **rationality**—"means-ends calculations that determine how decisions are made" (Geva, 2015, p. 172). Again, there are two types of rationality: **formal rationality** involves decisions and goals aligned with formal rules and economic gain (and guides instrumentally rational action); **substantive rationality** involves decisions based on values, honour, ethical principles, and "doing the right thing" even if it entails a personal sacrifice (guiding value-rational action). Formal rationality is seen as predominant in modern, capitalist societies, where action tends to be rule-driven and economic growth is prioritized over other values and principles. Workplaces are predominantly guided by formal rationality—work is conducted according to formal rules, and it is directed towards the achievement of specific goals, including efficiency

rational action
Weberian concept referring to social action that is goal-oriented

instrumentally rational action
Action pursued to achieve "calculated ends" (Weber, 1968, p. 24)

value-rational action
Action that is "determined by a conscious belief in the value for its own sake of some ethical, aesthetic, religious, or other form of behaviour, independent of its prospects of success" (Weber, 1968, pp. 24–25)

rationality
"Means-ends calculations that determine how decisions are made" (Geva, 2015, p. 172). Formal and substantive rationality are two types

formal rationality
Decisions and goals aligned with formal rules and economic gain. Formal rationality guides instrumentally rational action

substantive rationality
Decisions are based on values, honour, ethical principles, and "doing the right thing," even if it entails a personal sacrifice. Substantive rationality guides value-rational action

and profit-maximization. In such environments, substantive-rational principles (fairness, ethical conduct, concern for the well-being of others) are not necessarily absent, but they tend not to be the main forces driving decision-making (see Box 2.1). Formal rationality and substantive rationality are not mutually exclusive, and indeed both may simultaneously shape our actions. For example, we might seek a job to pay our rent but also pursue work that conforms to our values and/or allows us to help others. Nevertheless, formal rationality and value rationality are usually in tension, and there is a tendency for formal rationality to predominate.

rationalization
The ongoing search to find the optimum means to achieve a desired end (efficiency)

Sociologists often write about **rationalization** as a social trend, but when they do they are speaking about the spread of formal rationality. In this sense, rationalization entails the expansion of goal-oriented action shaped by formal rules, regulations, and laws (Ritzer & Walczak, 1988, p. 3; Weber, 1968). Rationalization is not inherently problematic; in fact, people acting in accordance with rules and laws contributes to social order and stability. However, both Weber and neo-Weberian scholars have shown how advanced rationalization in capitalist societies has become so focused on the end goals of efficiency and profit that the space available for other forms of rational action (especially value-rational action) may be diminishing (Ritzer, 1996; Ritzer & Walczak, 1988). The significance of these trends for work and workers may be best seen in Weber's writings on

A CLOSER LOOK

2.1 | Rationality and COVID-19

Although formal rationality tends to dominate in advanced capitalist societies, during certain moments substantive rationality may become more prominent. One such moment occurred during the early days of the COVID-19 pandemic, when acting according to purely economic motives was met with disdain. For example, when the pandemic first hit Canada and the United States in the winter of 2020, some people bought large quantities of disinfectant wipes, exacerbating local shortages, so that they could sell them at inflated prices online. In Weberian terms, this was instrumentally rational action aimed at maximizing personal gain. When these individuals were criticized, they defended themselves by appealing to formal rationality: they argued that their actions were simply business transactions and they were no different from any other actor who provided a needed service or good to customers in the marketplace. The public outcry at such behaviour reflects substantive rationality that defined such activity as dishonourable behaviour that put others at risk. Counter examples were abundant during the pandemic. For example, the "caremongering" movement entailed local groups mobilizing online to provide assistance to those in need (Sheldon, 2020). Moreover, many individuals worked—potentially risking their own well-being—to provide essential services, including health care, food, and delivery services. Some business owners continued to employ workers even when they had no work for them or little money to pay them, again because it was viewed as the right thing to do. These social actions are guided by substantive rationality: they reflect care and concern for others and adhering to values even when doing so involves personal sacrifices. If formal rationality often takes precedence, at certain moments substantive rationality can become pre-eminent and even, potentially, lead us towards positive social change.

bureaucracy and neo-Weberian George Ritzer's (1996) accounts of work in rationalizing organizations.

Weber saw **bureaucracy** as a product of the spread of formal rationality, emerging predominantly in the late 19th and early 20th centuries. Other, earlier forms of organization were less rule-driven and less focused on finding the most efficient means to meet their goals. Weber (1946, p. 215) linked the emergence of bureaucracies to the expansion of capitalist economies, claiming that the latter demanded that the "official business of the administration be discharged precisely, unambiguously, continuously, and with as much speed as possible." Although Weber believed that social action was shaped by a variety of factors, bureaucracies sought to ensure that decision-making was based on "purely objective considerations" (1946, p. 215). That is, when interacting with a bureaucracy (whether a government office, a university, health-care institution, or private company), it should not matter what your social background is, who you know, or how much money you have. The same rules should apply to everyone. Ideally, this should ensure that the operation of social institutions is fairer.

bureaucracy
Type of organization, discussed by Weber, characterized by advanced divisions of labour, hierarchies, and formal rules, among other characteristics

Weber provided an **ideal type** to describe the characteristics of bureaucracies; that is, he prepared a list of traits to capture the essence of bureaucracy, acknowledging that not all bureaucracies would necessarily possess all of these traits and many could possess traits not outlined. These traits included the following: reliance on formal written rules; hierarchical structures with clear chains of command; clear divisions of labour; expert workers with highly specialized roles; detailed rules and regulations to structure activity, promotions, and administration; and recruitment based training, skills, and ability (Weber, 1946, pp. 196–198, 214–216). Again, for Weber, bureaucracies were more efficient in achieving their goals and more orderly than other informal modes of organizing. Still, bureaucracies had some downsides. Their rule-driven nature could make them inflexible, unable to deal with exceptional circumstances, and too impersonal. They were instruments of power that could be used to dominate others. Moreover, workers within bureaucracies might find their work narrow and routine, without much scope for their skills and training. In fact, Weber described bureaucracies as an "iron cage" in which workers might become little more than "cogs" in the bureaucratic machine, subject to repeating "an essentially fixed route of march" (1946, p. 228).

ideal type
A description or list of traits to capture the essence of a social phenomenon or institution, while acknowledging that the phenomenon may not actually include all of the traits and the list provided is not exhaustive

These ideas were developed further by neo-Weberian scholar George Ritzer (1996), who sheds light on the impact of rationalization in his popular book, *The McDonaldization of Society*. Ritzer (1996) defines rationalization as an ongoing drive for efficiency wherein people strive to find the best means to reach a given end in a rule-driven way. **McDonaldization** is an extreme form of rationalization in which "the principles of the fast-food restaurant are coming to dominate" society and social institutions within it, from private enterprise to education and health care. He identifies four principles associated with McDonaldization: efficiency, calculability, predictability, and control, and considered their impacts on workers, social institutions, and citizens more generally.

McDonaldization
An extreme form of rationalization, characterized by efficiency, predictability, calculability, and control

Efficiency, Ritzer (1996) defines as finding the best means to achieve given ends. He argues that McDonald's and other fast-food restaurants have traditionally done this through their limited menus; mass-produced, standardized products; streamlined processes; and close management of workers, as well as having customers do unpaid work (like carrying trays of food to tables and disposing of their own garbage). He argues that

efficiency
Finding the best means to achieve a given end. Associated with doing more, faster, at less cost

other organizations and institutions are similarly concerned with efficiency and may adopt similar strategies. For example, Canadian universities in recent years have been reducing or narrowing course offerings, raising class sizes, streamlining and downsizing their staff and services, and finding ways to monitor the activities of their staff and faculty more closely.

calculability
An emphasis on quantity or quality, often to the point that quantity is taken as a measure of quality

Calculability refers to an emphasis on quantity over quality and even the belief that quantity is an accurate reflection or measure of quality. Fast-food restaurants have tended to emphasize the size of their meals, their low cost, and even how many people have been served. The emphasis is typically on cost and size, then, rather than on the quality of the food or its taste. Ritzer and many others show how these principles have been adopted in other fields as well. For instance, in education there is increased focus on test scores and grades, which are taken to reflect ability and learning but may not be closely correlated at all. Moreover, the focus in health care for some time now has been on "quality of care," which some attempt to measure in terms of number of people treated, how quickly they were treated, length of hospital stay, and use of available beds. All of these measures reflect quantity of care and actually have little to do with whether services provided are of good quality or not.

predictability
A component of McDonaldization and rationalization that aims to ensure that every similar firm functions and looks the same

Predictability reflects consistency. By and large, we should expect the menu at one McDonald's location to be similar, if not identical, to the menu at another. Moreover, our interaction with McDonald's employees tends to be the same from one location to the next. The problem here is that maintaining this kind of consistency can be stifling for workers who are required to follow scripts when interacting with customers and to produce food according to clear guidelines with robotic consistency. Predictability is increasingly evident in other sectors as well. Ritzer (1996) mentions cookie-cutter textbooks that all look the same, as well as the nature of testing, which also seems to be predictable from one course to the next.

control
The ability to determine one's own or others' actions

Finally, **control** is required to ensure that efficiency, predictability, and calculability is achieved. Formal rules and procedures are tightened to ensure that workers and customers follow rigid expectations, and technologies are used to control workers and ensure that products and procedures do not vary, regardless of who is doing the work. Enhanced control of workers and consumers is prevalent across a variety of industries, and technology is used to narrow variation, limit creativity, and increase surveillance to ensure that people are doing what managers want them to do. Ritzer (1996) discusses trends in US health care whereby medical doctors' actions are increasingly controlled by bureaucratic rules, insurance companies, and employers.

While increased efficiency and standardization can have many benefits, they also have downsides: more routine work, less creativity, managed social interactions, and less autonomy. The focus on quantity over quality can also lead to decreases in quality of services and products. For Ritzer, as for Weber, rationalization is potentially dehumanizing because it limits real human interactions and personal creativity. While rationalization brings societal gains, it is not without substantial costs.

Generally speaking, Weber, like Marx before him, saw the social organization and experience of work as tied to broader social forces and systems of social inequality. One's work shaped one's class position, life chances, and opportunities and could have a profound influence on well-being. Many subsequent social theorists continued to explore the link between the organization of work and social inequality.

Durkheim

Classical sociological theorist Emile Durkheim (1858–1917) touched on work in his writings on societies, social order, and social change. As work and employment were not his primary concerns, and his ideas have been less influential in the sociology of work, we will not review his theories in detail here. In his book *Division of Labour*, Durkheim (1933/1983) argues that modern societies were characterized by increased specialization and differentiation and moreover that these advanced divisions of labour brought dramatic changes that could undermine social order. Previously, social bonds were generated through similarity of experience. Because people in communities did similar work, they understood each other and shared an outlook. **Mechanical solidarity** was a form of social integration tying people in these simpler societies together. More advanced divisions of labour disrupted these traditional social bonds. However, Durkheim argued that this did not lead to conflict and chaos; rather, modern societies were characterized by a different form of social order—**organic solidarity**. With specialization, we become more interdependent and must rely on each other for survival. In the workplace, our labour is increasingly team-based and involves working with people who possess skills, knowledge, and expertise different from our own. It is only by working together that we can produce something of value. Our collaboration and mutual reliance form the basis of social cohesion, which in turn contributes to social order. Durkheim saw an important role for occupational groups and associations in this respect, arguing that they could foster common bonds among workers so that they would continue to have those linking social bonds; such associations could also facilitate people's interactions with other groups in society and the state.

mechanical solidarity Social bonds generated through similarity of experience, characteristic of simpler, pre-capitalist societies

organic solidarity Concept associated with Durkheim: social bonds arise from our interdependency in societies with advanced divisions of labour

Durkheim's contributions are valuable in linking the organization of work to societal organization and questions of social order. As our social divisions of labour become increasingly global, Durkheim's theories remind us that workers' experiences in Canada are bound up with those in other locales around the world.

Foucault

Michel Foucault (1926–84) was a French philosopher and social theorist whose major works were published in the 1960s and 1970s. While his work touched on many different subjects—from state power, through medical treatment, sexuality, and crime and punishment—themes of power and knowledge run through most of his scholarly contributions. Foucault explored many dimensions of the relationship between power and knowledge, including how power was used to produce, obtain, define, and attach meaning to knowledge. At the same time, he explored how knowledge could enhance and extend power. Foucault's ideas have been taken up in a variety of ways by scholars examining work—especially those studying "expert" workers with accepted claims to knowledge (Evetts & Dingwall, 2002; Fournier, 1999; Nettleton, 1992). These scholars examine experts' ability to use their knowledge to exert power over others but also their employers' efforts to seize that knowledge and exert control over them. Most influential within the sociology of work, however, have been Foucault's (1977) ideas concerning discipline and surveillance, most clearly articulated in his book *Discipline and Punish*.

In this book, Michel Foucault documents a shift within Western society away from rule by physical force towards rule through discipline. With a focus on the punishment of criminals and others deemed abnormal, Foucault describes how in centuries past, those convicted of wrongdoing were sentenced to physical punishment, which often entailed abuse, torture, and very public, brutal death. Over the past few centuries, however, there has been a move away from punishment of the body towards a form of discipline that aims to "correct, reclaim, 'cure' and improve" the soul (Foucault, 1977, p. 10). Discipline involves the exercise of power, as does physical punishment, but it operates more subtly and rests on a set of processes including surveillance, assessment, treatment, and self-discipline. Through surveillance, assessment, and treatment, people learn to discipline themselves or be judged lacking, in which case they are subjected to treatment to reform them. This is a more efficient and much less bloody exercise of power—one that rests on monitoring people and obtaining knowledge about them.

panopticon
An ideal prison design that facilitates surveillance and encourages self-discipline by ensuring that power is both visible and unverifiable

In *Discipline and Punish*, Foucault (1977) discusses the role of architecture and design in facilitating surveillance and generating discipline. To illustrate his point, he writes at length about a prison design by 18th-century philosopher Jeremy Bentham called the **panopticon**. While very few panopticons were ever built, Foucault believed the principles underlying the panoptic design were imbedded in other buildings and that these principles revealed broader trends in discipline and surveillance. In this way, the panopticon is an ideal that illustrates his broader argument about the societal shift from punishment to discipline. The panopticon was circular, with prisoners' cells arrayed along the circumference (see figure 2.1). In the middle of the building was a watch tower intended for a prison guard. Windows in the cells and in the watch tower ensured that prisoners were always in view of the guard. The design facilitated surveillance, allowing one or a few guards to monitor a large number of subjects. Blinds on the watch tower would allow the guards to look out and see the prisoners at a glance. While the prisoners could see the watch tower, they could not determine whether a guard was looking in their direction or not at any given moment.

Source: Photo by Underwood Archives/Getty Images

Stateville Correctional Center's "F-House" is one of the few examples of a panopticon. Built in Crest Hill, Illinois, in 1925, the cellhouse was in use until the 1990s before being officially closed in 2016, following criticism that the facility was dehumanizing and dangerous for both inmates and workers.

In this context, Foucault (1977) explains, power is both visible and unverifiable. It is visible because those being watched are aware of the fact that they are under surveillance and they know that if they are caught doing something they should not be doing, there will be consequences. It is unverifiable because those in the cells cannot determine exactly when someone is looking at them. As a result, Foucault argues, they begin to act as if they are constantly being watched and are more likely to follow the rules. Panoptic design, in this manner, is an efficient mechanism for the exercise of power. It allows the few (the watchers) to monitor and discipline the many (the watched) and, when necessary, to identify any wrongdoing and quickly correct it.

Foucault argued that while the panopticon was intended as a prison, elements of panoptic design came to be incorporated into other areas—hospitals, schools, factories, and other workplaces. Here, buildings were designed to render "subjects" (patients, students, workers) visible, enabling their overseers to watch them, judge or assess their behaviour, identify problems, and apply treatment, or discipline, to bring about conformity. Examples of such designs include large open spaces like factory floors or open office plans, both of which may incorporate two-way mirrors or platforms allowing supervisors to look out but limiting workers' ability to know when they are being watched. Such panoptic designs in workplace settings enable supervisors to monitor large groups of workers to make sure they are working consistently, following rules, and being productive. Any slacking or wrongdoing can be quickly identified by supervisors, with the unconscientious worker disciplined or fired. Such designs may facilitate productivity because workers who feel they are under surveillance are going to work harder—they are going to self-discipline.

Today, surveillance is further facilitated by technology, what Sewell and Wilkinson (1992) labelled the "electronic panopticon." Surveillance cameras also allow the exercise of power that is visible and unverifiable: workers may not know exactly when they are being watched remotely. Technology can track workers' computer and online activity and their movements. Work processes and outcomes are subject to audit. Sociologists who draw on Foucault to study work explore the ways in which workers are subject to discipline and constant judgment through technology and design, and they consider the impact of this surveillance on workers, identifying the ways they self-discipline (Salzinger, 2003) and the ways they seek to evade and manage this form of control, when and if they can. Research largely confirms Foucault's contention that while the exercise of power in a disciplinary society is efficient, its forced conformity and constant judgment create pressures that can be experienced negatively by those of us subjected to it.

Bourdieu

Pierre Bourdieu (1930–2002) was a French sociologist and contemporary of Foucault's whose career spanned decades. Most of his major works were published in the 1980s and 1990s, although some were published posthumously in the early years of this century. Bourdieu's impact on sociology over the past several decades has been significant. He wrote widely, but his main contributions have arguably been to the study of the reproduction of social inequalities across generations, the sociology of culture, and the sociology of education—all of which overlap, or have implications for, the study of work and employment. His theories have been most taken up in studies of how individuals navigate the labour market, find work, settle into occupations, and potentially earn promotions. Bourdieu's work shows us that labour markets and workplaces are part of broader social fields infused with power and inequality. To navigate these fields and acquire jobs, individuals draw on capital. Those with more capital have greater access to good jobs and opportunities, while others are disadvantaged.

Bourdieu's starting point is more conventional notions of "capital" used by economists and sociologists. Influenced by Marx, Bourdieu (1986, p. 46) describes capital as "accumulated labour in its materialized form"—that form being products whose value comes from the labour embedded within them (Marx, 1967). Economists and social theorists like Marx focus on capital as an economic phenomenon or set of resources integral to the reproduction and generation of social inequality in the labour market, the workplace, and society more generally. However, Bourdieu argues (1986, p. 46), if we want to understand "the structure and functioning" of society, we have to take into account "capital in all its forms." This includes cultural capital, social capital, and symbolic capital as well.

cultural capital A set of abilities, understandings, and dispositions related to a specific cultural setting that can be used to navigate that setting successfully

Cultural capital consists of a set of abilities, understandings, and dispositions related to a specific cultural setting. It consists of valued and prestigious knowledge—about cultural phenomenon, ways of speaking, pronunciation, food and drink, knowledge of art, and elite tastes—that is often taken for granted. Cultural capital is learned, but it is often acquired informally through family socialization. Individuals from privileged social backgrounds acquire this cultural capital as they grow up, and it benefits them in the school system and the labour market. People with cultural capital may be better able to relate to teachers and course material and to speak and write in a way that allows them to succeed in school. Cultural capital can also help people to navigate the job market; those with cultural capital might generate instant rapport with interviewers and leaders in important positions. They appear to fit in with those in positions of power and can navigate social and work situations successfully. Those without cultural capital might find themselves struggling in school or in the workplace unless they succeed in acquiring this knowledge themselves.

Cultural capital is a powerful mechanism in the reproduction of social inequality because it can be transferred easily from one generation to the next, but its importance is masked. Cultural capital facilitates school success, but school success is often perceived to be simply a matter of ability and/or hard work. Subsequent success in the labour market based on school success and the ability to fit in is seen by economists and others to be the product of **human capital**—accumulated education, training, and skills—and hard work. The role of cultural capital in facilitating the acquisition of skills and in generating school success is hidden. People with cultural capital can convert it into economic capital by landing high-paying jobs. Those without it may be locked into lower-paying jobs and experience difficulty finding anything better.

human capital Investments in skill acquisition, education, and training by individuals, organizations, and societies

social capital Connections and networks that individuals can use to navigate social fields of power for their own benefit

If cultural capital is related to what you know, **social capital** refers more to *who* you know—your social connections, networks, and group memberships. Social capital is also strongly shaped by your family background. Your family's kin, connections, and contacts can become yours. If your family members are well-connected and know important people, those people may be able to help you too, facilitating entrance into the best schools, institutions, and job opportunities. While in these settings, you will likely acquire more social capital. For instance, if you go to an elite school, you will meet other people your age who also have good social capital, and your friends and the families of your friends also become part of your extended network, providing potential sources for further opportunities in the labour market and beyond. Hiring based on social capital is a form of **nepotism**, in which those in power dole out opportunities to relatives and others in their social networks.

nepotism
A practice whereby people in power reserve opportunities for those in their social networks

Symbolic capital consists of resources related to prestige and recognition. This form of capital is linked to other forms of capital—economic, cultural, and social—and concerns how these forms of capital are recognized and rewarded in particular areas of social life. You may have cultural capital acquired through socialization and schooling, but how will others know you have this capital? In our society, we often rely on symbols like degrees and credentials to signal the possession of valued skills and knowledge. Various awards and accomplishments provide additional symbolic capital solidifying reputations and demonstrating the possession of valuable capital. Bourdieu (1989) applies this concept to the labour market explicitly in his book *The State Nobility*. Here he explains how academic credentials like a university degree have symbolic power in the labour market as "guarantee[s] of competence" (Bourdieu, 1989, p. 118). Credentials (as symbolic capital) are a form of labour market currency opening up job opportunities. In reality, Bourdieu (1989, p. 118) asserts, "the major portion of the necessary technical competence is often acquired on the job."

symbolic capital
Resources related to prestige and recognition. Symbolic capital shapes how economic, cultural, and social capital are recognized and rewarded

Symbolic capital is particularly powerful because credentials and other forms of recognition are perceived as legitimate. This legitimacy obscures the existence and importance of cultural, social, and even economic capital and makes it appear as if social inequalities are fair and based solely on merit and hard work. The systematic barriers disadvantaging some groups from obtaining university degrees or other forms of capital become invisible. Although Bourdieu acknowledges that educational facilities distribute knowledge, he also sees them as institutions distributing power. Those born into families lacking economic, cultural, and/or social capital are systemically disadvantaged. While it is not impossible for such individuals to acquire capital during their lifetimes, this is not an easy process, and they may continue to be disadvantaged as they progress in school and through their careers. Symbolic capital helps to hide the role of social class in transferring capital from one generation to the next.

As noted above, Bourdieu's ideas have been mostly taken up in the sociology of work in studies of people entering the labour market and pursuing careers (for example, Lehmann, 2019; Waterfield, Beagan, & Mohamed, 2019; Aslam, 2021). These studies draw on Bourdieu to show that cultural and social capital matter not only for locating jobs and opportunities but also for obtaining good jobs and thriving in them once hired. Those with less social, cultural, and economic capital are disadvantaged. Given the breadth of Bourdieu's theories (only a small portion of which are summarized here), there may be more opportunities to apply insights from his writings to understand experiences of work and working.

Symbolic Interactionism

symbolic interactionism
A set of theoretical approaches focusing on the meanings that people hold about themselves, their experiences, and their social world. These meanings are constructed through social interaction with others

Symbolic interactionism consists of a set of theoretical approaches that focus on the meanings that people come to hold about themselves, their experiences, and their social world—meanings that typically form and develop through social interaction with others (Blumer, 1969). Many of the sociological theories reviewed above focus on structures and social trends. They sometimes predict the response of people to these broad social forces (as Marx did when discussing alienation, for example), but they do not make these responses and meanings their central subject matter. Research shaped by symbolic interactionism takes experiences, meanings, and communication as its central focus and in so doing helps to shed light on what people think, feel, and experience while working.

Although scholars have traced the central ideas behind symbolic interactionism to various antecedents dating back centuries if not millennia (Dingwall, 2001; Prus, 2003; Reynolds, 2003), its modern form has been linked to the Chicago School in the opening half of the 20th century and especially the work of George Herbert Mead (1863–1931) and Herbert Blumer (1900–87); it was the latter who coined the term. Mead (1962) argued that humans interpret the things we hear, see, and otherwise experience as symbols: we attach meaning and significance to them. But the meanings we attach to objects, speech, or experiences are not generated in isolation; rather, they are structured and refined through social interaction. We anticipate how others might interpret what we say and what we see, and we adjust our interpretations and use of symbols accordingly (Blumer, 1969; Dingwall, 2001). In this manner, human experience and human understanding are shaped through social interaction—interaction shapes the meanings we attach to our experiences. For symbolic interactionists, meanings and interactions should be a fundamental focus of sociological investigation, since, as Thomas and Thomas (1928, p. 572) famously claimed, something that is perceived to be real is real in its consequences. Our perceptions and understandings shape social reality and our experiences of it.

Research on the sociology of work from a symbolic interactionist perspective has tended to focus on "the experience of work from the point of view of those who engage in it" (Shaffir & Pawluch, 2003, p. 894). This includes workers' socialization into occupational and workplace cultures, identity and work, careers, and the contradictions, tensions, and conflicts experienced by people in the daily course of their work (see for example, Becker, Geer, Hughes, & Strauss, 1976; Haas, 1977; Hughes, 1958). Research often consists of in-depth, ethnographic case studies of people in particular occupations, but contributions are inherently comparative as well, since similarities across occupations are highlighted (Hughes, 1958; Shaffir & Pawluch, 2003). Research from a symbolic interactionist perspective has provided insights into occupational and professional socialization, stigma and deviance attached to work, work identity, and many other topics that are of central concern to those who study work and working (see Box 2.2).

Feminist Theory

Some date Western feminist theory to Mary Wollstonecraft (1757–97) and her 18th-century feminist philosophical writings; however, more recent feminist theorizing is very much a collective effort. In the second half of the 20th century, feminist critiques of mainstream sociological theory grew louder. As impactful as the theories of Marx, Weber, Foucault, and others were, they tended to write as if everyone's experiences were the same. Yet this was clearly not the case. A growing body of evidence emphasized that men's and women's experiences of work, family, politics, and other areas of social life were different. Moreover, women appeared to be systemically disadvantaged compared to men in almost every social sphere. Feminists responded by revising and developing social theories. Some aimed to expand and alter established theories to incorporate a gender

A CLOSER LOOK

Box 2.2 | Learning Workers' Real Feelings

Influenced by symbolic interactionism, and especially the work of Erving Goffman (1959), sociologist Jack Haas (1974, 1977) conducted an ethnography to understand how high-steel ironworkers who construct high-rise buildings manage their fears when doing very dangerous work and how apprentices new to this work adapt to it. As Haas went undercover as an ironworker apprentice, he had to grapple with his own fears about this work where "workers are protected from certain death only by their skill in balancing on slender beams, a skill threatened by swirls of weather and wind" (Haas 1977, p. 148). Haas was surprised that the ironworkers he worked with demonstrated no fear. He wondered whether they truly experienced no fear—or had they learned to manage it? He found that ironworkers collectively managed their fears by denying and ignoring them. Because workers depended on each other for their own safety, they had to build trust with each other. Those who expressed fears or acted afraid were deemed untrustworthy. In the words of one of Haas's informants, "you get some ... guy who's afraid up here, and you have really got to watch yourself, because you don't know what the hell they're liable to do" (p. 154). Continuous demonstrations of fearlessness were expected as part of the work culture, and those who failed to control their fears faced "ridicule or ostracism" (p. 169). Apprentices had to prove their toughness and demonstrate their ability to handle challenges and manage their fear or they were sent packing.

By focusing on the meanings workers attach to their work, which they construct in interaction with each other, symbolic interactionists like Haas provide unique insights into the world of work.

Can you imagine other ways of applying symbolic interactionism to the study of work?

lens, producing Marxist-feminist, feminist neo-Weberian, and feminist neo-Foucauldian approaches. Others endeavoured to create new theories that placed women's experiences at the centre. The result was a broad array of feminist theories. Here, we touch on only a few, beginning with some feminist alterations to established theories.

In the 1970s and 1980s, many feminists were influenced by Marx's critique of capitalist society and his commitment to greater social equality but argued that the dominant theories of work did not pay adequate attention to women's experiences in the workplace and in the home. **Marxist-feminists** argue that it is crucial to consider women's work—in the labour force and outside of it—if we are to develop a clear, sociological understanding of work and social life in a capitalist economy (Luxton & Bezanson, 2006; Huws, 2001). Therefore, they expanded Marxist theory, especially by elaborating his discussion of work and labour to include domestic labour, done disproportionately by women in the home (Fox, 1980), and service work done by women for pay (Huws, 2001). For instance, Marxist-feminists argue that domestic labour is work that not only benefits men (who do less domestic labour and therefore can spend more time focusing on paid labour for economic gain) but also the capitalist system more broadly (Fox, 1980; Luxton, 1980). Women working in the home, raising children, cleaning, and cooking are doing productive labour crucial to the functioning of capitalist economies: their work ensures not only that today's workers are fed, rested, and ready to labour but that the

Marxist-feminist Theoretical approaches that blend Marxist and feminist theories to explore the intersection of gender and class in shaping work (and life) experiences

next generation of workers is raised to take their place (Luxton, 1980). The family unit is both a locus of production for women and a locus of consumption where capitalist goods are purchased and used (in part to produce workers ready to labour). Marxist-feminist theories encourage researchers to include a gender lens when studying work and to keep in mind that various dimensions of social inequality (like class and gender) are interlocking. If a more equal society is to be achieved, multiple dimensions of social inequality must be addressed simultaneously.

Feminist scholars have also drawn on and revised Weber's theories to shed light on women's experiences of working. For instance, feminists have adapted Weber's analyses of social action to explore how state policies reproduce gender inequality (Geva, 2015; Walby, 1986). Moreover, they have explored how formal organizations and organizational practices are infused with gender assumptions and biases.

Several scholars have also merged feminist theory with Foucault's writings to draw attention to, for example, the ways in which women's bodies are subject to disciplinary mechanisms that are infused with power. Constant surveillance, assessment, and judgment, combined with the sexualization and commodification of women's bodies, can have a profound effect on women, leading them to engage in everyday practices (work-outs, how to wear clothes and make-up) and more extreme practices (plastic surgery, bingeing and purging, not eating) to discipline their bodies to conform to unrealistic ideals (Bordo, 1993). These ideas have been applied to experiences in the workplace. For instance, Leslie Salzinger's (2003) research on Mexico's factories shows how the managers' disciplinary gaze and judgments are shaped by gender, aimed at producing good workers and good women simultaneously. "Good" women workers in some of the environments Salzinger studied not only perform their work diligently and quickly, but they look pretty and sexually available while doing so. The expectations placed on "good" men in the workplace are quite different. A feminist lens adds nuance to Foucauldian analyses of work and better captures the ways in which disciplinary mechanisms may impact men and women differently.

In a different vein, the influential work of West and Zimmerman on "doing gender" builds on the theories of symbolic interactionism and ethnomethodology (not discussed here). Their approach sees gender as an activity or set of performances accomplished within our daily social interactions (West & Zimmerman, 1987). This theory rejects notions of gender as a role or set of traits, rather seeing it as an accomplishment. It thereby draws our attention to the processes and interactions through which gender is done (or potentially undone) (Butler, 1990; Deutsch, 2007; Risman, 2009). The workplace can be an important setting for "doing gender" through social interactions. This theory has been extended to address the challenges experienced by transgender workers in the process of "doing transgender" (Connell, 2010).

Feminist theoretical innovations were spurred by the observation that dominant sociological theories aimed at explaining the experiences of men may be somewhat limited in capturing the experiences of women without revision. At the same time, however, it can be problematic to simply add women into theories intended to explain men's experiences. Recognizing this, Dorothy Smith (1990) recommended that sociologists begin from women's standpoint, making "our direct embodied experience of the everyday world the primary ground of our knowledge" (Smith, 1990, p. 22). Smith (1926–) is a UK-born and American- and UK-trained sociologist, who has produced her major works while living and working in Canada. According to Smith (1990, p. 22), "the only way of knowing a socially constructed world is knowing it from within." Therefore, if we are to understand our world, we need to start with personal experience—and especially with the experiences of the marginalized—and explore the structures, policies and practices that reproduce their marginalization. In so doing, researchers can reveal the relations of ruling in society. By "ruling relations," Smith (1996) means "the complex of objectified social relations that organize and regulate our lives in contemporary [capitalist] society." Since these social relations create structures that feel external to us, it may be difficult to even identify them, let alone understand their impact. Smith has sought to provide concepts and methodologies to reveal the relations of ruling without reproducing them.

Dorothy Smith (2005) has elaborated what was initially a "sociology for women" into a "sociology for people" and developed a methodology—institutional ethnography—to guide researchers in this project of identifying ruling relations and documenting the structures, relationships, and practices that reproduce power inequalities. **Institutional ethnography** is a methodology that aims to map institutional practices and ruling relations in a given setting. It has been adopted by sociologists and researchers in other fields to document the experiences of workers in a variety of settings. For example, Weigt (2006) explores the experiences of mothers in low-waged work, documenting how ideological expectations of mothering combine with work practices to subordinate them. Moreover, Corman's (2018) study of paramedics uses institutional ethnography to identify the meanings these workers attach to their work, explore their working conditions and work practices, and document how they utilize their knowledge in action. Using this methodology, Smith and colleagues uncover both the micro and macro aspects of social experience and blend theory and method to inform sociological research.

institutional ethnography A methodology that aims to map institutional practices and ruling relations in a given setting. Associated with Dorothy Smith and colleagues

Smith argued that gender infused the relations of ruling in a way that ensured men's experiences and women's experiences were often very different. These ideas have been expanded upon by feminist scholars who have elaborated theories of how social institutions are gendered (Acker, 1990). By **gendered organizations** or institutions we mean that expectations about gender—gender ideologies, traditional divisions of labour, gender relations, and so on—have become embedded within organizational structures and practices (discussed more in Chapter 4). These structures can then limit employment opportunities for women and others who do not fully conform to gender norms. Acker's insights on gendered organizations help to shed light on the relations of ruling identified by Smith (1990), revealing that these structures have assumptions about gender embedded within them that impact people's lives and work profoundly.

gendered organizations Expectations about gender—gender ideologies, traditional divisions of labour, gender relations, and so on—have become embedded within organizational structures and practices

Overall, feminist theory offers a wide-ranging approach to sociology and the sociology of work. However, feminists and others have noted the limitations of these theories that emphasize gender as a binary—when in fact gender is a great deal more fluid—and fail to challenge **heteronormativity** (the belief that heterosexuality is "normal" or preferred) (Butler, 1990). Moreover, scholars have argued that it is important to move beyond theories that focus on gender (and class) inequalities in order to incorporate other dimensions of inequality, including race and ethnicity, citizenship, immigration status, sexual orientation, gender identity, and age (Crenshaw, 1989; Glenn, 2002).

heteronormativity Assumptions that heterosexuality and the gender binary are normal or preferred

Critical Race Theory, Settler Colonialism, and Decolonization

There are a variety of theories addressing race, racial inequality, colonialism, and decolonization. Although they are separate strands of theory, they share a commitment to challenging racist and colonial institutional practices that subordinate and marginalize peoples on the basis of their (socially constructed and defined) racial and/or Indigenous status.

Critical race theory sees racism as a structural, institutionalized system that upholds the power of white people at the expense of racialized others. This theory emerged between the 1970s and 1990s, especially within the field of legal studies, in response to a scholarly and public discourse that saw racism simply as prejudice that could be easily corrected through education or as a relic of the past (Bonilla-Silva, 2015; Crenshaw, 2011; Delgado & Stefancic, 2013). In contrast, critical race theorists argue that racism is material and structural, continually reproduced through social practices and social institutions that are infused with racial power (Bell, 1995; Bonilla-Silva, 2015; Crenshaw, 2011, p. 1287; Omi & Winant, 1994). The theory has several core insights. First, racism is a pervasive and ingrained feature of social life confronting people of colour daily (Delgado & Stefancic, 2013). Second, race itself is a social construction (Omi & Winant, 1994) whereby those in power aim to uphold their power by not only defining and constructing race in a manner that positions whiteness as superior but by simultaneously suggesting that this superiority rests on merit—thereby justifying the subordination of racialized peoples (Crenshaw, 2011; Delgado & Stefancic, 2013). Third, white people will encourage advances for members of minorities only when they gain from these advances themselves. Fourth, it is crucial to pay attention to context and the details of minority people's lives to understand their experiences and combat the discrimination and disadvantage they experience (Delgado & Stefancic, 2013). Finally, the approach is critical of law and the legal order, seeing them as bolstering white privilege and reproducing minority subordination (Bell, 1995).

Racism is subject to contestation—the marginalized fight back—but it has been strikingly persistent (Bonilla-Silva, 2015; Glenn, 2015). Although racial ideologies and practices have changed over time, race and racial inequalities are continually made and remade (Bonilla-Silva, 2015; Glenn, 2015). Critical race theory reminds us that racial disadvantage is embedded within social institutions and legal structures and is therefore resistant to change (Bell, 1995; Crenshaw, 2011; Carbado & Gulati, 2013). Proponents of critical race theory have also noted that race interacts with other dimensions of inequality, like class and gender, to shape social experience.

Applied to the sociology of work, critical race theory has been used to show how seemingly objective hiring criteria actually reproduce racial inequalities through a focus on merit and accomplishments that themselves are racially infused and tend to privilege white people (see for example, Crenshaw, 2011). Within the workplace, minority workers can struggle to conform to ideal worker norms, since they are disadvantaged by stereotypes and biases that are difficult to overcome, despite extensive effort (Carbado & Gulati, 2013). Minority workers may have their competence questioned (Bell, 1995). Workplaces are racialized—racist assumptions are embedded within them—and this racialization can limit opportunities for employment, promotion, and work-related benefits among the marginalized.

One criticism that has been levelled against traditional theories of race and racism is that some tend to group the experiences of the marginalized together; however, as Glenn (2002, 2015) has argued, racism and racialization vary across social-historical period and social group. For example, the experiences of Indigenous peoples, Black people, and Asian people are not the same. Glenn (2015) proposes that a settler colonialism framework can better address variations across racial groups while simultaneously highlighting the centrality of racism against Indigenous peoples to the historical establishment and current structure of Canadian and American societies.

Settler colonialism is a form of colonialism in which the colonists seek land to settle on, establish new communities, and obtain resources. To obtain their ends, settlers remove Indigenous inhabitants through genocide, resettlement and exclusion, and assimilation tactics (Glenn, 2015). Settlers also undermine Indigenous knowledge, languages, and culture (Coburn, Moreton-Robinson, Sefa Dei, & Stewart-Harawira, 2013; Coulthard, 2014; Winder, 2020). These violent strategies pursued in Canada and the United States have had a devastating effect on Indigenous peoples while establishing white power. They were accompanied by ideologies that justified these tactics—ideologies that conceptualized Indigenous people as lesser beings and white settlers as progressive and enlightened (Glenn, 2015). Moreover, settler colonialism established whiteness as a racial category and laid the foundation for other racial divisions that followed in Canadian and American societies (Glenn, 2015).

settler colonialism
A form of colonialism in which the colonists seek land to settle on, establish new communities, and obtain resources

Colonization is not simply a historical relic but an ongoing phenomenon. In Canada, some view the focus on reconciliation as a continuation of state dominance and authority over Indigenous peoples, their communities, and their lands (Coulthard, 2014). Moreover, exclusion, marginalization, and discrimination have been embedded into Canadian laws, entrenching their continuation. Canadian settlers—descendants of European colonial settlers and others who benefit from the institutions established to maintain their power—continue to benefit from the oppression of Indigenous peoples in Canada (TRC, 2015; Vowel, 2016).[1]

colonization
A process of settling an area while subordinating Indigenous peoples who already inhabit it

Decolonization is a set of practices and processes aimed at dismantling colonial power and restoring Indigenous knowledge and ways of life. Decolonization challenges traditional sociological theories and ways of knowing and encourages Indigenization. Indigenous researchers are creating new research and knowledge to enhance understanding of their social experiences (Coburn et al., 2013; Kovach, 2009). In such research, there is a need to move beyond a "damaged-centred" approach that portrays Indigenous communities as broken and pathological (Tuck, 2009; O'Donnell & Perley, 2016). While it is important to acknowledge the continued impact of colonialism, research should not be one-dimensional and focus on deficits but rather acknowledge complexity, positives, and hope.

decolonization
A set of practices and processes aimed at dismantling colonial power and restoring Indigenous knowledge and ways of life

There is also a need to learn from Indigenous knowledges. Indigenous knowledges counter Western approaches. They are more "holistic and relational, interconnected and

[1] There are some differences of opinion surrounding the use of the term "settler." Vowel (2016) suggests that the term should be limited to European descendants and other white immigrants to Canada, while Black Canadians (especially those who are descendants from slavery) and non-Black people of colour should be categorized separately. Some, however, use the term more broadly, since even those who experience racism and oppression themselves may benefit from structural inequalities disadvantaging Indigenous peoples in Canada.

inter-dependent systems that encompass knowledge of the spirit, heart, mind, and body" (Johnston, McGregor, & Restoule, 2018, p. 7). The Truth and Reconciliation Commission of Canada (TRC) recommends integration of Indigenous knowledge into research and education (TRC, 2015; McGregor, Restoule, & Johnston, 2018).

While these theories have yet to be extensively adopted within the sociology of work, studies have documented the challenges Indigenous workers face due to the interplay of colonialism and discrimination. For example, Marom (2019) documents the resilience and resistance of Indigenous teachers navigating racist and colonialist work and education environments. Moreover, Voyageur's (2011) research on women in leadership positions in Indigenous communities shows how history, legislation, colonialism, sexism, and community values combine to shape women's experiences in these roles. She not only documents their challenges but highlights women's ability to cope with these challenges and succeed.

Both critical race theories and Indigenous approaches have been combined with intersectional analysis (Glenn, 2015), and it is to these theories that we turn next.

Source: © lev radin/Shutterstock

Civil rights scholar Kimberlé Crenshaw coined the term "intersectionality" in her 1989 paper "Demarginalizing the Intersection of Race and Sex" to describe how gender, class, race, and other dimensions of inequality and identity intersect to shape an individual's interactions with the social world.

Intersectionality Theories

Feminist theories have tended to focus on the experiences of white women, while race theories focus on the experiences of Black men. Minority women—and especially Black women—have been excluded from such theories, their distinct challenges going unrecognized (Collins, 2010; Crenshaw, 1989). Scholars like Patricia Hill Collins and Kimberlé Crenshaw encourage us to re-orient and have as our focal point the experiences of Black women because this provides a window into interlocking systems of oppression. In doing so, we can explore how race and gender interact to structure experience and reproduce social inequality.

Each of us has a gender identity, a racial or ethnic background, an age, a socio-economic background. These characteristics influence our identity, our social interactions, and the opportunities and barriers we experience within and across social institutions. All of these identities, interactions, and opportunities combine to shape who we are and how we experience our social world. Sociological theories that address these dimensions separately only tell part of the story. Intersectionality theory aims to bring these dimensions together. We experience them simultaneously, so we should try to theorize their connections and intersections.

intersectionality Theories advocating that multiple dimensions of inequality (like gender, race, class), and the ways they intersect, should be taken into account simultaneously

Intersectionality is the idea that multiple axes of inequality operate together, intersecting to such an extent that to study one dimension without considering the others creates a distorted picture of social experience (Crenshaw, 1989; Glenn, 2002). While this is an important goal, it may be difficult to do, since gender, class, race, and other dimensions of inequality operate on multiple levels (identity, social interaction, and social and institutional practices). Intersectionality theories have differed in precisely how they bring these different dimensions together (Choo & Ferree, 2010). For some scholars, the goal is to empower the marginalized by drawing attention to the ways in which interlocking inequalities disadvantage some groups—especially minority women of colour (Collins, 2010; Choo & Ferree, 2010). This is a worthy goal, but there is a potential to downplay the significance of intersectionality for the experiences of the privileged as well. Others focus on intersectionality in concrete circumstances, examining moments when gender, race, and class gain particular salience; however, such approaches risk ignoring intersectionality in everyday practices that may, on the surface, seem unexceptional (Browne & Misra, 2003; Choo & Ferree, 2010). Some intersectional approaches argue that class, gender, and race are co-created, equally important systems of inequality that run through all aspects of social life in contemporary society (Choo & Ferree, 2010; Glenn, 2002). Such approaches are valuable, but some would criticize them for being too academic and not focused enough on generating social change (Collins, 2019).

Although there are different approaches to intersectional research, there is increasing agreement that intersectional inequalities are created through simultaneous processes (Holvino, 2010). There is also agreement that intersectional inequalities are reproduced within and across organizations. Moreover, dimensions such as gender, race, and class are co-constructed to the extent that they gain meaning through their interaction in particular organizational, institutional, and social-historical contexts (Acker, 2006; Glenn, 2002; Holvino, 2010). For example, meanings attached to gender have been shown to vary across race and class, and perceptions of race vary across class and gender (Glenn, 2002).

One of the main trends within intersectional research is the expansion of dimensions considered. Intersectionality scholars have focused on gender and race (often including class as well). Such an approach leaves many other dimensions of inequality unaccounted for. While theoretically accounting for the intersection of multiple dimensions is a complex undertaking, advocates for intersectional theory argue that it is important that researchers try to do so (Choo & Ferree, 2010). While it may be impossible for every researcher to take into account every dimension of inequality all the time, researchers should remain aware of the fact that it is difficult to disentangle these interlocking systems of inequality. Pull on one strand, and you are likely to find that others are intimately bound up with it and cannot be entirely disentangled.

Studies from an intersectional perspective in the sociology of work explore the ways in which different dimensions of inequality intersect to shape the social experience of working. For example, Glenn (2002) explores experiences of work and citizenship among ethnic minority men and women and how these experiences varied by minority status, geographic location, and time period.

Theorizing Work

The theories reviewed in this chapter are by no means exhaustive. There are a wide range of theories that can be applied to the sociology of work, but those discussed above are among the most influential. The theories discussed will reappear in other parts of the textbook because they inform research and discussion of key characteristics and topics in the field. The work reviewed here is intended to provide a foundation for further study. The value of sociological theory can be seen in its application. When we apply theory to social experience, we begin to understand our social world better.

You may want to begin on a small scale and think about whether you learn something new about your own experiences of work by applying these theories.

Reviewing the Learning Objectives

After reading this chapter, you should:

- Understand that there are many different sociological theories that provide explanations for the organization and experience of work.
- Have a sense of the key arguments and important concepts advanced in different sociological theories.
- Understand that work has been tied to broader social trends and social inequalities.

Questions for Critical Thought

1. In Marx's discussion of alienation, he argued that workers were separated from the product of their labour, the labour process, themselves, and others. Are workers who perform service work alienated, since they don't produce a tangible product and they tend to work more closely with clients and customers? When might they experience alienation? Under what conditions might they experience less alienation?
2. Foucault discussed how architecture could be used to enhance the surveillance of workers. How might social media be used to monitor workers? Do social media allow for the exercise of power that is visible yet unverifiable? That involves assessment, judgment, treatment, and (self-)discipline? If yes, in what way?
3. How might your positionality (your gender, race, class background, citizenship status, age, etc.) influence your experiences of the labour market? Do you think it affects your ability to get work and the way people treat you when you are on the job? Why or why not?
4. Which of the above theories best captures, or sheds light on, your own work experiences?

Annotated Additional Readings

Ritzer, G. (2018). *The McDonaldization of society: Into the digital age*. (9th ed.). Thousand Oaks, CA: Sage Publications.

A readable, accessible look at rationalization in our society.

Crenshaw, K. (1989). Demarginalizing the intersection of race and sex: A Black feminist critique of antidiscrimination doctrine, feminist theory and antiracist politics. *The University of Chicago Legal Forum*, 140, 139–167.

A classic article documenting why an intersectional approach is needed to understand the experiences of the marginalized and to counter social inequalities.

Blumer, H. (1986). *Symbolic interactionism: Perspective and method*. Berkeley, CA: University of California Press.

An important text from one of the founders of symbolic interactionism.

Foucault, M. (1977). *Discipline and punish: The birth of the prison*. New York, NY: Vintage.

A fascinating look at the rise of disciplinary society.

Related Websites

Social Theory Applied, a UK website devoted to applying social theory to social life:

https://socialtheoryapplied.com/

Global Social Theory: a free resource for people interested in social theory from a global perspective:

https://globalsocialtheory.org/

Symbolic Interactionism: Thoughtco is a website containing articles on a wide range of ideas:

https://www.thoughtco.com/symbolic-interaction-theory-3,026,633

Purdue University, literary theory entry on critical race theory:

https://owl.purdue.edu/owl/subject_specific_writing/writing_in_literature/literary_theory_and_schools_of_criticism/critical_race_theory.html

3 Historical Trends in Canadian Work

Learning Objectives

After reading this chapter, readers will:

- Understand that pre-industrial life and work were quite different from work under industrial capitalism.
- Understand that the emergence of industrial capitalism and subsequent economic developments have profoundly altered the organization and experience of work.
- Understand that workers have resisted changes at work and endeavoured to improve their working conditions.
- Understand that experiences of transitions at work vary by class, gender, Indigeneity, race, and other factors and be able to describe how experiences differ.

Introduction

Several of the theories reviewed in Chapter 2 highlighted historical transitions that structured present-day experiences of working, including settler colonialism, the emergence of industrial capitalism, and the rise of large bureaucratic institutions. In this chapter, we take a closer look at these transitions by focusing on key moments in the history of work in Canada, including the following eras:

a) Pre-industrial work
b) Early industrial capitalism (mid-to-late 19th century)
c) The emergence of monopoly capitalism (late 19th and early 20th centuries)
d) 20th-century challenges and changes

If one is to understand the nature of work today, one must understand the historical events, contests, and crises that shaped it. Admittedly, these eras are somewhat artificial. Social change occurs gradually and unevenly; the working conditions prevalent during one era continue into the next, even as new trends emerge. Nevertheless, discussing trends by era is a useful way of capturing continuity and change over time. This overview highlights several recurring themes and foci that remain relevant today and will be explored further in subsequent chapters: most notably, (1) major changes in the organization of work; (2) worker autonomy, agency, and resistance; (3) variations in experiences across class, gender, Indigeneity, and race/ethnicity.

Pre-industrial Work (<1850s)

From our present-day viewpoint, work under capitalism appears inevitable, and it is hard to imagine other ways of living and working. It is valuable, then, to take a closer look at what work and life were like in Canada prior to the arrival of industrial capitalism in the mid-19th century. Although this section only provides a brief overview of work over several centuries, it highlights that pre-capitalist working conditions were quite different from those that prevailed under industrial capitalism.

Prior to the arrival of Western colonizers from Europe, Indigenous peoples in what became Canada lived and worked closely with the land. As in other pre-industrial societies, there was no clear separation between work and life (Knight, 1996), and there was much work to be done. People spent their time engaged in building housing, making clothing, preparing and preserving food, and otherwise obtaining the **means of subsistence**—ensuring that community members had what they needed to live. Different Indigenous nations had distinct traditions and cultures, but most were hunter-gatherers, meaning they were somewhat nomadic and lived off what they could hunt, fish, and gather from the land and waterways around them. They valued the land and nature and sought to live and work in a manner that drew from and honoured the natural world around them. The division of labour in hunter-gatherer communities was flexible, but there were typically differences in the work done by men and women or the young and old. Exactly what these roles were could vary depending on locale, community structure, and tradition. Among the Indigenous peoples living in the region now known as British Columbia, men had primary responsibility for hunting, trapping, and making implements needed in everyday life, including tools. Skilled craftsmen had primary responsibility for building big houses and canoes (Knight, 1996, pp. 45–47). Women often tended small traps and fishing nets closer to settlements, gathered mussels and clams along the coast, gathered berries, and did the complex work involved in food preservation, preparing pelts, and making clothing (ibid.). The organization of life and work was determined by the community and community leaders, and much work was shared by groups of people rather than carried out by individuals in isolation.

means of subsistence The ability to obtain what is needed to ensure human survival

Traditional ways of living and working were disrupted by the arrival of white settlers from Europe, especially with the establishment of permanent settlements in the 1600s. These settlers not only brought their own traditions but intentionally set out to destroy the traditions of Indigenous peoples in the name of civilizing them. By the 1600s, the economies of England and France centred on agriculture, as well as natural resource extraction. They saw in Canada a great source of raw materials and valued goods such as animal fur. Europeans aimed to extract resources from North America and ship them overseas to European markets. White settlers tended to view Indigenous peoples who lived off the land as potential barriers to the achievement of economic goals, although European settlers regularly enlisted the help of Indigenous peoples and benefitted from their knowledge. During this period, white settlers set up their own communities, disrupting natural ecosystems by denuding the Canadian landscape of trees and animals in order to establish farms. Through their actions, settlers altered Indigenous ways of living and working.

seigneurial system A mode of organization, production, and society common in New France, wherein the French king granted plots of land to elite nobles, or "seigneurs," who in return promised to settle, develop, and oversee the land and its inhabitants

Settlers in New France, the colony established by the French in what is now Quebec, introduced a **seigneurial system** to encourage settlement and agriculture in the region. The French king granted plots of land to nobles, or *seigneurs*, who in return promised to settle, develop, and oversee the land and its inhabitants (while pledging loyalty to the king and promising military service) (Canada Project, 2019). Tenants rented land from the seigneur and provided him with grain from their harvest, while the seigneur provided a mill and acted as a magistrate to settle disputes and keep order. This form of social organization resembled the feudalism that was prominent across Europe in medieval times, wherein nobles possessed land on which serfs lived and toiled. The primary difference between medieval feudalism and the seigneurial system of New France was that medieval serfs were not free: they could not leave the land and were subject to the authority of their lords. Feudalism declined in western Europe in the 14th century, but strong social inequalities in land ownership remained. In some respect, these inequalities were made worse over subsequent centuries as the nobility expanded their land use, impeding the ability of common people to eke out a living from farming in Europe. Many became landless and moved to urban centres looking for work. Others looked for opportunities to farm in the colonies and immigrated to Canada or elsewhere in successive waves.

In agrarian communities, as in hunter-gatherer societies, there was no clear separation between life and work. The focus was on obtaining the means of subsistence, and there was a division of labour across gender and age. The main "production unit" was the household, which typically consisted of a husband, wife, and children, although household structures varied and the children in the household might be servants, apprentices, and/or the couple's own children (Bennett, 1987). Within these households, men would focus their labour on a principal productive activity—farming for most, but fishing or work in a skilled trade were two alternatives. Women's labour was extensive and diverse. When needed, they joined men working on their main tasks, and they did a number of other household tasks that were crucial to family survival. These tasks varied by locale and time

Source: Library and Archives Canada, Acc. No. R9266-169 Peter Winkworth Collection of Canadiana

A watercolour sketch of habitants with a sleigh and hay cart in Montreal, March 1849. Although this sketch by artist Amelia Frederica Dyneley was completed just as the Industrial Revolution began to intensify in Canada, it reflects the agrarian focus of pre-industrial work in New France.

period but could include tending animals, gardening to produce fruits and vegetables for family consumption, cooking, foraging, laundry, dairying, spinning, and making items like clothes for household members (Bennett, 1987; Cohen, 1988). Children (including any household servants) primarily assisted with men's and women's work tasks. Household members relied on each other for survival. These households were embedded within larger communities in which there was some mutual support and community regulation of certain aspects of production, but landholders (outside feudal and seigneurial systems) were fairly independent and autonomous producers (Bennett, 1987; Hanawalt, 1986). Even where wage labour was employed on farms, work contracts were often seasonal or yearly, and workers tended to live and work alongside their employers, minimizing the social distance between employer and employee.

This pre-industrial organization of work and life was characterized by profound inequalities. Seigneurs and officials had substantial power, while individual households had little. Within households, male household heads held power and authority over all household members. Women had few rights (Bennett, 1987; Cohen, 1988). The products of their labour, their children, and all their worldly possessions were technically the property of their husbands (Cohen, 1988). Laws establishing greater gender equality and rights for women were not passed in Canada until well into the 19th century.

In early Canada, slavery was legal as well. For instance, when the British took over New France, thousands of slaves—predominantly Indigenous but also African—were documented in the region (see Box 3.1). Under the British, slavery continued, with African slaves becoming more common than Indigenous. It was not until 1834 that slavery was eliminated throughout the British Empire, although several Canadian colonies (such as Upper Canada and Prince Edward Island) had passed laws against the practice in decades prior. The elimination of slavery helped to spur the migration of African Americans from south of the border (both free Blacks from the northern states and runaway slaves) into Ontario between the 1830s and 1850s (Hepburn, 1999; Winks, 1997), Nova Scotia after 1814 (Whitfield, 2003) and British Columbia in the late 1850s (Winks, 1997).

African Canadians had mixed experiences when they arrived in Canada. In Nova Scotia in the early 19th century, African Canadians struggled to find employment and sufficient land to farm, experiencing considerable poverty (Whitfield, 2003). Black refugees from the United States may have fared slightly better when they came to southern Ontario in larger numbers in the 1820s and 1830s. They experienced racism, but under the law they were equal to other citizens (Hepburn, 1999). There is evidence that they integrated into Ontario communities, finding work in a variety of fields. Hill (1981) reports that an 1840 survey in Toronto found many African-Canadian men working as unskilled labourers, but also many working in skilled trades, and about 10 per cent owned businesses. However, an economic downturn in the 1850s, combined with increased immigration of other groups and changing social attitudes, resulted in increased discrimination. Segregated schooling was introduced in the 1850s, and the environment for African Canadians in Ontario deteriorated (Winks, 1997; Murphy, 1997). In British Columbia, experiences were similar. African Canadians were welcomed to the colony on Vancouver Island in the late 1850s. They engaged in a variety of economic pursuits and seem to have exercised full political rights (Winks, 1997). Some years later, prejudice and discrimination increased, and the province was less welcoming.

A CLOSER LOOK

3.1 | Slavery in Montreal: The Trial and Hanging of Angélique

Marie-Josèphe Angélique was an African-Portuguese slave in Montreal in the 1720s and 1730s. Born in Portugal, she was brought to New England by a Flemish trader and there sold to a Frenchman from Montreal (Cooper, 2006). She worked in his home as a domestic, continuing to serve his widow after his death. Her name, Marie-Josèphe Angélique, was given to her when she, like other slaves in New France, was converted to Catholicism. She was not given a last name, since she was the property of her owners. The historical record does not record her name of birth and tells us little of her opinions, experiences, hopes, and dreams. The historical record, however, does document the vulnerability of slaves in New France because Angélique was accused of a terrible crime and experienced brutal torture before a public, humiliating death.

In April of 1734, a fire broke out in Montreal. Forty-five houses and a hospital were burned, and while no one died in the fire, there was significant loss of property. Soon after the fire, a rumour began circulating that Angélique had deliberately set the fire, and the authorities arrested her. Testimony was taken from "witnesses," none of whom had any evidence against Angélique. Angélique had no lawyer to defend her—indeed, there were no attorneys in the colony at that time. She was left to defend herself, and she proclaimed her innocence. In the end, it was the testimony of a five-year-old girl, claiming that she had seen Angélique go into the attic with some embers, that sealed Angélique's fate. Angélique countered this testimony but to no avail. In the French criminal justice system of the day, the accused were guilty until proven innocent; rumours, evidence of antipathy between Angélique and her owner, and the story of a five-year-old were sufficient to sentence Angélique to death for arson. Angélique was tortured first, with the hope of identifying any accomplices; she named none. Then, she was publicly hanged. This sad tale sheds light on the vulnerability of slaves in early Canadian society and their lack of rights. It was not until a whole century after Angélique's death that slavery was prohibited in the British Empire, including Canada.

Generally speaking, conditions in the Canadas were similar to those in other societies for most of the pre-industrial period, except that frontier life entailed fewer amenities, few markets, minimal infrastructure, and less specialization (Cohen, 1988; Glazebrook, 1968; Heron, 2019a). While small-scale farmers and artisans in England and France may have been able to trade surplus goods for other items they needed, the lack of good roads and established markets meant that many early settlers had to produce most of what they needed and barter and trade with neighbours for the rest (Cohen, 1988; Heron, 2019a). People were "Jacks and Jills of all trades" (Cohen, 1988; Glazebrook, 1968).

Of course, there were other workers in pre-industrial societies, including craftspeople and skilled professionals like medical practitioners and land surveyors. These independent workers often began their training in an occupation as children by being indentured or apprenticed to a master craftsman (most of these skilled occupations were practised by men) with whom they lived and worked, learning the trade. After years of apprenticeship, workers were often employed for a period as journeymen, before becoming independent master craftsmen themselves. These skilled workers may have had more status and security than small-scale farmers, but in some respects their work was not dissimilar. The work was **task-oriented**, without a sharp division between work and life (Thompson, 1967), and it was characterized by general autonomy tempered by community, which in many cases included other workers in the form of guilds and societies. Those who did not farm or only did so on the side in addition to doing something else may have combined several careers, such as the early land surveyors in New France who also worked as architects, bailiffs, clerks, and, in some instances, even innkeepers or merchants (Vachon, 1962). Serving in the military was another common means of earning a living, especially during the colonial days when there were many garrisons stationed at strategic points throughout the Canadas.

task orientation
An approach to working that focuses on doing what needs to be done, without any substantial concern for time or other factors

After England defeated France in the Seven Years' War of 1756–63, Quebec became an English colony. Subsequently, England settled Ontario. English settlements had already been established in the Maritimes in the early 1600s. As settlements expanded and the colonies became more established, major public works were undertaken, including the building of roads, railways, bridges, dams, and canals. These public works required large numbers of workers—both skilled and unskilled labour (Bleasdale, 2018). The work was extremely physical and difficult, and the working conditions were terrible. Workers laboured outside, in all weather conditions, doing hard manual labour for 10 to 12 hours a day under the close supervision of often physically and verbally abusive overseers. The work was extremely dangerous, and many were injured, maimed, and killed on the job from cave-ins, equipment malfunctions, explosions, and disease (Bleasdale, 2018). The work was so back-breaking few could stay in the industry for their entire working lives (Bleasdale, 2018). For their efforts, however, they received decent wages. Many hoped to use their wages to buy farmland.

During this era, many settlers continued to work in resource-extraction industries such as logging, fishing, and the fur trade. This work was also physically demanding and often dangerous. French-Canadian voyageurs were indentured employees of fur-trade companies, travelling the country primarily by canoe in the 18th and 19th centuries especially, hunting and trapping animals (Podruchny, 2006; Englebert, 2007). Despite the challenges associated with the work, voyageurs celebrated their strength, skills, comradery, and connection with the land. Indigenous people were also active in the fur trade, trapping and trading with white settlers; in many instances, they were employed by fur-trading companies (Knight, 1996). St-Onge (2016) examined the participation of Mohawk men from Khanawake near Montreal. Men signed up as groups or teams on multi-year contracts to work as trappers, hunters, and canoeists. They were attractive employees due to their skills, expertise, and toughness, especially in an era when the fur trade was characterized by intense intercompany competition, often resulting in violence. This work allowed Mohawk men to live and work together in more nomadic fashion; in so doing, they could uphold Mohawk cultural norms for men by demonstrating expertise, skill, bravery, and independence. They were well paid for their efforts.

Overall, pre-industrial work and life in Canada was physically demanding, precarious, and dangerous. However, it was also characterized by a balance of independence and community, autonomy for many, and task orientation. All of this gradually changed with the emergence of industrial capitalism.

The Emergence of Industrial Capitalism (1850s–1890)

Industrial Revolution Period of massive economic, technological, and social change occurring in Western countries in the 18th and 19th centuries under capitalism

In the Western world, the capitalist system emerged first in England, transforming agricultural production in the 1600s, before spurring the Industrial Revolution, which transformed the production of goods beginning in the 1700s (Wood, 1999). The **Industrial Revolution** entailed the use of technology—initially steam-powered—to manufacture products for the market on a grand scale. This change in production, however, was associated with considerable upheaval, impacting how people lived and worked (Thompson, 1967). The efficiency and power of the new work systems—combined with their potential to generate capitalist profit—led to their adoption around the world.

Industrial capitalism arrived later in Canada than in countries such as Britain and the United States, and its development was slow and uneven (Heron, 2019a; Rinehart, 2001). Poor roads, few railways, and the sparse population spread across a broad territory limited the growth of markets and market-oriented production. As in England, capitalist production methods were first introduced in agriculture and resource industries. Resource extraction and farming became more market-oriented, and production relied increasingly on wage labour; innovation was pursued to increase efficiency, productivity, and profit. Manufacturing facilities emerged in the mid-19th century, but they were often seasonal and initially quite small—some having only four or five employees (Heron, 2019b). Gradually, manufacturing expanded, and firms producing everything from furniture, textiles, and food to cigars, agricultural equipment, and clothes became more common, especially in urban centres. They came to employ more workers and embraced mechanization to increase production efficiency.

Although looking back we can see the transition to industrial capitalism as a gradual one in Canada, it seemed sudden and revolutionary to those that lived through the change (hence the term industrial *revolution*). To people used to working on farms or in skilled trades, wage labour in factories was a shock. The working conditions were terrible. Factories did not have electricity until late in the 19th century, so factories were often dark, poorly ventilated, dirty, and dangerous. Work hours were long, with days averaging 12 to 14 hours in length, six days a week. People used to working by the task (task orientation) were now asked to work by the clock, putting in a steady work effort throughout the day under the watchful eye of a foreman or overseer. E. P. Thompson (1967, p. 73) has argued that when people work independently, their work pace tends to be uneven as they "alternate bouts of intense labour and of idleness," but industrial capitalism required **time discipline**. Owners wanted to synchronize the work of their employees to enhance efficiency and profit. The adjustment to working according to regimented and strict time schedules was not easy (Thompson, 1967). **Mechanization**—the introduction of steam-powered (and later electric) machines—further controlled the speed and conduct of work, since people had to keep up with the pace of the machinery (ibid.).

time discipline Working according to the clock and the schedules of others

mechanization The alteration of work processes through the introduction of machinery

Work changed dramatically. Manufacturers faced many challenges producing for local markets given Canada's small population, including limited sources of labour, skill shortages, and the unpredictability of local markets (Heron, 2019b). To secure profit, they restructured work to make more use of unskilled labour, which was readily available. Jobs formerly done by one person were subdivided into a narrow range of tasks, which could be done by less-skilled workers at lower wages. In some industries, employers used the **putting-out system** whereby they subcontracted work to people in households or smaller workshops, who sent completed work back to their employer. Nevertheless, there were efficiency gains to be made by bringing workers into factories and mechanizing aspects of production. Machinery could save on labour costs by doing work formerly done by humans and could set the work pace, ensuring that labourers worked steadily (Heron, 2019b; Thompson, 1967).

putting-out system Production system wherein workers are subcontracted to produce goods from their homes or small workshops and then to send completed work back to their employer

Workers and contemporary observers were ambivalent about these changes. On the one hand, they were amazed by the technological advances revolutionizing production. One news reporter, after visiting a factory in Toronto in 1888, described the "marvelous" "labour-saving machinery," saying "it really looks as if it was the machines that are human and the men that were machines" (quoted in Heron, 2019b, p. 69). Another reporter extolled the superiority of machines that "can work the whole twenty-four hours without stopping" and made "no distinctions between Sundays, holidays and any ordinary day" (Heron, 1980, p. 23). Others remarked on the coordination of labour, describing it as scientific and like clockwork and comparing workers to ants and bees (Bleasdale, 2018). Yet, as the language used here implies, contemporaries also regarded these changes as alarming and potentially dehumanizing. It was this aspect that concerned theorists like Karl Marx: the autonomy and creativity of workers appeared to be undermined by mechanization and the relentless dictates of industrial capitalism.

Mechanization also made work more dangerous. Machinery was unpredictable, prone to breakdowns and malfunction. It was also often large and cumbersome, with moving parts that could harm people. There were few safety provisions. Workplace injuries were commonplace, and could have grave consequences when limbs got caught in machinery or were trapped by it, necessitating amputation (Bleasdale, 2018; Hallgrímsdóttir & Adams, 2004). In this period, there was no "social safety net." A worker who lost a limb did not have workers' compensation, unemployment insurance, or other sources of income to fall back on. A family who lost their primary wage earner could be left destitute. For employers seeking profit, added safety provisions could be viewed as an unnecessary expense. Canadian Pacific Railway engineer Sir Sandford Fleming was critical of employers' refusal to accept any responsibility for the safety of their employees and cynically summarized their attitude: "It cost nothing to kill a man, but it would cost something to make use of a mechanical contrivance that might save his life" (Fleming, 1878). Profit margins were tight, and employers sought to use whatever means to increase them. Workers were sacrificed in the process.

The early industrial attitude to worker safety is far removed from the paternalism that characterized pre-industrial (and some early industrial) work relationships. Here, employers were expected to provide for their employees, ensuring that they had food, shelter, and other necessities of life, as well as providing a paycheque and often imparting skills. Employees were expected to work hard for their employers, do what was asked of them, and demonstrate some loyalty. It was an unequal relationship but one with reciprocal responsibilities (Heron, 2019b). The idea that employers owed workers anything beyond a wage for their services was not consistent with capitalist ideology, and hence such notions gradually disappeared. In return, workers felt less loyalty to their employers and were more willing to leave unpleasant jobs when they could find alternative work or stay and fight for better working conditions.

In the late 19th century, workers resisted employer exploitation and workplace change that resulted in deteriorated working conditions. Skilled craftsmen traditionally enjoyed autonomy in the exercise of advanced skill; they used existing craft guilds and formed new associations for collective protests when employers tried to routinize their work, mechanize in a manner that threatened to undermine their expertise, or substitute less-skilled workers to do aspects of their work (Heron, 2019b; Morton, 1998). They also fought for more reasonable working hours. Some achieved limited successes, while others failed. Some skilled and less-skilled workers tried to form unions to bargain for better working conditions and remuneration. However, they faced considerable opposition. Union organizing was deemed a "conspiracy in restraint of trade" and, hence, illegal (Heron, 1996). Employers were aggressive in undermining unions, firing anyone rumoured to be involved in union organizing and colluding with other employers to prevent such workers from obtaining work elsewhere. Such tactics were successful for a time, but unions still managed to gain a toe-hold in this era, especially in the 1880s when the Knights of Labor gained popularity and signed up thousands of workers across workplaces, sectors, and regions in Canada and the United States (Kealey & Palmer, 1982) (see Box 3.2).

The period between the mid-19th century and the 1890s was characterized by urban growth, expanding education, immigration, and other important social changes. Gradually, more Canadians came to live in urban centres, and that brought different employment opportunities. With more people living in close proximity, the market for

A CLOSER LOOK

3.2 | The Knights of Labor

Everywhere, the implementation of industrial capitalism has met with resistance from workers (Thompson, 1967). One important labour movement was the Knights of Labor (KOL). The KOL was founded in Philadelphia in 1869 and subsequently spread throughout the United States, into Canada, the United Kingdom, and Australia. While worker organizations were traditionally organized by occupation or industry, the KOL was different in that it sought to unite all workers, across occupation, industry, region, and even across gender and race. The KOL was open to almost everyone—lawyers and liquor salespeople excluded—and fought for better working and living conditions for labourers and their families (Kealey & Palmer 1982; Kealey & Gagnon 2006). The Knights of Labor reached their heyday in the mid-1880s, with a Canadian membership estimated to be 12,000 to 14,000 in the years preceding 1888. On principle, the Knights of Labor were ambivalent about strikes, preferring to bargain with employers and to seek legislative change to improve working and living conditions (Kealey & Palmer, 1982; Hallgrímsdóttir & Adams, 2004). The popularity of the Knights of Labor was short-lived, and in the 1890s the movement declined in the face of employer hostility and an economic downturn. By the end of the 19th century, most workers did not have the protection of a union. With so much employment unstable and low-paid, many workers could barely make ends meet. They were not in a strong position to stand up to employers because if they lost their jobs, they and their families could starve.

many services expanded, as did the number of stores and other businesses. Growing towns and cities needed new homes and roads, opening up opportunities in construction. The growth of education created jobs for teachers. Expanding infrastructure brought jobs for professional workers like engineers, land surveyors, and architects. Urban centres also provided more opportunities for medical doctors, dentists, pharmacists, and other educated, skilled workers. These educated workers were able to maintain considerable autonomy and exercise creativity in the conduct of their work. Work in stores and businesses had its challenges, including long hours spent standing, but it was less dangerous than manual labour. In this era, Canada's middle class emerged (Holman, 2000), and those who had more wealth and education were able to obtain and even create jobs that were more fulfilling and less exploitative. Others were not so fortunate. Experiences of the rise of industrial capitalism varied not only by class but gender, age, and minority status.

Gender divisions of labour were long-standing, but in the early industrial period they became more entrenched as the locus for production shifted away from the home towards centralized workplaces, including factories, often in urban centres. An influential gender ideology, **separate spheres ideology**, which gained popularity among the middle class in Western countries beginning in the 18th century, shaped gender divisions of labour (Davidoff & Hall, 1987). Separate spheres ideology held that men and women were biologically different—with different natures, temperaments, and abilities. Men were inherently independent, rational, and ideally suited for the public sphere of politics and work. In contrast, women were seen as inherently dependent, emotional, and caring, making the private sphere of home and family ideal for them. While necessity sometimes pulled women out of the home into the public sphere, it was expected that their public roles would correspond to their private sphere responsibilities and link in some way back to home and family. This ideology shaped employment trends: since men and women were perceived to be so different, it followed that their work should be different as well.

separate spheres ideology
The belief that there are two spheres in society and that men are ideally suited for the public sphere and women for the private sphere because of their "innate" characteristics

In early capitalism, men specialized in productive labour, and while many continued to engage in farming or work in other primary industries (such as fishing, forestry, and mining), others found work in factories and other workplaces. Married women stayed close to home, continuing many of the same tasks they had done previously—looking after animals (even in urban areas), maintaining a garden to grow food for the family, and running the household (Bradbury, 2000; Cohen, 1988). Separate spheres ideology cast women as nurturers, ideally suited for child-rearing. As children came to be seen as beings that required care, attention, and education before they could be launched into the adult world, raising children became a task requiring women's careful attention (Ryan, 1984). Married women had so much to do in the household that it was difficult for them to work outside the home, but out of economic necessity they sometimes took in work under the putting-out system, making clothes or other items or taking in others' laundry (Bradbury, 2000; Cohen, 1988). While women's labour force participation was discouraged by separate spheres ideology, many single women needed to earn a living (Bradbury, 2000). When working for pay, single women were predominantly found in a narrow range of occupations deemed suitable for them: such as domestic service or in clothing and food manufactories. Women also found work in the growing service economy. For their efforts, women were paid roughly half of what men made—in part because it was assumed they would have a male breadwinner to support them.

In the early industrial era, many children also worked outside the home. As in the past, their labour contributed to household survival. There was no general consensus as to when children were adult enough to work (Heron, 2019b, p. 85). By and large, boys over 12 and girls over 14 were treated as adults and eligible for employment, but many younger children also went to work. Children found work assisting adult workers in factories, and they worked in shops as well as running errands and doing other odd jobs. They were paid very poorly for their work, but nonetheless made an important contribution to household income (Bradbury, 2000). Some social commentators from more privileged classes criticized parents for stopping their children from getting a good education, but the reality was that wages were so low and work so precarious that many families required all family members to earn income in order to put food on the table and keep a roof over their heads (ibid.).

Experiences of industrial capitalism also varied by race and ethnicity. Immigration to Canada in the mid-19th century was predominantly from Britain and the United States, but the diversity of Canada's population was increasing. Immigrants came to Canada from other European countries like the Netherlands, Germany, and Eastern Europe. Chinese men immigrated to British Columbia beginning in the late 1850s. At times, the Canadian government actively recruited people to immigrate to Canada, not only with the aim of settling the country but to make up for labour shortages and spur the growth of capitalist industry. The challenges faced by immigrants were strongly shaped by racial prejudice. While many of the British and American immigrants settled in Canadian society with few difficulties, others experienced systemic racism, including Irish Catholics, African Canadians, and the Chinese. Racist ideologies, however, were variable, and the experiences of different minorities were not the same (Goutor, 2005).

There is evidence that African Canadians' work opportunities decreased with the rise of industrial capitalism (Adams, 2011). In London, Ontario, in 1861, while roughly 50 per cent of African-Canadian men worked as labourers and 15 per cent were farmers, there were also a few professionals (minister, doctor, dentist, pharmacist), several businessmen, and many working in skilled trades. By 1871, 84 per cent of African-Canadian men in the city were clustered in five jobs: labourer, barber, farmer, plasterer, and gardener. Despite major transformations of the Canadian economy, African-Canadian men continued to be clustered in these and similar occupations 30 years later (Adams, 2011). African-Canadian women's labour was even more clustered. They worked predominantly as laundresses and servants—similar to their counterparts in Nova Scotia (Morton, 1993). In some census years, their opportunities were broader, including work as seamstresses, dressmakers, and hairdressers. It seems that for African-Canadian men and women, opportunities for semi-skilled work using new machinery in factories and other settings were few and far between. With decreasing opportunities and the changing political and racial environment for African Americans in the US after the Civil War, many African Canadians moved to the US in search of better opportunities.

While opportunities for African Canadians were limited, they were at least afforded the rights of citizenship. The same could not be said for Chinese and Japanese immigrants to Canada, who were treated very poorly (Creese, 1987; Goutor, 2005). Systematically denied citizenship and discouraged from bringing their families over to join them, Chinese men worked in some of the least popular, most back-breaking, and most dangerous jobs: building railways, working as farm labourers, in mines, in canneries, and in other undesirable jobs, such as domestic service, mostly in British Columbia. For their labour they were paid one-third to one-half of what white men earned (Creese, 1987). They were formally excluded from pursuing better jobs, including professions like law, accountancy, and pharmacy. Other workers excluded them from unions and fought against their immigration (Goutor, 2005). Their situation was dire during this period.

Indigenous men and women also faced discrimination and shifting opportunities during this era. Knight (1996) has argued that as more settlers moved into British Columbia, Indigenous people experienced a decline in their political autonomy and traditional ways of supporting themselves. Nevertheless, Indigenous peoples were "essential to the capitalist development of British Columbia" (Lutz, 2000, p. 236); moreover, they were integrated "into virtually every major resource industry in the province as workers and owner-operators" (Knight, 1996, p. 9). These industries included fishing and canning (the latter employing Indigenous men and women), work as seamen and sealers, farming and ranching, mill work, freighting and packing, boat-building, and logging. In this era, Indigenous peoples also established small businesses and engaged in the production of handicrafts and carvings for sale. They also found work in the Nanaimo coal mines (Lutz, 2000). Here and elsewhere, Indigenous men found work in railway and bridge construction (Knight, 1996; Blanchard, 1983). Much of this work was seasonal, and Indigenous peoples might move between wage work in different sectors, and other subsistence activities, seasonally (Lutz, 2000). Blanchard (1983) has also documented the employment of Indigenous peoples, including those living in Kahnawake (discussed earlier in this chapter), in high-steel construction, building bridges and high rises in Quebec and the United States. This work required skill, teamwork, and bravery and hence may have appealed to Mohawk and other Indigenous men whose opportunities for work that allowed them to work collectively and demonstrate culturally valued characteristics had dwindled because of colonization and discrimination. Indigenous women were also active in the labour force, employed in canneries, farming and agriculture, and many other industries (Knight, 1996; Patrias, 2016). Despite these opportunities, Indigenous men and women faced considerable discrimination.

To summarize this lengthy discussion, the rise of industrial capitalism transformed work in Canada, but there were some continuities as well. New jobs were created with mechanization and the rise of industrial production: for instance, semi-skilled jobs for machine tenders and unskilled and skilled work in manufacturing, construction, and emerging high-status professions. With the spread of employment under industrial capitalism, worker autonomy decreased. Some workers saw their skills decline with workplace change and mechanization. Opportunities for work varied by class, race, gender, and age, with women and minorities (and children) typically earning less and having a narrower range of occupations open to them. The new world of work was unsafe, and workers were left to bear the brunt of the responsibility for these conditions as they risked injury for their employers with few protections; in fact, many were blamed for their own injuries (Bleasdale, 2018). Working conditions in many sectors were poor, and work was often precarious. Workers fought for change but found only limited success in this era. Fortunately, they had more success in the subsequent decades.

Issues at Work

3.3 | Royal Commission on the Relations of Labor and Capital

In December of 1886, the federal government established a commission to inquire into and report on "the subject of Labor, its relation to Capital, the hours of labor, and the earnings of laboring men and women, and the means of promoting their material, social, intellectual and moral prosperity, and of improving and developing the productive industries of the Dominion so as to advance and improve the trade and commerce of Canada" (Canada, Royal Commission on the Relations of Labor and Capital, 1889, p. 3). This was a broad remit, and the commissioners held hearings in many Canadian cities, hearing testimony from workers and employers. The commissioners were particularly distressed by the testimony of child workers, as can be seen in this excerpt from their report (Canada, Royal Commission on the Relations of Labor and Capital, 1889, p. 36):

> Many children of tender age, some of them not more than nine years old, were employed in cotton, glass, tobacco and cigar factories, and in other places. At one place in Ontario children, certainly less than eleven years of age, were employed around dangerous machinery. Some of them worked from six o'clock in the morning till six in the evening, with less than an hour for dinner, others worked from seven in the evening till six in the morning. At Montreal boys were employed all night in the glass works. In the cotton factories . . . sometimes the afternoon work is continued till 7:15, without stopping for supper, and less frequently the machinery is in continuous operation from 12:45 till 9 p.m., making eight and a-quarter hours of uninterrupted work, though it is in evidence that operatives are permitted to take a little lunch while the machinery is in motion.
>
> The testimony respecting children employed in cigar and tobacco factories was of a very painful nature. Boys and girls not more than ten years of age, were found in these places in considerable numbers. . . . The evil in these instances was accentuated by the evident fact that the tobacco had stunted the growth of the witnesses and poisoned their blood. They were undersized, sallow and listless, wholly without the bright vivacity and rosy hue of health which should animate and adorn children.

The Royal Commission provided many recommendations for reform, but virtually none were implemented.

Monopoly Capitalism and the Administrative Revolution (1890s–1920s)

monopoly capitalism Period of capitalist development in which the concentration of capital spurred the rise of larger, more international firms able to restrict the workings of a free competitive market

By the 1890s, the slow and uneven growth of industrial capitalism had progressed, and it was more fully established in Canadian cities. Scholars argue that this era witnessed the rise of **monopoly capitalism**, characterized by a gradual decline in smaller firms and the emergence of larger ones, which provided goods and services not just to local markets but, increasingly, regional, national, and even international markets (Braverman, 1974; Heron, 2019a). These changes have continued to the present day and are at the heart of what we now refer to as **globalization**—processes through which businesses and other organizations extend their influence and operations internationally (*Oxford English Dictionary*, 2020b). In the late 19th century, such changes were only nascent, but they nonetheless transformed work. Some refer to this era as a second industrial revolution (Vallas, Finlay, & Wharton, 2009) to highlight rapid technological change (electricity, telephones, and so on) while others call it an **administrative revolution** (Lowe, 1987) to capture shifts in organizational structures and divisions of labour. During this era, new jobs were created, old jobs were transformed, and the regulations surrounding work changed.

globalization
A set of processes in which production, capital, labour, communication, and culture are increasingly occurring on a global level

administrative revolution
Period of organizational change in the early 20th century, which saw the expansion of white-collar, managerial, and other administrative jobs

You may remember Max Weber's (1946) argument about rationalization and the rise of bureaucracies to increase efficiencies through advanced divisions of labour, hierarchies, and formalization from Chapter 2. The era of monopoly capitalism was also an era of bureaucratization. Pre-industrial and early industrial firms were usually small, with few hierarchical levels or formal rules. Bosses and overseers had a great deal of authority over their workers, and they set and enforced rules largely as they saw fit. However, as firms started growing, they came to resemble those bureaucracies described by Weber: jobs were subdivided, new jobs were created, formal rules and policies were implemented, and hierarchies grew. The implications of these changes for work can be seen through a few examples.

First, consider the case of clerical or secretarial work. In early industrial times, the owner or his assistants would have handled a firm's correspondence and may also have taken on the book-keeping, purchasing, marketing, bill payments, and other similar tasks. When firms had a secretary, this position was held by an educated man who worked closely with the owner, and the job description would have been very broad (Lowe, 1987). As firms grew larger, however, it became more difficult for one person to complete all of these tasks. With a large workforce, handling payroll alone might be a full-time job for several people. As firms hired more people to complete all of this clerical work, the job was transformed. The position was subdivided so that there were several clerical or secretarial workers, each specializing in a particular area and supporting different departments. By subdividing the tasks and narrowing the work, employers could hire less-skilled workers and pay them lower wages. During this period, middle-class, single women began to take over these roles, and clerical work came to be defined as "women's work." The number of women doing clerical work in Canada increased from 9000 in 1901 to 79,000 in 1921 (Frager & Patrias, 2005, p. 65). Women were deemed an ideal workforce because they had the required education, were paid much less than men, and were thought to be less likely than men to complain about narrow, repetitive work (Cohn, 1985; Frager & Patrias, 2005; Lowe, 1987). Women were also believed to have fewer expectations about career progress than men since many left the labour force upon marriage. Some companies even implemented formal policies terminating women's employment when they married (Cohn, 1985). In this manner, the job of secretary was transformed during monopoly capitalism from a high-status, broad job for middle-class men to a lower-status, lower-paying, narrower job for women.

Second, this was an era when the job of manager became more established. In previous eras, workers were often supervised directly by their employer, a hired overseer, or perhaps one of their own promoted to fulfill duties as foreman. However, as companies expanded their workforce, it became difficult for employers or their direct agents to ensure that workers were working diligently and efficiently at a steady pace all day long. Firm hierarchies expanded to create managerial levels lying between the firm's leadership and the workers underneath.

scientific management
Management philosophy associated with the writings of F. W. Taylor (also called Taylorism). It is associated with separating conception from execution, management appropriating knowledge about the labour process and closely directing the work of workers

Taylorism
Management philosophy associated with the writings of F. W. Taylor (also called scientific management). It is associated with separating conception from execution, management appropriating knowledge about the labour process and closely directing the work of workers

Fordism
A manner of organizing production characterized by advanced divisions of labour, automation, mass production, and managerial control

semi-skilled
Requiring some skills and training but not a lot

deskilling
Process of job degradation through which workers are denied the opportunity to use skills (and autonomy) formerly exercised on the job

A new science of management also emerged during this era. **Scientific management** was a set of principles through which managers sought to make work more efficient (Braverman, 1974). The goals of scientific management (sometimes called **Taylorism**) were articulated by its founder, Frederick W. Taylor (1911).

(1) Managers need to acquire knowledge about the work they manage, "gathering together all of the traditional knowledge which in the past has been possessed by the workmen and then classifying, tabulating, and reducing this knowledge to rules, laws, and formulae" (Taylor, 1911, p. 39).
(2) Jobs should be altered so that workers labour without bearing any responsibility for planning. That is, "all possible brain work should be removed from the shop [meaning the workers] and centred in the planning . . . department" (Taylor, 1911, p. 63).
(3) Work should be planned by managers and other experts who then tell workers exactly what to do: "each [worker] receives in most cases complete written instructions describing in detail . . . Not only what is to be done, but how it is to be done and the exact time allowed for doing it" (Taylor, 1911, pp. 98–99).

These goals may call to mind the arguments made by Marx and Weber. The defined steps involve planning, formalization, and rationalization, as highlighted by Weber. At the same time, scientific management entails the separation of conception from execution (the "thinking" work from the "doing" work), which Marx saw as so alienating under capitalism. These trends were taken further under **Fordism**, characterized by mass production and the use of assembly lines, beginning in the early 20th century (and pioneered by the Ford Motor Company). Although firms varied in the extent to which they implemented scientific management and Fordism (Braverman, 1974), these principles reflect broader changes at work in this era and reveal the drive to alter the work of lower-level workers by creating a new layer of managerial workers tasked with increasing efficiencies.

In addition to the expansion of the managerial workforce, several other new jobs emerged in large firms. These jobs tended to be **semi-skilled**—requiring some knowledge, education, training, or expertise but not necessarily the several years of training required by master craftsmen or professional workers (doctors, lawyers). That said, workers in some jobs experienced **deskilling**—a reduction in the skills demanded of them on the job (including the reduction in planning recommended under scientific management; Braverman, 1974). Workers also experienced a further loss of control at work, since their activity was subject to the direction of others. Trends at the heart of scientific management—subdivision of tasks and increasing managerial authority over workers who have less ability to direct their own work—continue today in a variety of occupations, as we will see in later chapters (7 especially).

Scientific management provided one set of solutions to the challenge of managing labour to ensure steady, consistent, and speedy production. Another solution—called

welfare management—involved making workplace improvements with the goal of enticing employees to work diligently. We have seen that in the early industrial era, workers organized to demand better working conditions. These demands continued, and some employers believed that if they provided better facilities and some benefits, they could win loyalty and increased productivity from their semi-skilled and skilled workers (there was less motivation to woo unskilled workers, since they could be more easily replaced). Employers began to invest in improving workplaces by making them lighter, cleaner, and safer and providing their employees with some benefits. It was hoped that such changes would discourage **unionization** and improve workers' willingness to work hard for their employers.

welfare management A strategy to encourage worker compliance and commitment by making workplace improvements and providing some work-related perks

unionization The process of organizing workers into a union

Despite such changes, workers continued to fight for workplace change, and in this era they won some policy concessions. In Canada, federal and provincial governments had been reluctant to regulate workplaces, preferring to allow employers freedom to do as they pleased. However, when government commissions and media reports revealed conditions in the factories, the government was eventually compelled to act—albeit in a very limited manner. Workers' compensation and minimum wages for women were both implemented during this period. Widespread concern over children (and women) working in factories resulted in legislation to limit working hours. These laws seem lax by modern standards. For instance Ontario's Factory Act, passed in 1884 but not enforced until 1887, aimed to prevent the factory employment of boys under 12 and girls under 14 (Tucker, 1988). Children and women were restricted from working more than 10 hours a day, six days a week; however, exceptions to these rules were allowed under certain circumstances. These restrictions were not tightly enforced (Tucker, 1988), and it seems that the law did little to discourage child labour. More effective were laws eventually passed to force children to attend school. Moreover, worker campaigns gradually resulted in improvements to men's wages, raising them to a level where they could support their entire families and making it more affordable for working families to send their children to school.

Other changes to working conditions were brought about through workers' unionization. In the opening decades of the 20th century, industrial workers began forming unions to fight for better working conditions, pay, work hours, and the right to **collective bargaining**. Employers still opposed unions vociferously, but by World War I, union activity, strikes, and protests increased. The climax of these was the Winnipeg General Strike in May and June of 1919, which saw 25,000 to 30,000 (unionized and non-unionized) workers, across industries, walk off the job: factory workers, postal workers, retail workers, and many others joined the strike (Morton, 1998). They primarily sought better wages and working conditions, union recognition, and collective bargaining rights. Although the strike was a peaceful one, with no picketing, it culminated in violence: a worker parade was broken up by the North-West Mounted Police and other officers; two people died and many more were injured (Morton, 1998). Several people were arrested, although many of those targeted for arrest were not strike leaders. In this era, Canadian state actors opposed worker protests, and they were quite willing to support employers through the use of repressive force. State leaders' fear of unions and worker protests only increased after the Russian Revolution in 1917. In the 1920s, the combination of state and employer hostility, and a recession, provided major setbacks for the labour movement.

collective bargaining Negotiations between employers and workers' unions concerning the terms and conditions of employment

Source: Royal Canadian Mounted Police/Library and Archives Canada/e004666108

NWMP officers on horseback charge to break up a worker parade during the Winnipeg General Strike, killing two people and injuring many others. Between May and June 1919, more than 30,000 men and women went on strike for the right to collective bargaining, better wages, and better working conditions. They were opposed by local and federal business leaders and politicians, who blamed the strike on eastern European immigrants and "Bolsheviks" and used these allegations to block negotiations with the strike committee.

Although unions made some minor gains in this period, those gains were not shared among all workers; it was predominantly white men working in industrial jobs who had the opportunity to join unions. Members of racial minorities and white women worked in different sectors and were overrepresented in jobs deemed "unskilled." Unskilled workers had less bargaining power with their employers, since they were more easily replaceable. They still resisted poor conditions, however, engaging in activism when possible (Creese, 1987).

In the late 19th and early 20th centuries, women were clustered in a narrow range of occupations, but they did see their job opportunities grow. In addition to their work in domestic service and food and textile manufacturing, they found work in teaching, clerical work, nursing, and retail stores. A very small number of women entered formerly male-dominated professions such as medicine, law, and dentistry in the 1880s and 1890s; by the 1920s, the number of women in professions like medicine and dentistry had grown. White women had access to the best jobs, while minority women were relegated to a narrower range, including domestic service, laundry work, and manual farm labour (to name a few). Immigrant women also found work in factories and in agriculture. Married women were less active in the workforce than single women, except when circumstances and economic necessity required their participation (Buddle, 2010; Frager & Patrias, 2005).

The jobs open to white, and especially middle-class, men diversified with growth in the manufacturing sector and the expansion of administrative, white-collar jobs. New jobs for men included management and jobs in urban centres as police officers. Professional work also expanded in this era as new specialties arose and were regulated by provincial governments—including work in law, medicine, dentistry, pharmacy, land surveying, architecture, engineering, accounting, and veterinary science (Adams, 2018). Professional workers enjoyed better working conditions, pay, autonomy, and social respect. They had advanced education and the opportunity to use and develop their skills on the job. They were truly privileged workers in Canadian society.

There were few opportunities for minority men in professions. While there is evidence that work opportunities did open up for minority men in this era, in the context of general labour market expansion, their opportunities remained limited. As noted earlier, African-Canadian men worked as labourers but also on railways as porters, as barbers, and in various service industries (Adams, 2011; Fingard, 1995; Winks, 1997). In this period of rising prejudice in Canada, African-Canadian women's work opportunities were still limited. Chinese men continued to work in domestic service and perform manual labour but also opened up laundries, restaurants, and fruit and vegetable businesses. Indigenous men and women often combined independent production (agriculture, fishing, trapping, and other activities in their communities) with wage labour in a variety of low-paying positions in industry, on construction, or in resource industries (logging, fishing, mining), and transportation (High, 1996; Knight, 1996). Much of this work was seasonal: men might "alternate commercial fishing during the summer and fall with logging in the early winter and spring" (Knight, 1996, p. 125) or combine seasonal wage work with independent production (High, 1996). Indigenous women, like their white counterparts, performed a lot of unpaid labour, including housekeeping. They also obtained food for the family through gardening, small-scale farming, fishing, and so on (Knight, 1996). In terms of wage work, employment in fish canneries was a major source of employment for Indigenous women; they also found work seasonally on commercial farms. Overall, minority men and women had few opportunities to obtain positions in emerging industries and new jobs.

To summarize, this era witnessed some improvements in working conditions for workers, with skilled workers, especially professional workers, benefitting the most. New jobs were created, and old jobs were restructured and subdivided. There is evidence of deskilling and **routinization** of work in some sectors. At the same time, some jobs requiring skill expanded. One of the main trends concerned organizational changes that brought more workers under managerial control. Such enhanced workplace surveillance is consistent with the theories of Foucault, but also Marx and Weber. These workplace trends would continue in subsequent decades.

routinization Processes making work more routine and repetitive

Twentieth-Century Transformations

The subsequent century witnessed continuing change as wars, economic booms and downturns, and continued technological developments further altered how and where Canadians worked. This section highlights only a few such changes; others are discussed in subsequent chapters.

Job Shifts

Through the pre-industrial and early industrial eras, most Canadians worked in agriculture. This gradually began to change with the growth of the services and manufacturing sectors. Figure 3.1 provides an overview of the dramatic shifts in work during the 20th century. As this figure shows, agricultural employment has declined over time, while work in the services sector has steadily increased. Employment in goods-producing industries, including manufacturing and primary industries (like

FIGURE 3.1 Employment shifts 1911–1981

Source: Leacy, F. H., Buckley, K. A. H., & Urquhart, M. C. (Eds). (1983). Historical Statistics of Canada (2nd ed.). Ottawa: Statistics Canada and Social Science Federation of Canada, 08–58.

forestry, fishing, and mining), has been important, but this sector has never employed a majority of Canadian workers. The percentage of Canadians working in these industries has declined fairly steadily since the 1950s. Today, about 19 per cent of Canadian workers are in industrial jobs (Plecher, 2019).

The term **deindustrialization** was coined to refer to the systematic disinvestment in production within Western countries like Canada and the United States (Bluestone & Harrison, 1982, p. 6). The decline of manufacturing accelerated in the 1970s and 1980s as firms that once provided good-paying jobs to unionized workers began shutting their doors, many moving production to areas of the world where labour was not unionized, laws regulating production were more lax, and workers earned low wages (ibid.). This trend is an aspect of globalization but also reflects capitalists' continuing search for profit through technological innovation and the reduction of labour costs (as discussed in Chapter 2).

deindustrialization The systematic disinvestment in production (manufacturing) within Western countries like Canada and the United States

Scholars have been divided on how to view these trends and what they mean for Canadian workers. For some, these were positive developments, since many service jobs were less routine and physically taxing, providing opportunities for workers to exercise skills and knowledge at work (Bell, 1976). White-collar jobs in professions, management, and business services and other high-status service jobs tend to require high levels of education, pay good wages, and allow workers some autonomy. Others expressed concern. Jobs in the service sector are of mixed quality (Myles, 1988). Work in restaurants, retail sales, tourism, and cleaning occupations tends to be lower-paid and less autonomous. Some of these jobs are part-time, and many have unpredictable work hours. Workers who lost semi-skilled jobs in manufacturing usually ended up in low-paying, low-skilled service jobs earning a fraction of what they once had (Bluestone & Harrison, 1982).

post-industrial Term used to describe societies in which labour is predominantly found in the services or tertiary sector

The expansion of work in the services sector has led many scholars to declare our economy both **post-industrial**—in light of the declines in domestic manufacturing—and a **knowledge economy**, since many jobs require workers to hold advanced education. Nevertheless, it must be noted that manufacturing is still an important component of the Canadian economy. These trends also highlight that Canada is part of a **global economy**, interdependent with other nations and reliant on production and services generated by workers around the world. The goods that Canadians buy are often fully or partially manufactured elsewhere in the world.

knowledge economy Economy dependent on information and educated workers

global economy The world economy

Bound up with these sectoral shifts are changes in workforce stability in Canada. Deindustrialization was associated with mass lay-offs, followed by organizational restructuring intended to achieve increased efficiencies. As part of these trends, employers began offering fewer workers full-time, full-year contracts. Full-time employees were increasingly seen as a burden for companies: they require benefits and must be paid even during periods when there may be less work for them to do. By hiring part-time or contract workers, companies have the workers they need when they need them, have minimal responsibility for benefits, and can easily let workers go when there is no longer a need for their services. The decline of the standard work-contract is one of several forces contributing to labour market precarity among workers (discussed in Chapters 4 and 6).

Unionization

Trends in unionization and **collective bargaining** were influenced by the two world wars and the Depression in the opening half of the 20th century. They are also wrapped up with the emergence of the welfare state in the early to mid-20th century. The **welfare state** is a system of governance whereby state actors believe they have a responsibility to implement policies that better the well-being of the population they govern.[1] Protections for workers include employment insurance (originally *un*employment insurance), workers' compensation (for work-related illnesses and injuries), and legislation establishing employment standards (like minimum wages, maximum work hours, and rules about breaks and vacation time). Rights to collective bargaining are part of a broader set of policies aimed at improving workers' working conditions.

collective bargaining Negotiations between employers and workers' unions concerning the terms and conditions of employment

welfare state A system of governance whereby state actors believe they have a responsibility to implement policies that improve the well-being of the population they govern

Earlier in this chapter, we saw that union activity increased in the 1910s, culminating in a series of strikes in 1919, including the Winnipeg General Strike. Unions experienced a set-back in the succeeding eras—the volatility of the economy in the 1920s and early 1930s did little to encourage union growth. Unionization increased during the Second World War (1939–45), with the expansion of wartime employment in manufacturing facilities. Conditions were not ideal during wartime, however, and workers protested against poor working conditions and wage freezes. Workers sought rights of collective bargaining and other concessions from their employers, engaging in strikes to achieve their aims (Heron, 2019a). Workers were persuasive as they "seized on the war-time rhetoric of combating fascist tyranny and began to demand more democracy in the workplace" (Heron, 2019a, p. 24). Public support for unions increased as well. The federal government responded by enacting policies to benefit workers, including unemployment insurance, children's allowances, and a wartime order-in-council to enable the recognition of unions and compulsory collective bargaining (Heron, 1996, 2019a; Morton, 1998). This landmark achievement finally legalized unions and compelled employers to negotiate with them. The order-in-council was confirmed through legislation in the late 1940s but not before unions fought employers across industrial sectors for recognition (Heron, 2019a; Morton, 1998).

The new legislation was not a complete victory for unions, however. While they won the right to organize and engage in collective bargaining—allowing workers to fight for fair wages, fair treatment, and better working hours—they were also faced with restrictions on when and under what conditions they could strike, and they had little voice in shaping

[1]The welfare state emerged in the post–Second World War era in a period of relative economic prosperity, and it was intended to counteract the worst effects of recessionary periods so prominent in Canadians' minds after the Great Depression in the 1930s.

the labour process. The mechanisms that emerged for dealing with disputes were also heavily bureaucratized and cumbersome and hence largely unsatisfactory from workers' point of view.

Despite the limits placed on collective bargaining, workers benefitted from unionization, acquiring better working conditions and improving their earnings in the succeeding decades. By the 1950s, the workforce seemed more secure and stable. The welfare state provided a safety net for workers in need of assistance. In some ways, this period was a "golden age" when Canadian workers enjoyed stable, secure work with prospects for advancement. This stability gradually declined as the 20th century progressed.

For the next several decades, unionization grew in manufacturing and related industries before spreading to the public sector in the 1960s and 1970s. Initially, men were the main benefactors of collective bargaining rights, since they composed the majority of union members. As unionization spread to the public sector, more of women's occupations—including nursing and teaching—were covered. In 1981, almost 38 per cent of Canadian workers were union members. However, unionization rates have decreased since then. By 2018 only 28 per cent of Canadian workers were unionized (Morissette, 2018). The drop has been particularly dramatic in the private sector, where only 15 per cent of workers are unionized.

Most unionized workers today are women working in the public sector: government workers, nurses, teachers, professors, and other white-collar and professional workers (Statistics Canada, 2015). Public-sector unions have resisted pressures towards precarity, declining real wages, and deteriorating working conditions; however, their efforts have only tempered these trends, not stopped them. The shift in union activity towards the public sector has led to declining public support for unions and their activities. In the past when manufacturing workers went on strike, they cut into their employers' profitability, often with little impact on the consumer. In contrast, when public sector employees go out on strike, the public is affected. Moreover, government support for the principles of collective bargaining is on the wane, in part because governments are frequently the employers accused of unfair work practices. Over the past 50 years, governments have repeatedly passed legislation that undermines collective bargaining.

These legislative developments are part of a broader trend towards neoliberal governance in the West. **Neoliberalism** is a theory of governance that holds that "human wellbeing can best be advanced by liberating individual entrepreneurial freedoms" and embracing

Source: THE CANADIAN PRESS/Michael Bell

SaskTel employees walk the picket line in downtown Regina during a 2019 strike at seven Saskatchewan Crown corporations. Today, the majority of unionized workers are women working in the public sector.

free market principles; therefore, state interventions should be minimal (Harvey, 2005, p. 2). While welfare state theories argued that state policy could be used to protect the disadvantaged, neoliberalism has a philosophy of independent responsibility. State supports are said to hinder the economy and prevent individual self-sufficiency to the detriment of all. Such philosophies have encouraged policy that whittles away employment protections, exacerbates social inequalities, and benefits the capitalist class at the expense of workers. Major corporations benefit through deregulation and lower taxes, resulting in higher profits stemming from cuts to costly programs investing in worker training and safety and environmental protection (Bakan, 2020). As a result, people are put at risk, and the planet is damaged, perhaps beyond repair. Neoliberalism also "responsibilizes" workers, blaming them for their own misfortune and deflecting attention away from structural inequalities and deteriorating working conditions. Individuals are encouraged to work harder to attain success, despite the uneven playing field. This philosophy, then, further marginalizes the disadvantaged in the workforce and society more generally.

neoliberalism
A theory of governance that holds that "human wellbeing can best be advanced by liberating individual entrepreneurial freedoms" and embracing free market principles (Harvey, 2005, p. 2)

Experiences by Gender and Race/Ethnicity

Throughout the 20th century, experiences of work and labour market trends continued to vary by gender and race-ethnicity. Differences were also evident by class, as the earlier discussion of sectoral shifts intimated. Members of the working class—long employed in manufacturing, other goods-producing industries, agriculture, and lower-level service work—have been particularly disadvantaged by 20th-century trends. However, the expansion of white-collar work appears to point to growing opportunities for educated, middle-class Canadians.

One of the predominant labour market shifts to occur over the 20th century concerns labour market diversity. At the turn of the 20th century, the majority of workers in the Canadian labour force were white men. Since then, women have entered the labour force in large numbers, and because of Canadian immigration patterns, the Canadian labour force has become more diverse. The intersection of gender and race-ethnicity continues to shape labour market experiences.

Turning first to trends in women's employment, in 1901, only about 14 per cent of working-age women were in the labour force (Connelly, 2006). That percentage increased fairly steadily over the course of the next century. Women's work outside the home increased during both the First and the Second World Wars. With many young men joining the war effort and white men preferred for military service (Winks, 1997), manufacturers had to hire workers they might not have favoured in the past, including women and minority men. Having been shut out of much manufacturing employment in years past, these workers did not have experience doing this kind of work. Employers seized this opportunity to restructure work and cut costs; they "reorganize[d] work to a degree unimaginable in . . . pre-war markets" (Heron 2019c, p. 328). To staff factories, "thousands of untrained workers were recruited to run narrowly specialized machines on piecework" (Heron, 2019c, p. 328). Women were pleased to have the opportunity to perform different kinds of work and earn higher wages. To meet labour shortages during the Second World War, married women were enticed into the labour force with offers of state- and employer-sponsored daycare, after-school care, and tax benefits (Pierson, 1986). These initiatives contributed to an increase in women's labour force participation from 20 per cent in 1941 to 33 per cent in 1943. Nevertheless, when the wars ended, women were encouraged to leave the labour force altogether or, if they had to work, to return to their low-paying female-dominated jobs. In the post–Second World War period, governments cut women's daycare benefits and tax benefits, and formally barred them from some civil service jobs, all with the goal of pushing them out of the labour force (Sangster, 2010, p. 18; Pierson, 1986). Many returned to work in the home. By 1946, women's labour force participation rate had dropped to 25 per cent (Sangster, 2010, p. 18).

Women's labour force participation expanded in the 1960s and 1970s, with married women driving the trend (Sangster, 2010). The women's movement of the 1960s, the expansion of service sector jobs, and deindustrialization that led to a decline in men's wages (making it difficult for families to survive on one income) helped to drive women's entrance into the labour market. The Charter of Rights and Freedoms, which made discrimination illegal on the basis of gender, race, citizenship status, sexual orientation, and other characteristics, has also helped formerly disadvantaged workers (including women) to find more opportunities. Nonetheless, women still face barriers in the workforce, and it is clear that their opportunities vary by class, race, and other factors.

Minority workers continued to be marginalized in the Canadian labour force throughout the 20th century. Immigrants of South Asian background increased after 1920, especially in BC, but they had few citizenship rights and limited labour market opportunities (Das Gupta, 1994). Moreover, both Indigenous and African-Canadian men and women experienced substantial barriers in the 1920s and 1930s. During this period, some of Indigenous peoples' traditional employment in transportation, fishing, and canning started to dry up; to make ends meet, Indigenous men tended to combine (often seasonal) work for wages in logging, fishing, and transportation with work in other sectors and independent production (Brownlie, 2008; High, 1996). Indigenous peoples' own businesses and enterprises floundered during the Depression of the 1930s (Knight, 1996). African-Canadian men also continued to face barriers in the first part of the 20th century, and their labour was highly segregated in a few industries; many were employed as railway sleeping car porters (Calliste, 1987; Winks, 1997). African-Canadian men and women found that there were few to no opportunities for advancement in Canada: employment discrimination was widespread and perfectly legal. It was not until the 1940s and 1950s that legislation began to be passed to counter racial discrimination. Until then, many had to move to the United States to progress (Winks, 1997).

While the Second World War provided more work opportunities for minority workers because of labour shortages, many of these gains were temporary and were reduced upon the return of white soldiers. With increased immigration after the war, the diversity of Canadian society increased, but immigrants tended to face several barriers obtaining work in Canada. In some professional occupations, for instance law and architecture, citizenship requirements for entry-to-practice effectively barred immigrant professionals until they had obtained citizenship and undergone additional training (Adams, 2016). Experiences of immigrant men and women varied somewhat by ethnicity, but many immigrant men and women were overrepresented in cleaning jobs, manufacturing, restaurant work, and other similar jobs (Iacovetta, 2000). Generally, members of minorities had few opportunities for white-collar and professional work. Immigrant men and women from eastern and southern Europe were often viewed as inferior and experienced discrimination, which relegated them to less attractive jobs in the labour market (Patrias, 2016). The same was true for racialized workers.

Since the 1960s, there has been not only increased immigration to Canada but a shift in our newcomer population from its former western European base to include peoples from around the world. This means that the Canadian labour force is more diverse than ever before. Research has highlighted the challenges these workers—many of them racial minorities—experience in the labour market (Grant & Nadin, 2007; Teelucksingh & Galabuzi, 2007). Racialized workers are overrepresented in precarious jobs, experience more discrimination in finding work, and are more likely to have difficulty landing jobs in the fields for which they were trained. Nevertheless, experiences can vary across ethnicity and locale. For instance, there is evidence that South Asian women immigrants were able to find work opportunities doing professional and white-collar work, especially in Ontario and the Atlantic provinces in the 1980s (Das Gupta, 1996). Overall, as in previous eras, minority workers are disadvantaged in the labour market.

Moreover, state policy combined with economic change and discrimination has worsened the labour market opportunities for Indigenous workers (Sangster, 2010). Traditional opportunities for work have diminished, but new opportunities have been limited and are disproportionately found in the least attractive areas of the Canadian economy. Thus, it is not surprising that studies identify higher unemployment rates and lower incomes among Indigenous peoples, especially those living on reserves (Lamb, Yap, & Turk, 2018). Indigenous workers continue to be under-represented in well-paying, unionized jobs and continue to face unemployment and labour market disadvantages (McCallum, 2014; MacKinnon, 2015; Mills, 2017).

To summarize, this chapter has explored the history of work in Canada, with a focus on the rise of industrial capitalism, to provide a foundation for the discussion of more recent workplace change in subsequent chapters. Throughout, the ways in which workplace change impacts workers and reproduces social inequalities have been emphasized. Workers' efforts to improve their circumstances have also been highlighted. These themes will continue to be relevant as we turn our attention to experiences of working in Canada today in the following chapters.

Reviewing the Learning Objectives

After reading this chapter, you should:

- Understand that pre-industrial life and work was quite different from work under industrial capitalism.
- Understand that the emergence of industrial capitalism and subsequent economic developments have profoundly altered the organization and experience of work.
- Understand that workers have resisted changes at work and endeavoured to improve their working conditions.
- Understand that access to jobs and experiences of working have varied across class, gender, race, Indigeneity, and other factors and be able to describe how experiences differ.

Questions for Critical Thought

1. Many of the battles at work historically have been about time: how long people work, when people work, and who controls the time and pace of work. Do you think time is still a focus of contention and conflict at work? If so, in what ways?
2. As noted at the beginning of this chapter, sociological theories have attempted to explain important historical transitions in the sociology of work. Can you make linkages between the two and connect sociological theories and concepts to actual historical trends?
3. At times, the federal and provincial governments have passed legislation to regulate aspects of work, but historically they were reluctant to do so. Why do you think this was the case?

Annotated Additional Readings

Calliste, A. (1987). Sleeping car porters in Canada: An ethnically submerged split labour market. *Canadian Ethnic Studies*, *19*(1), 1–20.

This article explores the discrimination experienced by Black workers in Canada during the 20th century and their challenges working as sleeping car porters.

Cooper, A. (2006). *The hanging of Angélique: The untold story of Canadian slavery and the burning of Montréal*. Toronto, ON: Harper Collins.

An accessible, impactful book detailing Angélique's story, providing rich detail about slavery, and life, in 18th-century New France.

Frager, R. A., & Patrias, C. (2005). *Discounting labour: Women workers in Canada, 1870–1939*. Toronto, ON: University of Toronto Press.

This book provides an accessible overview of the history of working women in Canada.

Kealey, G. S., & Palmer, B. D. (1982). *Dreaming of what might be: The Knights of Labour in Ontario, 1880–1900*. Cambridge, UK: Cambridge University Press.

A well-written book providing the fascinating history of the Knights of Labour in Ontario.

du Preez, M., & Dronfield, J. (2016). *Dr. James Barry: A woman ahead of her time*. London, UK: Oneworld Publications.

This book follows the life and career of Dr Barry, who had a very successful career as a military surgeon in the early to mid-1800s and became infamous upon death when it was discovered he was born a woman.

Related Websites

Royal Commission on the Relations of Labor and Capital in Canada. 1889. Report, Volume 1. Ottawa: Queen's Printer.

http://publications.gc.ca/site/eng/472984/publication.html

Canadian Labour Congress website with information on the history of labour in Canada:

https://canadianlabour.ca/uncategorized/why-unions-history-labour-canada/

Canadian Encyclopedia entry on working-class history:

https://www.thecanadianencyclopedia.ca/en/article/working-class-history

Historica Canada's educational portal respecting Indigenous History:

http://education.historicacanada.ca/en/collections/18

4 The Context of Work

Labour Markets and Organizations

Learning Objectives

After reading this chapter, readers will:

- Have a sense of key labour market characteristics and dominant trends.
- Understand that these trends have implications for how work is experienced.
- Understand the nature of organizations and their significance for the experience of work.
- Comprehend that organizational structures can reproduce social inequalities.
- Know about the existence of alternative organizational forms.

Introduction

The previous chapters provided context to inform our understanding of work in Canada through an exploration of theories and historical trends shaping work as we know it. This chapter fleshes out our understanding of the contexts in which work takes place by looking at labour markets and organizations. **Labour markets** are places (more virtual than literal) where workers meet employers and are sorted into jobs. The study of labour markets centres on the distribution of workers into employment, their experiences of unemployment and underemployment, and a consideration of the characteristics of the jobs available. **Organizations** are collectivities established to pursue specific goals. Most work takes place within organizations, and organizational structures can profoundly shape experiences of working. The study of organizations within sociology has focused on their characteristics, as well as organizational cultures, change, and organizational alternatives.

labour markets
Where employers and employees come together and workers are distributed into jobs

organizations
Collectivities deliberately created to achieve a set of goals or objectives

By studying labour markets and organizations, we can better understand the core contexts workers must navigate when they seek and find work and when they are working. The first half of the chapter is devoted to labour markets while the second examines organizations.

Labour Markets

Are men more or less likely to be unemployed than women? How do Indigenous peoples fare in the labour market? Are there good job opportunities available for youth? All of these important questions can be answered through the use of labour market statistics. Fortunately, Statistics Canada and other agencies regularly analyze trends in work and employment so that Canadians and policy-makers can become informed. Many labour market trends are not merely national but global. For instance, the growth of non-standard work and high youth unemployment rates are trends found in many countries. Indeed, while labour markets have historically been local in nature—since people look for work close to home—they are increasingly national and international, with people seeking work opportunities far from their birthplace.

While it is commonplace to refer to "the labour market" as a singular entity, some scholars argue there is value in focusing on labour market*s*, plural. In doing so, we acknowledge that workers might engage in local, regional, provincial, national, or international labour markets and that not all workers are competing for the same jobs in a single market. A skilled-trades worker, retail salesperson, and someone with a university degree in business are unlikely to be applying for the same jobs. **Labour market segmentation theory** argues that not only are there multiple labour markets, but their characteristics differ. For example, we can distinguish a *primary* labour market from a *secondary* labour market. The primary labour market is characterized by stable and secure jobs with opportunities for promotion, while the secondary market is less secure and stable. While most of us would like to participate in the primary labour market, we may be locked into the secondary labour market if we have fewer resources, face discrimination, or have less education. Such a distinction is valuable in highlighting divisions within the labour market and the disadvantages experienced by some. However, it is a distinction that may be less useful now than in the past, as the lines between the primary and secondary labour markets appear to be blurring. Secure work and insecure work can occur in the same sectors, in the same occupations, and even in the same firms: Permanent workers can work on a project, manufacture a product, or teach a university class alongside temporary workers hired to do the same tasks. Such practices reflect broader labour market changes, several of which are discussed below.

labour market segmentation theory Argument that there are at least two labour markets: a primary one characterized by good jobs and a secondary one characterized by less attractive jobs

employment rate The ratio of people age 15 and over who are working to the overall population aged 15 or over (including those who are not working)

labour force participation rate The ratio of those working for pay and those available and looking for work, divided by the total population

unemployment rate The percentage of workers in the labour force who do not currently have a job but are actively seeking work

economic cycle The movements between periods of economic growth and recession

Trends in Employment and Unemployment

To understand labour market trends, especially trends respecting employment, it is necessary to define a few key terms. First, the **employment rate** is the ratio of people who are working to the population of working age (usually those aged 15 and over). Second, the **labour force participation rate** measures the percentage of people of working age who are either working or who are *actively* looking for work. Third, the **unemployment rate** identifies the percentage of workers in the labour force who do not currently have a job but are actively seeking work. All of these measures can be used to assess the health of a region's economy, but also to track trends in working over a period of time. All of these rates vary according to the **economic cycle**—movements between periods of economic growth and recession. When the economy is booming, employment rates tend to be high and unemployment low. The reverse is true during recessionary periods.

The long-term trend in the employment rate over the past 50 years has been upward, primarily because of the movement of women into the labour force during this period.

Over the past 15 to 20 years, employment rates have been fairly flat—there is little evidence of a consistent upward or downward trend (Bernard & Morissette, 2018). In the winter of 2019–20, the *employment rate* in Canada was about 62, not far below the all-time high of 63.7 (Trading Economics, 2019a). At this time, then, approximately 62 per cent of working-age Canadians were working. What about the remaining 38 per cent of Canadians? Only some of them were unemployed. In fact, at the time Canada had a relatively low unemployment rate of 5.5 (Trading Economics, 2019b). The remainder of Canadians of working age were not, for whatever reason, in the labour force—some were in school, others raising children, some unable to work due to disability or injury, and others were retired. Some were unemployed but discouraged by the failures of previous searches to the point that they did not actively look for work in the previous month. The labour force participation rate during this period was calculated at 65.7 per cent, meaning about one-third of Canadians of working age were not in the labour force.

In March of 2020, Canada—like other countries in the world—experienced a dramatic change in employment and unemployment rates due to the COVID-19 pandemic. The unemployment rate jumped from 5.5 per cent in February 2020, to a high of 13.7 per cent in May, before rebounding to 9 per cent in the early fall, before the second wave (Statistics Canada, 2020a; Trading Economics 2020). The employment rate dropped from 62 per cent in February 2020 to a low of 52 per cent in April before rising to 59 per cent in September and hovering around that rate into the spring of 2021 (Statistics Canada, 2020a; Trading Economics, 2020). However, these statistics are somewhat misleading: the fact is that the circumstances of those employed deteriorated. Many employed workers had their hours cut back due to the pandemic. Minority and low-wage workers were particularly impacted (Koebel & Pohler, 2020; St. Denis, 2020). Moreover, job growth in the summer of 2020 was primarily in part-time work, not full-time work. The pandemic thrust Canada into an economic depression, with many negative impacts on workers that persisted in 2021.

Source: © illuminaphoto/Shutterstock

A closed seating area in Vancouver's Granville Island Public Market in April 2020. Rates of full-time employment dropped as public spaces closed and stay-at-home orders were issued to prevent the spread of COVID-19.

Variations in Employment and Unemployment

Although national-level statistics are illuminating, labour markets are still often local in nature, and regional labour markets can differ significantly. Table 4.1 shows employment and unemployment rates across the provinces in Canada in 2018. In general, provinces with the lowest

TABLE 4.1 Employment and Unemployment Rates in Canada by Province, 2018

	Employment Rate	Unemployment Rate
Canada	62.0	5.5
Newfoundland and Labrador	51.8	11.1
Prince Edward Island	60.8	8.4
Nova Scotia	57.7	8.0
New Brunswick	56.0	8.1
Quebec	61.8	5.0
Ontario	61.5	5.3
Manitoba	62.7	5.3
Saskatchewan	65.3	5.1
Alberta	66.5	6.7
British Columbia	62.3	4.7

Source: Statistics Canada, 2018b.

employment rates are in Atlantic Canada. These provinces also have higher than average unemployment rates. The highest employment rate in 2018 occurred in Alberta, and the lowest employment rate was found in Newfoundland and Labrador. Newfoundland and Labrador also had the highest unemployment rate—twice the national average. The lowest unemployment rate was in British Columbia. These numbers confirm the regional nature of labour markets and hint at the different economies found across the country.

Gender, Education, and Age

Employment and unemployment rates vary by worker characteristics, including gender and education. Those with more education tend to have higher employment rates and lower unemployment rates than others. Those with university degrees (bachelor or graduate degrees) enjoy the lowest unemployment rates; post-secondary education clearly brings employment gains. Rates also vary by gender (which Statistics Canada measures as a binary). Women have lower employment rates than men, except at the highest education levels. Women's unemployment rates are higher than men's at the lower education levels, lower than men's among high school graduates and post-secondary diploma levels, before climbing above men's again at the graduate degree level (see Table 4.2). These statistics reveal that gender intersects with education to shape labour market opportunities (see also Chapters 9 and 10).

These numbers do not tell us about how social crises affect men's and women's employment rates, but there is evidence that the impact differs. Many 20th-century recessions impacted men disproportionately because they reduced employment in the manufacturing, financial, and resource extraction industries where men predominate. The pandemic-induced recession appears to have impacted women more (Settersten et al., 2020; Bahn, Cohen, & van der Meulen Rodgers, 2020). Lockdowns led to job loss (temporary or permanent), within retail stores and accommodation and food services especially—fields that employ many women. Moreover, some women appear to have left the labour force in order to care for children in the home, with the closing of daycares and

TABLE 4.2 Employment and Unemployment in Canada by Education and Gender, 2018

Education	Employment Rate	Employment Women	Employment Men	Unemployment Rate	Unemployment Women	Unemployment Men
All Levels	62.5	58.0	67.1	5.0	4.8	5.1
0–8 Years	19.0	11.5	27.8	8.7	9.2	8.4
Some High School	38.8	28.0	48.2	8.1	8.5	7.9
High School	56.0	47.6	64.7	5.7	5.7	5.7
Some Post-secondary	60.4	54.0	66.5	5.9	5.7	6.1
Post-secondary Diploma or Certificate	68.2	64.8	71.7	4.8	4.5	5.0
University Degree (bachelors)	74.0	72.1	76.2	4.1	4.0	4.1
University Degree (above bachelor)	74.4	74.4	74.4	4.1	4.5	3.8

Source: Statistics Canada, 2018c.

schools (Desjardins and Freestone, 2020), exacerbating the gender gap in employment rates, especially among working-class parents (Qian and Fuller, 2020).

Employment and unemployment also vary across age. Age is a hidden factor in Table 4.2 (that is, it is not explicitly accounted for). Many individuals in the labour force with very low levels of education are older Canadians, and their poor employment outcomes could be shaped by the combined impact of both education and age (see Chapter 11 for more on older workers).

Workers with Disabilities

Workers with disabilities tend to have lower employment rates and lower labour force participation rates compared to other workers (Zarifa, Walters, & Seward, 2015; Benoit, Jansson, Jansenberger, & Phillips, 2013). While a lack of workplace accommodations for workers with disabilities is a barrier, research suggests that discrimination and stereotyping about workers' abilities and skills have a more deleterious impact on employment opportunities (Shier, Graham, & Jones, 2009; Lindsay et al., 2014).

Young Workers

In Canada and elsewhere in the Western world, particular attention has been given in recent decades to the experiences of youth. Youth unemployment levels are sometimes twice the national average, and concerns have been raised about the labour market opportunities available to youth. This is particularly the case internationally; worldwide, an estimated 71 million young workers were unemployed in 2016 (ILO, 2019) (see Box 4.1). In Canada, the 2019 youth unemployment rate was 11.9 (twice the adult national average of 5.5) (Trading Economics, 2019b). Among employed youth, more are working part-time than in the past, at least in part because of the expansion of youth in post-secondary education (Statistics Canada, 2018c). Youth may work part-time while still in school.

Global Perspectives

4.1 | Youth Unemployment

Intational bodies including the International Labour Organization (ILO), the United Nations' Office of the Secretary-General's Special Envoy on Youth, and Plan International have all expressed concern over youth unemployment rates worldwide. For example, Plan International (2019) contends that "in the next decade one billion young people will enter the labour market and large numbers of young people face a future of irregular and informal employment." This is particularly the case in developing countries but is nonetheless a problem in every region of the world. As the below figure shows, rates of youth unemployment vary from a low of 11 per cent in North America and sub-Saharan Africa to highs of 30 per cent in Northern Africa and Arab States (United Nations, 2016). Rates of youth working but still living in poverty are also high in some regions. Furthermore, there are gender gaps in employment and unemployment, with young women particularly disadvantaged, especially in Southern Asia, Northern Africa, and the Arab States (United Nations, 2016).

Youth unemployment around the world

		Unemployment Rate, 2007–17 (percentages)			Unemployed Youth, 2015–17 (millions)		
Region	2007-14	2015	2016	2017	2015	2016	2017
World		12.9	13.1	13.1	70.5	71.0	71.0
Africa							
Northern Africa		29.4	29.3	29.2	3.7	3.7	3.7
Sub-Saharan Africa		10.9	10.9	10.8	11.1	11.3	11.6
Americas							
Latin America and the Caribbean		15.7	16.8	17.1	8.5	9.2	9.3
North America		11.8	11.5	11.7	3.0	2.9	2.9
Arab States		30.6	30.6	29.7	2.6	2.7	2.6
Asia							
Eastern Asia		10.6	10.7	10.9	11.9	11.4	11.0
South-Eastern Asia and the Pacific		12.4	13.0	13.6	7.4	7.7	8.0
Southern Asia		10.9	10.9	10.9	13.7	13.8	13.9
Europe and Central Asia							
Central and Western Asia		16.6	17.1	17.5	2.1	2.1	2.2
Eastern Europe		17.1	16.6	16.2	2.0	1.8	1.7
Northern, Southern, and Western Europe		20.6	19.7	18.9	4.5	4.3	4.1

Source: United Nations, 2016.

Involuntary part-time employment
When a worker would prefer full-time hours, but can only secure part-time work

However, there are also signs that **involuntary part-time employment** has risen for youth. We call part-time work "involuntary" when a worker would prefer to work full-time hours but cannot secure full-time work. Employers often prefer to hire workers who already have work experience, disadvantaging youth.

Figure 4.1 shows unemployment rates for youth over time. Ignoring the ups and downs throughout this period—shaped by economic cycles and other factors—one can see clear, general patterns. Youth under 25 have consistently higher unemployment

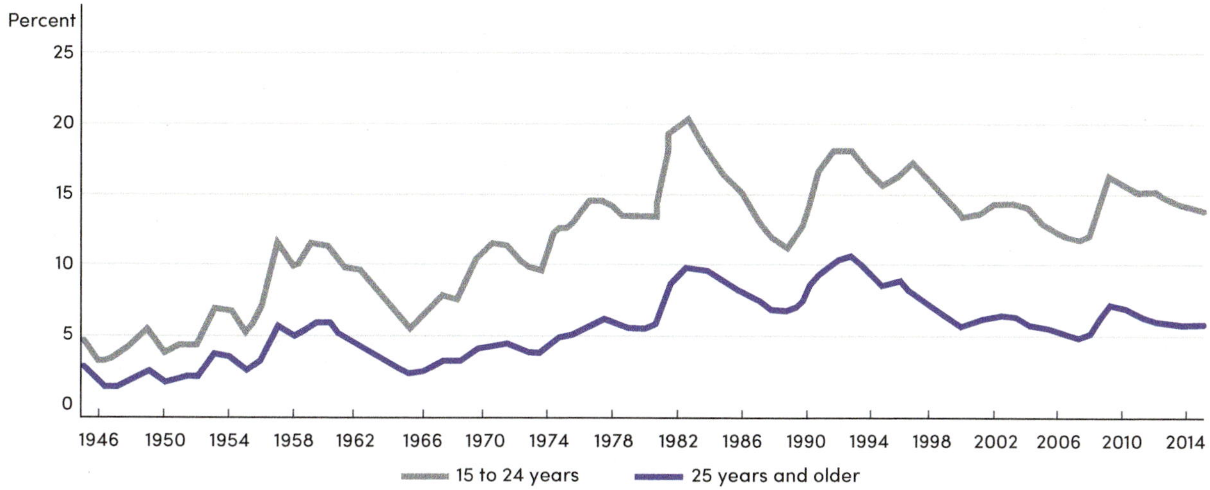

FIGURE 4.1 Unemployment rate by age group, 1946 to 2015

Source: Statistics Canada, 2018g.

rates, indicating that they have more difficulty finding work. Those over 25 have lower unemployment rates, suggesting they have more success landing work. Nevertheless, workers in both age categories have experienced higher unemployment in the past 30 years than in decades past.

Indigenous Peoples

Employment and unemployment rates also vary by Indigeneity, with Indigenous peoples having lower employment rates than non-Indigenous people nationally (National Indigenous Economic Development Board, 2019). The gap between Indigenous peoples and settler Canadians widens during periods of recession (Moyser, 2017), as Indigenous men and women experience higher rates of job loss than do others. In 2016, only about half (52 per cent) of First Nations[1] people living outside reserves were employed (Moyser, 2017; Statistics Canada 2017). Reflecting these employment rates, unemployment among First Nations people living off-reserve was high at 15 per cent. Young and older First Nations workers appear to be particularly disadvantaged: 64 per cent of **core working age** adults (aged 25–64) were employed but only 40 per cent of youth, and one-third of older adults (Moyser, 2017). Indigenous workers with higher education levels have more opportunities: those with a post-secondary education had an employment rate of 78 per cent, while those with less than high school had a rate of 43 per cent (Moyser, 2017). Statistics Canada has also gathered data on other economic activities pursued by Indigenous peoples in Canada, from fishing, hunting, and trapping, to gathering wild plants and making clothes and handicrafts. Activities pursued varied across regions (both rural/urban and Canadian province). As in the past, Indigenous peoples, especially those living in rural areas, engage in a variety of economic activities to make ends meet.

core working age
Adults aged 25–64

[1]The term First Nations excludes Indigenous peoples who identify as Inuit or Métis.

pluriactivity
The practice of combining two or more economic activities to make a living

The term **pluriactivity** can be used to describe the practice of combining two or more economic activities to make a living.

First Nations people living on-reserve appear even more disadvantaged: those on-reserve have employment rates 10–15 per cent lower than members of First Nations living off-reserve (National Indigenous Economic Development Board, 2019). Inuit fare slightly better, but their employment rates are still just under 50 per cent. Métis have employment rates that compare to the non-Indigenous in Canada (ibid.). Unemployment rate data tell a similar story: First Nations individuals living on-reserve experience high unemployment (about 25 per cent), with Inuit peoples not far behind. The unemployment rate among Métis is 11 per cent (ibid.).

These labour market statistics highlight the disadvantages endured by Indigenous peoples in Canada. Discouragingly, employment rates were lower and unemployment rates higher among Indigenous peoples in 2019 than they were a decade earlier (National Indigenous Economic Development Board, 2019). As noted, Indigenous peoples appear highly vulnerable to economic shifts, suffering considerable job loss during poor economic times. Geographic distance from many jobs combines with other barriers, and discrimination, to limit opportunities.

Visible Minorities

Members of visible minorities have higher unemployment rates than white Canadians (9.2 per cent compared to 7.3 per cent in 2016). Employment rates are similar between visible minority and white Canadians (60.4 per cent and 60.7 per cent, respectively). These numbers, however, hide considerable variability. Most disadvantaged are Black Canadians and people claiming Arab and West Asian backgrounds. The intersection of gender and race is also important: for example, Black women have higher employment rates but also higher unemployment rates than others (Statistics Canada, 2019a; Katshunga, Massaquoi, & Wallace, 2020). Table 4.3 compares employment and unemployment rates for select groups in 2016. These variations are reflective of employment discrimination in Canada (see Chapter 10). Members of the most disadvantaged visible minorities (including Asian and Black workers) were also harder hit by job loss and reduced hours during the pandemic (Hou, Frank, & Schimmele, 2020).

Immigrants in Canada

Labour market statistics also reveal variations in employment and unemployment across immigration status: immigrants have been disadvantaged in terms of both employment

TABLE 4.3 Employment and Unemployment Rates for Select Minority Groups

	Employment Rate	Unemployment Rate
White Workers	60.7	7.3
Visible Minority (total)	60.4	9.2
Arab	52.9	13.5
Black	60.4	12.5
South Asian	61.0	9.2
West Asian	56.1	11.0

Source: Statistics Canada, 2016 Census of Population, Catalogue no. 98-400-X2016286.

and unemployment rates compared to Canadian-born workers (Statistics Canada, 2018d). They are overrepresented in lower-quality jobs (Malambwe, 2017). These trends have been a topic of some discussion in the literature exploring barriers to immigrants' labour market integration (Madibbo, 2020; Fuller, 2015; Nakhaie & Kazemipur, 2013). The supply of educated immigrant workers appears to outstrip the demand for their labour (Lu & Hou, 2020). The most recent statistics may provide grounds for optimism because there is evidence of an incline in employment rates among immigrants to Canada (Statistics Canada, 2018d; Wong, 2020). Figure 4.2 shows employment rates for Canadian-born and for immigrant workers between 2006 and 2017. This figure also compares the employment rates of immigrants by their length of stay in Canada. Employment rates are higher for immigrants who have been in Canada longer. Those who have been in Canada five years or less have lower employment rates than other immigrants and the Canadian-born (Statistics Canada, 2018d). It may be the case, then, that employment rates improve over time with length of time in Canada. Unemployment rate statistics show a similar trend, with the Canadian-born having an unemployment rate of around 5.0, while immigrants who landed more than 10 years ago have a rate of 5.6 and those who immigrated five or fewer years ago have an unemployment rate of 9.6 per cent. Still, challenges in the early years after immigration can have a lasting impact on immigrants' subsequent labour market trajectories (Fuller, 2015).

Data from 2019 show that immigrants to Canada reported higher labour force participation and employment rates than the Canadian-born; however, immigrants' unemployment rates were also higher than the Canadian-born (Wong, 2020).

Higher levels of unemployment for immigrant workers occur despite the fact that immigrants have higher education levels than the Canadian-born on average. Immigrants' credentials are not always recognized, ensuring that they do not often see full returns on their education acquired outside of Canada. Those with social capital in addition to human capital fair better (Akkaymak, 2017; Nakhaie & Kazemipur, 2013),

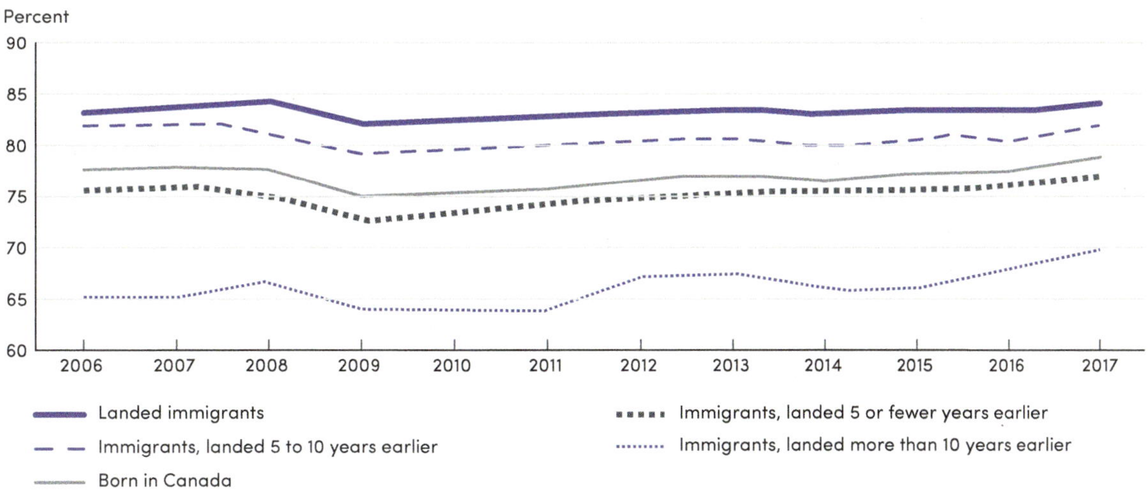

FIGURE 4.2 Employment rate for core-aged immigrants and Canadian-born, Canada, 2006–2017

Source: Statistics Canada. Table 14-10-0085-01 Labour Force Characteristics of Immigrants by Sex and Age Group.

as do immigrants who arrive in Canada before they are adults and receive some of their education here (Cousineau & Boudarbat, 2009). Immigration class may also be important; for example, privately sponsored refugees to Canada report better outcomes than government-assisted refugees (Kaida, Hou, & Stick, 2020). Visible minority immigrants are particularly disadvantaged (Nakhaie & Kazemipur, 2013; Creese & Wiebe, 2012; Teelucksingh & Galabuzi, 2007). Systemic barriers and discrimination result in more limited opportunities for immigrants of colour.

Work Opportunities, Work Hours, Non-standard Work, and Income

Labour market statistics documenting employment and unemployment rates can tell us a lot about who is working, but they tell us nothing about the kinds of jobs people work in. Therefore, it is helpful to look beyond employment rates to learn about the occupations workers hold, how much people work, what they earn, and how stable those jobs are. Labour market statistics can also document trends in jobs to illuminate where Canadians are working.

Table 4.4 summarizes the most common occupation categories[2] for the Canadian labour force according to the 2016 census. As this table shows, more Canadians work

TABLE 4.4 Most Common Occupations in Canada, 2016

	NOC Code	Occupations
1	642	Retail salespersons
2	751	Motor vehicle and transit drivers
3	673	Cleaners
4	122	Administrative and regulatory occupations
5	403	Teachers
6	421	Paraprofessionals in legal, social, community, and education services
7	141	General office workers
8	671	Food counter attendants, kitchen helpers
9	111	Auditors, accountants, investment professionals
10	661	Cashiers
11	217	Computer and information systems professionals
12	124	Office administrative assistants
13	416	Policy and program researchers, consultants, and officers
14	341	Occupations assisting in health services
15	301	Home care providers and educational support

Source: Statistics Canada, 2018a.

[2]Based on National Occupational Classification (NOC) three-digit codes. https://www12.statcan.gc.ca/census-recensement/2016/dp-pd/dt-td/Rp-eng.cfm?TABID=2&LANG=E&APATH=3&DETAIL=0&DIM=0&FL= A&FREE=0&GC=0&GK=0&GRP=1&PID=110696&PRID=10&PTYPE=109445&S=0&SHOWALL= 0&SUB=0&Temporal=2017&THEME=124&VID=0&VNAMEE=&VNAMEF=

in retail sales than in any other category, with drivers and cleaners the next most common. Many Canadians engage in skilled professional work in teaching, accounting, and information technology. Office and administration jobs are also common (falling at numbers 4, 7, and 12). So too is less-skilled work as food counter attendants, cashiers, and home care aides. These trends reflect labour market shifts that have seen expansion in less-skilled service-sector work but also growth among skilled knowledge workers (Lapointe & Bach, 2016; Livingstone, 2019a).

When one disaggregates this data by gender, one finds that men and women predominate in different kinds of jobs. Women are often found in administration and regulation occupations;[3] para-professional jobs in legal, social, and community services;[4] and teaching. Men are overrepresented among drivers, cleaners, and in computer information systems jobs. These occupational differences between men and women will be explored more in Chapter 9.

Non-standard Work

In addition to where Canadians are working, labour market statistics also shed light on how much they are working and what the nature of their jobs is. Researchers distinguish between "standard" and "non-standard" work. Generally speaking, **standard** work is stable and secure work, with steady full-time hours (roughly 35–40 hours a week). **Non-standard jobs** differ from standard work in terms of their hours and/or stability: this work tends to be temporary, contract, and/or part-time. The rise of non-standard work is related to the rise of neoliberalism mentioned briefly in Chapter 3. Non-standard work is often insecure and precarious and hence may lead to uneven income and unusual work hours that can have negative implications for workers' personal lives. Workers who are involuntary part-time workers or otherwise consigned to non-standard jobs might find they have to take on several jobs just to make ends meet. Labour market statistics have documented the increase in non-standard work over the past few decades. Since the 1990s, for instance, non-standard work has been growing at a faster rate than standard work. That is, while job growth has been evident both among standard and non-standard jobs, the latter are growing as a proportion of all jobs in the labour market, composing 13 per cent of all jobs in 2017/18 (Statistics Canada, 2019c); however, some estimates have the number of people in temporary and precarious work much higher (Lewchuk et al., 2016). The growth in temporary and contract work is shown in Figure 4.3 (Statistics Canada, 2019c).

standard employment A situation in which workers have full-time, full-year employment with one employer with the expectation that this work will continue to be available to them

non-standard work Work that differs from standard work because of its instability, irregular hours, or temporary nature

The substantial increase in temporary work has resulted in a drop in the percentage of the Canadian labour force holding full-time, permanent jobs (Morissette, 2018). Non-standard work is explored more in Chapter 6.

Multiple Jobs and Hours Worked

A linked trend is the increase in the number of workers holding multiple jobs (or pluriactivity). Workers who are involuntarily part-time and those who do not make enough to support themselves with one job may pick up a second. The number of individuals with a second job has increased in the past 20 years to 5.7 per cent of

---

[3]Among the jobs included in this category are administrative officers, human resources personnel, jobs in purchasing, event planning, and other similar work.

[4]This category includes paralegals, social service workers, and early childhood educators.

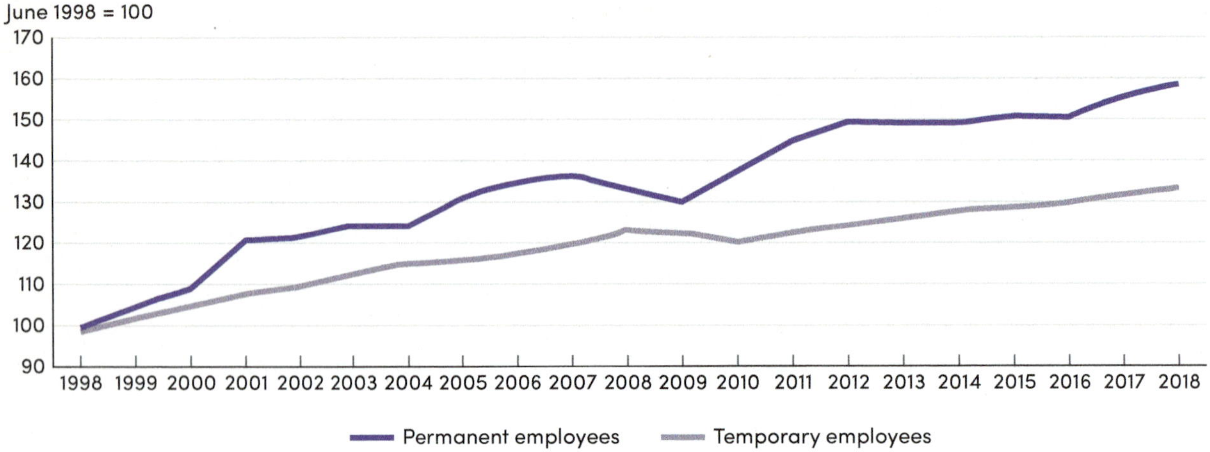

FIGURE 4.3 Job growth in temporary and permanent jobs since 1998

Source: Statistics Canada, 2019c.

workers—more than a million Canadians. Official statistics likely underestimate the full extent of pluriactivity because measures focus on work activity in the previous week and hence miss secondary employment that is more sporadic or seasonal. Multiple job holding is more likely among workers who are in temporary or part-time jobs, younger workers, and the self-employed. It is also a growing phenomenon among women, who are more likely than men to hold more than one job (Fulford & Patterson, 2019).

These trends are very much connected with trends in hours worked. In Canada, average hours worked weekly has remained fairly steady over the past several years. The average Canadian worked 35.8 hours per week in 2018. These averages hide a fair amount of variation. Some Canadians find that they have too little work, while others feel overworked, putting in 50 hours a week or more. Differences are evident by occupation and industrial sector. Workers in agriculture and natural resources, trades, management, and protective services tend to have the longest average weekly hours (more than 40 hours a week) (Statistics Canada, 2019b). In contrast, jobs in customer service and sales have the lowest average hours per week. Although there was evidence in the 1980s and 1990s of a polarization of work hours, with growth at both the high and low end of the hours distribution, this trend has reversed in recent decades, resulting in a moderate decline in overall hours worked by workers in Canada (Usalcas, 2014). Still, considerable variation in hours worked remains, and long work hours are associated with physical and mental health challenges (see Chapter 8).

Self-Employment

self-employed Individuals who are not employed by another company but rather earn a living by providing services or products to clients and customers

Many Canadians are **self-employed**, meaning that they are not employed by another company but rather earn a living by providing services or products to clients and customers. Sometimes self-employment is intertwined with non-standard work. Consider, for example, the case of an engineer who used to be employed full-time by a company but is let go, only to be hired as an independent contractor providing similar services when needed. Uber drivers are also independent contractors with little security,

Source: © Tyler Olson/Shutterstock

A harvester filling a grain truck on a farm in Alberta, one of the provinces where the decline in farm employment is most evident. While the agricultural sector still makes up the largest percentage of self-employed Canadians, stagnant profits, an increase in second-job farming, and an aging workforce means that this number is in decline.

low pay, and no benefits. Other self-employed individuals work independently to provide services to clients (for example, hairdressers who work out of their own homes, landscapers providing services directly to clients, or chiropractors who work independently). When the self-employed work on their own, without paid employees, they are sometimes called "own account workers"; some self-employed individuals, however, employ others to support their businesses. About 15 per cent of Canadian workers are self-employed (Yssaad & Ferrao, 2019). The largest single percentage can be found in agriculture, although self-employment in farming has decreased over the past 30 years. Self-employment is also fairly common in professional and technical services, construction, and business, finance, and insurance (ibid.). Men are more likely to be self-employed than are women, but women's involvement in self-employment has increased over time. In 2018, women composed 38 per cent of all self-employed workers (up from 30 per cent in 1987).

There are a several "push" and "pull" factors that shape decisions to enter self-employment. In surveys, self-employed workers highlight factors "pulling" them towards self-employment, including a desire for autonomy and independence, flexibility, and work-life balance (Hughes, 2003; Yssaad & Ferrao, 2019). There are also many factors that "push" people away from employment, including job loss, lack of good employment alternatives, poor working environments, and bad bosses (Hughes, 2003). Resources are also important in shaping opportunities to engage in self-employment. Establishing a business requires capital and resources, and possession of these varies across gender, race-ethnicity, immigration status, and sexual orientation. For instance, Abada, Hou, and Lu (2014) find that unemployment (exacerbated by discrimination and other barriers) pushes immigrant men into self-employment; however, self-employed immigrants tend to be more highly educated and have more resources than other immigrants (Li, 2001). Moreover, research suggests that visible minority men and women are less likely to be self-employed compared to those from European backgrounds (Nakhaie, Lin, & Guan, 2009); discrimination and lack of resources can limit opportunities for self-employment. Research also finds that self-employment in Canada varies by sexual orientation: lesbian women are more likely, while gay men are less likely, to be self-employed compared to heterosexual men and women (Waite & Denier, 2016).

Self-employed workers have fewer benefits and less access to employment insurance, meaning that in periods of hardship, they can be quite vulnerable. Although some self-employed workers are independent and well-off, others are barely scraping by (Huws, 2001).

Income

Trends in earned income are generally positive, with median hourly wages (in real dollars) for full-time workers increasing from $22.76 in 2001 to $25.00 in 2018 (Morissette, 2018). Trends are uneven among part-time workers, where median hourly wages dropped between the 1980s and 1990s, only to increase in the 2010s (in accordance with recent changes to legislated minimum wage levels in most provinces). The median hourly wage increased for part-time workers from $13.63 in 2001 to $15.00 in 2018 (Morissette, 2018). These increases have been, in part, prompted by workers' campaigns for fair wages (see for example, https://fightfor15.org/). It is not all good news, however, because over the past several decades employer-sponsored pensions have declined fairly substantially for Canadian workers (Morissette, 2018). Moreover, wage increases have not kept pace with the cost of rent in urban areas, meaning that the standard of living of many Canadians is declining (Macdonald, 2019).

Labour market statistics on income also show persistent income inequalities related to labour market outcomes. For example, men still make more, on average, than do women (women earn 87 per cent of what men do). Indigenous peoples make less than non-Indigenous workers in Canada. The gender wage gap persists among Indigenous peoples, with Indigenous women earning less than Indigenous men (Haan, Chuatico, & Cornetet, 2020). However, when education and occupation are taken into account, gender differences among Indigenous peoples disappear (ibid.). Such findings reveal that the intersection of Indigeneity and gender (in combination with other factors like education) is important in shaping outcomes (see also Chapter 10).

Unions

Before concluding this section, it is valuable to note one other important labour market trend over time. In Chapter 3, we briefly reviewed the history of unionization in Canada. Laws and policies surrounding collective bargaining in Canada were introduced during the Second World War and the years that followed. In the 21st century, however, the dominant trend has been a decline in unionization. Morissette (2018) reports that the proportion of Canadian workers in unionized jobs has decreased from 37.6 per cent in 1981 to 28.3 in 2018. This decline is primarily driven by the drop in the percentage of men in unionized jobs. In 1981, 42 per cent of men workers held unionized jobs. By 2018, that percentage had declined to 26 per cent. Women's employment in unionized jobs has been fairly stable during this same period: 31.4 per cent of working women held unionized jobs in 1981, and 30.7 per cent were in such jobs in 2018. Hence, the decline among women is less than 1 per cent. Declines in union participation have been primarily driven by drops in private sector unions; most union members now work in the public sector. The decline in unionization is associated with other work trends—the expansion of work in the services sector and the rise of non-standard work—and likely contributes to observed declines in pensions.

Overall, the world of work in Canada is always changing, and labour market trends help us to understand these changes. Trends in employment, unemployment, occupations, type of work, work hours, and income tell us about the opportunities Canadians have for obtaining paid work and the ways in which social inequalities are reproduced through work opportunities and labour market trends. We will consider the causes and impacts of many of these trends in subsequent chapters. The next section on organizations talks about what Canadians might experience in the workplace once they have a job.

Organizations

Most of us work for, or with, organizations. Even if we are self-employed or work from home, chances are that we are contracting or interacting with organizations in the course of our work. What exactly are **organizations**? Sociologists have created a number of definitions, typologies, and lists of characteristics to provide us with some clarity, although at times these detailed lists can muddy the waters a bit (see Box 4.2). At the most general level, we can define organizations as "a type of collectivity" deliberately created to achieve a set of goals or objectives (Jary & Jary, 2005a, p. 435; Jones, 1996, p. 4). Through organizations, people come together to pursue their interests, mobilizing resources and navigating complex environments to achieve their goals (Hall, 1999; Jones, 1996; Pfeffer & Salancik, 2003). Individuals within organizations have several goals—for example, organizational survival, profit (or, in non-profit firms, financial solvency), producing goods or services, pleasing clients and consumers, and so on. These goals may, at times, be contradictory. For example, pleasing clients may require expenditures that threaten solvency. The goals of individuals within organizations may also conflict (Jary & Jary 2005a; Selznick, 1948; Thornton & Ocasio, 1999). Front-line workers may be

A CLOSER LOOK

4.2 | Characteristics of Organizations

Many scholars define organizations in terms of their major characteristics (Hall, 1999; Weber, 1946; Selznick, 1948; Pfeffer & Salancik, 2003). The following are some of the principal characteristics they have identified:

• identifiable boundaries	• clear, formal rules
• hierarchy and authority systems	• communications systems
• systems of control and consent	• ongoing operations
• interaction with surrounding environment	• goal-seeking
• specialized, trained workforce	• division of labour
• impersonal	• trained management
• concern for rationalization, efficiency	• harnessing resources to achieve aims
• limited membership	• internal co-ordination

Do you think these characteristics accurately describe the organizations you have worked in? Are there characteristics that do not apply or ones that are missing?

more concerned with client well-being and personal fulfillment, while their managers may prioritize profit and their own promotion opportunities. Hence, organizations are complex entities, infused with social inequalities, competing interests, and various norms and social practices. The impact of organizations on workers, therefore, is quite complex.

Definitions of 'organization' tend to be broad. This is helpful to the extent that such definitions can encompass a broad array of social formations and organizing activity. Nevertheless, most of us work in a particular type of organization—bureaucratic organizations—and it is this type that has received most attention in the scholarly literature. Thus, our look at organizations focuses especially on bureaucracies; however, alternative organizational structures are touched on briefly at the end of the chapter.

The study of bureaucracies usually begins with Max Weber, whose theories we reviewed briefly in Chapter 2. Weber (1946) provided an ideal type of bureaucracies outlining core characteristics shared by many, including advanced divisions of labour, specialization, hierarchical authority structures, reliance on written rules and regulations (formalization), expert management, and so on. Weber argued that bureaucracies were a product of rationalization—processes aimed at enhancing efficiency to achieve stated goals in a formal, rule-driven way (Ritzer, 1996; Weber, 1946). For Weber, bureaucracies were instruments of power through which people in positions of authority sought to achieve their goals, even in the face of resistance from others.

Organizational theory has adapted and built upon Weber's typology to provide a better rounded picture. Scholars have elaborated on how organizations interact with their environment and other organizational entities, illuminated processes of organizational change, and shed light on the importance of organizational cultures and interpersonal relations for shaping activity. The sociology of organizations is a distinct area of research and theorizing, and there is an extensive literature on each of these areas and others. Here, we are interested in how organizations shape work and impact workers—with a focus on organizational inequalities, cultures, and change.

Organizational Cultures

Early discussions of organizations and bureaucracies tended to focus on their structure and formalization, going as far as arguing that interactions within modern bureaucracies were impersonal (Weber, 1946; Selznick, 1948). There is some truth to this, since rule-driven organizations proceed from the principle that personal relationships should matter little in hiring, promotion, and service provision. Hiring and promotion should be based on merit, not your friendship with the boss, where you come from, or who your parents are. Similarly, as consumers we expect that organizations will treat each of us the same, regardless of who we are or who we know. While many bureaucratic organizations have adopted these principles, interpersonal relationships are still consequential (Selznick, 1948). Good communication and positive relationships with colleagues are important to organizational functioning, and they contribute to workers' job satisfaction. Relationship-building with clients and customers can also contribute to organizational success. Social interaction and relationships matter a great deal within organizations.

organizational cultures
Values, attitudes, meanings, and norms shared by members of an organization

Organizational cultures shape relationships and interactions. **Organizational cultures** consist of norms, values, attitudes, meanings, and ways of behaving shared by members of an organizational community (Jary & Jary, 2005a; Schein, 1993). Cultures frequently develop somewhat spontaneously through the interactions and relationships of members of an organization. Nonetheless, since the 1980s at least, organizational leaders have viewed organizational cultures as phenomena that can be manipulated to achieve organizational goals (Jary & Jary, 2005a). Organizational cultures, however, are somewhat resistant to manipulation (Schein, 1993; Trice & Beyer, 1993). Companies can try to formulate and enforce an organizational culture—for example, one that values long working hours and a commitment to efficiency—but alternative cultures may still emerge. Organizations, then, may have several cultures—some imposed from above, others developed from below. Different groups or departments within an organization may develop their own cultures, known as **subcultures**. Organizational cultures can be powerful, driving activity within organizations, or weaker, shaping organizational policy and interactions to only a limited extent. Organizational cultures are most likely to develop where employment is stable and workers interact with each other regularly over a lengthy period of time (Schein, 1993).

subcultures
The cultures shared by a subgroup of members in a broader organization or occupation

For workers, organizational cultures can be experienced positively. Sharing norms and values with your colleagues can provide a foundation for strong working relationships and can make work more meaningful. Sharing terms and slang can make us more effective at work as well. For example, our colleagues might understand what we need without a detailed explanation—a few choice phrases or words may suffice. Strong cultures frequently develop in work that is challenging, skilled, fast-paced, and dangerous; carries a stigma; or, conversely, is high status (Rothman, 1998; Papp, 2003). Cultures in these contexts may provide workers with a sense of belonging and safety, a positive identity, or even prestige.

Organizational cultures can have their downsides. They may be exclusionary. People who do not fit into the culture, whether new to the organization or not, may be treated poorly and have difficulty working alongside colleagues who embrace the culture completely. Workers who are minorities in the workplace—especially due to their gender identity, race, immigration status, sexual orientation, or Indigeneity—are more likely to be excluded and may face incivility, harassment, and discrimination as a result (Faulkner, 2009; Papp, 2003; Marom, 2018; Melaku, 2019). Moreover, workplace cultures can encourage work activity that is otherwise not personally (or even socially) beneficial—working unpaid overtime, not taking leaves of absence when required for health reasons, taking short-cuts and not following procedures, regulations, or laws. Long working hours, for example, are part of many organizational cultures (encouraged by management/employers eager to enhance surplus value), but these long working hours not only undermine workers' work-family balance (Hochschild, 1997) and health (Dembe, Erickson, Delbos, & Banks, 2005) but have also been linked to environmental disasters like the Exxon Valdez oil spill in the 1980s (Alaska Oil Spill Commission, 1990) and medical errors causing harm to patients and health care practitioners (Landrigan et al., 2004).

Organizational subcultures are similar, with parallel advantages and disadvantages. However, it is worth noting that organizations may have several subcultures within them, and they can be contradictory, leading to internal conflict across departments or work teams.

Organizational Change

Because bureaucratic organizations are heavily formalized, rule-driven, and characterized by advanced divisions of labour, they are often depicted as rigid and resistant to change (Hall, 1999). However, change is essential within organizations. Regulatory change, market shifts, variations in consumer or client demands, workforce alterations, technological innovation, resource availability, and changing organizational priorities or personnel require organizations to be adaptable. Organizations may also generate change: creating change may be one of the over-arching goals of individuals driving organizations. Thus, while there are organizational pressures resisting change, there are also many that provoke or invoke change within organizations.

One theory of organizational change was proposed by Max Weber and neo-Weberians discussed in Chapter 2. Rationalization was said to be an overarching process driving organizational change. Scholars have argued that organizations are constantly changing to find efficiencies. However, these are not the only changes that occur. DiMaggio and Powell (1983) developed a theory of **institutional isomorphism** to account for organizational change that does not result in greater efficiencies. Isomorphism is a process whereby one element comes to resemble others within a broader population (DiMaggio & Powell, 1983, p. 149). By institutional isomorphism, DiMaggio and Powell are referring to processes that encourage an institution or organization to become more like other organizations in the same (or a closely related) field. These processes may be *coercive*—that is, political and other elites may force an organization to conform—or *mimetic*—organizations may intentionally copy others that appear legitimate and effective (DiMaggio & Powell, 1983). Isomorphic processes may also be shaped by workers within organizations; professional workers in particular may share educational and credential pathways, as well as networks within and across organizations. This similarity in training and connections across networks exerts *normative* pressures generating similarities across the organizations in which these professional workers work (DiMaggio & Powell, 1983, p. 152). These three isomorphic processes encourage organizations to change in similar ways and adopt the strategies, principles, cultures, and goals of others in their fields. These changes do not necessarily make organizations better or more efficient, although change-agents may believe they will. Organizations can still differ in their day-to-day operations, their personnel, and their cultures. Nonetheless, as DiMaggio and Powell (1983) explain, it is often the case that changes made by some organizations in a sector or field are adopted by others who do not want to be left behind.

institutional isomorphism Processes that encourage an institution or organization to become more like other organizations in the same (or a closely related) field (beyond rationalization processes) (DiMaggio & Powell, 1983)

Organizational change generates challenges. It may require new rules, new relationships, new workers, new resources, and other subsequent changes. Organizational cultures can provide barriers to change. When proposed organizational change runs counter to organizational culture, it is likely to fail (Schein, 1993; Trice & Beyer, 1993). Workers will resist changes if they feel those changes alter their working conditions, increase workloads, or result in poorer services to clients/customers. For example, several studies have documented change within health care organizations that has added a considerable amount of paperwork (computer work), reporting, and documentation to health professionals' already long and busy days (McGivern & Ferlie, 2007; Cruz and Sawchuk, 2021). Health care workers have been resistant to these changes, which can limit the time they spend caring for patients—dimensions of their work that are important and meaningful to them—by requiring them to fill out what many believe are unnecessary reports. While they may resist such workplace change when they can, their ability to do so can be limited. The result appears to be declining job satisfaction and increased workplace stress. As noted, while managers and organizational elites invoke change to increase efficiency or to match what other organizations are doing, workers will find ways to protect their working conditions when they can.

Organizations and Inequality

Organizations are instruments of power and domination. This is true by definition as individuals seek to mobilize resources to achieve their ends through organizations. Weber (1968) defined power as the ability to achieve your goals despite the resistance of others. Corporations are a particular type of organization that reproduces inequalities in society more broadly. Corporations are legal entities whose main purpose is to generate profit and benefit shareholders (Bakan, 2004, 2020). Even when corporations embrace other values—as Joel Bakan (2020) argues they are increasingly doing, voicing concern over climate change and social inequalities—these priorities are routinely sacrificed in the interests of making money. Corporations fight for tax breaks and less oversight over their activities, freeing them to cut corners with respect to worker and environmental safety to achieve their goals. Their activities, then, can undermine worker well-being, are destructive for the environment, and can even undermine democracy (Bakan, 2020). Corporate concentration is particularly potentially harmful in this light. In Canada, a small number of large firms control the majority of corporate assets: for example, at the turn of the 21st century, 41 per cent of business assets were held by the top 25 companies (Carroll, 2017, p. 15). Large, global, and powerful corporations are difficult to regulate, but they make decisions that have significant consequences for billions of people around the world, putting all of us at risk. Their profits come at the expense of societal well-being (Bakan, 2020).

Inequality is also produced and reproduced within organizations. Bureaucratic organizations tend to be characterized by entrenched hierarchies, which grant individuals in the upper echelons more authority or power than those below them. Within organizations there is a tendency for elites to rise and impose their will upon others. Robert Michels (1915, p. 407) called this the **iron law of oligarchy**, arguing that "the majority of human beings, in a condition of eternal tutelage, [is] predestined by tragic necessity to submit to the domination of a small minority, and must be content to constitute the pedestal of an oligarchy." Power is used within organizations to achieve the elite's goals, and the well-being of employees or clients is sometimes sacrificed in the process (as cases of corporate irresponsibility and long working hours cultures illustrate). Such dynamics reproduce inequalities by social class.

iron law of oligarchy The tendency for organizations to be governed by a few, despite efforts towards democracy

Inequalities by gender, race, and other dimensions are evident as well. In the 1970s, Rosabeth Moss Kanter (1977) explored gender inequalities within organizations and challenged arguments that men and women workers had different orientations to work. Her research showed that women were disadvantaged in many organizations due to limited opportunities for promotion, stereotypical work roles, and token status in positions of influence. Joan Acker (1990) took these insights further when she argued that organizations were **gendered**: traditional practices and ideologies surrounding gender were embedded into organizational structures to the advantage of many men and the disadvantage of women. To illustrate the gendering of organizations, Acker points to the prevalence of occupational segregation—wherein men and women tend to do different types of work—as well as gendered interactions on the job and the presence of gender ideologies. She also takes a critical look at job evaluations used by management to define

gendered organizations Expectations about gender—gender ideologies, traditional divisions of labour, gender relations, and so on—have become embedded within organizational structures and practices

jobs, establish skill and pay levels, and shape hiring decisions. These job evaluations, she argues, are cast as gender-neutral: they are simply descriptions of what a job entails, ignoring the characteristics of the workers who fill these jobs. These evaluations assume an abstract, disembodied, hypothetical worker who is always available for work, has no outside obligations, and exists simply to do the tasks assigned to them. Far from being gender-neutral, however, Acker (1990) argues that these job evaluations are quite gendered because they assume a traditional gender division of labour whereby men are free to work because they have wives, mothers, and others in their lives who can meet their personal and family obligations. Acker argues that women have a tougher time reaching the upper echelons of organizations precisely because they cannot easily fit the mould of the abstract or hypothetical worker. They are perceived to have other obligations—children and other family members who demand their time. Organizations may be gendered in a manner that disadvantages women, even in female-dominated fields (Stokes, 2015, 2017).

The main argument advanced by Acker (1990) and other scholars like Britton (2000) is that organizations are structured in a manner that has disadvantaged women. The same structures disadvantage transgender and gender-diverse individuals as well. These organizational structures increasingly disadvantage men too. While 50 years ago, many working men had a wife at home to raise children and do domestic labour, this is less often the case today. Men too have outside obligations that interfere with their ability to be always available to work. They may prioritize family and a life outside of work more than in the past. Available data suggest that men who have a partner at home earn more money and win promotions more quickly than their counterparts without partners or with working partners (Chun & Lee, 2001; Vandenbroucke, 2018). Increasingly, the structure of organizations may disadvantage most workers.

Research has also begun to explore other structural inequalities within work organizations. For example, many organizations are not only gendered but heteronormative (Priola & Lasio, 2018). They valorize heterosexuality and assume heterosexual relationships among workers (Williams & Giuffre, 2011). LGBTQI workers are disadvantaged in these work environments by being excluded from organizational cultures, included in ways that marginalize them, and subject to harassment and discrimination (discussed further in Chapter 10). Organizations are also **racialized**, or structured in a manner that favours white people and disadvantages members of racial-ethnic minorities (Crenshaw, 2011; Carbado & Gulati, 2013). These dimensions of disadvantage may intersect. Scholars have argued that inequalities by gender, class, and race (along with other dimensions of inequality) are "simultaneous processes of identity, institutional and social practice" (Holvino, 2010, p. 249). These inequalities have become embedded within organizational contexts where they combine to shape work opportunities and work roles (Acker, 2006; Glenn, 2002; Holvino, 2010). The intersection of gender, class, and race not only may limit opportunities for employment and advancement for the disadvantaged but may shape the nature of their work and interrelationships with colleagues.

racialized
Having experienced a process through which racial markers have been identified as problematic and grounds for subordination

racialized organizations
Assumptions and biases concerning race and ability have become embedded in organizational processes and practices

Ultimately, it is important to recognize not only that organizations are institutions infused with power but that they both reflect and reproduce existing societal inequalities. Workers who are disadvantaged in society more generally face fewer opportunities within bureaucratic institutions. They may be treated like outsiders in organizational cultures, excluded from some social interactions, and even be asked to do different kinds of work than others in similar jobs. Disadvantaged workers may also find themselves struggling to adapt to organizational norms because these norms are not necessarily their own. Dorothy Smith (1990) introduced the concept of "bifurcation of consciousness" to describe women's experiences in male-centric organizations. She argued that women navigated these institutions by learning how to see the world from men's perspectives as well as their own. This concept is similar to that of **two-eyed seeing** (Bartlett, Marshall, & Marshall, 2012), used to describe the practice whereby Indigenous peoples learn to see the world through two perspectives: one rooted in their Indigenous ways of knowing and one in Western knowledge systems. According to Bartlett, Marshall, and Marshall (2012), this can be a strength, allowing people to see two perspectives on important issues and work towards reconciling them to create solutions. While difference is often taken as a disadvantage for those deemed non-normative in organizations, the concept of two-eyed seeing allows us to see this difference as a strength that could enable us to overcome social inequalities to create meaningful organizational practices and change.

two-eyed seeing The practice whereby Indigenous peoples learn to see the world through two perspectives: one rooted in their Indigenous ways of knowing and one in Western knowledge systems

Alternative Organizations, Including Collectives and Co-operatives

Rejecting the power inequalities inherent within bureaucracies, many people have attempted to establish less hierarchical, more democratic organizations. Collective and co-operative organizations are two common alternatives. Technically speaking, a **co-operative** is a type of organization owned by its members who govern it democratically—each member has a vote on major decisions (Cooperative Development Institute, 2015). Despite this democratic structure, co-operatives might still have a hierarchy: members may agree to appoint specific individuals as leaders to run the co-operative on a daily basis or appoint a board of directors, even as major decisions are referred back to the members. **Collectives** are a form of co-operative that operates without hierarchy. No single person or group is awarded managerial or oversight authority; rather decision-making power is spread evenly across group members (Cooperative Development Institute, 2015). Decision-making tends to be by consensus and not majority, especially in small collectives.

co-operative A type of organization owned by its members, who govern it democratically

collective A form of co-operative that operates without hierarchy

Many co-operatives start out as small organizations in which people with common interests or concerns get together to form an organization through which they can work together to achieve their goals—from providing shelters for abused women, to running a restaurant, providing taxi services, opening a store, or providing credit. Democratic decision-making may be easier when member numbers are low. However, some co-operatives are large and even international in scope. Credit unions are one of the most visible types of co-operative, formed to provide members with credit and financial services at competitive rates. Desjardins Group (2019) is a Canadian co-operative that is in fact a federation of hundreds of local credit unions providing financial services primarily in Quebec and Ontario to 7 million members and clients. As a co-operative institution, Desjardins has clearly defined values including cooperation, ethics, integrity, community, and democracy. Desjardins Group (2019) is run by a board of directors, but co-op members do have a voice in company affairs. Clearly, this is a highly formalized company that has a hierarchy but one that intentionally operates according to a different structure and distinct values.

Union Cab in Madison, Wisconsin, is a worker co-operative that is much smaller in size. It is a worker-owned taxi company, and each driver for the company is a part-owner (Union Cab Co-op, 2019). The company was formed by taxi drivers who left a previous

A CLOSER LOOK

4.3 | Co-operatives

The International Cooperative Alliance (ICA) (2019) has articulated a "Statement on the Cooperative Identity," including seven values or principles of the co-operative movement (excerpted from website).

Core Principles of Co-operatives

1) Membership in co-operatives is *voluntary and open*. There should be no barriers to participation, regardless of gender, politics, religion, or other social factors.
2) Co-operatives are *democratic*, and members should actively participate in decision-making and policy development.
3) Members *democratically control (and contribute to) the economic capital* of the co-operative.
4) Co-operatives are *"autonomous*, self-help organisations controlled by their members" (International Cooperative Alliance, 2019). Any agreements to partner with third-parties, must maintain member democracy.
5) Co-operatives are *committed to education*, and should provide training and other learning opportunities for members and employees. Moreover, they should inform the public about the benefits of co-operatives.
6) Co-operatives are encouraged to *collaborate* with other co-operatives.
7) Co-operatives should demonstrate *concern for their communities*.

https://www.ica.coop › cooperatives › cooperative-identity

employer because they were fed up with their working conditions. When starting their own co-operative company, they established clear rules to ensure that workers do not work excessive hours, are paid a fair wage, and have safe working conditions. A further example is the Moosewood collective based in Ithaca, New York, which is owned by 19 members who share the jobs required to run the natural-food restaurant owned by the collective as well as its other business endeavours (Moosewood, 2019). The collective also has additional employees who work there as well. This collective has a non-hierarchical structure and responsibilities are rotated (Moosewood, 2019).

Co-operatives and collectives tend to differ from other organizations not only in terms of their structure but in terms of their values. Member-workers view co-operatives as providing better work environments, more learning opportunities, and quality goods and services (Sommer, Schlanger, Hackman, & Smith, 1984). These businesses often privilege social values and ethical practice over efficiency. Indigenous communities also engage in co-operative businesses that merge cultural values with economic activity (Berge, 2020).

Co-operatives are part of an international movement and can be found in countries around the world. They have a long history in North America; for instance, early cooperatives were encouraged by the Knights of Labor (Curl, 2009). In the 19th century, workers formed both consumer (for purchasing goods) and worker co-operatives (providing goods and services). Co-operatives also became popular among farmers in the late 19th and early 20th centuries (Curl, 2009). In the US, African Americans established many cooperatives tied with broader civil rights social movements (Nembhard, 2014). Co-operatives had a resurgence in the 1930s during a period when many became disillusioned with the failures of capitalism and hence more open to principles of socialism, including fairness and democracy. This trend was an international one that also saw the kibbutz movement in Palestine and collectivization in the Soviet Union. In Canada, this trend may be seen in the establishment of the Co-operative Commonwealth Federation (or CCF), a social democratic political party (and predecessor of the NDP) in Alberta in 1932 by farmer, co-operative, and labour groups (Morley, 2006). Co-operatives have continued to grow and thrive over the past century and may be gaining in popularity. The Canadian Co-operative Association (CCA) has been around since the 1960s and continues to support co-operatives in Canada (Canadian Co-operative Association, 2019).

This section has summarized the characteristics of organizations in which we work, paying particular attention to organizational culture, change, and social inequalities. Our experiences of work are profoundly influenced by the structure and nature of these organizations. While sociological research has tended to focus on bureaucratic organizations, many of us work in smaller firms or alternative organizations, like co-operatives, that are frequently overlooked. It is important to remember that there are meaningful and successful alternatives to bureaucratic organizations.

Reviewing the Learning Objectives

After reading this chapter, you should:

- Understand key terms like "employment rate" and "unemployment rate" and have a sense of current rates and variations across provinces.
- Understand that trends in employment, unemployment, working hours, job availability and so on have implications for how work is experienced.
- Understand the characteristics of organizations and have a sense of their impact on workers.
- Comprehend that organizational structures can reproduce social inequalities.
- Know that organizational alternatives like co-operatives exist.

Questions for Critical Thought

1. Youth unemployment rates are higher than rates for other age groups. Are there changes that Canadian organizations could make to encourage the employment of youth? What kinds of changes do you think might be effective? If organizations were going to make changes to encourage the employment of youth, what factors might affect their ability to make such an organizational change?
2. Thinking back to organizations you might have worked for, what kinds of organizational cultures did they have? Did these cultures improve your work experience or not? Why or why not?
3. Co-operatives are structured very differently from other organizations. Do you think workers' experiences of working in these organizations are different? How?

Annotated Additional Readings

Creese, G., & Wiebe, B. (2012). Survival employment: gender and deskilling among African immigrants in Canada. *International Migration*, *50*(5), 56–76.

This article reveals the intersection of gender, education, and immigration status in shaping African immigrants' labour market outcomes.

Haan, M., Chuatico, G., & Cornetet, J. (2020). Aboriginal earnings in Canada: The importance of gender, education and industry. *Canadian Ethnic Studies*, *52*(2), 1–27.

The authors explore gender differences in Indigenous workers' earnings, exploring the role of industry and education in shaping outcomes.

Bakan, J. (2020). *The new corporation: How "good" corporations are bad for democracy.* Toronto, ON: Penguin Canada. imprint: Allen Lane.

This book (and the documentary that accompanies it) provides a provocative look at corporations, revealing how even when they purport to further social causes, they operate in a manner that prioritizes profit and is detrimental to societies, people, and the environment.

Williams, C., & Giuffre, P. (2011). From organizational sexuality to queer organizations: Research on homosexuality and the workplace. *Sociology Compass*, *5*(7), 551–563. doi:10.1111/j.1751-9020.2011.00392.x

This article provides an overview of research on heteronormativity in organizations, suggesting new directions to further research in the field.

Related Websites

International Co-operative Alliance, statement on identity, values and principles:

https://www.ica.coop/en/cooperatives/cooperative-identity

Statistics Canada, Labour Statistics-Research Papers: Annual Labour Market Review:

https://www150.statcan.gc.ca/n1/pub/75-004-m/75-004-m2019002-eng.htm

Trading Economics (Labour market statistics):

https://tradingeconomics.com/canada/forecast

Fight for $15 (Organization fighting for better wages for low-paid workers):

https://fightfor15.org/

5 Occupations
Blue-Collar, White-Collar, Service, and Professional Jobs

Learning Objectives

After reading this chapter, readers will:

- Develop a general understanding of the characteristics of different kinds of blue-collar, white-collar, service (personal, protective, and interactive), and professional work.
- Understand that these categories are not firm but flexible, with jobs that that might fall into more than one category and shared characteristics.
- Understand that recent workplace change is altering some aspects of these jobs, while other characteristics persist.

Introduction

When you were little, what did you want to be when you grew up? When we are very young, our knowledge of jobs can be quite restricted. We likely have only a vague sense of what our parents and others do. We are exposed to some jobs in storybooks, movies, and shows. We learn about other jobs as we live our lives. Thus, while there are thousands of jobs, there is only a small number that the average child would know: teacher, daycare worker, police officer, firefighter, construction worker, truck driver, garbage collector, doctor, nurse, grocery cashier, farmer, to name a few. Even as adults our knowledge of jobs may not be extensive. We know jobs held by family and friends and those popular enough to figure in stories, movies, and the news.

Nonetheless, there is a wide array of jobs in Canada, and to capture some of the similarities and differences among them people have tended to use colloquial categories like "blue-collar" and "white-collar." These are somewhat vague and ill-defined, but they are useful because they capture some real differences. **Blue-collar work** has traditionally been physical, requiring workers to use their muscles and get their hands dirty. Wearing a dark-coloured shirt to do this kind of work just makes sense—hence the name. In contrast, **white-collar work** generally involves working with information, people, and computers. This work often takes place in a clean office, and so people can dress up if they want to—wearing white to work, for example. To this simple dichotomy we can add two other categories. Professionals are often hands-on workers, but they also have advanced education and work with information and ideas. Surgeons definitely get their

blue-collar work
Traditionally, physical work taking place in the primary or secondary sector

white-collar work
Work that typically takes place in office settings and involves administration, the processing of information, and the management of organizational operations, across industries

hands dirty, as will an engineer on a construction job site or the nurse working closely with the ill; however, when they do so they are putting their knowledge into action to help people. Finally, **service workers** provide services to others: researchers tend to distinguish between those who deliver **personal services** (like cleaners), **interactive service work** (such as retail workers who interact with customers), and **protective services** (policing, firefighting).

service worker Worker whose job involves providing services to others, especially interactive, personal, or protective service work

personal service work Work that entails providing personal services to clients and/or employers

interactive service work Service work requiring interaction with members of the public (such as retail, food services, and hospitality)

protective services Work directed towards protecting people and society (for example, policing and firefighting)

This chapter provides an overview of these different types of work, identifying some of their principle characteristics, documenting workers' experiences, and discussing recent workplace change. In some instances, the changes experienced alter the nature of these jobs, blurring the distinctions between these job categories.

Blue-Collar Work

Blue-collar jobs are found predominantly in the primary industries (farming, fishing, forestry, mining, and related industries) and the secondary or manufacturing sector, as well as construction. In 2016, about 21 per cent of Canada's workforce worked in blue-collar jobs; the percentage among men, however, was 35 per cent (Statistics Canada, 2018a). What has traditionally distinguished all of these jobs is that they are physical in nature and that the work is tangible. Blue-collar workers use their bodies and their hands to harness and manage natural resources for human use (food, lumber, metals, and minerals), to manufacture goods for human consumption, or to contribute to the construction and maintenance of buildings, bridges, roads, and other structures. Although these jobs may be physically challenging, they can also be rewarding.

Primary Industry Work

Table 5.1 provides a snapshot of a sample of jobs in the primary sector. As the table shows, work in this industry is quite variable respecting training and pay. Job prospects vary between limited and good. Some provinces have been reluctant to allow unionization among farm workers, contributing to lower wages and poor working conditions in this sector (Makin, 2011). Unionized jobs tend to benefit from higher wages.

As Table 5.1 shows, some primary sector workers earn decent wages without extensive post-secondary training. Here, workers may find fulfilling work that enables them to work in/with nature, engage in meaningful, socially necessary work, and enjoy a sense of accomplishment. Nevertheless, some jobs are dangerous, with higher than average rates of workplace injury, illness, and mortality (see Chapter 8). Moreover, some primary sector work is seasonal. As a result, workers may need to combine these jobs with others to make ends meet year-round.

The seasonal nature of farm work, combined with the fact that it is onerous work offering low pay, has resulted in a shortage of (skilled) Canadian workers willing to do this work. To address this shortage—without raising wages and increasing the price of food—the Canadian government established the Seasonal Agricultural Workers Program (SAWP). This program imports tens of thousands of agricultural workers from Mexico and the Caribbean to work on Canadian farms during the agricultural season for low pay—often in poor working and living conditions. This program has been highly criticized for its exploitative nature. Migrants' work is arduous and their housing substandard;

TABLE 5.1 Select Primary Industry Jobs

Occupation	NOC	Description	Education	Prospects	Median Wage
Farm Hand	8431	Plant, cultivate, harvest	High school	Limited-fair	$16.60/hr
Forestry Worker	8422	Reforestation, forest management	High school & training	Limited-fair	$22.00/hr
Mining	8231	Drill, blast, operate machinery	College/apprenticeship	Fair-good	$34.00/hr
Oil and Gas Drilling	8412	Operate rig, machinery +	High school & training	Limited	$32.00/hr
Fishing	8262	Operate fishing vessels to fish	College/apprenticeship	Limited-fair	$25.00/hr

Source: jobbank.gc.ca; NOC = National Occupational Classification code.

this combination compromises migrant workers' health (Preibisch & Hennebry, 2011). Stark evidence of this emerged during the COVID-19 pandemic when outbreaks occurred among migrant workers, overcrowded in housing and work settings, leading to illness and death (Doyle, 2020). Migrant workers are often vulnerable to abuse and overwork (Basok, 2002; Hennebry, 2006; Belanger & Candiz, 2014). Workers in this program have no input into where they will work, when they will come to Canada, and when they will return home. They are not entirely free, since all aspects of their work are determined by others. Although these workers are viewed as skilled and important by employers and officials, they are also racialized and largely invisible, such that their circumstances are too easily ignored (Belanger & Candiz, 2014).

The SAWP is just one component of the broader Temporary Foreign Worker Program (TFWP) in Canada. There are roughly half a million temporary workers in Canada in any given year (Lu, 2020), and they are overrepresented in not only agriculture but other primary industries such as forestry and fishing. Temporary foreign workers are also employed in accommodation and food services, domestic service, and several other fields. Many temporary foreign workers experience precarious and exploitative working conditions (Fudge & MacPhail, 2009; Strauss & McGrath 2017). Fudge and MacPhail (2009, p. 43) describe the TFWP as "an extreme version of labour flexibility" providing "employers with a pool of unfree workers who are disposable at will." Temporary workers typically do important work that Canadian workers are reluctant to do because of poor working conditions and low pay.

Source: THE CANADIAN PRESS/Graham Hughes

Erick Lopez, Noe Arteaga, and Henry Aguirre (left to right) of Guatemala, who entered Canada through the Temporary Foreign Worker Program, speak out against the abuse of the rights of agricultural workers at a 2017 protest in Montreal. Although the Canadian government promised to protect the rights of foreign workers, the measures taken have been inadequate. 2020 saw fatal outbreaks of COVID-19 among temporary foreign workers in the agricultural sector because of poor working and living conditions.

Work in Skilled Trades

Skilled trades are distinguished from other blue-collar jobs by the many years of training and experience required and the fact that they are regulated. Workers in these fields must obtain certifications, and their work is guided by codes and regulations (see Table 5.2).

Wages for jobs in skilled trades are good. Job prospects are also typically promising: in fact, Canada has experienced shortages of some skilled workers (Howcroft, 2019). Workers in these jobs often enjoy a measure of autonomy, the opportunity to exercise creativity and problem-solving, a sense of accomplishment, and job satisfaction. Still, in some types of work (especially construction), turnover is extensive, leading to employment instability (Charest, 2008).

Occupations in Manufacturing

Jobs in manufacturing and assembly are less advantaged than some other types of blue-collar work (see Table 5.3). Unionized jobs in manufacturing (such as in auto assembly) pay well and have good benefits, but the job prospects in this sector are poor and the future uncertain. Manufacturing used to be a good source of jobs for people with limited education; however, the decline of employment in this sector in Canada—only about 9 per cent of working men and women were in these jobs in 2020—has reduced opportunities. Canada imports most of its manufactured goods from other countries (see Box 5.1).

TABLE 5.2 Select Jobs in the Skill Trades

Occupation	NOC	Description	Education	Prospects	Median Wage
Auto Service	7322	Repair and restore motor vehicles	College/apprenticeship	Fair-good	$22.50/hr
Carpenters	7271	Construct, erect, install, repair wood structures	College/apprenticeship	Limited-fair	$25.00/hr
Electricians	7241	Lay out, assemble, install, test, repair electrical wiring, etc.	College/apprenticeship	Limited-fair	$32.00/hr
Heavy Equipment Operators	7521	Operate heavy equipment	High school, training	Fair	$27.00/hr
Machinists	7231	Operate machine tools to make parts/products	College/apprenticeship	Fair-good	$25.68/hr
Plumbers	7251	Install, repair pipes and plumbing	College/apprentice	Limited-fair	$30.00/hr

Source: jobbank.gc.ca.

TABLE 5.3 Manufacturing Jobs

Occupation	NOC	Description	Education	Prospects	Median Wage
General Labourers in Processing & Manufacturing	9619	Basic activities in processing, manufacturing, and utilities	On-the-job training	Limited	$14.50/hr
Motor Vehicle Assembly	9522	Assemble & install prefabricated parts	High school and/ or training	Uncertain	$23.50/hr
Manufacturing Painter	9536	Operate machines, equipment to paint manufactured products	High school and/ or training	Fair	$21.40/hr

Source: jobbank.gc.ca.

Global Perspectives

5.1 | The Global Assembly Line

The movement of manufacturing production to developing countries increased substantially beginning in the 1970s and 1980s. In these locales, workers are paid less, and regulations and taxes are lighter, allowing goods to be manufactured abroad cheaply and shipped to the West for consumption (Bluestone & Harrison, 1982; Seneviratne, 2019; Salzinger, 2003). In these transplanted factories, the labour force disproportionately consists of young women (aged 14–24), said to be ideal employees because of their "nimble" fingers, docility, obedience, and hard work (Seneviratne, 2019). As Salzinger (2003) contends, this docility is described as something innate among Third World women, but it is not. Rather, docility is manufactured on the job through gendered labour management strategies. In a recent study of young women's manufacturing work in Sri Lanka, Seneviratne (2019) documents the difficult working conditions in which workers were driven to achieve impossible targets and then subjected to harsh discipline when they could not reach them. For example, Seneviratne (2019) describes one factory where women were asked to sew 70 articles an hour—more than one a minute. Anyone who fell behind was verbally abused and denied breaks—of which there were precious few. The work was very strenuous and the pace difficult to sustain eight hours day, six days a week. Seneviratne's (2019) study, and many others, lay bare the challenging conditions workers on the global assembly line endure to provide goods to Canadians and others in Western countries.

Manufacturing jobs used to be regarded as semi-skilled and routine. At times, they are also physically strenuous. Continued implementation of automation within manufacturing, however, is altering both job content and job availability.

Distinguishing Features of Blue-Collar Jobs

Blue-collar jobs are variable, but they have some characteristics in common. Notably, work in this field is highly male-dominated: only 6 per cent of workers in skilled trades and 20 per cent of workers in the primary industries were women in 2016. Women compose about 30 per cent of workers in manufacturing jobs. Researchers have also flagged the following as significant: (1) the presence of strong occupational cultures; (2) dirty work, identity, and dignity; and (3) social inequalities.

Many blue-collar jobs involve work in teams. In fact, teams take on a special importance in dangerous blue-collar jobs because workers rely on their team members to help keep them safe. Occupational cultures and subcultures emerge in these settings. As you may remember from Chapter 4, workers who share a culture often have similar values, use terms and phrases outsiders would not understand, and have strong norms governing social interaction (Haas, 1974; Steiger, 1993; Papp, 2003; Thiel, 2012). Cultures in these jobs often emphasize white, working-class masculinity, including toughness, physical strength, and hard work (Ackroyd & Crowdy, 1990; Deery, Kolar, & Walsh, 2019; Lucas, 2012; Thiel, 2012). Shared cultures bind groups together and can enhance their ability to work effectively (Haas, 1974). Social networks and group ties can also help workers employed on seasonal and temporary contracts to obtain work (Jones, 1984; Thiel, 2012; Berntsen, 2016). Workers are socialized into these work cultures during apprenticeships and on-the-job training (Haas, 1974). Here, they may need to prove their toughness and strength to their counterparts and even undergo hazing rituals to be accepted by others (Haas, 1974; Vaught & Smith, 1980; Thiel, 2012). Strong work cultures can help to protect workers in dangerous jobs by encouraging workers to look out for one another (Haas, 1974), but they can also encourage workers to take unnecessary risks to demonstrate their toughness and bravery (Papp, 2003). On the positive side, work cultures can imbue jobs with a sense of meaning and increase job satisfaction. More negatively, they can be exclusionary, making it difficult for outsiders to succeed in these fields.

dirty work
Job tasks that are "physically disgusting . . . a symbol of degradation, something that wounds one's dignity" (Hughes, 1958, p. 49)

Some blue-collar work requires what Everett Hughes (1958, p. 49) called **dirty work**—job tasks that are "physically disgusting . . . a symbol of degradation, something that wounds one's dignity." Work can be "dirty" in different ways (Ashforth & Kreiner, 1999; Deery et al., 2019). Physically dirty work involves working with actual dirt or noxious substances. Socially dirty work involves working with people deemed undesirable or working in subservient positions. Morally dirty work requires doing things people find morally repugnant (for example, evicting people). Not all blue-collar work is dirty work, but some of it is physically dirty. Hughes (1958) and others have argued that dirty work can be discrediting—that is, people may look down upon those who do dirty work. How do workers cope with this disrespect? Studies find that strong work subcultures help workers to distance themselves from the discrediting aspects of their work and focus on the positives: their toughness, their physical and emotional strength, how hard they work, how they treat others, their ability to make an honest living through their labour, and, when they have it, their autonomy (Deery et al., 2019; Lucas, 2012; Ashforth & Kreiner, 1999). Workers who spend time hanging out with colleagues shield themselves from negative feedback from others and enjoy the camaraderie that comes from sharing experiences that others cannot fully understand (Ashforth & Kreiner, 1999; Deery et al., 2019). The result may be improved job satisfaction, whatever the working conditions.

The blue-collar work cultures that value white, working-class masculinity, including physicality and toughness (Ackroyd & Crowdy, 1990; Papp, 2003, Thiel, 2012), can result in the exclusion of people based on gender identity, race, sexual orientation, disability status, and Indigeneity. Blue-collar masculinities may denigrate and devalue femininity and alternative masculinities (Connell, 1990). The result can be physical and verbal aggressions against coworkers, especially in contexts characterized by job insecurity, high work demands, and insufficient social support (Cloutier & Marchand, 2020). The accounts of women entering male-dominated work environments are rife with examples of hostile treatment, failure to recognize skills and training, sexism, discrimination, even sexual assault (Vaught & Smith, 1980; Martin, 1997; Trumpener, 2020). Visible minority and Indigenous women have had a particularly difficult time (Kong, 2020). Indigenous men and women may find that the cultures valued in blue-collar work do not match their own values, as studies of Indigenous workers in the forestry sector have argued (Booth & Skelton, 2011). Racial minority men may need to "prove" their toughness, physicality, and roughness within the context of the work culture (Thiel, 2012; Haas, 1974). The situation of racial minority men may be improved when they can work in teams with others who share their ethnic-racial and/or religious background (Thiel, 2012; Haas, 1974; Berntsen, 2016). Social exclusions can reproduce social inequalities. For example, racial minority and immigrant men are clustered in the least attractive blue-collar jobs—including low-paying factory work and agricultural work—exacerbating their societal marginalization and vulnerability (Thompson, 2010). Recently, there has been a concerted effort to bring more women and minorities into skilled trades and primary industries to prevent anticipated labour market shortages and increase diversity and inclusion (Kong, 2020; Canadian Institute of Forestry, 2018).

Recent Changes in Blue-Collar Jobs

Work in these sectors is very much influenced by the global economy and trade such that international trends (like the movement of manufacturing to other countries or the international market for wood) shape employment opportunities and experiences. Workplace change spurred by rationalization and technology also impacts workers.

The decline of employment in the manufacturing sector is one notable change that has accelerated over the past several decades. Rationalization and technology has ensured that many manufacturing facilities can produce more with fewer employees. Much **labour-intensive manufacturing** work (that which requires many workers) has been moved outside of Canada to countries around the world where labour is cheaper (see Box 5.1). Manufacturing work in the past tended to be routine and repetitive much of the time, but it also provided opportunities for social interactions and even fun and games to break up routines (Burawoy, 1979; Roy, 1959; Ackroyd & Crowdy, 1990). If some workers were bored on the job, they at least had opportunities to daydream and occasionally slack off (Molstad, 1986; Burawoy, 1979). With rationalization, production accelerated. For instance, Rinehart, Huxley, and Robertson (1997) describe jobs at the CAMI plant in Ingersoll, Ontario, in the early 1990s that took 57 seconds out of 60 to complete, allowing workers three seconds of rest time every minute before they had to repeat the same tasks again. This was an intense work pace that was difficult for workers to sustain without injury. In such facilities, workers were divided into teams and rotated through a series of mundane but intense jobs throughout the day (Rinehart et al., 1997; Crowley, Tope, Chamberlain, & Hodson, 2010).

labour-intensive manufacturing Manufacturing in which labour is a (or the) main cost of production

These changes were part of broader processes of rationalization—a drive to achieve greater efficiencies—and what Crowley et al. (2010) label **neo-Taylorism**. The latter trend represents a renewed adoption of scientific management, wherein workers are chosen very carefully—with attention to their work effort and ability to handle intense work pressures—and then subjected to speed-ups and work intensification (Crowley et al., 2010; Braverman, 1974). A commitment to constant innovation, whereby workers are encouraged to identify ways to increase their own work pace and pass their knowledge on to management, is encouraged. Here, workers are asked to contribute to their own exploitation. Rationalization contributes to a decrease in the size of the labour force, since efficiencies allow companies to do more with less, and it alters the nature of the work.

neo-Taylorism A renewed adoption of scientific management, wherein workers are chosen very carefully, with consideration for their work effort and ability to handle intense work pressures, and subsequently subjected to speed-ups and work intensification (Crowley et al., 2010)

Rationalization trends like streamlining processes and standardizing products and procedures lay the foundation for automation and greater use of technology (Susskind, 2016). **Automation** not only replaces workers, but it changes the nature of jobs left behind. For example, researchers have documented the transformation of work in slaughterhouses, which used to be messy, physical, boisterous, and autonomous work environments with strong work cultures (Ackroyd & Crowdy, 1990; Hamilton & McCabe, 2016). Increasingly, these environments are automated (Hamilton & McCabe, 2016). Workers monitor the machines; as such, their work is less physical. Instead of a permanent workforce with a strong work culture, workers are predominantly temporary workers with little attachment to the work. Sennett (1998) documents similar changes in

automation The use of labour-saving technology, usually to cut costs and/or speed up production

a US bakery, where the work has become so automated that workers need no knowledge of baking. They are machine-tenders.

Automation, then, is altering many blue-collar jobs, especially manufacturing. Rationalization trends are also common. While trades, crafts, and much primary sector work required time and effort for a person to become skilful (Sennett, 2008), rationalizing processes subdivide and standardize tasks, undermining quality and workers' fulfillment in exercising creativity and skill on the job. Moving forward, blue-collar workers will continue to be impacted by technological and workplace change.

White-Collar Work

White-collar work typically involves administration, the processing of information, and the management of organizational operations across industries. About 31 per cent of Canadian workers are employed in these jobs. Like blue-collar work, white-collar work is variable in nature. Some is highly skilled and involves advanced training and education, while other jobs are more routine—the latter have been decreasing over the past several decades.

Clerical and Administration Jobs

Table 5.4 lists some clerical occupations. In the mid-20th century, large numbers of women were employed to do clerical work; however, computerization and automation have been used to replace many of those who formerly handled correspondence, answered phones, greeted visitors, and processed paperwork. As the table shows, these jobs tend not to require a great deal of formal education. Nevertheless, it is increasingly common to see people with post-secondary diplomas in these jobs. The median pay for clerical work is above minimum wage but lower than the pay in other white-collar jobs.

What this table cannot capture is the hidden skills and training that clerical workers are expected to possess: these include customer service, social, and communication skills, to name a few. Self-presentation has also been important in this job in the past. Those who meet with clients are expected to look nice: their appearance is viewed as a reflection of the company and the people they work for. In her classic study of men and women in large US organizations, Kanter (1977) identified two different types of secretaries or clerical workers. Some were partnered with a specific (usually male) manager and worked as his "office wife." Others were more akin to factory workers, unattached and working in a division completing routine work on orders from others. Today, most clerical workers are assigned specialist roles in which they work with a variety of other white-collar workers

TABLE 5.4 Clerical and General Office

Occupation	NOC	Description	Education	Prospects	Median Wage
Payroll Clerk	1432	Collect, verify, & process payroll	High school &/or training	Good	$25.00/hr
Bank Clerk	1434	Compile, process, & maintain financial information	High school &/or special training	Fair	$20.67/hr
Office Clerk	1411	General office	High school &/or special training	Fair	$20.51/hr

Source: jobbank.gc.ca.

and clients providing support, processing claims, forms, and requests, and administering aspects of organizational affairs.

Business and Administrative White-Collar Work

Other white-collar workers include financial analysts, workers in sales, purchasing, and marketing, insurance agents, and administrative officers, to name a few. As Table 5.5 shows, these white-collar workers tend to have higher educational requirements than clerical workers. They collate, analyze, and interpret the information clerical workers collect and process and make decisions (to support clients and other white-collar workers). Wages earned are only slightly higher than those of clerical workers. Job prospects in these fields are fair to good. Many of these workers are also public-facing and may be required to represent their companies through their appearance and demeanour.

Managerial Work

The literature on managers often distinguishes between lower-level, mid-level, and upper-level managers. Their roles can be somewhat ambiguous, since they spend some of their time trying to solve unanticipated problems that arise, but typically their jobs entail planning, organizing, coordinating, reviewing information and deciding on a course of action, and managing people (Konrad, Kashlak, Yoshioka, Waryszak, & Toren, 2001). On average, managers tend to have post-secondary education, and they hold jobs where they are granted considerable responsibilities. For these responsibilities, they can be very well-paid, as Table 5.6 shows. Nevertheless, these median wages conceal a great deal of

TABLE 5.5 Administrative and Other White-Collar Jobs

Occupation	NOC	Description	Education	Prospects	Median Wage
Administrative Officer	1221	Oversee and implement admin processes	College	Fair-good	$24.04/hr
Financial Analyst	1112	Collect and analyze financial information	University	Fair-good	$33.65/hr
Sales (wholesale)	6411	Sell goods & services to retail, wholesale, commercial, industrial, and other clients	High school &/or training	Fair-good	$23.12/hr
Insurance Agent	6231	Sell insurance	College/apprenticeship	Fair-good	$23.56/hr

Source: jobbank.gc.ca.

TABLE 5.6 Managerial Work

Occupation	NOC	Description	Education	Prospects	Median Wage
Banking Manager	0122	Manage financial establishment/department	University	Fair-good	$45.64/hr
Financial Manager	0111	Manage financial & accounting departments	University	Fair-good	$46.64/hr
Human Resources Manager	0112	Manage HR & personnel departments	University	Limited-fair	$45.06/hr
Construction Manager	0711	Manage construction companies, depts.	University	Fair-good	$40.00/hr
Manufacturing Manager	0911	Manage manufacturing facilities, depts.	University	Fair-good	$39.74/hr
Retail Manager	0621	Manage retail establishments	University	Fair	$32.69/hr

Source: jobbank.gc.ca.

variation across firms and managerial levels. For instance, retail and manufacturing managers are among the lowest paid—although they still earn much more than the white-collar, service, and blue-collar workers they supervise. Managers in banking, financial and human resources earn more on average. Despite job losses among other types of white-collar workers, managers have increased in number over the past several decades, especially at the middle-manager level (Livingstone, 2021; Goldstein, 2012). Today about 11 per cent of all Canadian workers are in managerial jobs—although some claim this is an underestimation (Livingstone, 2021).

Traditionally, managerial work was dominated by white men, but this is (slowly) beginning to change, with the entrance of white women into managerial jobs. Other workers continue to be strongly under-represented, especially in upper management.

Key Job Characteristics

Writing decades ago, C. Wright Mills (1951, p. 182) argued that white-collar work differed from blue-collar work because in the former, employers not only sought "labor, energy and skill" but also certain "social personalities." That is, white-collar workers must complete their work while projecting a certain image and demeanour that reflects well on their employers. In this manner, expectations on white-collar workers for dress, demeanour, and social interaction can be high. Research has documented that these displays are racialized: the "right" appearance was traditionally a "white" appearance (Jones, 1998, p. 324; Moss & Tilly, 1996). Moreover, expectations surrounding white-collar jobs are gendered. In clerical work, traditionally gendered female, workers have been expected to present a more feminine and subordinate display and demonstrate caring and conciliation. In contrast, among managers—traditionally gendered male—assertiveness and confidence are expected. Contradictions can be experienced by men doing traditional women's work and women doing traditional men's work, even when they attempt to adopt the demeanour expected in their jobs (Henson & Rogers, 2001; Pierce, 1995). Assertive women are sometimes denigrated as "bitches," while non-assertive, caring men can be ostracized for not being manly enough. LGBTQI workers experience additional challenges fitting into these "gendered" work boxes (Connell, 2010, 2012). The gendering and racialization of work creates many contradictions and pressures for workers.

emotional labour Work (especially work under the direction of others) requiring the suppression of personal emotions and the manipulation of others' emotions to benefit one's employer

Many (but not all) white-collar workers must perform **emotional labour** in their jobs. Emotional labour has two central components (Hochschild, 2003): workers are expected to control or manage their own emotions while simultaneously managing or even manipulating the emotions of those they are interacting with. When you are feeling grouchy, tired, frustrated, or angry and you suppress these feelings to appear pleasant and positive while on the job, you are engaging in emotional labour. When you soothe an angry client, endeavour to calm your boss, or try to cheer up your colleague, you are also engaging in emotional labour. Alternatively, emotional labour—especially in male-dominated jobs—can take the form of "strategic friendliness"—being outwardly friendly with someone to get what you want (Pierce, 1995) or even being authoritative and intimidating to achieve your goals (Hochschild, 2003).

Emotional labour can be complex, and performing it successfully can take considerable skill and effort (Bolton, 2005). Some emotional labour may be closely prescribed by the employer, but workers with discretion may perform some emotional labour to connect and help others, to express themselves, and to feel good about themselves and what they do (Bolton, 2005; Jenkins, Delbridge, & Roberts, 2010). To some extent emotional labour can be experienced as positive by workers: sometimes acting happy can make you *feel* happy and distance you from negative emotions (Wharton, 1999). However, manipulating your own emotions and those of others can come at a cost and enhance stress and burnout (Hochschild, 2003). Emotional labour can be gendered and racialized, with different emotional displays required across the gender and race of the worker as well as the nature of the job (Pierce, 1995).

The most privileged white-collar workers appear to be managers, who not only benefit from higher pay but also report more autonomy than other workers (Livingstone, 2021). Networking can be very important for managers, not only to the conduct of their jobs but also in obtaining upward mobility. Those disadvantaged by race, class, immigration status, and other structured social inequalities may have more limited networks, negatively impacting their opportunities for promotion. Few top managers are members of racial minorities or other disadvantaged groups (see Chapters 9 and 10).

Workplace Change

White-collar workers have been impacted by rationalization and technological change. Technological change alters not only what workers do but how they do it and when and where they do it. Surveillance of office work has increased—key strokes can be counted, online activity tracked, and phones monitored—to accelerate the pace of work. Beginning in the 1980s and progressing from there, office work increasingly came to resemble an assembly line in which workers performed repetitive, simple tasks, broken down using scientific management principles, in a manner that minimized creativity and variety (Garson, 1988; Carter et al., 2013). Garson (1988) called this a white-collar "sweatshop" when she detailed how automation threatened to reduce autonomous office workers into drones. As automation proceeds, some jobs are eliminated, but those workers left behind may find their jobs narrowing in scope (Carter et al., 2013). The combined impact of this job redesign to achieve more **lean work environments** with higher work demands, performance targets, and increased surveillance has been to workers' disadvantage. In some contexts, office workers may spend "staggeringly long periods . . . at the workstation engaged in . . . mind-numbing repetitive tasks" (Carter et al., 2013, p. 759). Workers' physical and mental health has been negatively impacted by these rationalization trends: workers in rationalizing organizations report more physical ailments, including musculoskeletal disorders, and stress (ibid.).

lean work Environments environments where staffing is kept to a bare minimum in an effort to cut costs

For others, technological change combined with organizational restructuring has broadened jobs as well as increased pressures to perform. To maximize efficiency, organizations are relying increasingly on computer technology and software innovations to cut down on office staff. This has been accompanied by the transfer of some work to remaining white-collar workers, who must now add tasks formerly done by colleagues to their workload (work intensification). As a result of organizational rationalization and technological change, work increasingly encroaches on workers' personal and home lives. With smartphones, laptops, and other devices, workers can be constantly available to clients, supervisors, and others and may be expected to keep up with work, long after formal work hours are over—evenings, weekends, and even during vacations. This combination of organizational and technological changes is exacerbating workloads and work pressures.

A key element of organizational restructuring, alluded to above, is **downsizing**—cutting back on the permanent workforce. Organizations aim to be "lean" and keep their permanent workforce to a minimum. Permanent, full-time workers may earn good wages

downsizing Reducing the number of permanent staff members at an organization

and have benefits and opportunities for promotion up organizational hierarchies. When there is more work than these workers can accomplish, companies rely on contract and temporary workers—people hired on limited term contracts, at fixed wages, with few to no benefits, to do specific tasks for their employers. Relying on contract workers can be cheaper for organizations, but these jobs are precarious. Workers have little job security. In some cases, workers are downsized only to be hired back as temporary contract employees. This trend is an important contributor to labour force **precarity** (discussed more in Chapter 6) and is another factor increasing workplace stress.

precarity
Situations and work that are precarious

outsourcing
Organizations contracting other firms and individuals to do work formerly done in-house

Ironically, this downsizing and **outsourcing** of the white-collar labour force appears to be one of the drivers for the expansion of managers (Goldstein, 2012). Managers are hired in larger numbers to oversee this disparate and changing workforce, as well as to handle the human resources demands of a shifting workforce with frequent hiring and firing. Thus, firms are letting go of some workers, only to hire managers, who demand higher salaries. Although these workforce changes are done in the name of enhancing efficiency, firms continue to engage in practices that go against this goal. Indeed, control and surveillance of workers appear to have become an end itself (Garson, 1988; McGivern & Ferlie, 2007).

These employment shifts are altering hiring practices. Employers want to make sure they hire the "right" workers—with the right skills, attitudes, demeanour, and work ethic. Some hire full-time workers from competitors, since they have a proven track record. Some may hire from their pool of temporary workers, who have already proven their worth. For entry-level jobs, taking on low-paid or unpaid interns is another strategy to allow employers to screen potential employees. As an alternative, job candidates may be asked to do some work for the company for free as part of an evaluation process, in addition to several rounds of interviews, résumé review, and vetting references (see for instance Ashley & Empson, 2016). This is in line with neo-Taylorism discussed by Crowley et al. (2010). The "right" worker not only possesses valued skills and education but the right attitude, including a tolerance for high work demands. These extra layers of hiring—and the focus on hiring not only for skill but for company "fit"—amplify exploitation and discrimination (as Chapter 10 discusses in more detail). Minority, transgender, Indigenous, and working-class workers, and those with disabilities, may not be deemed to "fit" to the same extent as others.

Service Work

Service work entails the provision of services to customers and clients. About 23 per cent of Canadians work in these occupations. There are many different types of services workers: some interact directly with members of the public (for example in retail and food services), while others provide services to people more indirectly (for example, cleaners). While much service work is female-dominated, some protective service work (like that of firefighters and police officers) is traditionally male-dominated.

Personal and Interactive Service Work

Table 5.7 lists several service-oriented jobs. This work tends to be low paid, with earnings right around minimum wage or slightly above. Education requirements are often basic,

TABLE 5.7 Interactive and Personal Services

Occupation	NOC	Description	Education	Prospects	Median Wage
Cashiers	6611	Operate equipment to scan, record, & accept payment	On-the-job training	Fair	$12.00/hr
Food & Beverage Servers	6513	Take orders, serve food	High school &/or specialized training	Fair-good	$14.00/hr
Retail Salespersons	6421	Sell, rent/lease goods to consumers	High school &/or specialized training	Fair	$14.00/hr
Cleaner	6731	Clean buildings, residences	On-the-job training	Fair-good	$15.00/hr
Home Health Care Worker	4412	Personal care to seniors, people with disabilities, others	High school or specialized training	Fair-good	$16.50/hr
Personal Support Aide (health)	3413	Assist hospital and care home staff with basic care of patients	Some high school or college; some additional training (i.e., first aid)	Good	$20.23/hr

Source: jobbank.gc.ca.

although workers develop skills and acquire valued experience (Gould, 2010). Job prospects consistently range between "fair" and "good." Although these jobs rarely get the respect (or remuneration) they deserve, they are important; during the 2020 pandemic, they were frequently referred to as "essential services" along with jobs in health care. To survive in today's society, we need to purchase food and goods, and we rely on cleaning and disinfecting now more than ever before.

Work in these sectors is race- and sex-segregated. Minority workers—especially racialized and immigrant workers—are overrepresented in cleaning and health aide work especially. Immigrant workers may have qualifications in other fields but cannot get their credentials recognized and hence are forced to accept low-wage jobs. Immigrants are often highly valued in these jobs because they are regarded as cooperative, competent, and hard-working employees who rarely complain (Shih, 2002). Cleaning work is undertaken by both men and women, but job titles and locales of work vary, with more women working in jobs as "light duty cleaners" and domestic workers in private homes (including those brought in under temporary foreign worker schemes: Grandea & Kerr, 1998; Stasiulis & Bakan, 1997), while men are more common in janitorial occupations.

Women (and youth) predominate in jobs in retail sales and food and beverage service and as cashiers. They may be seen to possess the right personality and social skills to perform this kind of work. Indeed, Moss and Tilly (1996) argue that Black men are discriminated against in many interactive service work jobs; they are stereotyped as lacking the requisite demeanour and interactive skills to succeed, despite no evidence that this is the case. Low wages in these fields (and often part-time hours) are predicated on the idea that workers are "secondary earners" and may not be relying on these jobs entirely to survive (Williams & Connell, 2010); it is assumed they have family members with better-paying jobs who help to pay the bills. These assumptions are not always accurate; these low-paid workers do not typically earn enough to live on.

Home health care aides and personal support workers (PSW) are disproportionately women—especially minority women—and their wages are typically low. About 10 per cent of PSWs are men, most of them visible minority (Storm, Braedley, & Chivers, 2017).

The interaction of gender and race (in combination with workplace setting) shapes experiences of doing the work (ibid.). Work in these jobs is arduous, intense, risky, and low paid (Armstrong & Day, 2017; Banerjee et al., 2012). Privatization of long-term care in many provinces has resulted in deteriorating working conditions, exacerbating health concerns for workers (see Box 5.2). Media attention during the COVID-19 pandemic illuminated the plight of personal support workers, who provide important services in poor conditions, putting their own health at considerable risk.

Protective Services Work

This category includes jobs that aim to serve and protect; they are an interesting mix of routine and challenging work (Huey & Broll, 2015) (see Table 5.8). Job characteristics and pay differ substantially across jobs in this field in accordance with the racialization of

Issues at Work

5.2 | Workers in Long-Term Care

A number of studies have identified terrible working conditions for a variety of personal service and social care workers in long-term care facilities (Armstrong & Day, 2017; Banerjee et al., 2012). In Canada over the past several decades, long-term care has been privatized and corporatized; thus, care of the elderly and infirm is increasingly a for-profit endeavour (Armstrong, Armstrong & Kehoe MacLeod, 2015). As in other for-profit businesses, the emphasis is on efficiency, cost-cutting, and doing more with less. Workers in these facilities, from nurses, through personal support workers, to laundry workers, have faced deteriorating working conditions. They have more work than can reasonably be done in the time allotted, forcing unpaid overtime, working through breaks, and leaving work undone or not done well. The pace of the work exacerbates health risks for workers, including over-exertion, muscle pain, repetitive strain injuries, and musculo-skeletal problems, to name a few (Armstrong & Day, 2017; Banerjee et al., 2012). These workers are also subject to violence. In fact, Banerjee et al. (2012) in their study of long-term care in three Canadian provinces found that 43 per cent of workers said they experienced violence from residents *daily*, while an additional 23 per cent experienced violence weekly. Thus, for two-thirds of workers, violence was a common occurrence. However, employers and managers tended to downplay this violence as "part of the job," demonstrating little concern for workers' well-being. Moreover, workers experienced verbal and emotional abuse, including racism and harassment (Sethi, 2020). By comparing the Canadian situation with that in Scandinavian countries, Banerjee et al. (2012) determined that Canadian PSWs' experiences were directly related to working conditions and under-staffing (see also Armstrong et al., 2015; Armstrong & Day, 2017). Because they had too much to do and too little time to do it, workers were forced to rush their work or follow rules that ensured that care was substandard. In these situations, residents were more likely to lash out. In addition to the physical abuse, workers also experienced physical strains and the mental anguish of being forced to provide care that was not to the level they or their clients expected or deserved.

Overall, workers in long-term care experience job insecurity, health risks, low pay, and poor working conditions. The system is rife with abuse from owners and insufficient state oversight. The consequences for workers and clients can be devastating. The COVID-19 pandemic demonstrated this all too clearly, with PSWs forced to work short-staffed, without sufficient personal protective equipment (PPE), suffering illness and death (Pinto, 2020).

TABLE 5.8 Protective Services Work

Occupation	NOC	Description	Education	Prospects	Median Wage
Firefighters	4312	Fight fires, fire prevention	College/apprentice	Fair	$40.06/hr
Police Officers	4311	Protect public, detect and prevent crime	College/apprentice	Fair-good	$42.24/hr
Security Guards	6541	Guard & implement security measures to protect property, establishments	High school or specialized training	Fair	$16.50/hr

Source: jobbank.gc.ca.

the work. Fields in which white men predominate—policing and firefighting—are well paid. Education and entry requirements for these jobs have risen in recent decades to include some post-secondary education and for supervisory roles, a university degree. Educational requirements and pay among security guards is much lower; minority men are overrepresented in these jobs.

Job Characteristics

For public-facing service work—interactive and some protective service work especially—emotional labour and **aesthetic labour** are highly relevant. Service workers are expected to present a particular visual and emotional display to others, one that simultaneously represents their employers in a good light and encourages the client to act in a desired fashion—to purchase a retail item, enjoy an experience, or follow orders and obey rules, as the case may be. Stores aim to build customer loyalty through the emotional displays of their workers. Of course, emotional labour goes beyond this, requiring workers not only to control their own emotions but to evoke the desired emotions in their customers and clients. In protective services, workers are expected to be stern, intimidating, or caring, depending on the situation, and to act in a manner that elicits desired, lawful behaviour from members of the public.

aesthetic labour
Work performed by workers so that their appearance and demeanour reflects their employers' image and brand

Hochschild (2003) argued that emotional labour could require "surface" acting or "deep" acting. For most short-term encounters, such as cashiers might have, surface acting may suffice: A friendly smile and some rote phrases (Have a nice day!) are often enough. Other service work may require "deep acting" whereby workers not only display the right emotions but are expected to actually *feel* them. Feeling angry when you are supposed to be happy? Workers are encouraged "to draw on their emotion memories so as to induce the required feeling" (Williams, 2003, p. 516). Hochschild (2003) argues that deep acting may take worker alienation to new levels not envisaged by Marx: workers can become alienated from their own feelings and emotions, forced to pretend to be someone who they are not for the profit of others. However, as Bolton (2005) argues, emotional labour can also be an expression of self and therefore not experienced as alienating.

The demands of emotional labour can be a challenge for workers with heavy care demands in their work and personal lives and others like those with disabilities. Wilton (2008) finds that a lack of workplace accommodations can force workers with disabilities to do extra emotional labour to conceal their impairments and "fit in." LGBTQI, Indigenous, and racial minority workers may experience similar challenges if they feel compelled to conceal their identity to produce the emotional display expected by their employers.

Emotional labour can look very different in male-dominated jobs but may be no less taxing. Police officers and firefighters, for example, are expected to be stoic, tough, and brave, even in the face of traumatic and stressful situations. Showing fear or emotion is not acceptable. Indeed, considerable deep acting is required of officers who are not expected to experience fear or distress. Recently, attention has been drawn to the mental health challenges experienced by police officers, including PTSD. Unresolved (and denied) mental health challenges take a significant toll on officers and other first responders. It will require a cultural shift within policing to improve the situation (Bikos, 2020).

Aesthetic labour is also required by many interactive (and other) service workers whose jobs require them to "look good and sound right" (Williams & Connell, 2010). Service workers are expected to reflect middle-class values as well as the company brand or lifestyle it is trying to sell to others. They often need to follow "scripts" in their interactions with customers. Even workers who interact with customers over the phone, at call-centres, must have the appropriate tone, say the right things, and have the correct attitude (Jenkins et al., 2010). Retail workers may be required to spend part of their salary buying clothes from the stores they work in to represent the brand better. Even those in uniforms (personal and protective service workers) are expected to dress in a way that upholds their occupational and/or company image. How people wear their hair, whether they have (and how they wear) their facial and body hair, the presence of tattoos and piercings can all become matters of company concern. Employers of service labour seek to manage not just what people do but how they do it as well as what they sound and look like as they are doing it. These expectations not only add an additional layer of control over employees in these jobs, but they are also invasive of self, adding new layers of alienation and exploitation. These expectations are shaped by class as well as gender, race, ability status, and so on (Williams & Connell, 2010; Huzell & Larsson, 2012).

Another striking feature of service work concerns the presence of customers. To some extent, service workers serve two masters—their managers/employers and their customers/clients. This can be a challenge for service workers because the expectation that the customer is always right can place demands on workers that may go against company rules and supervisor expectations. Indeed, sometimes workers can get in trouble for following company rules if they upset customers by doing so (Williams, 2003). Service workers are subject not only to direct oversight, including monitoring of their sales, service, speed, and other visible outputs (Price, 2016) but also to management by customers who rate performance, provide online reviews, and/or complete satisfaction surveys. Thus, workers in interactive service jobs are subject to considerable scrutiny.

Complicating interactions with customers for interactive and personal services workers is an "asymmetry in exchange of respect" (Macdonald & Sirianni, 1996, p. 17). The fact is that workers are required to be courteous and respectful to customers; however, customers are under no such constraints and are often rude and short-tempered with service workers (Macdonald & Sirianni, 1996; Tannock, 2001). Customers also sometimes unfairly treat these low-wage workers as though they were of below-average intelligence. Protective services workers usually receive more respect from others (Huey & Broll, 2015).

Personal service workers face similar challenges. They may be treated with disrespect and expected to cater to others to the point of being asked to do tasks that lie outside their job description (Armstrong & Day, 2017). Even when not directly interacting with customers and clients, the latter can influence the content, nature, and pace of their work and contribute to its variability (Sherman, 2007). Personal service workers also often engage in dirty work: both physically and socially. Work that is physically dirty work may be unpleasant but also dangerous for those working with toxic substances. Their health may be put at risk, even as their cleaning work creates a healthier work environment for others. Personal services work can also be socially "dirty" due to workers' subordination and the people they come into contact with. People may look down on them (Armstrong & Day, 2017). Like their blue-collar counterparts, they may seek ways to redefine their jobs, emphasizing their skills and highlighting how important their work is to client/customer well-being (Carter et al., 2013; Armstrong & Day, 2017); however, doing so may be difficult when they have little autonomy, pay, or recognition. The gendering and racialization of skill also mean that people may not recognize the skills of women, non-binary workers, and visible minority men.

Although personal service and interactive service workers are discredited, they have many unrecognized skills (Nickson, Price, Baxter-Reid, & Hurrell, 2017). For instance, Fuller and Smith (1996, p. 75) explain that "interactive service workers are required to make on-the-spot, subtle judgments about what would please individual customers [and clients] hundreds . . . of times daily." They acquire skills to manage customers, deal with tricky situations, and get work done in challenging situations (see also Nickson et al., 2017, and Chapter 7). In a similar vein, personal service workers often develop good interaction skills to deal with difficult clients and tricky situations (Storm et al., 2017). Cleaners acquire knowledge of cleaning techniques, products, and processes (Armstrong & Day, 2017). These workers deserve more respect and recognition than they normally receive.

Workplace Change

Among the trends impacting service workers, two deserve particular mention: technology-enhanced surveillance and the impact of the pandemic. First, technological change is making it easier for supervisors, managers, and owners to supervise workers remotely. In-store cameras can be accessed through computer software and phone apps to ensure close supervision, even when owners are far away. Body cameras allow direct surveillance of police officers who formerly enjoyed considerable autonomy and discretion. Personal service workers can be watched closely through cameras as well. Thus, surveillance of service workers has increased in recent years, and this trend is likely to continue. The electronic panopticon is extending, encouraging workers to self-discipline, since they never know exactly who will be watching or when.

Second, the future of in-person services will be shaped by concerns about the spread of viruses and disease. Cleaning has been given new emphasis in light of the COVID-19 pandemic, and work in this field of disinfecting public areas may increase. In contrast, with public gatherings now viewed as unsafe, there may be a decline in service jobs linked to amusement parks, public events, and even in-person retail shopping and restaurant visits. More people may prefer to shop online. Fewer people may eat out, leading to a decline in employment in restaurants and bars. At the time of writing, the impact of the pandemic on service work over the long term is uncertain.

Source: © Andriy R/Shutterstock

The COVID-19 pandemic accelerated workplace change in 2020, exposing service workers to new health risks and placing a new emphasis on cleaning and disinfecting as a part of in-person services.

Professional Work

Professions are occupations traditionally distinguished from others by their advanced education, expertise, and social and regulatory status, which grants them a privileged market position (Adams, 2020a). Specific characteristics of professions vary across social-historical context and locale and, to some extent, type of work done. Still, professional workers have traditionally enjoyed autonomy, good earnings, and the authority to exercise their skills as they deliver important services to clients (Freidson, 1970; Weeden, 2002). Their autonomy in part stems from their powers of self-regulation (Larson, 1977; Freidson, 2001). Professionals like medical doctors, nurses, lawyers, and engineers are self-governing: legislation has been passed to allow professionals themselves (in cooperation with members of the public and the state) to make important decisions about entry to practice and the conduct of professional work, as well as professional education, training, and discipline (Adams, 2017, 2018). If we limit our count to these **self-regulating professions**, professionals comprise about 18 per cent of the labour force. If we use an expanded definition and include scientists, artists, and others, then that percentage increases to about 26 per cent.[1]

self-regulating professions
Occupations for which legislation has been passed to allow practitioners (in conjunction with members of the public and the state) to govern their own affairs and regulate aspects of professional practice and discipline

Self-regulating professions date from the late 19th century in Canada. The first professions created were male-dominated, and they provided services that people (and the state) in a nascent country could not easily live without—medical care, legal services, surveying the land (Adams, 2018). The influence these professionals acquired was reflective of their social authority as middle- and upper-class white men and their prominent social roles in local leadership and provincial and federal governments (ibid.). Female-dominated professions did not emerge until the 20th century. The earliest female-dominated profession, nursing, was regulated around the time women earned the vote, in the second decade of the 20th century, and their authority and influence was limited at first. Teachers were also regulated early but lacked powers of self-regulation and hence were more controlled. Although women now represent a majority in many formerly male-dominated professions, it is helpful to distinguish between traditionally male-dominated and female-dominated professions, since the former have long had more autonomy and authority than the latter.

---

[1]We will not be discussing the work of artists, athletes, and scientists here.

Traditionally Male-Dominated Professions

The earliest and most prominent self-regulating professions in Canada were medicine and law; however, dentistry, pharmacy, land surveying, architecture, accounting, and (to a lesser extent) engineering all emerged in the late 19th century. Table 5.9 provides an overview of their job characteristics today. All of these jobs require university education and an additional period of practical training before a licence to practise (or full registration) can be obtained. Job prospects are fair to good for all, and incomes are high.

These professional jobs have long been regarded as some of the best in the labour force, although managers appear to be gradually edging professionals out in this respect. As noted, many of these traditionally male-dominated jobs are now more gender-balanced: for instance, 44 per cent of lawyers in Ontario are women (LSUC, 2016), and 47 per cent of family physicians in Canada and 38 per cent of medical specialists are women (CIHI, 2019). Women make up about one-third of architects but only 14 per cent of engineers in Canada (Statistics Canada, 2019a).

Female-Dominated Professions

Traditionally, female-dominated professions were subordinate to male-dominated professions and management. It is only in the past few decades that some female-dominated professions like nursing earned more autonomy and respect. Table 5.10 lists a few female-dominated professions. Here we can see that they too require university education, they have fair-to-good prospects, and their incomes have climbed to the point

TABLE 5.9 Traditionally Male-Dominated Professions

	NOC	Description	Education	Prospects	Median Wage
Accountants and Auditors	1111	Accounting, auditing	University & practical experience for CPA)	Fair	$33.65/hr
Architects	2151	Conceptualize, plan, & design buildings	University & internship	Fair-good	$31.79/hr
Civil Engineers	2131	Plan, design, develop projects for construction of infrastructure	University & practical experience	Fair-good	$39.42/hr
Electrical Engineers	2133	Plan, design, evaluate electrical & electronic equipment & systems	University & practical experience	Fair	$44.27/hr
Lawyers	4112	Lawyer, notary	University & practical experience	Good-fair	$116,940/yr
Pharmacists	3131	Compound, dispense pharmaceuticals	University & practical training	Fair-good	$104,646/yr
Medical Doctors (GPs)	3112	General practitioners, family physicians	University & practical training	Good	$211,111/yr
Medical Doctors (specialists)	3111	Medical specialists in a variety of fields	University, practical experience, & additional certifications	Good	$273,138/yr

Source: jobbank.gc.ca; note that pay was given in yearly income rather than hourly wage for some professions.

TABLE 5.10 Traditionally Female-Dominated Professions

Occupation	NOC	Description	Education	Prospects	Median Wage
Registered Nurses	3012	Nursing	University, practical training, licence/exam	Fair-good	$37.60/hr
Physiotherapists	3142	Treat patients to maintain, restore, & improve physical functioning and mobility	University, practical training, licence/exam	Fair-good	$38.00/hr
Elementary Teachers	4032	Teach at elementary level	University & practical training	Fair	$37.50/hr
Social Work Officers	4152	Help people develop skills, resources for social functioning	University & practical experience	Fair-good	$33.33/hr

Source: jobbank.gc.ca.

that they are now comparable with men's. Still, it is important to note that teachers' median wages are misleading. Teachers' rate per hour reflects the hours they spend actively teaching children. Teachers, then, technically work several hours a day unpaid. They are not remunerated for lesson planning, curriculum development, classroom preparation, marking student work, and the many other tasks they do outside core school hours. If these hours are accounted for, then their "per hour" rate drops substantially.

Good pay and prospects, combined with doing work that is socially meaningful, helping others, have long made professions attractive jobs. Yet professionals also experience considerable stress and work-family conflict. Workplace change appears to be undermining many of the characteristics that have made professional work so attractive.

Key Characteristics

Like the service workers discussed earlier, professionals provide a service to the public, and they may engage in emotional labour as they do so. However, they tend to approach the service encounter from a position of authority, unlike most service workers. Nonetheless, because professionals provide services and care to people and often work under stressful conditions, they are not immune to stress from client interactions. Care providers—especially those in female-dominated health and social care professions—appear particularly prone to burnout. The high demands and emotional exhaustion of providing care on the job combines with family care demands to exacerbate the situation (Cottingham, Chapman, & Erickson, 2020; Olakivi & Wrede, 2019). Other professionals are prone to burnout as well because there are long-hours cultures in many professions that see them working extended hours, missing sleep, and sometimes meals. Mental stress can lead to additional problems—including errors—which have dire consequences given the areas in which professionals practise. Like those in protective services, professionals are sometimes reluctant to seek help when they have difficulty, which allows their stress and burnout to compound. Mental health issues can be alleviated by leaves of absence, but many professions—especially the classically male-dominated professions—have few mental health accommodations and leave policies available to them. Even when they are available, they may be reluctant to take these leaves for many reasons (Bourgeault, 2018).

Professions also reproduce social inequalities in Canadian society. Entry into professions requires a considerable amount of schooling and work practice, and most professionals acquire substantial debts because the cost of this training is very high. Setting up an independent practice (for those who do so) can also be costly. This structure provides an inherent barrier to the economically disadvantaged and members of the working class. Those who are foreign-trained also experience challenges trying to enter professional practice in Canada. Oftentimes, their training is not recognized, and they may need to take additional training once here. This additional training can be lengthy and expensive, and not everyone can afford it. Inequalities are also reproduced through professional training because gender norms, transphobia, and racism against Indigenous peoples and members of visible minorities can be embedded within curricula and social relations (Acker, 2017; Beagan, 2001; Vallee, 2018).

Additional barriers face minority and working-class professionals after they receive their training. For instance, studies of elite professional service firms have identified significant biases against people who have limited social and cultural capital and who do not "fit in" with current employees and clients (Rivera, 2012; Ashley & Empson, 2016). This has the effect of limiting diversity and weeding out minority and working-class professionals. Moreover, research shows that racial minority professionals are at a substantial disadvantage because they experience racism (from patients/clients and colleagues) and skill-discounting. Women of colour are particularly impacted (Beagan, 2001; Kwon & Adams, 2018; Crenshaw, 2011; Melaku, 2019), and they may need to engage in aesthetic and emotional labour to "fit in" when their bodies do not match the traditional white, male image of "professional" (Melaku, 2019). The lack of family-friendly flexibility, combined with expectations for unpaid overtime, further disadvantages women (Legault & Chasserio, 2013; Olakivi & Wrede, 2019). Barriers experienced in school, entering practice, and on the job accumulate, disadvantaging minority workers and women across their careers (Purkayastha, 2005; Henry, 2012). Such barriers are reflected in practitioner statistics. For instance, the LSUC (2016) reported that lawyers in Ontario identify predominantly as white, heterosexual, and anglophone. Only 3 per cent identify as LGBTQI and 5 per cent as francophone, only 4 per cent claimed a disability, and only 1.6 per cent were Indigenous. About one-third of lawyers practising in Ontario in 2016 identified as racialized: 12 per cent were South Asian, and only 4 per cent were Black. On average, the professions are not fully reflective of Canadian society, and hence, professions play a role in reproducing social inequality. Effective policies are needed to encourage the entrance and continued participation of the racialized, LGBTQI, Indigenous, and other disadvantaged workers (Connell, 2012).

Workplace Change

A number of workplace and social changes are affecting professions. Here we highlight two: the crisis of expertise and workplace change that is undermining the characteristics that traditionally distinguished professionals from other workers.

First, professionals are impacted by the same rationalization trends affecting other workers. The ongoing drive for efficiency has meant that professionals and their workplaces are constantly striving to do more with less. Lawyers and accountants working in professional services firms are seeing their opportunities for promotion dwindle, while their workloads increase (Muzio & Ackroyd, 2005; Allen, Faulconbridge, & Thomas, 2019). Performance pressure has exacerbated both workloads and stress (Allen et al., 2019). Professionals in the private sector especially—such as lawyers, engineers, and accountants—have seen a decline in permanent jobs; more professionals are being employed on a temporary and contract basis (Crowley et al., 2010; Barley & Kunda, 2004). The public sector, though, has experienced similar trends, notably in health care and education. In higher education, for example, there is a clear trend towards temporary and contract work (see Box 5.3). At the same time, professionals are subject to more surveillance and audit. While they used to be able to work somewhat autonomously, their actions are more closely scrutinized, not only by supervisors but by efficiency specialists continually seeking ways to cut costs (Allen et al., 2019; McGivern & Ferlie, 2007). There is also evidence of neo-Taylorization in professions (Crowley et al., 2010). Professionals face more competition for jobs—especially in the private sector—where they need to demonstrate that they not only have the right skills but also possess a willingness to work long hours and prioritize their professional work above all. Failure to meet these rising expectations not only limits promotion opportunities but can lead to job loss. Precarity in professions—largely unheard of a generation ago—is on the rise. These changes have the effect of reducing professional autonomy and job security and increasing mental health challenges. These pressures have implications for social inequalities within professions as well because those with less social and cultural capital (due to class, race, immigration status, and so forth) may be particularly impacted (Waterfield et al., 2019).

Second, people in Western society are becoming increasingly skeptical of experts and their claims to expertise. Despite professionals' training and advanced education—indeed because of it—a significant minority of the population regards them as untrustworthy and

A CLOSER LOOK

5.3 | Precarious Professionals: Academics

Although university professors are not regulated, they are often regarded as professional workers. However, the percentage of full-time academics at Canadian universities has declined steadily since the early 2000s. Over the same period, university enrolments have grown. Grappling with budget shortfalls and shifting perceptions of what the university's mission should be, universities have hired temporary instructors to teach courses in larger numbers. The number of part-time, temporary academic staff in Canadian post-secondary institutions jumped 79 per cent between 2005 and 2015 (Foster & Birdsell Bauer, 2018). Part-time instructors are precarious workers: they are hired on short-term contracts, at pay rates substantially lower than full-time faculty, to teach courses with no guarantee of further employment. To make a living, most contract instructors must acquire several contracts a term, sometimes at multiple universities. They work long hours and prepare a variety of courses, frequently on short notice, with little recognition or reward. Moreover, part-time instructors are often expected to engage in unpaid labour, like sitting on university committees, without remuneration. They are provided with few resources, including adequate office space in which to meet with students and complete other job-related activities. This precarity contributes to mental health challenges for many part-time academic workers.

Professionals in contract positions in other fields face similar challenges and may become locked in a cycle in which they move from one short-term contract to another throughout their careers.

believes they are out to achieve self-gain by misleading the public (see also Chapter 7). This trend is contributing to the enhanced surveillance of professionals' work. The **crisis of expertise** has been linked to the rise of **populism**—a political approach that challenges elite authority and triumphs the cause of ordinary people (while failing to challenge economic elites). The crisis of expertise has been exacerbated by right-wing politicians who endeavour to cast doubt on science and professional expertise for their own gain. Members of the public, then, are increasingly skeptical of experts and may refuse to seek their services or heed their advice (even to their own detriment). The crisis of expertise is combining with rationalization trends to decrease professional authority and autonomy and increase professional precarity.

With these changes, professionals are increasingly coming to resemble other white-collar and service jobs in the Canadian workforce.

To conclude, this chapter has reviewed different types of occupations and the social trends impacting them. Many themes raised, including skill trends, precarious work, health, and discrimination, are explored in more detail in the following chapters.

crisis of expertise
Although we are more dependent on science and experts than ever before, we are increasingly skeptical and even dismissive of scientific findings and expert claims

populism
A political stance appealing to the "common people" who may feel disenfranchised. Often associated with anti-elite sentiments (especially against political elites and experts, not economic elites)

Reviewing the Learning Objectives

Now that you have read this chapter, you should:

- Be able to identify the characteristics of blue-collar, white-collar, service (personal, protective, and interactive), and professional work.
- Understand that these categories are not firm but flexible with jobs that that might fall into more than one category and shared characteristics.
- Understand that recent workplace change is altering some aspects of these jobs.

Questions for Critical Thought

1. How is workplace and technological change impacting occupations in Canada? To what extent does the impact appear to be the same across occupational categories, and to what extent does it differ?
2. When are work cultures positive for workers, and when might they be negative?
3. Do you think that some types of workers are more alienated than others? If so, which ones and why?
4. Research has focused on how emotional labour is gendered. Do you think it is racialized as well? If so, in what way?

Annotated Additional Readings

Deery, S., Kolar, D., & Walsh, J. (2019). Can dirty work be satisfying? A mixed method study of workers doing dirty jobs. *Work, Employment and Society, 44*(4), 631–647.

Deery, Kolar, and Walsh examine cleaners' responses to performing dirty work in the US and UK.

Hochschild, A. R. (2012). *The managed heart: Commercialization of human feeling* (3rd ed.). Berkeley, CA: University of California Press.

This book introduces and explores the concept of emotional labour and its applications at work.

Melaku, T. M. (2019). *You don't look like a lawyer: Black women and systemic gendered racism*. Lanham, MD: Rowman and Littlefield.

Melaku explores systemic racism in the legal profession.

Williams, C. L., & Connell, C. (2010). "Looking good and sounding right": Aesthetic labor and social inequality in the retail industry. *Work & Occupations, 37*(3), 349–377.

Williams and Connell explore aesthetic labour and social inequalities in retail.

Related Websites

Canadian Council for Refugees, information on migrant workers and the issues they experience:

https://ccrweb.ca/en/migrant-workers-issues

British Columbia information on Temporary Foreign Worker Programs:

https://www.workbc.ca/employer-resources/your-workforce/temporary-foreign-workers.aspx

British Columbia Institute of Technology, information on working in skilled trades:

https://commons.bcit.ca/news/2020/08/cool-things-about-working-in-trades/

Government of Canada, profile of service industries in Canada:

https://www.ic.gc.ca/eic/site/si-is.nsf/eng/home

6 Non-Standard, Unpaid, and Discredited Work

Learning Objectives

After reading this chapter, readers will:

- Have a clearer sense of what makes work non-standard and precarious and understand the implications for workers in Canadian society.
- Understand when crime is a form of work.
- Understand that some work is unpaid and how unpaid work and paid work are connected with each other.
- Know what sex work is and have a sense of the skills required and challenges experienced by those who do this work.

Introduction

The previous chapter began by asking, "When you were little, what did you want to be when you grew up?" Chances are that your childhood aspirations did not include the work reviewed in this chapter. Few of us dream of precarious jobs, unpaid work, sex work, or drug-dealing. If we dreamed about gaming all day or doing something else creative, we may not have imagined actually making a living from doing so. If we did, probably the adults in our lives would have suggested otherwise. Nevertheless, these forms of work are not uncommon. Some—like unpaid work—we do every day. Many of us have held precarious jobs; all of us know someone who has worked precariously. Other types of work discussed here are not uncommon, whether or not we are familiar with them. Still, there are some who would question whether these work activities are *real* work.

If there is a unifying theme cutting across these different types of work, it is probably this: These jobs are either non-standard or their legitimacy as real work has been questioned. Some members of Canadian society likely regard them as illegitimate, unappealing, or unimportant. Beyond this over-arching commonality, however, the types of work reviewed in this chapter are very different. We begin by looking at non-standard and **precarious work**. Here we are focused not on what people do but on how their work is organized. We review the features that distinguish standard from non-standard employment relationships and consider their implications for workers. Next, we look at

precarious work
There is no guarantee that employment will continue, and wages may be uneven and discontinuous

work that is discredited, including sex work and work that is illegal (like drug-dealing). We consider who does this work and review the challenges and opportunities for workers in these fields. Following this, we take a look at unpaid work, with attention to two aspects: domestic labour and volunteer work. Finally, we consider the blurry line between work and leisure through the concept of **productive leisure** and consideration of income-generating hobbies, such as playing video games. The lines between paid and unpaid work appear to be narrowing. To the extent that workers are not properly remunerated for what they do, these trends are not only worrisome, but they exacerbate social inequalities.

productive leisure Engaging in hobbies that involve work (whether paid or unpaid)

Non-Standard Work and Precarity

Since the years following the Second World War, in the West we have had this mental image of a standard or "normal" job. This is one in which workers have a formal work contract with an employer, who expects them to work regular, full-time hours at their place of work. For their roughly 40 hours of work per week, workers earn a consistent wage (formally stipulated in their employment contract) and are entitled to paid vacation, regular breaks, and additional paid benefits. Workers with standard contracts typically expect to keep their jobs until they get promoted or find another job. Since the 1980s, more and more jobs do not fit this "standard" ideal. They may require fewer hours. Wages may vary. There may be no job security or even a steady contract, and workers may not actually work at a single location for the company that employs them (Cranford, Vosko, & Zukewich, 2003; United Way, 2011). Precarious work is on the rise.

Examples of **non-standard work** include temporary and contract work, self-employment, and gig work (Cranford et al., 2003; Kalleberg, 2000, Lewchuk et al., 2016). Temporary, contract, and gig work (and, to a variable extent, self-employment) are inherently precarious—there is no guarantee that employment will continue, and wages may be uneven and discontinuous. **Gig work** consists of platform-mediated work, such as driving for Uber or delivering food for Skip the Dishes. Here one is hired to do specific, very short-term jobs—like drive someone to their destination. Many gig workers are not employed, but rather they are **independent contractors**: people who contract their services to others. Since they are not employed, rules about vacation pay, benefits, and consistent work assignments are not applicable (Kessler, 2018). With few guarantees of hours and shifting (often low) pay levels, gig workers experience precarity (Kessler, 2018; Healy, Nicholson, & Pekarek, 2017; Wood, Graham, Lehdonvirta, & Hjorth, 2019b; see Chapter 12). Other independent contract workers may sign limited-term contracts with organizations to work on a specific project or provide services—like the precarious academics profiled in Box 5.3, as well as home daycare workers, construction workers, and many others. Even when workers move from one short-term contract to another, they have no guarantee of continued employment, and their benefits are usually limited. Some independent contractors can make good money, especially where their skills are highly coveted, but many have limited pay and autonomy (Anderson & Hughes, 2010; Kessler, 2018).

non-standard work Work that differs from standard work because of its instability, irregular hours, or temporary nature

gig work Work in which individuals do a series of short-term tasks for others as assigned through digital platforms. Often used interchangeably with the term "platform work"

independent contractors Workers who contract their services to a company but are not technically employed by them. A form of self-employment

Zero hours contracts are not uncommon in some countries, like the UK and US. For example, workers (especially "independent contractors" with no formal employment contract) might agree to work with or for an organization with no guarantee of pay or work. Harvey, Rhodes, Vachhani, and Williams (2017) describe the experiences of self-employed personal trainers working at fitness centres in the UK who actually pay rent for the privilege of working with clients at a specific facility. While there, they interact with centre clientele and do considerable unpaid labour around the facility. This unpaid work allows fitness centres to employ fewer people. Harvey et al. (2017) call this "hyper flexible" and precarious work "neo-villeiny"—drawing parallels between independent contractors today and medieval serfs who were bonded to a lord, worked his land (and their own) for free, with no guarantee of reward. Personal trainers labour long hours, with no guarantee they will win clients and make a living. These kinds of contract arrangements appear to be increasing over time in a variety of sectors. Indeed, Bruckert (2002) describes similar contract arrangements among exotic dancers in Canada.

temporary work
Work conducted for a company on a short-term basis; typically, workers are hired by an agency that contracts their work out to other companies

Temporary work is different: here, temporary employment agencies hire workers whom they then send out to work for other companies on a short-term basis—for example, to fill in for sick employees or to cover a job that is temporarily vacant. Temporary workers' direct bosses, then, are not their employers. They may be working alongside other, more permanent employees, even doing the same job, but for a different wage, receiving different benefits, training opportunities, and treatment. All of these dimensions add layers of complication and uncertainty to their labour process. Temp workers can be attractive to employers: companies usually pay lower wages and no benefits, and can easily let the temp worker go when they no longer need them. Temp work can also be appealing to some workers because it enables them to secure employment, provides variety, and allows workers to acquire labour market experience (Vosko, 2000). However, temp work is also limiting for workers. Most workers prefer more secure, steady employment, finding temporary work stigmatizing (Glaymann & Grima, 2008) and at times dangerous (because of a lack of on-the-job training and experience). Temporary foreign workers are particularly vulnerable to exploitation (Strauss & McGrath, 2017).

All of these forms of non-standard work are precarious. Precarious work has been defined as "employment that is uncertain, unpredictable, and risky from the point of view of the worker" (Kalleberg, 2009, p. 2). Unfortunately, this description is applying to more and more types of work such that even standard work is increasingly experienced as uncertain and unpredictable, with no promise of continuity

Source: © Dusan Petkovic/Shutterstock

While many associate temp work with offices, temporary workers are employed in many industries. In 2017, a *Toronto Star* investigation found that Fiera Foods, a large industrial bakery, was employing workers from a temp agency without providing adequate workplace safety training, leading to the deaths of multiple temporary employees. At the time, employers using temporary workers were not held liable for on-the-job injuries by the Workplace Safety and Insurance Board.

(Alberti, Bessa, Hardy, Trappmann, & Umney, 2018; Kalleberg, 2009; United Way, 2011). People may *feel* precarious in a variety of jobs and employment settings. As the 2019 House of Commons committee report on precarious work in Canada asserts, "no-one is immune" (May, 2019, p. xiii). Thus, Alberti et al. (2018) suggest that we focus less on precarious work as a subset of jobs and rather focus on **precarization** as a process, or set of processes, raising insecurity across jobs in capitalist economies. These processes include explicit efforts on the part of managers, and other employers including states, to move from standard to non-standard employment contracts and changing government legislation (including employment regulations) with implications for worker security (Alberti et al., 2018; Vosko, 2005; Kalleberg, 2009). Changing laws around citizenship and migrant workers' rights also contribute to precarization. Even privileged workers—like managers and professionals—are experiencing precarization today as employers attempt to manage their own risks, by downloading them onto workers. For instance, managers may feel that their jobs are constantly on the line: failure to generate sufficient profit for shareholders or cut costs to meet stipulated targets could result in dismissal. Precarization is a global trend, but OECD data show that among OECD countries, Canada has a higher-than-average rate of temporary work and less of a social safety net to compensate compared to many (May, 2019).

FIGURE 6.1 Three dimensions of precarious employment

Source: Library of Parliament, Precarious Work, Understanding the Changing Nature of Work in Canada, Figure 7. Retrieved from https://www.ourcommons.ca/DocumentViewer/en/42-1/HUMA/report-19/page-93.

The impact of these trends include "low-wages, income volatility, insecure working arrangements, unsafe work, lack of access to social protections, lack of opportunities for career advancement and skills training as well as vulnerable workers" (May, 2019, p. xiii). Non-standard workers are less likely to be unionized than standard workers, to their disadvantage (Coiquaud, 2011; Boivin, 2017). Temp workers, even in good public sector jobs, have lower incomes and fewer benefits (Stecy-Hildebrandt, Fuller, & Burns, 2019). A spell as a non-standard worker can negatively impact earnings years later (Fuller & Stecy-Hildebrandt, 2014). These impacts have ripple effects that can affect every aspect of people's lives (Kalleberg, 2009). For example, insecurity and low earnings associated with precarity discourage marriage and relationship formation, as well as child-bearing (Lewchuk et al., 2016). Unstable living conditions and even social isolation are additional consequences. Precarious workers report poorer health, more workplace risk, and more workplace discrimination (Lewchuk et al., 2015). Precarious workers with disabilities report fewer workplace accommodations (Shuey & Jovic, 2013). Figure 6.1 summarizes dimensions of precarity and its impacts related to security, income, and opportunity (May, 2019, p. 25).

One aspect that distinguishes non-standard and precarious work is flexibility. On the one hand, flexibility can be construed as a good thing. Flexibility could mean that you have the ability to combine work with family responsibilities, other work commitments, hobbies, or opportunities to develop new skills. In fact, workers may intentionally seek out work as independent contractors for precisely these reasons (Kessler, 2018; Anderson & Hughes, 2010; Tremblay, Chênevert, & Hébert, 2012). However, the flexibility that comes with precarious work is *usually* not freeing in this sense because it is associated with insecurity, uncertainty, and anxiety (Alberti et al., 2018; Kalleberg, 2009; Lewchuk et al., 2015). On the other hand, non-standard work provides flexibility for employers, and this kind of flexibility does not typically benefit workers. Non-standard work allows employers the flexibility of paying workers less for doing the same job as full-time workers, reducing costs by not paying benefits, and cutting back on worker training (companies are reluctant to invest in workers who they expect will only be with them for a short time). Such practices can even help employers keep the wages of their permanent workforce down, since these workers could be replaced by temporary workers willing to work for less (adding to permanent workers' perceptions of precarity despite their standard contracts). Thus, the flexibility associated with precarity enables for-profit firms to increase their profits (and surplus value) and non-profit organizations to balance their budgets, but it provides few benefits for workers.

The marginalized are particularly impacted: the less-educated, women, youth, older workers, immigrants and the racialized (May, 2019; Vosko 2000). Lewchuk et al. (2015) estimate that only about 60 per cent of workers in the Greater Toronto–Hamilton Area (GTHA) have stable, secure jobs. That means four in 10 experience precarity. While some studies find women experience more precarity than men (May, 2019), Lewchuk et al. (2015) find no gender difference in the GTHA. However, there are significant differences by race. That is, members of racialized groups are more likely to be found in precarious employment than white workers (United Way, 2011). Black women appear to be particularly impacted (Katshunga, Massaquoi, & Wallace, 2020). Non-standard work reproduces systemic racism in Canadian society (Cardona, 2018). Immigrants are also much more numerous among the precariously employed, particularly those who have been in Canada only a short time. The rates of the Canadian-born and those who immigrated 10 plus years ago are similar (United Way, 2011). Nevertheless, gender interacts with immigration status in nuanced ways to shape outcomes (Fuller & Vosko, 2008). As we will see in later chapters, the discounting of immigrants' credentials and education combines with outright discrimination to reduce their opportunities for full-time, secure work (Buzdugan & Halli, 2009; Madibbo, 2020; Vosko, 2005). Workers aged 55 and over are more likely than workers in younger age groups to be working precariously; however, workers 25–34 are not too far behind. Young workers just entering the labour force may have difficulty landing full-time, standard jobs. They may first need to spend time in internships and limited-term contracts to gain experience (see Box 6.1). International students in the labour market also predominate in precarious jobs, experiencing uneven

Issues at Work

6.1 | Experiences of Young Workers in Internships

There has been little research on youth internships, but that which exists has highlighted their exploitative potential (Siebert & Wilson, 2013; Jacobson & Shade, 2018; May, 2019). With the goal of obtaining experience, building networks, and "getting a foot in the door," many young workers and newcomers look to internships. Interns do the work of a paid employee but for little (or sometimes no) remuneration. These practices can be especially common in creative industries where jobs for young people are highly coveted and scarce (Siebert & Wilson, 2013; Jacobson & Shade, 2018). Engaging in unpaid work to gain experience and build social capital has been normalized and accepted as just something one needs to do to break into the field. However, low-paid or unpaid internships do not necessarily impart skills or increase social capital. What they do is exploit young workers and lower the pay and security of paid established workers in the field. Some companies rely on a string of unpaid interns to do more routine work instead of hiring permanent employees (Jacobson & Shade, 2018). Young workers may have to piece together several internships, with no paid job guarantee at the end. Such practices reproduce social inequalities because middle-class women are disproportionately employed in unpaid intern positions in the creative industries and they can only pursue this option with financial support from their parents (ibid.). Those with fewer financial resources may not have the opportunity to pursue internships now seen as a normal stage in the career path in these sectors. Internships are a source of precarity, prone to abuse, and often low quality in terms of job content (May, 2019).

Do you think the trend towards experiential learning in education will exacerbate the problems with unpaid internships or mitigate them by providing work-relevant experience in the context of education?

hours, low pay, unpaid work, and exploitation (Maury, 2020). Workers 35–54 enjoy the most stability (United Way, 2011).

Unpaid work, internships, and temporary work contracts are all part of a continuum of precarious work. The predominance of young and older workers, immigrants, and racialized workers in these jobs is cause for concern and contributes to social inequality.

Sex Work

sex work Work that entails selling sexualized services to others

Sex work is a term that encompasses an array of jobs linked to sex: selling sexual services, pornography, exotic dancing, and related activities. These are semi-skilled jobs in which a worker sells (or is hired to provide) sexualized services for money (Visano, 1987; Bruckert, 2002; Law & Raguparan, 2020). Some aspects of this industry are legal (if highly regulated, like exotic dancing), while the legality of others is contested. In the past several years, courts have argued that prevailing laws surrounding prostitution are unconstitutional, prompting change to national laws in 2014 and encouraging further revision more recently (Perkel, 2020; Dubinski, 2021). It is not illegal to sell sexual services in Canada (that is, to engage in prostitution). It is illegal, however, to advertise sexual services or to live off the income from others' sexual services. The latter laws are aimed at minimizing

The legality of sex work has undergone significant change in the past decade. Left to right, Nikki Thomas, Terri-Jean Bedford, and Valerie Scott attend a press conference after the Ontario Court of Appeal struck down a ban on brothels in 2012. Bedford and Scott, along with Vancouver sex worker Amy Lebovitch, were the three principals in the case, arguing that the ban on brothels created unsafe working conditions for sex workers by forcing them onto the street. The decision was upheld by the Supreme Court of Canada in December 2013.

Source: THE CANADIAN PRESS/Aaron Vincent Elkaim

"pimping," but they have been criticized for preventing partnerships and limiting organizations that employ (and potentially protect) sex workers and for restricting women's ability to earn a (safe) living from providing sexual services (Perkel, 2020; Raguparan, 2017).

Some forms of sex work are more precarious than others. Working conditions, organizational settings (if any), and security are all highly variable both within and across different categories of sex work. Most studies of sexual services draw a clear distinction between *inside* and *outside* work, with the latter deemed more vulnerable and insecure. Outside sex workers may be more vulnerable because of the clientele they cater to, where they work, and also their personal circumstances (for example, drugs, homelessness: Brewis & Linstead 2000; Visano, 1987). Drug addictions can force sex workers to make compromises about which clients they provide services to, what they will do, and how much they charge. Their safety and autonomy is undermined as a result. Police may offer little protection. Despite a shift towards protection in the policing of sex workers, there is still evidence that sex workers are blamed for sexual violence perpetrated against them, limiting their access to police protection (Krüsi, Kerr, Taylor, Rhodes, & Shannon, 2016). Indoor work tends to be safer, caters to a higher-class clientele, and is often better paid. Workers can have considerable autonomy in determining what they will do, when, and with whom. In this capacity, it may be viewed as more "professional" or even as "community service" (Dunn, 2012). Still, violence is a lingering concern (Manning & Bungay, 2017). Transgender and other LGBTQI sex workers are particularly vulnerable to violence (Davis, Miles, & Quinley, 2019; NSWP, n.d.) and face unique challenges (Capous-Desyllas & Loy, 2020); there is need for more attention to these issues (Jones, 2020).

Working conditions in exotic dancing are also variable depending on the venue, management, clientele, and other factors (Bruckert, 2002). Exotic dancers have a fair amount of autonomy, since they are often hired as independent contractors and hence can determine the content of their work to a certain extent. The downside, however, is that income in these jobs is unpredictable: strippers' income comes predominantly from tips, which can vary substantially from one day to the next (Bruckert, 2002). Workers in clubs may feel safer because they are surrounded by other workers and bouncers (although safety risks are not entirely eliminated in these settings: Law & Raguparan, 2020). People who dance at private parties and others' homes may experience personal safety fears (Chapkis 2000).

Although the experiences of sex workers are variable, there are some commonalities across the sector. Emotional labour is an important one. Sex workers manage their emotions and feelings while simultaneously influencing the feelings of their clients. Moreover, as with other service workers, this emotional work can vary somewhat from client to client. Being able to read their clients and pick up on what they need is a skill workers acquire with experience. Taking charge of situations to ensure their own safety, maintain control, and secure payment are other valuable skills (Law & Raguparan, 2020; Bruckert, 2002; Dunn, 2012; Manning & Bungay, 2017). Sex workers often "use impression management skills to create an illusion that will allow them to control / manipulate their audience" (Lewis, 1998, p. 51; Law & Raguparan, 2020).

A second commonality concerns aesthetic labour. Physical appearance is of utmost importance, and sex workers may spend a considerable amount of time cultivating their appearance and developing an image or brand that will appeal to clients. This can involve hyper-sexualized, overtly feminine displays for women in the sex industry and overtly masculine displays for men. Hair, body hair, make-up, clothes, and shoes all contribute to this image. Some businesses employing sex workers, like exotic dancers, have formal rules around shaving, hair length, tattoos, breast size, and weight (Chapkis, 2000; Bruckert, 2002). For indoor sex workers, these ideals reflect middle-class, white, gendered expectations, and this might involve an outlay of money for more expensive clothes, or sexy costumes for exotic dancers. It could also involve changes to modes of speaking and knowledge of etiquette. Body expectations in sex work are highly racialized as well, with whiteness valued but some racial minority statuses fetishized. In response, minority workers may foster an appearance that reflects whiteness (Law & Raguparan, 2020). Alternatively, since there is a clientele for women viewed as "exotic" and foreign, some minority workers may try to serve this niche market and construct their appearance accordingly. Sex work is shaped by the intersection of race, class, and gender in a way that typically disadvantages minority women and men (see Box 6.2). Nonetheless, racialized and Indigenous sex workers find creative ways to resist and navigate the system to ensure their livelihoods (Raguparan, 2017).

abject labour Work that is simultaneously repulsive and attractive

Third, sex work can entail "dirty work" to the extent that it is morally and at times social discrediting. Tyler (2011), however, argues that to truly capture sex work (and some other types of dirty work), the concept of **abject labour** is preferred. Abject labour is that which is simultaneously repulsive and attractive. Sex holds a fascination for many and may be experienced as titillating and pleasurable. At the same time, it can be repulsive to be physically intimate with people you find unattractive, and some even regard this work as immoral. The concept of dirty work may not go far enough in capturing this duality, which can shape the labour of those in various parts of the industry—from the sex shop workers studied by Tyler (2011) to those who provide exotic dances or sell sex services for a living (Bruckert, 2002; Brewis & Linstead, 2000).

How do people get into this line of work? Research has pointed to several paths. There is a tendency in media, and even some scholarship, to see sex work as a last resort for those who are very vulnerable or victimized by abuse and/or drug addiction (Hallgrímsdóttir, Phillips, & Benoit, 2006; Raguparan, 2017). There is some evidence to support these depictions; however, they do not provide a complete picture. Research on sex workers in

A CLOSER LOOK

6.2 | Men Who Provide Sexual Services

Research on men who do sex work is not plentiful, partly because women are more numerous in this field. However, it is unfair to assume that men's experiences are identical. Emotional labour and aesthetic labour are relevant for both women and men, as are concerns for safety and violence (Peters, Kessi, & Boonzaier, 2019; Walby, 2012). Nevertheless, masculinity norms are powerful influences on men who provide sex services to men and women (Minichiello, Scott, & Callander, 2013; Peters et al., 2019). Peters et al.'s (2019) interviews with Black men sex workers in South Africa highlighted narratives of violence and hyper-masculinity whereby men felt the need to justify their manhood because of their involvement in what might be construed as feminine work. Race strongly shaped their experiences, influencing rates charged and harassment from police (Peters et al., 2019). The experiences reported by the self-employed, white, college-educated male escorts (based in Canada, the US, and the UK) studied by Walby (2012) were somewhat different: they emphasized the benefits of self-employment over employment, the challenges of marketing themselves and obtaining clients, and the income-generating potential of this work, treating it as an "efficient way to make money" (quoted in Walby, 2012, p. 88). These men, then, approached sex work as a business. For them, relationship building was key. Many offered companionship as well as sex, with some forming friendships with clients. The intersection of gender, race, and class profoundly shapes experiences of workers in this sector.

Canada identifies three sets of motivators (Benoit, Ouellet, Jansson, Magnus, & Smith, 2017): the need for money, critical life events, and the personal appeal of the work. The need for money appears most common. The fact is that women can make more money from sex work than in most other female-dominated jobs (Ham & Gilmour, 2017). Men also report making good money compared to other opportunities open to them (Walby, 2012). Transgender workers report financial need as a primary motivator for their entry into sex work (Davis et al., 2019). Still, research findings show that sex work is not only an option for the desperate but can be appealing for those aiming to fund a post-secondary education, buy things for their children, and achieve a middle-class lifestyle.

Critical life events prompting people to engage in sex work include rejection from family, being homeless, being preyed upon by others (including sexual abuse), and extreme poverty. Although these events push people into prostitution, scholars argue that it should still be viewed as a choice, structured by limited options. Moreover, women may choose to stay in the industry even when push factors like homelessness are no longer relevant. Finally, some sex workers do the work because they obtain enjoyment and satisfaction from it. This can include sexual pleasure (Benoit et al., 2017; Dunn, 2012) but also identity confirmation (the latter especially among transwomen, for example: Brewis & Linstead 2000; Benoit et al., 2017; Capous-Desyllas & Loy, 2020). Many sex workers report that their work provides more autonomy, income, and job satisfaction than other jobs they have held (Benoit, Smith, Jansson, Healey, & Magnuson, 2021). If entry into sex work is a choice (Benoit et al., 2017), exit is as well. Some engage in sex work for a short period of time to reach financial and life goals and then stop, while others work for longer periods (Ham & Gilmour, 2017). Demand for older sex workers is limited, however, so few pursue this career past middle age.

To conclude this section, it is important to highlight how sex work, like other forms of work, is shaped by intersectional inequalities. The experience of Indigenous, white, Black, Asian, and other sex workers differs in many respects—as do the push and pull factors that lead men and women into the sector.

Illegal Work

underground economy Unrecorded and untaxed economic exchanges; illegal trade in goods or services

When we think about work, most of us imagine legal activity, but the **underground economy** is extensive in Canada, totalling almost $52 billion in 2016 (Statistics Canada, 2018e); many people earn a living through work they do "under the table" or through illegal activities. Scholars of crime and work—or crime *as* work—argue that not all crime is work. The crimes that most resemble work are those that require a steady time commitment and generate an income (Fagan & Freeman, 1999). Such activities include white-collar crime (employee theft and embezzlement), fencing and selling stolen goods, theft, drug-dealing, fraud, kidnapping, and tax evasion. Someone engaging in a crime of opportunity—a one-time theft, for example—would not usually be classified as an illegal worker. Those who engage in theft for a living may spend a considerable amount of time planning, making contacts, and making sales. In such contexts, we can regard theft as work.

Some of the illegal work activities mentioned might be a person's full-time job—like selling stolen goods or theft—while others can or must be combined with legal employment. Drug-dealing could be a full-time job; however, it might also be something one does on the side while engaging in other activities (Fagan, 1995; Fast, Shoveller, & Kerr, 2017). In fact, employment might help expand to networks and hence open up new opportunities for selling. Fencing stolen goods requires a legitimate business, and white-collar crime is usually done by employees. In this manner, illegal work can be a supplement to legal work or an alternative.

The nature of illegal work is variable. Some work requires considerable skill and ingenuity—for instance, the safecrackers interviewed by Letkemann (1973; see also Conwell & Sutherland, 1937). Other forms of illegal work may require resources and contacts, such as fencing stolen goods. Some work is more semi- or low-skilled, including drug-selling, although there are skills involved in learning the work and navigating these environments as well (Duck, 2016; Fast et al., 2017).

Research on crime and work, similar to the literature on crime, emphasizes that young men from low socio-economic status backgrounds, out of school, with limited skills that would benefit them in the legal job market are overrepresented in illegal work activity, including drug-selling. Fast et al. (2017) explain that the young Vancouver-based male drug-sellers they studied had low levels of education (high school diploma or less) and difficult childhood family circumstances that limited their opportunities. Some were recruited young, with the promise of good incomes for easy work, right from group homes or school (Fast et al., 2017). Others saw their legitimate job opportunities dry up in the face of drug addictions. Regardless of the circumstances, all of these young men could make considerably more from their illegal work (drug-selling, theft) than they would in the low-wage legal job market (Fagan & Freeman, 1999; Fast et al., 2017). While some drug-sellers continue to combine legal work with illegal work, opportunities for the former can dry up once someone is convicted for the latter, leading to enhanced reliance on illegal sources of income.

Researchers contend that the decision to engage in illegal work is often a rational one whereby people weigh the benefits (such as good pay) against the costs (potentially getting caught and punished) (MacDonald & Pyle, 2000). Those who have opportunities for illegal work have few opportunities for legal work (due to low education: Lochner, 2004), and believe that the benefits outweigh the costs are more likely to pursue criminal activity (until such time as their cost-benefit analysis changes). Decisions to partake are also influenced by a desire to live a certain lifestyle and/or achieve status and respect among others in their community. Among illegal workers, jail time could be viewed as largely inevitable and, in this sense, may not constitute a deterrent (although individuals lose much when they serve time) (Fast et al., 2017; Fagan & Freeman, 1999). The pressures of young parenthood create financial incentives for continued involvement in illegal work activity.

The economic incentives for illegal work are confirmed through data analysis suggesting a positive correlation between unemployment and crime such that some property and income-generating crimes increase during periods of high unemployment (MacDonald & Pyle, 2000). More pertinent, however, are local employment opportunities (Fagan & Freeman, 1999); local conditions and cultures can shape decisions around work. For young, unskilled workers with few job opportunities—especially those from low socio-economic backgrounds—crime really does appear to pay, encouraging young people's participation in this work.

Researchers also suggest that illegal work differs by gender: women are more likely to engage in crimes like shop-lifting, or in prostitution, rather than in other forms of theft and drug-dealing, although this appears to be changing (Caputo & King, 2011; Fagan 1995; Ferraro & Moe, 2003). Illegal work is also racialized; opportunities for legal and illegal work vary by neighbourhood, and these are also racially segregated (Duck, 2016; Fast et al., 2017).

white-collar crime Crime committed in employment or other commercial situations for economic gain

White-collar crime is different from other forms of illegal work to the extent that it is disproportionately done by middle-aged men with skills and education who work full-time. The term "white-collar crime" is generally used to refer to illegal activity committed in employment for economic gain. The term was coined by Edwin Sutherland in the 1940s. He was trying to draw attention to crimes done by the more powerful in society, since the marginalized were centred out for more attention and punishment. Sutherland argued that the damage wrought by people in positions of high status using their power for personal gain was substantial. His focus was more on what we would now call corporate crime: "misrepresentation in financial statements of corporations, manipulation in the stock exchange, commercial bribery ... misrepresentation in advertising, embezzlement" and so on (Sutherland, 1940, p. 2). Corporate crime is committed "by, and on behalf of" corporations (Croall, 2001, p. 160). Not infrequently, corporations and the wealthy get away with such crimes.

Today, the term "white-collar crime" is used to describe a range of activities, some of which are done at work (embezzlement, insider trading) and some carried on outside of a legitimate workplace like credit card fraud. White-collar criminals are typically working- or middle-class people looking for ways to increase their earnings (Weisburd, Waring, & Chayet, 2001).

Issues at Work

6.3 | Professional Misconduct

Professional misconduct may be seen as similar to white-collar crime because it involves people engaging in illegal and/or unethical conduct at work for their own or others' gain. Professionals like doctors and lawyers have been placed in positions of social trust. Misconduct abuses this trust and has the potential to do significant societal damage. Professional misconduct is defined as "behaviours, legal or illegal, that contravene normative expectations and professional codes of conduct" (Muzio, Faulconbridge, Gabbioneta, & Greenwood, 2016, p. 143). In this manner, the term covers behaviours ranging from the unprofessional (discrediting a colleague) to the criminal (assaulting someone, stealing money) (Currie, Richmond, Faulconbridge, Gabbioneta, & Muzio, 2019). To understand different types of professional misconduct better, it is helpful to focus on outcomes and intentions. For example, professional misconduct may be undertaken by a professional for their *own gain* or satisfaction. Whether abusing a patient, taking advantage of a client, or stealing funds from their employer, professionals may gain, like other white-collar criminals, from nefarious deeds at work. This type of misconduct has received the most attention in the media and the academic literature. Alternatively, professional misconduct may *benefit a client*; some professionals break the law or find loopholes in the rules for their clients' gain. This situation has been described as "client capture," and it occurs when professionals prioritize the interests of their clients over the interests of the public (Dinovitzer, Gunz, & Gunz, 2014). Professionals may or may not benefit from these activities (beyond being able to keep their jobs). Finally, professionals may engage in misconduct for *their employers' benefit*. Especially in rationalizing companies, professionals can be encouraged to take shortcuts, turn a blind eye to rule violations, or even falsify test results (Adams, 2020b). Again, professionals may not benefit from this type of misconduct (beyond maintaining employment), and some have been sent to jail for following the orders of their bosses. These latter two dimensions of misconduct have received too little attention in the literature. The organizational contexts and social inequalities shaping misconduct at work are deserving of more attention.

Crime can be an important source of income for people, but it is important to recognize that legal and illegal work exist along a continuum and people may move back and forth along that continuum over the course of their careers.

Domestic Labour and Volunteer Work

domestic labour
The tasks involved in running a household, including housework, home maintenance, childcare, and consumption work

volunteer work
Work we do for free that contributes to our neighbourhoods and communities

Unpaid work can take many forms, but two of the most common are **domestic labour** and **volunteer work**. Unpaid domestic labour encompasses work we do to take care of ourselves and others in our households, as well as the work we do to maintain those households and our residences. It includes tasks such as cooking, cleaning, laundry, and home maintenance. It also includes childcare and child-rearing. Of course, domestic labour can be done for pay: people who can afford to do so might hire one or more personal service workers to do these tasks for them. Most of us, however, do at least some of this work ourselves, unpaid. Volunteer work, in contrast, is work we do for free that contributes to our neighbourhoods and communities. Some scholars distinguish between volunteer work done with formal organizations and that done informally to help neighbours and others on occasion (Wilson & Musick, 1997). This work is, by definition, unpaid.

Domestic Labour

Without taking time to feed and clothe ourselves and maintain residences, we would not have the energy to work for pay, earning the money we need to survive. The work of child-rearing ensures that we have future generations of workers. Domestic labour, then, is essential to the cycle of production and consumption that keeps society going (Luxton, 1980). To elucidate the importance of domestic labour, feminist scholars have turned to Marx (1967) who in *Capital* clarified that labour power bought and used in capitalist workplaces must itself be produced on a daily basis (Luxton, 1980): if someone uses up their energy on the job on Monday, the following day they "must again be able to repeat the same process in the same conditions as regards health and strength" (Marx, 1967, p. 168). Domestic labour ensures that workers have the food, clothing, and energy necessary to labour day after day. Thus, domestic labour is productive labour that produces labour power for the workplace (Luxton, 1980).

Domestic labour is gendered labour, since the tasks of cooking and cleaning still disproportionately fall on women and even when done by men are often seen to represent "women's work" (Luxton, 1980; Fox, 1980; Moyser & Burlock, 2018). In 2015, women spent on average four hours a day on unpaid work (as a primary activity), compared to 2.5 hours a day of unpaid work completed by men (Moyser & Burlock, 2018). Women also do more "multi-tasking" than men, combining unpaid domestic work with other activities. A gender division of domestic labour still exists whereby men do more of the outside tasks while women do more of the inside jobs (Hochschild, 1989; Moyser & Burlock, 2018). That is, women report doing more meal preparation and cleaning than men, while men do more outdoor maintenance, repair, and renovation. This division of labour helps to account for gender differences in daily totals of domestic labour: women's tasks are done daily, while men's are more likely to be weekly or occasional. Still, the gender gap in domestic labour is decreasing: women are doing less domestic labour today than they were 30 years ago (especially cleaning), while men are doing more (especially meal preparation) (Moyser & Burlock, 2018). Women's reduction in domestic labour is related to their increased hours spent in paid work (ibid.).

Domestic labour is racialized as well. Meanings attached to the work may vary across culture and/or immigration status: in some contexts, housework is not recognized as real work (Nichols, Etemadi & Tyyskä, 2018). Moreover, when domestic labour is done for pay, it is disproportionately done by visible minority women, who have the double burden of doing both paid and unpaid domestic work. There is also evidence that experiences of domestic labour (what is done, how, and by whom), vary by class as well (Luxton, 1980; Luxton & Corman, 2001). Thus, the intersection of gender, race, and class shape the organization and performance of domestic labour.

In general, the literature on the domestic division of labour has tended to focus on heterosexual married couples, but this is changing, and some studies explore dynamics within LGBTQI relationships (Pfeffer, 2010; Kurdek, 2006, 2007). There is some evidence, for example, that lesbian couples have more egalitarian household divisions of labour (Kurdek, 2006, 2007), although some argue that the reality is often more complex (Pfeffer, 2010; Moore, 2008). Pfeffer's (2010) study of women in relationships with transmen finds a gendered division of labour, with most women doing more domestic labour than their transgender partners but justifying this division of labour as a matter of preference rather than inequality. Gender continues to shape the division of domestic labour in complex ways among LGBTQI couples.

Many years ago, Luxton (1980) created a typology of domestic labour, arguing that it had three central components: (1) housework, including cooking, cleaning, and home maintenance; (2) child-rearing, the work of raising and caring for children; (3) consumption work: managing money and making ends meet by stretching income to meet expenses. Some may be reluctant to regard each of these activities as work. Housework appears as routine drudgery, and many of us do it without thinking about it. Child-rearing is seen as an extension of love and caring, and hence, for some, it seems wrong to depict it as work. Consumption work involves shopping and budgeting, and the former at least might be cast as leisure, although labour is clearly required (Ritzer, 2015; DeVault, 1991). The failure to recognize domestic labour as work devalues it, resulting in lower respect for stay-at-home moms and dads and leading to lower levels of remuneration and respect for those who do this work for pay. It is important to recognize that domestic labour is work.

While studies of domestic labour often cast it as routine, there can be a fair amount of skill and planning that goes into it. For instance, research on food preparation highlights how much planning and forethought is required when feeding the family to ensure nutritious meals that balance likes and dislikes within a budget, to say nothing of shopping and the work of preparing meals (DeVault, 1991; Kwon & Adams, 2021; Bowen, Brenton, & Elliott, 2019). This research has also revealed the extent to which this work is value-laden, with heavy expectations placed on those who prepare meals for their families. The situation is even more challenging for racialized families who may feel others are judging their food choices or immigrant families who may need to cook meals in contexts where the ingredients they are familiar with are not only in short supply but potentially expensive (Bowen, Elliott, & Brenton, 2014; Kwon & Adams, 2021).

intensive mothering An ideology that sees appropriate child-rearing as child-centred, expert-guided, emotionally absorbing, financially expensive, and labour intensive (Hays, 1996, p. 8)

The work of child-rearing is also heavily value-laden. Hays (1996) argues that parents, and especially mothers, are subject to the pressures of **intensive mothering**. This is an ideology that holds that child-rearing requires considerable time and resources and should be done predominantly by mothers, who prioritize child-rearing above paid work and are guided by experts. Of course, parents resist these expectations. Fathers *can* take primary responsibility for childcare, mothers typically *do* engage in paid work, especially once their maternity leaves are over, and they may resist the advice of experts. However, mothers and fathers are aware of the ideology and may even feel guilty when they do not meet its expectations. Further, some may feel defensive when they account for their child-rearing practices (Elliott & Bowen, 2018). Child-rearing is, therefore, labour-intensive, and high childcare demands combined with paid work demands, can create work-family conflict and stress for parents (discussed in Chapter 11). In light of these ideologies, it is perhaps not surprising that time spent on childcare by parents has increased over time for both men and women—but especially the latter (Moyser & Burlock, 2018).

Consumption work is also complex and may involve considerable unpaid labour, especially for those with limited means: learning prices, budgeting, hunting bargains and sales, actually purchasing goods, and so on (Luxton, 1980). This unpaid labour entails some amount of exploitation because people end up paying more for goods and services than they should (Ritzer, 2015) and even potentially more than they can afford. The fact that this work tends to go unrecognized does not make it easier to complete.

Domestic labour is particularly challenging today because many people combine it with other work. Researchers use the term **double day** to capture the fact that many engage in paid work and follow it up with a **second shift** of domestic labour at home. The double day is particularly challenging for those with others to care for (children or other dependents).

double day
A shift of paid work combined with a second shift performing domestic labour.

second shift
Performance of domestic labour after a "first shift" doing paid work

The COVID-19 pandemic raised new concerns about domestic labour as many workers worked from home during lockdowns while simultaneously caring for children with the closure of daycares and schools. Working parents found it nearly impossible to work, engage in childcare and domestic labour, and home-school children simultaneously. While men working from home did expand the amount of domestic labour and childcare they performed (Shafer, Scheibling, & Milkie, 2020), the heavier burden appears to have fallen on women (Feng & Savani, 2020). Stay-at-home mothers too struggled as their workloads increased (home-schooling, entertaining children at home all day, and doing more domestic labour with partners at home) while cut off from their usual outlets and supports (Aslam & Adams, 2021). Outcomes included deteriorating mental health, increased domestic violence, burnout, and pressure on working parents, along with potentially negative career implications (including the retreat of some working women with young children from the labour force, as described in Chapter 4).

Volunteer Work

Some question whether volunteer work is real work, but since it is productive labour directing human effort towards adding use value to goods and services, it meets the definition provided in Chapter 1 (Tilly & Tilly, 1998). The challenge with theorizing volunteer work is that its content can be similar to paid work: for example, office work, coaching, fundraising, firefighting, baking, or providing services for sale are all types of work regularly performed both for pay and on a volunteer basis. Moreover, volunteer work may (or may not) be done under the supervision or management of others, who themselves are paid, within formal organizations. What distinguishes volunteer work, then, is not what is done, or even how it is done, but the conditions under which it is done—the fact that this labour is freely given to aid a cause for the benefit of others. Although this work is unpaid, it may be rewarding in more intangible ways: people may acquire a sense of accomplishment or feel good about helping others. Volunteer work, then, may be guided by substantive rationality, as discussed in Chapter 2. Nonetheless, volunteer work might also be shaped by formal rationality, especially when it takes place within formal organizations.

Volunteering is a fairly common activity. Statistics Canada reports that just under half of all Canadians aged 15 and over volunteered in the year 2010 (Vézina & Crompton, 2012). The number of volunteers (more than 13 million) has been increasing over time. These data apply to formal volunteering only, specifically, involvement with formal organizations. The most common areas for formal volunteering are sports and recreation, social services, education and research, religion, and health. The distribution of volunteering is uneven, with a small percentage (10 per cent) completing more than 50 per cent of all volunteer hours in the country (Vézina & Crompton, 2012).

People are more likely to volunteer during certain life stages, as young adults and adults with young children. More than half of those 15–24 and 35–44 volunteer (Vézina & Crompton, 2012). Youth may have high school volunteering requirements to fulfill, or they might hope that by volunteering they will be gaining valuable job experience (see Box 6.1). Those 35–44 are likely to have school-aged children in the home and volunteer to support their kids' recreation activities. Moreover, those most likely to volunteer are well-educated, healthy, and from higher socio-economic backgrounds (Wilson & Musick, 1997; Vézina & Crompton, 2012). However, these findings reflect formal volunteering; it is not surprising that employed individuals, with more human and social capital, may be more likely to volunteer in this capacity. It must be noted, however, that while more people in higher income groups volunteer, volunteers from lower income groups devote more hours to the cause (Vézina & Crompton, 2012). The more religious are also more likely to volunteer than others.

There is some evidence that men's and women's volunteering differs. Women's volunteering is more likely to involve preparing and serving food or clothing, raising money, or assisting at events. Men are more likely to be found volunteering in leadership positions, doing maintenance work, and coaching (Rotolo & Wilson, 2007).

Informal helping is even more common than formal volunteering, with more than 80 per cent of Canadians reporting that they provided informal help to others in 2010. Common areas of help include house or yard-work and household maintenance (60 per cent), unpaid babysitting, health or personal care (53 per cent), running errands or helping someone get to an appointment (47 per cent), and help with paperwork (29 per cent) (Vézina & Crompton, 2012). The caremongering movement that emerged out of the COVID-19 pandemic in Canada is another example of this type of volunteering (Sheldon, 2020). The percentage of people offering informal help is fairly steady across ages, but it declines among seniors.

People who volunteer find it rewarding. It not only provides opportunities to contribute to the community but may also build social ties, encourage the development of new skills, and provide people with the opportunity to engage in work that confers autonomy and meaning (Thompson & Bono, 1993; Neysmith & Reitsma-Street, 2000).

As with other forms of unpaid work, volunteering is connected with paid work. Paid work can shape our opportunities and resources to engage in volunteering, as noted. Volunteering can potentially lead to paid work, allowing people to acquire skills and contacts leading to employment. Like paid work, volunteering can contribute to communities and provide valuable services.

Productive Leisure and Prosumption

The lines between work and leisure are blurrier than they once were. Or, at the very least, they are blurring in different ways thanks to innovations in information and communication technologies (ICTs). There are a few concepts that capture this trend.

First, some speak of **productive leisure**—engaging in hobbies that involve work (whether paid or unpaid). That blog you write, crafts you make, or pictures you take that you post online—those are all hobbies that involve unpaid labour. Of course, there are opportunities for this work to earn you some money. That blog may pay you pennies per view, or you may sell your crafts online or game on Twitch.tv for some small remuneration. In this way, leisure can involve work, and in the course of working, we may experience leisure. The term "playbour" has also been used to capture this blending of play and labour (Kücklich, 2005; Bolton & Houlihan, 2009). However, this term is also used by scholars to describe the increased use of games in the workplace to enhance productivity. Referring specifically to gaming, Taylor (2018) prefers the term "serious leisure" to capture the investment of time, resources, and identity by those engaging in it.

productive leisure Engaging in hobbies that involve work (whether paid or unpaid)

A more sweeping term, but one that captures the trends on a theoretical level, is **prosumption**. This term blends the words "production" and "consumption" to highlight the centrality of both to our lives under capitalism (and other economic systems) (Ritzer, 2015). Increasingly, because of technological and social changes, we engage in production and consumption at the same time. To provide a common real-world example, when you use the self-checkout line at the supermarket you are acting as a prosumer: you are engaging in unpaid work for the store—which now needs fewer cashiers, since you and many others are willing to do cashiers' work for free—while simultaneously purchasing food as a consumer.[1] This prosumption is occurring more and more in different areas of work and life (Ritzer, 2015).

prosumption The performance of both production and consumption simultaneously (Ritzer, 2015)

Prosumption is particularly clear when we think of productive hobbies or serious leisure. When we upload something to Instagram or Facebook or Twitter, we are doing unpaid work for these entities, while simultaneously consuming items posted by others. When we game online for hours, we are similarly contributing to a game's success as we hone skills and build relationships. Social media sites and gaming companies profit immensely from all of this unpaid work, benefitting from our exploitation both as free labourers and avid consumers (Ritzer, 2015). We can be so focused on our own consumption on these sites, we lose track of the free labour we are providing and the profit we help to generate. Even if we are aware of it, we may not care as long as we see what we are doing as fun or productive. Having something to show for our efforts can be satisfying in and of itself. In Marxist terms, as prosumers we may be exploited but not alienated if the products of our labour still belong to us.

However, the significance of prosumption or productive hobbies goes deeper than this because the fact is that some of us manage to turn our hobbies into careers; many more of us may engage in considerable unpaid labour with the hope of living the dream. Instagram and YouTube influencers were working for free on these platforms before they began earning money. Competitors in esports or streamers on Twitch.tv who can make a living at these activities had to put in many an hour playing video games to hone their skills. The fact that people have been able to carve out a living from gaming and other

[1]Using online checkouts is also an example of what Craig Lambert (2015) calls "shadow work": unpaid work we do for the benefit of businesses and other organizations. Shadow work eats into our leisure time, to our detriment.

leisure pursuits is a testimony to hard work and creativity, but it also reflects prosumption. People work hard at developing a skill set for their own and others' consumption—all to the benefit of major corporations who prosper in these burgeoning industries.

For example, modders—people who modify video games—have been around for decades. These gamers use their skill and creativity to modify commercial video games for their own and others' enjoyment, typically making them available for others within a gaming community for free. Game companies may encourage modders because their innovations can extend the life and popularity of a game (Kücklich, 2005). Modders who produce popular modifications could earn a coveted job in the gaming industry; that is, their unpaid work could eventually bring them paid work. However, this appears to be exceptional. Many modders labour for free, to the benefit of companies, for no monetary reward (Kücklich, 2005). Some may do so because they hope to get full-time work in the industry. Others may do it for the love of the game and the community. Either way, modding blurs the line between work and leisure and generates profit for others (see also Box 6.4).

Only some can afford to invest the time and effort into acquiring gaming skills, and these people are disproportionately male and middle-class. Gaming costs money, and time spent gaming is time not spent engaging in other pursuits. The industry's assumption that workers will acquire skills on their own time, working for free, before even entering the industry (where they may also be expected to work long hours for low wages), privileges young men who have families to help support them. Women and the economically disadvantaged have fewer opportunities to acquire these skills (the former in part due to the gendering of the industry) and hence fewer opportunities for employment (Harvey & Shepherd, 2017; Haight, 2021). The industry is also not considered LGBTQI-friendly (Haight, 2021). The structure of the gaming industry reproduces social inequalities.

Global Perspectives

6.4 | Blurring of Leisure and Work in Gaming

Studies of gamers as workers are growing. For example, Lee and Lin (2011) examined "gold farmers" or people who play digital games to acquire in-game items that they then sell for cash to other players who want these items to advance but do not want (or cannot afford) to spend the time in-game to acquire the items themselves (Lee & Lin, 2011). These workers may be self-employed, or they might work for a company who offers in-game items for sale. This is a global industry: gamer-workers are typically based in developing countries, and they use their in-game skills and techniques to sell to consumers in wealthier countries. Haight (2021) examined gamers and other workers in esports internationally. Both studies show that work in gaming tends to be precarious and can require long hours for uncertain remuneration. For many, the ability to play for pay is appealing; however, there are challenges for these paid gamers beyond precarity, including the blurring of leisure and work. Indeed, one's enjoyment of the game usually wanes when leisure is perceived as work (Lee & Lin, 2011; Haight, 2021). Some manage this by trying to draw clear separations between the two in terms of when they game, where they game, and what game they play (Lee & Lin, 2011). Still, when your main leisure activity no longer provides an escape from work, you can lose your primary means for alleviating stress (Haight, 2021). For some, the solution is to cultivate new hobbies (such as being active and getting exercise) to achieve a new balance (Haight, 2021). These new activities, of course, may also be productive leisure involving unpaid work.

Whether in gaming or other creative pursuits, the fact is that many people engage in hobbies that might be deemed productive, and many may hope to turn these hobbies into paid employment. Corporations gain from the faint hope that prosumption could turn into employment as prosumers continue producing and consuming at high rates. Here we can see not only the exploitation inherent in prosumption but also the blurry line between leisure and work. People may labour for free, for small amounts, or get paid for doing essentially the same activities. In this sense, productive leisure is similar to the internships reviewed in Box 6.1 through which young workers and newcomers seek to acquire skills and social capital to make a living. Like these internships, productive leisure also benefits employers and disadvantages paid workers, whose wages may be kept low because of the large "reserve army of labour" eager to take their jobs should they ask for more (Haight, 2021). Companies are the real winners. However, because this unpaid (or low paid) work is fun, creative, and sometimes fulfilling, it is unlikely that workers, or prosumers, will challenge the status quo anytime soon (Ritzer 2015).

To summarize, the jobs in this chapter straddle various lines between work and leisure, paid and unpaid, legal and illegal work. This liminal status can contribute to labour market precarity. Workers in many of these jobs are potentially vulnerable; some are marginalized. Participation in these discredited jobs reflects and reproduces intersectional social inequalities. In the following chapters, we explore workers' experiences in more detail, focusing on key dimensions of work.

Reviewing the Learning Objectives

After reading this chapter, you should:

- Have a clearer sense of what makes work non-standard and precarious and understand the implications for workers in Canadian society.
- Understand when crime is a form of work.
- Understand that some work is unpaid and how unpaid work and paid work are connected with each other.
- Understand the nature of sex work and have a sense of workers' experiences in these jobs.

Questions for Critical Thought

1. There are a number of social trends contributing to work precarity. Are there steps you think we as a society could take to address this issue? What are they? Do you think such change is likely?
2. Do you think that societal attitudes are changing in a manner that will make sex work less "object" than it was in the past? Are some forms of sex work likely to be de-stigmatized before others?
3. We say that workers who work for pay and engage in domestic labour are engaging in a double day. How might volunteering impact workers—especially those volunteers with school-aged children in the home?
4. Do you agree that the lines between leisure and work are blurring with advances in information and communication technologies? What are the advantages and disadvantages of productive leisure?

7 Skill, Expertise, Knowledge, and Education

Learning Objectives

After reading this chapter, readers will:

- Be able to define the core concepts of skill, knowledge, and expertise and understand their connection to education.
- Understand that skill, expertise, and knowledge are socially constructed and socially contested constructs that are shaped by, and in turn shape, social inequalities.
- Know some of the ways in which scholars have tried to measure skill over time and have a sense that measuring skill is difficult.
- Understand that there is evidence of both deskilling and skill upgrading among workers.
- Know that a sizeable minority of Canadian workers are underemployed and overqualified in their jobs.
- Be aware of changing social attitudes towards expertise.

Introduction

Many would argue that we live and work in a "knowledge economy" in which education, knowledge, and skill are not only prized and rewarded but in fact essential for economic survival. While physical work in agriculture and manufacturing dominated work in decades past, jobs in these sectors are disappearing, replaced by high-tech occupations and jobs working with information, data, and people. As a result, the labour force is more skilled, educated, and expert than ever before.

There is a great deal of evidence to support such arguments (Liu & Grusky, 2013; Livingstone & Watts, 2018; Oesch & Piccitto, 2019; Lapointe & Bach, 2016); however, there are also grounds for skepticism. We live in a society in which expertise and skill are highly lauded and yet routinely questioned, in which education is perhaps more important than ever before yet not always recognized or rewarded in the labour market, and skill appears to be both expanding and contracting depending on where you look. This chapter will explore conceptualizations of skill and expertise, consider their connection to knowledge and education, and explore their relevance to the labour market. Trends in skill and the significance of education within the labour market have long been areas of interest to sociological theorists and historians. Labour market analysts have also followed these trends closely. Most of us hope to have opportunities to exercise acquired skills and expertise in our work and feel frustrated—even alienated—when we cannot. For these reasons, skill and expertise are areas of considerable interest and concern. They are also areas of contradiction and debate.

Conceptualizing Skill, Knowledge, and Expertise

Researchers need a clear definition of skill in order to understand its distribution in the labour market and trends in skill demanded in the economy over time. However, they have not always agreed on precisely what skill (or expertise) is or how it is best measured. Drawing on dictionary definitions we can describe **skill** as an ability to do something well, based on one's knowledge, aptitude, and practice (*Oxford English Dictionary*, 2020d). While we often speak of skill in the singular, there are a multitude of skills individuals might possess. Most people are specialists—skilled in some areas, unskilled in others. Focusing on job-relevant skills, we might distinguish manual skills (like those skilled foresters or carpenters possess) from social skills prized among those who work with people or critical-analytical skills valued among those who analyze data and information. Moreover, it is not uncommon in the world of work to distinguish between "hard" skills—usually cast as technical in nature—and "soft" skills, which include interpersonal, social, and managerial skills. Understanding that there are many different types of skill is important if we are going to assess how much skill workers have or whether the skills in demand in the labour market are changing.

skill
An ability to do something well, based on one's knowledge, aptitude, and practice (*Oxford English Dictionary*, 2020d)

Sociologists have typically gone beyond dictionary definitions to add nuance to our understanding of skill, influenced by symbolic interactionism, labour process theory, and feminist theory. When conceptualizing skill, labour scholars include both task complexity (acknowledging that different tasks require different types and amounts of skills) and autonomy (Spenner, 1983; Vallas, 1990; Ikeler, 2015). **Autonomy** is an important, if sometimes downplayed, aspect of skill: it entails the independence or freedom to utilize one's knowledge and experience. Workers may possess many skills, but if they do not have autonomy, they won't be able to use their skills (and knowledge and experience) in the conduct of their work.

autonomy
The independence or freedom to utilize one's knowledge and experience

Researchers have identified many different types of skill, as noted. For example, Liu and Grusky (2013) in their study of skill trends over time in the United States identify four main types and several subtypes of skill: *cognitive* (verbal, quantitative, analytical), *creative* (which includes innovation, originality, and creative thinking), *technical* (computer science and engineering), and *social skills* (managerial and care work). While this typology is broader than many, it ignores important manual skills as well as autonomy and some service skills. To augment such depictions, other studies have highlighted skills required in service work, including *emotional labour* and *aesthetic labour* (discussed previously in Chapter 5) among others (Hochschild, 2003; Williams & Connell, 2010; Gatta, Boushey, & Appelbaum, 2009; Nickson et al., 2017). For example, researchers have

tacit skills
Often unrecognized skills acquired through close familiarity with technology, work practices, coworkers, or customers/clients

knowledge
Familiarity with, or understanding of, a particular subject matter, branch of learning, set of experiences, or principles (*Oxford English Dictionary*, 2020c)

Indigenous knowledges
"The understandings, skills and philosophies developed by societies with long histories of interaction with their natural surroundings ... [and which are] integral to a cultural complex that also encompasses language, systems of classification, resource use practices, social interactions, ritual and spirituality" (UNESCO, 2017)

expertise
Special skill, knowledge, or judgment; the skill and knowledge claimed by experts (*Oxford English Dictionary*, 2020a)

argued that emotional labour (inducing or suppressing feelings to influence customers' or clients' feelings) involves both technical complexity and autonomy (Bolton, 2005; Ikeler, 2015). Researchers have also identified **tacit skills,** which often go unrecognized because they typically emerge when one is familiar with work practices, cultures, and technology: they may include having a "feel" for technology, work routines, or customers so that one knows the right touch to make a piece of equipment work effectively or the right turn of phrase to win over a client. Such skills are built up through experience and may be invisible to observers—until a new worker comes along and cannot achieve the same results (Hampson & Junor, 2010; Armstrong, 2013; Juravich, 2017). Hampson and Junor (2010) provide a detailed typology of skills demanded in various jobs across the service sector, showing how even jobs that appear lower-skilled require considerable practical expertise as well as explicit and tacit knowledge learned through experience (see also Nickson et al., 2017). They highlight often unrecognized skills, including "shaping awareness"—which includes being able to read situations, monitor and guide reactions—and interacting and relating with others (Hampson & Junor, 2010; Nickson et al., 2017). It may take service workers years to hone these skills (even in jobs that to others might appear low-skill). The diversity of skills, and the fact that many can—like tacit skills—go unrecognized, complicates the study of skill and skill trends.

We may be on firmer definitional footing when we examine related concepts like knowledge and expertise. **Knowledge** is a component of skill, as dictionary definitions indicate. By knowledge we usually mean familiarity with, or understanding of, a particular subject matter, branch of learning, set of experiences, or principles (*Oxford English Dictionary*, 2020c). Knowledge can be acquired through texts, education, interaction, and practical experience. Knowledge is both exercised on the job and (at least partially) acquired on the job (Adams & Sawchuk, 2020; Nickson et al., 2017). Although it is closely related to skill, the two are not synonymous. Knowledge is also socially constructed and shaped by culture and structural inequalities. There is a hierarchy of knowledge and, in Canada, Western, rational, and scientific knowledge has been privileged over other ways of knowing, including Indigenous knowledges.

UNESCO (2017) defines **Indigenous knowledges** as "the understandings, skills and philosophies developed by societies with long histories of interaction with their natural surroundings ... [and which are] integral to a cultural complex that also encompasses language, systems of classification, resource use practices, social interactions, ritual and spirituality." Indigenous ways of knowing are distinct from Westernized knowledge more commonly imparted through education curricula. Although variable, they tend to be more holistic, local/contextual, linked with the land and nature, intuitive, and inclusive compared to the analytical, positivistic emphasis of Western knowledge (Semali & Kincheloe, 1999; Maurial, 1999; Watts, 2013). Indigenous knowledges have been marginalized and are often unrecognized in Canadian society (see Photo 7.1). Efforts to celebrate Indigenous knowledge and skills can lead to a greater appreciation and understanding.

Expertise is a similar concept, defined here as special skill, knowledge, or judgment or the skill and knowledge claimed by experts (*Oxford English Dictionary*, 2020a). This concept has received more sociological attention in recent decades, with scholars tracing the emergence of the term in the 20th century and its association with the rise of a group of workers advancing claims to social authority based on their knowledge (Eyal, 2013,

2019). For Eyal (2013, p. 872), expertise reflects not skill per se but the organizational contexts and institutional arrangements that allow some to accomplish specific tasks (see also Eyal, 2019). It is a social construction shaped by social interaction and networks (Eyal, 2013, 2019). Expertise is also shaped by power, and who claims expertise (and whose claims are accepted) is subject to debate and disagreement. Thus, for Eyal and others, expertise can be distinguished from skill (as well as knowledge), although they are closely related; the study of expertise requires a focus on networks, social organization, and negotiations between and among experts, as well as parties within states and other social institutions.

Source: THE CANADIAN PRESS/Christopher Katsarov

Filmmaker Alethea Arnaquq-Baril has used her work to highlight how Indigenous knowledges have been marginalized by colonial societies. In her 2016 documentary Angry Inuk, Arnaquq-Baril highlights how European and Canadian animal rights activists' failure to meaningfully engage with Inuit opposition to anti-sealing campaigns have threatened the social, economic, and ecological health of Arctic communities.

All three of these key concepts—skill, knowledge, and expertise—are connected with education but are not reducible to it. Skill and knowledge are both acquired through formal education but also through more informal learning and practical experience. Expertise (when defined in terms of skill) can also be acquired, at least in part, through education. When expertise is defined in terms of networks and spatial arrangements, we can see educational institutions as part of a larger set of institutions shaping the acquisition and exercise of expertise and structuring relationships within networks between and among experts and their clients, patients, and others.

Now that we have a clearer sense of what is meant by skill, knowledge, and expertise, we can begin to explore their significance to work in Canadian society.

Measuring Skill

Skill is a social construction. As a result, skill is not easily measured. Our cultural understandings (and our biases) about what is worthwhile and important tend to get in the way. We prioritize some skills over others and fail to recognize certain skills when we see them (Hampson & Junor, 2010). For instance, we might say that someone who is a good artist has "natural talent" and fail to recognize the years they have spent training and honing their skills. We might recognize the strength of an agricultural worker but not their expertise. The same is true for those who seem to have an affinity for dealing with children; we tend to see this as reflecting temperament (patience, sense of fun) rather than skill (Armstrong, 2013; Gatta et al., 2009). Few of us make similar judgments about brain surgeons and rocket scientists—workers who are culturally viewed as highly skilled and trained after years of formal education and practical experience. Our culture's respect for science is one of the factors leading us to recognize the skills of the latter workers while ignoring those of artists, manual workers, and childcare providers. What is culturally viewed as skilled or not skilled work can be shaped by how rare an ability is (Gaskell, 1983; Braverman, 1974). It can also be influenced by who is exercising a skill, or what job they hold (Armstrong, 2013).

social closure Processes through which groups (of workers) seek to maximize their own rewards and opportunities by delimiting others' access to resources, opportunities, and group membership

Skill is also the product of social campaigns and **social closure** (Vallas, 1990; Cockburn, 1983; Armstrong, 2013). Social closure is a neo-Weberian concept referring to a set of processes through which privileged people cut off others' access to opportunities and rewards. In this instance, workers with skills cut off others' access to training, education, and opportunities to use skills at work (see also Chapter 5). Groups of elite workers—especially professionals—may also invest in advertising to tell us about their skills. Among recent advertising campaigns is one that tells us that chartered professional accountants (CPAs) do more than work with numbers. Ads that talk about how government cutbacks undermine workers in health care and teaching similarly draw attention to these workers' skills. Workers who are less organized may not have the same capacity to advertise their skills to others. Such advertisements and campaigns can shape public opinion concerning who has skills and disrupt our ability to measure skill objectively.

Research has shown that our perceptions of skill are profoundly shaped by social inequalities. For instance, the (often manual and service) skills exercised by working-class men and women are frequently undervalued. Moreover, skill and competence are gendered. Occupations that have traditionally been female-dominated (office work, teaching, childcare work, nursing) have long been viewed as less skilled than jobs done by men (engineering, computer science, and medicine). Scholars have shown how such perceptions are only loosely related to job content and are rather related to gender bias, length of training, and men's success at limiting access to skills in certain jobs (Gaskell, 1983; Creese, 1999). Scholars have also documented a "gendering of competence." In male-dominated settings, men are viewed as more competent than women regardless of training and performance (Ridgeway, 2001; Kmec, 2013). While it may be the case that women are perceived as more competent than men in certain fields like working with young children, this is too often seen as a matter of innate ability, not skill.

Azocar and Ferree (2016) have argued that expertise and skill are shaped by power and privilege along a variety of dimensions, including gender, class, and race. They take an intersectional approach, urging scholars to consider skill and expertise as concepts shaped by networks and social relationships infused with power and structured by gender, race, and class inequalities. Skill and expertise are not gender-neutral, class-neutral, or race-neutral (Gatta et al., 2009; Sherman, 2007). Support for their arguments is found in research documenting the downgrading of the culture and competence of Indigenous workers (Lahn, 2018). The racialization of skill is also evident in studies documenting stereotyping in hiring that disadvantages minority workers. For example, Moss and Tilly (1996) show how Black men have been disadvantaged in obtaining jobs when soft skills are emphasized; employers stereotyped such workers as deficient in these skills and unable to do certain types of work (see also Shih, 2002). Research on migrant farm workers has shown that they are regarded as unskilled labourers, and yet they possess agricultural skills and knowledge that few Canadians possess (Basok, 2002). In a similar vein, studies of minority women in medicine highlight that their competence, credentials, and toughness are frequently questioned (Beagan, 2001; Kwon and Adams, 2018). Such stereotypes foster bias, downgrading the skills minority men and women have, and contributing to the **concrete ceiling** whereby members of minorities have difficulty breaking into the upper echelons of companies, making it difficult for them to advance in certain professions.

concrete ceiling
Similar to the glass ceiling, the concrete ceiling consists of impenetrable barriers preventing members of minorities from being promoted to organizations' upper echelons

Tilcsik's (2011) study documenting discrimination in hiring among gay men in the United States also found evidence of skill-related stereotyping: job applicants perceived to be gay were less likely to receive job offers when the work called for assertiveness. Transgender workers experience similar stereotyping, since work colleagues sometimes question their ability to perform gendered skills effectively (Connell, 2010). Such stereotyping reflects cultural beliefs about ability, which can have implications for hiring, work experience, and promotion. The result can be reduced access to desired jobs for LGBTQI workers.

Additional examples can be seen in the treatment of immigrants; employers and professional regulatory bodies downgrade their skills when acquired through foreign education and experience (Reitz, 2001). The downgrading of immigrants' skills has been seen as a significant contributor to their poorer labour market outcomes (discussed in Chapter 4) and social inequalities by immigration status more generally. Disability status is also pertinent here. The term "disabled" implies a lack of ability. Individuals with disabilities may face stigma and have their skills downgraded, leading to difficulties in finding meaningful employment commensurate with their skills (Benoit et al., 2013; Williams, 2006). This leads to negative outcomes in terms of employability and economic security (Maroto & Pettinicchio, 2015; Shuey & Willson, 2019).

Since our cultural perceptions get in the way, it may be impossible to produce unbiased assessments of skill and expertise. However, we need good measurements of skill to track trends over time and to understand the distribution of skill in the job market. Such information is not only of interest to academics but valuable to policy-makers, planners, and educators and has the potential to shape funding decisions, educational planning, and training programs.

Many studies use education as a proxy for skill, but this approach has been widely criticized; some skills are acquired in school, but others are acquired through informal learning, practical experience, and on the job. Moreover, just because someone has an advanced education does not mean they are exercising skills on the job. Three concepts are particularly useful here. The first is **credential inflation**. Over time, the education requirements for jobs have increased—often irrespective of changes to job content. Education requirements for jobs can be affected by supply and demand: when there are many applicants for jobs, companies often select those with more education, regardless of whether that education is necessary to perform the work. Education may signal other characteristics (ability to learn, status, stability, even class background) that are appealing to employers but not necessarily essential for job completion (Ashley & Empson, 2016). Second and third are the related concepts of underemployment and overqualification. Workers are said to be **underemployed** when they have more skills and abilities than their job actually utilizes. Such workers may also be **overqualified**: They have higher credentials (more education) than their job requires. Recent national

credential inflation
The tendency of firms to demand higher credentials from workers, even when job requirements do not change

underemployment
Employment that does not utilize the skills and training that workers possess

overqualification
When workers have more qualifications (for example, academic credentials) than their jobs require, they are overqualified

figures suggest that more than one in three Canadian workers report being overqualified for their jobs (Livingstone, 2019b). In light of credential inflation, underemployment, and overqualification, researchers who use education as a proxy measure of skill likely overestimate skill requirements in the labour force by some margin.

Researchers have tried to develop other, better measures of skill (Hampson & Junor, 2010; Liu & Grusky, 2013). However, in doing so they may focus on different "units" of analysis. Some seek to measure skills by examining characteristics of individual workers, while others look at characteristics of certain jobs. Ideally, we would examine a combination of the two—assessing both job content and the abilities individuals bring to, and develop within, specific jobs (Nickson et al., 2017; Armstrong, 2013). However, this is complicated. Researchers have developed occupational classification systems—including the NOC (National Occupational Classification) in Canada and O*NET in the United States—to identify skills required within jobs. These classifications attempt to define distinct skills and distinguish occupations based on their complexity, types of skills required, and the education and training required. These assessments can still be biased along the lines discussed above (Gatta et al., 2009; Steinberg, 1990; Vallas, 1990).

Generally, research must acknowledge that measurements of skill are imperfect and that the best measures consider a variety of factors and dimensions, including education, training and practical experience, and autonomy and job discretion, as well as a mixture of skills.

Skill Distributions

Cultural biases and stereotypes about skill contribute to social inequalities and occupational segregation (discussed in Chapter 9), channelling people into jobs for which they may be perceived to have a "natural" affinity or the right skills (Baird, 2012; Charles, 2005). Older studies found that a skill gap existed across gender in the labour force such that men dominated both high-skill and lower-skill jobs, while women were overrepresented in semi-skilled occupations (Boyd, 2003). The gender gap in skill was even evident within broadly similar occupations, to women's disadvantage. The gendering of competence that downgrades women's skills is important to keep in mind. With women's increased participation in management and traditionally male-dominated professions, we might expect that this gender gap in skill has lessened. However, there have been few recent studies examining gender gaps in skill. While gender differences in skill appear to persist, these differences do not entirely account for different labour market outcomes.

A growing number of studies has also documented the discounting of skills held by members of racial minorities and especially visible minority immigrants. For instance, historical and contemporary studies have documented numerous instances of Black men and women not being able to find work utilizing their skills and education (Das Gupta, 1996; Calliste, 1987; Creese, 1999); stereotypes about race and skill disadvantage Black workers especially (Moss and Tilly, 1996, 2001). Moreover, Vallas (2003) has shown how workers of colour can be disadvantaged in acquiring tacit skills on the job because their white colleagues may not share their accumulated experience. Add to this literature a large body of evidence that immigrants' skills and credentials are not recognized in the Canadian labour market (Buzdugan & Halli, 2009; Teelucksingh & Galabuzi, 2007).

As a result, they end up working in jobs that do not use their skills. When they are in skill-relevant jobs, they receive lower remuneration than Canadian-born workers with similar skills and education (Reitz, 2001).

There is also evidence that younger and older workers, those with disabilities, and Indigenous workers are disadvantaged. They experience skill discounting—that is, others assume they lack important skills (Berger, 2009; Benoit et al., 2013; Hu, Daley, & Warman, 2019), and this can encourage their channelling into low-skill, low-paid jobs (see also Chapter 11). Indigenous workers with lower levels of education are particularly vulnerable to underemployment (Park, 2018). At times, underemployment is viewed as a skill mismatch, provoking additional training, with the latter shaped by cultural norms. For example, Bell (2017) describes how "soft skills" training programs have been introduced in some sectors to encourage Indigenous workers to adopt corporate and settler norms. Such programs can be portrayed as positive skill development, but they demonstrate a lack of appreciation for existing Indigenous skills and knowledge and entail a concerted effort to alter Indigenous ways of knowing. As such, they reproduce discrimination and disadvantage.

Skills also vary across and within occupations. Hampson and Junor (2010) categorize service work into skill categories, distinguishing high-skill jobs in professions and management from mid-range skill support work in health care and teaching and less-skilled work in retail sales and call-centres. At the same time, they emphasize that even so-called low-skill jobs require many skills and practical expertise. In contrast, Lloyd and Payne (2009) caution against over-attributing skill to jobs that are highly controlled, arguing that personal attributes like "enthusiasm" and "patience" are increasingly labelled as skills by managers seeking a pliable workforce. Skill differences are also apparent within occupations. As an illustration, Box 7.1 presents data from a recent survey of professional engineers and engineer degree holders in Ontario. As this data show, members of visible minorities are less likely to report that they exercise skill and autonomy on the job than their racial majority counterparts.

More research remains to be done to unpack skill differences within and across gender, race, Indigeneity, disability, and other structured social inequalities.

A CLOSER LOOK

7.1 | Skill and Autonomy Differences among Canadian Engineers

In 2016–17, an online survey of professional engineers and engineering degree holders was conducted in Ontario. There were approximately 700 respondents to this survey exploring the work and learning of these professional workers. Several questions asked about their skill and autonomy. Crosstabular analyses of survey findings revealed several differences among respondents by visible minority status and gender. As Table 7.1 shows, visible minority engineers were less likely to participate in decision-making than engineers who were not members of visible minorities. Minority workers were also less likely to indicate that the knowledge they used at work as very complex and that they were able to use their skills and knowledge "fully"—suggesting that their work may demand fewer skills and knowledge than work performed by white workers.

(Continued)

box 7.1 *(Continued)*

Comparisons were also made between men and women engineers. Men were more likely to report that they had the autonomy to participate in decision-making and the ability to use their skills fully; they were also more likely to rate their knowledge as complex. While engineers have similar training and education, these data show that the skills exercised on the job can still vary by gender and visible minority status, reflecting not only discrimination, but the downgrading of minority workers' skills.

TABLE 7.1 Skill Use and Knowledge Complexity among Professional Engineers by Visible Minority Status and Gender

	Visible Minority	Racial Majority		Men	Women
Knowledge Is Very Complex	17.0%	28.4%**		29.2%	13.5%**
Skill Used "Fully" on the Job	15.9%	26.7%*		24.6%	18.8%*
Participate in Decision-Making	32.1%	50.4%***		50.0%	30.8%**

Data based on CWKE online survey of Ontario engineers.

*** p<.001,

** p<.01,

* p<.05

Trends in Skill

deskilling
Process of job degradation through which workers are denied the opportunity to use skills (and autonomy) formerly exercised on the job

There has been considerable academic debate about skill trends, some of which has been briefly touched on in previous chapters. Claims of **deskilling** date back to early political economists Karl Marx and Adam Smith, A (2000). both of whom contended that manufacturing under industrial capitalism requires specialization, simplification, and repetition of tasks to such an extent that the average worker loses the ability to exercise broad skills on the job. Such concerns were revived in the 1970s and 1980s with the publication of Harry Braverman's *Labor and Monopoly Capital*. Braverman (1974) argued that under industrial capitalism, work has been reorganized in a way that reduces workers' autonomy and control over the labour process. Employers have adopted managerial techniques, including scientific management and Fordism, that simplify tasks and remove decision-making away from workers and into the minds of management. Workers are increasingly required to follow the instructions of others and discouraged from thinking on their own. A plethora of studies provided support for Braverman's arguments documenting losses in craft skills historically and decreasing autonomy in manufacturing, clerical work, computer programming, and a variety of other occupations (Cockburn, 1983; Kraft, 1977; Glenn & Feldberg, 1977; Heron, 2019a). This approach, influenced by Marxist and labour process theory, paints a dim picture of work under capitalism.

A counter argument emerged. Daniel Bell (1976) and others argued that the major story of the latter part of the 20th century was one of market expansion in skilled jobs:

employment in professions, management, and white-collar work. The rise of new technologies had scholars proclaiming a third industrial revolution in which new technology ushered in a knowledge economy in which skilled workers would be in demand. **Skill upgrading** or upskilling is the dominant trend, this literature argues. Workers without skills are seen as increasingly expendable in a globalizing economy.

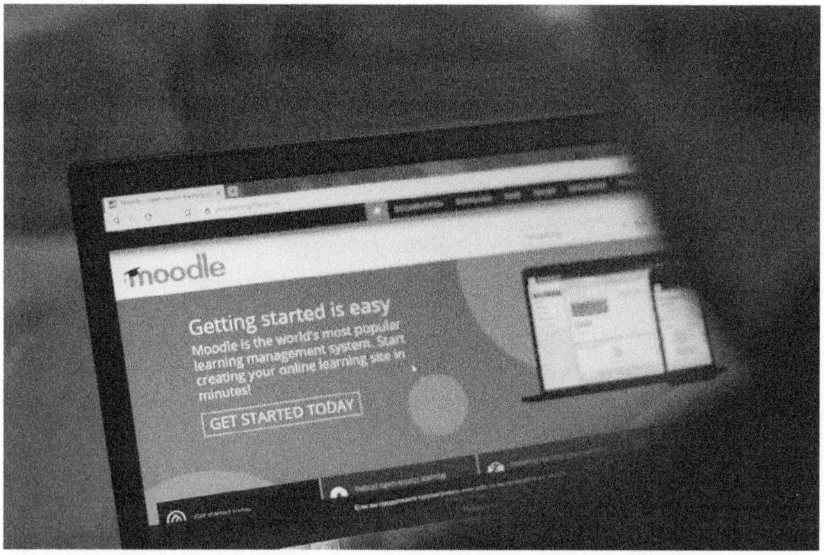

Technological advances have led to deskilling in industries previously considered immune, such as academia. Learning Management Systems like Moodle have been seen as an attempt to deskill professors' teaching work by systemizing teaching and moving it online.

Source: © Postmodern Studio/Shutterstock

Does the empirical evidence support arguments of skill upgrading or deskilling? The answer depends on what measures are used (Vallas, 1990). Studies have found evidence of both upskilling and deskilling. The demand for some skills in the North American labour market is increasing: especially computer, analytical, and social skills, as well as creativity (Liu & Grusky, 2013). Jobs for workers with education and analytical skills, like managers and professionals, have grown (Oesch & Piccitto, 2019; Livingstone, 2019b); however, lower-skill interactive service work has grown as well (Lapointe & Bach, 2016). Fewer researchers focus on autonomy as a dimension of skill, but here the research findings appear even more mixed. Through a series of surveys, Livingstone (2019a) has documented a substantial reduction in worker autonomy for managers and professionals, while some service and manufacturing workers have experienced an increase. Many formerly autonomous workers have been negatively impacted by rationalization, intensified surveillance, and an extension of (upper) managerial control. These trends have combined to alter professionals' work and skills (Crowley et al., 2010; Barley & Kunda, 2004; Adams & Sawchuk, 2020). Any autonomy gains among service workers appear modest at best. Indeed, the literature on autonomy in service work has generated conflicting findings. Ikeler (2015) documents skill and autonomy decline among retail workers with the rise of discount chains, while other studies document skill and autonomy among some service workers (Nickson et al., 2017; Hampson & Junor, 2010).

skill upgrading Sometimes called upskilling. Demand for new, enhanced skills in a workplace or occupation

Individual studies of specific occupations and professions continue to find evidence of within-occupation deskilling (Gale, 2012; Ikeler, 2015), but the trend for the labour force as a whole appears to be upward—with analytical and social skills increasing, while some others (science and craft skills, autonomy) are decreasing or remaining flat, on average (Liu & Grusky, 2013; Livingstone, 2019b; Sennett, 2008).

Although the literature has focused on deskilling and upgrading, some argue that this debate is not particularly helpful (Sawchuk, 2006; Vallas, 1990; Armstrong, 2013). A focus on skill shifts and organizational constraints on the exercise of skill may be more fruitful.

Shifting organizational demands, rationalization, and technological change alter workers' skills and learning (Armstrong, 2013; Adams & Sawchuk, 2020). There is evidence, for instance, that employers are increasingly reluctant to train workers on the job; instead they hire people with the skills they need, only to fire them when they no longer need them (Adams, 2021; Barley & Kunda, 2004). Moreover, the skills needed to perform work today may be different from—but not necessarily higher or lower than—what they were in the past. Some skills are lost or reassigned to other workers, while new skills are acquired (Barken, Denton, Brookman, Zeyinoglu, & Plenderleith, 2015). Workers can experience deskilling and upskilling simultaneously (Vallas, 1990). A case in point is provided in nursing, where the work of registered nurses is shifting in a manner that pulls RNs away from the bedside and requires more record-keeping and computer-mediated work (Cruz & Sawchuk, 2021; O'Neill, 2015). Such task shifts bring a loss of some skills (or at least fewer opportunities to exercise a skill set) and the acquisition of others. In this instance, other health care workers, including licensed/registered practical nurses (titles vary by province) and personal support workers, have new tasks assigned to them, which could result in skill upgrading (Barken et al., 2015).

Also, when considering skill trends, it is helpful to take into account evidence of underemployment and overqualification. If the skill *demanded* of workers in the labour force is, on balance, increasing, it appears to be the case that the skills *held* by the labour force are also increasing and perhaps at a faster rate. Livingstone (2019b) reports that approximately 45 per cent of Canadian workers with a post-secondary education were overqualified in 2016, working in a job that did not require their credentials. Underemployment among Canadian workers generally has increased over time, rising from 20 per cent in 1998 to 35 per cent in 2016 (Livingstone, 2019b). Thus, Canadian workers, on average, appear to have more skill than they have opportunity to use in their jobs, despite increased skill demands in the labour market. The Canadian labour force is among the most educated in the world (Livingstone, 2019b). The supply of skilled labour in Canada appears to outstrip the demand (Lu & Hou, 2020). At the same time, policy reports suggest that skill shortages in some areas persist (Antunes, 2013). Skill mismatches in the labour market are therefore evident, with shortages in some areas and oversupply in many others.

It is difficult to predict future trends in skill, especially in light of ongoing technological change. On the one hand, there is reason to believe that skill upgrading will continue, especially in light of labour market growth in some high-skill areas of the economy. Technological change will likely result in continued demand for people to innovate, maintain, program, and utilize technology and for analysts to assess the voluminous amount of information and data produced as different technologies and data repositories are brought together. Still, there is evidence that technological change, including artificial intelligence (AI) is replacing skilled workers (Susskind & Susskind, 2015). There is reason to believe that this may be an important future trend (see Chapter 12). One potential outcome of technological change is skill polarization—jobs for experts who can program and fix technology will remain, as will low-skilled personal service jobs for which technology is not cost-efficient or appropriate (Gatta et al., 2009). Under such a scenario, some will be deskilled while others will experience continual skill upgrading (Dunkerley, 1996; Castells, 2000). Job loss could result. This is not the only potential outcome, however. At present, the impact of technology on workers' skills is not entirely clear.

The Future of Work

7.2 | Skills for Tomorrow's Economy

It is difficult to predict what skills will be in demand in the workplace of the future; nevertheless, predictions have been made (Conference Board of Canada, 2020; World Economic Forum, 2016). Most prognosticators point to rapid technological change, and especially artificial intelligence, as shaping work in years to come. Demand for people with technological skills—artificial intelligence, blockchain, continuous integration, web development, and so on—is expected to be high. However, several soft skills have also been highlighted. Most emphasized are the following:

- communication skills (written and verbal)
- critical and analytical thinking
- information management, numeracy
- teamwork skills
- active learning orientation
- creativity and innovation
- leadership
- judgment and decision-making

Some reports also emphasize emotion management, emotional intelligence, and attitudes including adaptability and flexibility (Gilchrist, 2019; Marr, 2019; World Economic Forum, 2016). Ability to work with AI may be important, but many jobs will still require a human touch in the years to come.

Do you think your education and work experience is providing you with these skills to succeed in the future? If not, what would you like to see changed?

The Changing Nature of Expertise

Expert workers are not only in demand in the labour market generally, but they have long held important roles in societies. Some are members of regulated professions providing highly specialized services to the general public (see also Chapter 5). Within schools, universities, hospitals, research facilities, and other institutions, experts generate research to inform social practice, and they develop innovations that drive technological and other social change. In for-profit businesses, experts may contribute significantly to company profitability. Within government, they inform policy. Expertise is growing over time, with advanced divisions of labour and growing specialization (Weber, 1946; Sandefur, 2015). There is so much to know—so much information, research, and science being produced—that it is difficult for us as individuals to keep up. In this context, we may increasingly rely on experts who are specialists in their fields, not only to produce new knowledge but to interpret it for us so that we can understand its relevance. We may heed the warning of scientists about the dire impact of climate change or follow health-care professionals' advice about healthy eating and exercise, and we seek out engineers' assessment about the stability of buildings and bridges. Throughout the 20th century, there was a movement towards evidence-based policy-making at the government and workplace level; for instance, the adoption of evidence-based policing has been revolutionizing police practices in the past few decades (Kalyal, 2019). Historically, the rise of evidence-based policy-making intensified around the mid-to-late-20th century with growing demand for expertise in shaping policy, the employment of experts to oversee government programming, and the expansion of the welfare state more generally (Head, 2010; Eyal, 2019).

This expansion of expertise—and the influence of experts on our lives—has been met with a backlash (Larson, 2018; Eyal, 2019). People question the evidence on climate change or dismiss their doctor's advice, and governments pursue legislative change despite the warnings from experts that certain policies could have dire consequences. During the COVID-19 pandemic in Canada, millions followed the advice of medical public health experts; however, a minority rejected their advice, resenting stay-at-home orders, and refusing to believe that the pandemic was serious enough to warrant such measures. As this example illustrates, we live in an age when expertise is both valued and dismissed. The dismissal of expertise has long been a phenomenon characteristic of the United States, which has experienced ebbs and flows over the past several centuries. It has become increasingly evident in other parts of the world with the expansion of neoliberalism and the rise of populism. Both ideologies are associated with a distrust of experts, cast as elites seeking self-gain by providing questionable advice to others (Müller, 2020; Harvey, 2005).

Distrust of experts is also a characteristic of our information age. When we are bombarded by information from a variety of sources online (and elsewhere), who can we believe? Many people have claims to knowledge in a certain field, and different experts may disagree with each other about what the evidence shows; the array of expert advice can be bewildering (Larson, 2018; Eyal, 2019). Expertise, like skill, is after all a social construction and hence subject to social contestation (Larson, 2018; Eyal, 2019). On any given issue there may be many different expert workers and various non-experts, weighing in, offering contradictory guidance. Whose advice you follow (if any) may be based in part on your trust in experts and your ideological views about the credibility of some over others as much as (if not more than) your assessment of the evidence they use to support their claims. In fact, people often find personal experience particularly compelling: the tale of a random stranger may resonate more with us than the results of a random clinical trial providing scientific evidence. The social authority of experts has been challenged.

Also relevant is the phenomenon of what we might call "expertise by crowd." We may base some of our decisions not on a body of evidence, or the advice of an expert, but by how many "likes" or positive ratings a person, place, or experience receives online. Many of us refer to consumer ratings when making restaurant or hotel reservations or purchasing various products. It is less clear that such ratings are as valuable when they pertain to evidence or expertise. Ratings of your doctor or psychologist may reflect some assessment of popularity and not their ability to provide you with quality services when you need them. Nonetheless, such ratings appear to be increasingly relied upon.

Eyal (2019) and others contend that we are experiencing a "crisis of expertise." On the one hand, we are more dependent on science and experts than ever before. On the other hand, we are increasingly skeptical and even dismissive of scientific findings and expert claims. Eyal traces the current crisis in the United States to the "scientization of politics" characteristic of the mid-to-late-20th century: scientists and other experts were brought into government institutions to inform policy. Close ties between politicians and scientists have led to the politicization of science. Whether you believe in science or not is increasingly shaped by your political beliefs. To curtail the influence of experts, or at least to ensure that their expertise is not used for self-gain, the involvement of citizens and other stakeholders in decision-making has been increased. However, the success of such strategies has been mixed. Overall, these are complex issues, but it seems clear that science and expertise have been politicized, thereby exacerbating public suspicion of expertise (Eyal, 2019; Strassheim & Kettunen, 2014).

As evidence-based policy-making transforms into policy-based evidence-making, trust in the impartiality of science and its ability to produce truth is undermined (Strassheim & Kettunen, 2014). Rather, science and expertise are seen as forces either supporting or threatening power regimes and social inequalities. Of course, these trends are also strongly gendered and racialized: conflicts around expertise, perceptions of bias, and the politicization of science frequently break down along the lines of race, class, and gender (Bonilla-Silva, 2019). To elaborate, Bonilla-Silva (2019) speaks of an "emotional racial economy" and explains how beliefs (even falsehoods) can be embraced if they produce "emotional well-being among members of the dominant race" and contribute to the upholding of their power. We might believe something—even in the face of evidence to the contrary—if that belief brings us a sense of emotional or psychological satisfaction. In these instances, evidence and expertise that challenge existing power hierarchies and established social practices are rejected in favour of opinions that uphold the status quo, or that buttress the special interests of segments of the population.

Canada has historically been more open to expertise than the US. Nevertheless, in Canada science and expertise are increasingly associated with elites and hence viewed suspiciously by some. While in the past many Canadians trusted experts to shape policy that would benefit the people (Jones, 2019), increasingly experts are dismissed as out of touch with real people's concerns or as self-interested. Politics and policy-making are frequently driven by emotion, values, and interests, as well as structured social inequalities by race, class, and gender, among others (Bonilla-Silva, 2019; Geva, 2015). Evidence that does not match one's world views, interests, or emotions may be rejected as irrelevant. The result is that while "expertise" has long been socially valued, experts increasingly face a societal backlash, resulting not only in bad press but also in funding cuts to the institutions where they can be found—universities, research enterprises, government and non-profit agencies, and other such institutions—affecting the training and employment of experts in Canadian society. It is also leading to greater surveillance of expert workers and feeds decreases in autonomy. The "crisis of expertise" is, at least in part, a crisis of trust. Some of us still trust experts to provide sound advice to guide personal and societal decision-making, but that trust has lessened over time.

The COVID-19 pandemic has implications for the crisis of expertise. For example, there is evidence to suggest that regions where governments' pandemic response was guided by health experts had more success in reducing COVID-19-related mortality and morbidity in 2020 (Adams & Wannamaker, 2020). In this manner, it has become apparent that expert-guided policy can have a valuable societal impact. Moreover, research from the autumn of 2020 indicated that public respect for scientists had increased in the West, including in

Issues at Work

7.3 | Politics, Expertise, and the "Muzzling" of US Scientists

A 2019 report on research in US government-related bodies raised alarm about political interference and its impact (Brennan Center, 2019; Milman, 2019). The report finds that the US federal government administration under President Trump interfered with research, suppressing findings that ran counter to political priorities, to an extent that "the value of scientific and technical research, and of objective data itself, is now contested" (Brennan Center, 2019). For example, the Environmental Protection Agency reportedly told scientists who found that there were economic benefits to protecting wetlands to alter their findings. The report also revealed the suppression of another study that identified toxic chemicals in water. In another instance, the federal Department of the Interior apparently reassigned a climate scientist to a non-research role when he issued a warning about the impact of global warming on communities in the Arctic. The Brennan Center (2019) report is critical of political efforts to "recast the scientific and research communities as little more than special interest groups whose conclusions carry no more weight than those of other such groups."

This report supports Eyal's (2019) arguments about the "scientization of politics" and the "politicization of science," resulting in a crisis of expertise. Economic and right-wing political elites are discrediting scientists to further their own political and economic agendas. While the scientists affected may not have experienced deskilling—measured as a loss of acquired skill—they clearly have less autonomy than in the past. Those who have been fired or reassigned for their views likely have experienced deskilling as a result of political interference.

Canada, while skepticism towards experts had declined as a result of the pandemic (3M, 2020). It is too soon to predict whether these trends will continue post-pandemic.

Although expertise may be regarded with suspicion by many, skill tends to be rewarded in the labour market (Stier, 2015). By and large, those with more skill, education, and training earn more and have better opportunities to obtain stable employment—as human capital theory contends. The connection is not a perfect one. As we have discussed in this chapter, not all skills are rewarded to the same extent, and pervasive social inequalities mean that not everyone benefits from skill and training to the same extent. Cultural biases disregard the skills of some and fail to reward or recognize the skills of others.

Overall, this chapter has emphasized that skill is multi-faceted and socially constructed. What abilities are recognized as skills, and which ones are valued, are defined through social debate, culture, and social movements. The social construction of skill is also determined by social inequalities: those in positions of economic and political power benefit from downgrading the skills of those beneath them because low skill is associated with less cultural and social influence and lower remuneration. Recall from Chapter 2 that capitalists increase surplus value by replacing skilled workers with less-skilled workers. While there is empirical evidence that some dimensions of skill are increasing, it is also true that autonomy (and some other dimensions of skill) is diminishing, at least for some. Observed trends appear contradictory. While skills are typically rewarded in the labour market, claims to expertise may be met with skepticism. Moreover, the pandemic disrupted patterns in skill and expertise: jobs formally viewed as unskilled (such as cashier and cleaner) were labelled "essential," and trends in public perceptions of science appear to be reversing. Whether previous trends in skill and expertise will become re-established post-pandemic, or whether new trends will take hold, is not yet known.

Reviewing the Learning Objectives

After reading this chapter, you should:

- Be able to define the core concepts of skill, knowledge, and expertise and understand their connection to education.
- Understand that skill and expertise are socially constructed—shaped by social inequalities, campaigns, and culture.
- Know some of the ways in which scholars have tried to measure skill over time and have a sense that measuring skill is difficult.
- Understand that there is evidence of both deskilling and skill upgrading among workers.
- Know that a sizeable minority of Canadian workers are underemployed and overqualified in their jobs.
- Be aware of changing social evaluations of expertise.

Questions for Critical Thought

1. Marx, Weber, Foucault, and other social theorists provided explanations of workplace change that have implications for skill trends. Drawing on your knowledge of the theories reviewed in Chapter 2, what would these theorists predict about skill and autonomy in the labour market? To what extent does evidence about skill trends support or challenge their theories?
2. In the jobs you have held, are there any tacit skills that you and/or your coworkers developed to make your work easier? What were they, and how did they improve your ability to do your work?
3. Thinking about your own jobs, try to identify the job-relevant skills you have. Then classify these skills by type: for example, hard versus soft skills, or manual, cognitive, creative, technical, or social skills.
4. What implications does the skepticism surrounding expertise and science have for expert workers? Do you think they are experiencing deskilling? Under what conditions might this occur?

Annotated Additional Readings

Azocar, M. J., & Ferree, M. M. (2016). Engendering the sociology of expertise. *Sociology Compass*, *10*, 1079–1089.

This article argues for adopting an intersectional and gender lens when studying expertise.

Eyal, G. (2019). *The crisis of expertise*. Cambridge, UK: Polity Press.

This book explores the factors contributing to the recent, and seemingly growing, skepticism towards experts and expertise in Western societies.

Gatta, M., Boushey, H., & Appelbaum, E. (2009). High-touch and here-to-stay: Future skills demands in US low wage service occupations. *Sociology, 43*(5), 968–989.

This article explores skills in the context of gendered and racialized interactive service work.

Liu, Y., & Grusky, D. B. (2013). The payoff to skill in the third industrial revolution. *American Journal of Sociology, 118*(5), 1330–1374.

This article examines the distribution of skills in the American labour force and the payoffs to skill.

Related Websites

Government of Canada website for immigrants and refugees outlining occupations and skill requirements in Canada:

https://www.canada.ca/en/immigration-refugees-citizenship/services/immigrate-canada/express-entry/eligibility/find-national-occupation-code.html

United States website for O*NET documenting occupations and their skill characteristics:

https://www.onetonline.org/

UBC blog discussing Indigenous knowledge:

https://blogs.ubc.ca/traditionalknowledgetechnology/revaluation-of-indigenous-cultures/what-is-indigenous-traditional-knowledge/

Conference Board of Canada webpage discussing employability skills:

https://www.conferenceboard.ca/edu/employability-skills.aspx?AspxAutoDetectCookieSupport=1

8 Health, Well-Being, and Resistance

Learning Objectives

After reading this chapter, readers will:

- Be able to identify the characteristics of work that contribute to job satisfaction.
- Know what characteristics of work contribute to stress.
- Be aware that people respond to unpleasant work through a variety of responses, both individual and collective in nature.
- Comprehend the complex relationship between work and health: work contributes to well-being but can also undermine health.
- Understand which jobs are among the most dangerous in Canada and have a sense of the incidence of workplace injury, illness, and mortality in Canada.

Introduction

The impact of work on health and well-being is complex. On the one hand, people who work tend to be healthier and happier than those who do not. On the other hand, work is a source of stress, injury, and, for some, even death. Although it might be tempting to map these opposing outcomes onto a simple good-job/bad-job dichotomy, reality is not that straightforward. Well-paying, good jobs can be a source of stress and injury. Many routine, low-paying jobs can be satisfying and safe. Thus, it is important to look more closely at the factors contributing to stress and satisfaction on the job. It is also valuable to look at how workers react to work that is unpleasant and unsatisfying because workers do not passively acquiesce but often engage in multiple strategies of resistance—some collective and others individual. Through resistance, workers find ways to invest meaning and carve out autonomy in jobs in which both may be in short supply.

In Chapter 2, we saw that social theorists such as Karl Marx believed that work could be a means through which people exercised creativity and achieved fulfillment but that the way in which work was organized in a capitalist society stripped many workers of their creativity, turning them into drones, or, in Weber's (1946, p. 228) terms, "cogs in a machine" with an essentially "fixed route of march"—potentially resulting in alienation (Marx) and dehumanization (Weber). Although the world of work has changed in many ways since Marx and Weber were writing, recent scholars continue to highlight how the organization of work can influence our experiences. Moreover, researchers find that worker autonomy is a significant contributor to job satisfaction and potentially a factor mitigating workplace stress. The organization of work also has implications for workplace health and safety.

This chapter explores job satisfaction, job stress, work and health, and worker resistance, paying particular attention to the ways in which the structure of work affects workers and shapes their experiences.

Job Satisfaction

job satisfaction
An indicator measuring how satisfied workers report they are with their jobs

Surveys of workers frequently ask how satisfied they are with their jobs. Consistently, surveys find that most workers say they are "very satisfied" or "somewhat satisfied." For example, the 2016 *Changing Workplaces in a Knowledge Economy* (CWKE) survey of employed adult workers in Canada found that 81 per cent are very or somewhat satisfied. Statistics Canada (2020b) data similarly indicate that 83 per cent of Canadian workers aged 15 and over are satisfied. It may be the case that **job satisfaction** has declined over time. A Canadian survey from the early 1970s found that almost 90 per cent of Canadian workers found their jobs satisfying (Burstein, Tienharra, Hewson, & Warrander, 1975), and a 1997 survey found that 87 per cent were satisfied (Lowe, 2000, p. 55).[1] Regardless, the percentage of workers who find their work satisfying is generally high. What exactly does this mean?

When people indicate their job is satisfying, do they mean it is fulfilling? That they gain pleasure from their work? Or that their job is better than available alternatives or better than having no job at all? Researchers have no clear answers, but there is reason to think that "satisfied" does not mean "fulfilled and happy." In fact, a recent study found that three-quarters of workers were either actively looking for a different job or would consider one if recruited (CBC, 2018). Thus, many of those who agree they are satisfied with their jobs are actively looking for other jobs. How people feel about their jobs can be complex (Hodson, 1989). You might love what you do but feel underappreciated and underpaid. Or you could be thankful to have a job even when you are not enjoying it because of the economy. Our ratings of job satisfaction may be shaped by implicit comparisons with others or by our vision of our ideal job. Our satisfaction on any given day could also be influenced by recent work events: it might be higher after completing a project for which we are praised and lower when we are working overtime to meet a pressing deadline that seems out of reach.

In light of these considerations, most researchers do not put too much faith in job satisfaction ratings. However, measures of job satisfaction are valuable in at least two ways. First, they provide a measure against which we compare workers across jobs. Once we know that roughly 80 per cent of Canadian workers are satisfied, we can explore whether workers in specific occupations are more or less satisfied than average. For instance, the 2016 CWKE national survey had companion 2017 surveys of professional engineers and registered nurses in Ontario: 74 per cent of engineers and 68 per cent of nurses indicated they were satisfied with their jobs. Such findings open lines of research, raising questions about why some workers are less satisfied than other workers and what challenges nurses experience on the job that result in lower rates of satisfaction.[2]

[1] Others suggest that the rate of job satisfaction has recently increased (Conference Board of Canada, 2019).
[2] Data are drawn from the Changing Workplaces in the New Economy national survey and the companion engineering and nursing profession surveys, stored at the University of Toronto.

Second, we can learn a lot by exploring what job characteristics are positively or negatively correlated with job satisfaction. Understanding what organizational and work features shape satisfaction is important because job satisfaction reduces absenteeism and turnover and may increase job performance (Wang & Jing, 2018).

Contributors to Job Satisfaction

What work characteristics contribute to job satisfaction? Research has identified several—from autonomy and pay to work-life balance and trust in managers. Two characteristics that are among the most important are opportunities for interesting and self-directed work and positive social interactions. These intrinsic characteristics tend to be ranked above more extrinsic characteristics such as pay and benefits. People are more satisfied with their jobs when they have the opportunity to do work they find *interesting and diverse* (and learn new things) and when they can exercise *autonomy* in the conduct of work without having their every action closely monitored (Conference Board, 2019; Ross & Mirowsky, 1995; Wang & Jing, 2018). Furthermore, people are more likely to enjoy their jobs when they are provided opportunities for positive *social interactions* with, and support from, coworkers and superiors (Wallace & Lemaire, 2007). Conversely, when interactions are negative, toxic, or discriminatory, or if there are few opportunities for social interaction, workers are less satisfied (Wang & Jing, 2018). These research findings are consistent with Marx's arguments about worker alienation and the negative impact of declining autonomy and altered social relationships on workers labouring in a capitalist system.

While job qualities tend to be more strongly correlated to job satisfaction than rewards, *pay and benefits* are still important contributors to job satisfaction. People are more likely to be satisfied with their jobs when they feel their remuneration is fair (Wang & Jing, 2018; Levy-Garboua & Montmarquette, 2004). This may be especially true for men (Conference Board, 2019). Less tangible rewards such as *status* or a positive identity are also positively correlated with job satisfaction (Hoyle, 2001).

Work-life balance can be positively related to job satisfaction too. Workers who feel that their jobs allow them to have a life outside of work and to meet family obligations are more satisfied (Mas-Maschuca, Berbegal-Marabent, & Alegre, 2016). Workers, especially women, whose jobs offer work-life balance are more satisfied than others (Fang, Lee, Timming, & Fan, 2019; Conference Board, 2019). Those whose jobs require non-standard hours—including unpredictable hours or having to work evenings, weekends, and overnight—are less satisfied (Jamal & Badawi, 1995). These workers are not only forced to keep odd hours, but they may have less time to hang out with friends and family because of their schedules. Workers with small children may struggle to find daycare. These associated difficulties decrease job satisfaction.

Relationships with managers and supervisors are also important predictors of job satisfaction. Workers who believe they have the *support* of their superiors and coworkers are more satisfied (Wang & Jing, 2018). Related to this is social trust in managers: satisfied workers are more likely to report that they trust their managers and supervisors (Helliwell & Huang, 2011). Satisfaction has also been linked with opportunities to participate in decision-making and supervisors' willingness to accept worker input and recognize hard work (Conference Board, 2019).

Finally, research finds that workers experiencing rationalization and increasing workloads tend to be less satisfied than workers whose companies are not undergoing change to increase efficiencies and whose workloads are more manageable (Zeytinoglu et al., 2007). Taylorism and rationalization strategies to increase efficiencies at work not only reduce workers' satisfaction but also increase workplace stress. These factors may partially account for the lower job satisfaction among registered nurses in Ontario because they have experienced workload increases in recent years (Rhnima, Wils, Pousa, & Frigon, 2014; Zeytinoglu et al., 2007).

Which Workers are More Likely to Be Satisfied?

We can also use survey data on job satisfaction to compare across social categories. Are men more satisfied with their jobs than women, and do members of visible minorities have lower levels of satisfaction? Research has found some differences in satisfaction rates, but, on average, men and women tend to be equally satisfied. Some Canadian studies suggest that women are slightly more satisfied with their jobs than are men (Magee, 2015); however, US studies find the opposite (Conference Board, 2019). Furthermore, there is evidence that gender intersects with age to shape job satisfaction: younger women are more satisfied than younger men, but mid-life and older women tend to be less satisfied than men (Magee, 2015). Mid-career and older women may experience work-family conflict and stalled career progress, diminishing their job satisfaction. There are also gender differences in the factors contributing to job satisfaction. For women, job satisfaction is strongly shaped by coworkers, work-life balance, and workload; men's satisfaction is more closely tied to income and promotion opportunities (Conference Board, 2019).

Other research on job satisfaction and age finds that younger workers are less satisfied, on average (Statistics Canada, 2020b). This is not surprising given high rates of youth underemployment and concentration in entry-level jobs. Researchers suggest that older workers have either moved into more fulfilling, interesting roles over the course of their careers or they have adjusted their expectations and resigned themselves to accept what they have. Both paths may result in job satisfaction (Hodson & Sullivan, 1994). According to recent Statistics Canada (2020b) data, only 77 per cent of workers 15–24 report being satisfied with their jobs compared to 87 per cent of those aged 45–54.[3]

There is evidence of differences across ethnicity and immigration status. For example, Yap, Holmes, Hannam, & Cuker (2013) find that immigrants have lower job satisfaction than native-born Canadians, with visible-minority immigrants having lower satisfaction than other immigrants. Magee and Umamaheswar (2011) find that workers born in the Philippines and China are less satisfied, possibly because their jobs do not meet their expectations or desires. Immigrant job satisfaction may be especially low in the initial years post-migration, but there is some evidence that it increases with time spent in Canada (Wang & Jing, 2018). Immigrants who experience discrimination and unfair treatment, underemployment, a lack of organizational support, a lack of autonomy in the workplace, and fewer learning opportunities on the job are especially less satisfied than other workers (Wang & Jing, 2018).

There has been limited research on Indigenous and LGBTQI workers' satisfaction and well-being. Not surprisingly, research does find that LGBTQI-supportive policies in the workplace have a beneficial impact, reducing discrimination and improving worker well-being (Lloren & Parini, 2017). Recent research on Indigenous workers has highlighted

[3]In contrast, the Conference Board of Canada (2019) found that younger workers in the US had higher job satisfaction than older workers between 2015 and 2018.

Issues at Work

8.1 | Satisfaction and Jobs

When people look for jobs, they do not have the literature on workplace satisfaction and stress at their fingertips, but they nonetheless have a general sense of what intrinsic and extrinsic qualities they seek in a job: some autonomy and self-direction, good colleagues, sense of purpose or meaning. Researchers at the University of Chicago's National Opinion Research Center (NORC, 2007) have identified which jobs seem to have the highest job satisfaction rates, and most are jobs that involve helping people and that allow workers autonomy and/or creativity. Workers in the following jobs reported the highest levels of satisfaction: clergy/religious leaders, firefighters, and physical therapists, as well as education administrators, teachers, painters and sculptors, authors, and psychologists. In contrast, roofers, waiters, labourers, retail sales workers, packagers, and freight, stock and material handlers were among those reporting the lowest rates of job satisfaction. The latter workers tend to have little autonomy, and many experience high work demands and low levels of meaningful social interaction.

Does learning about the correlates of job satisfaction impact your own ideas about the jobs you would like to hold in the future or what careers to pursue? If so, how might you use this knowledge to shape your job search in the months and years to come?

that current workplace models of well-being are Westernized and do not take cultural differences into account (Overmars, 2019). Indigenous workers report valuing workplaces where their cultures are accepted and where there are opportunities to build relationships with people and communities; these characteristics increase their satisfaction and contribute to Indigenous workers' well-being (ibid.).

Workplace Stress

Satisfaction tends to be inversely correlated with stress. Sociologists define **stress** as "a state of tension produced by pressures or conflicting demands with which the person cannot adequately cope" (Jary & Jary, 2005b, p. 611). There are many features of work that induce stress, including close supervision, low levels of control and autonomy, hazardous working conditions, job insecurity, work-family conflict, and toxic colleagues.

stress "A state of tension produced by pressures or conflicting demands with which the person cannot adequately cope" (Jary & Jary, 2005b, p. 611)

Studies indicate that stress is fairly common among Canadian workers. For example, in a 2015 survey conducted by the *Globe and Mail*, 59 per cent of respondents said they felt stressed and that they found it difficult to balance their work and private lives (Livingston, 2015). Thus, it appears that a majority of Canadian workers find their jobs stressful and claim that work impacts their mental health negatively. Stressed workers more commonly report that job expectations are too demanding, work cultures are negative, and they do not trust their managers (ibid.). Stress is a major contributor to mental health issues (Howatt, 2018). One in five Canadian workers reports experiencing a mental health problem or illness (Morneau Shepell & Mental Health Commission of Canada, 2018). Stress and mental health problems are major causes of absenteeism and lost productivity (Howatt, 2018; Morneau Shepell & MHCC, 2018). Managers are often ill-prepared to cope with workers' mental health challenges adequately (Malachowski, Boydell, Sawchuk, & Kirsh, 2016).

Research on workplace stress has linked it to work characteristics and especially job demands, resources, and job control. Pioneering work in this area was done decades ago by Robert Karasek (1979). One might expect that workers in the most demanding jobs would experience the most stress and strain; however, Karasek (1979; Karasek & Theorell, 1990) argued this was not necessarily the case. Rather, he suggested, it was the combined impact of work demands and **job-decision latitude** that was important. Specifically, if a worker has high job demands but also the autonomy, or the latitude, to solve problems that arise, then they can cope. For example, high demands may be placed on surgeons, firefighters, and top managers, but given that these workers have the latitude to use their skills and knowledge to meet those demands, they are able to manage their stress levels. Indeed, high work demands may make work invigorating and fulfilling, without negatively impacting worker health. The truly disadvantaged are workers who have high demands but lack the autonomy to address those demands, according to Karasek. They are prone to exhaustion and depression. Workers subject to the control and demands of others—including personal support workers, agricultural workers, and wait staff, to name a few—may be particularly vulnerable to harmful workplace stress. Workers with low job demands (with or without autonomy) are not prone to workplace stress, according to Karasek (1979).

job decision latitude The extent to which workers experience high job demands as well as the autonomy or latitude to solve problems that arise

Karasek (Karasek & Theorell, 1990) refined and extended his model over time to include a role for social support and job insecurity. The literature on stress has long noted the important role of social support in mitigating stress (Thoits, 1995); support from friends, family members, coworkers, and bosses can reduce workers' stress. In contrast, job insecurity exacerbates stress. Karasek has found a lot of support for his model, documenting high-demand, low job decision latitude impacts on both mental and physical health over time. Subsequent researchers have elaborated Karasek's model. The job-demands-resources model sees workplace stress as a function of job pressure and job resources. The latter include not only workplace control but autonomy, challenge, and other rewards that might allow workers the ability to cope with work-related pressures effectively (Marmot, 1994; Schieman, 2013). Lower-status workers may be particularly vulnerable (Marmot, 1994).

More recent research, however, has begun to raise questions about these models. Reported rates of worker stress have climbed—especially among those workers Karasek identified as more immune to stress from high demands, such as professionals and managers. Such developments have prompted the **stress of higher status model**. This explanation posits that some job resources might actually *increase* job pressures (Schieman, 2013; Schieman, Kurashina Whitestone, & Van Gundy, 2006). Schieman and colleagues define job pressures as having more work tasks than can be reasonably done in the time available (Schieman, 2013). While some job-related resources might enable workers to stay on top of job pressures, certain resources—like job authority—bring additional job pressures. In this manner, higher-status workers with high job resources may actually have more job pressures than others.

stress of higher status model Higher-status, high-demand jobs may entail resources that increase, rather than decrease, job pressures

There is empirical support for both the *stress of higher status model* and the *job demands-resources model* (Schieman, 2013). More specifically, while professionals and executives (who have higher-status jobs) experience more stress, autonomy lessens those pressures—as Karasek and others indicate. Nevertheless, high-status workers with challenging work and job authority actually experience increased pressures—consistent with the stress of higher status model. Job authority increases job pressures instead of mitigating them.

Schieman's work is helpful in understanding high stress rates among high-status workers. Other factors, like work environments, also contribute to the stress experienced by educated and high-skill workers. Research has found that rationalization and work intensification in these fields may be reducing professionals' autonomy while increasing the amount of work they need to do (Konzelmann, Wilkinson, & Mankelow, 2011; Ogbonna & Harris, 2004; Adams, Lugsden, Chase, & Arber, 2000). Work intensification can lead to stress as the demands on workers increase while the time available to do those tasks does not. Workers in these situations then end up extending their work hours, bringing work home, and potentially exacerbating work-family conflict, leading to more stress. Work cultures that stress long hours and high commitment may further foster stress (Schieman et al., 2006).

The impact of high status may vary by gender. For example, researchers have found that women with job authority are particularly prone to stress; indeed, evidence indicates that they are more likely than women without authority to have depressive symptoms (Pudrovska & Karraker, 2014). Women with job authority are also more likely to experience depression than are men when they are under-compensated (Schieman, Taylor, Narisada, & Pudrovska, 2020).

Although high-status workers may be vulnerable to stress, they are not alone. Research shows that workers in helping professions (including paramedics, firefighters, police officers, and others such as social workers and nurses) can experience traumatic events and "compassion fatigue" that contribute to stress and post-traumatic stress disorder (PTSD) that can result in devastating effects on their long-term mental health and well-being (Conference Board of Canada, 2015; Bikos, 2020). On a smaller level, studies show that women who work in part-time and casual jobs are vulnerable to stress and associated health problems (Zeytinoglu, Seaton, Lillevik, & Moruz, 2005). Moreover, across occupations, stress has been linked with job characteristics including job insecurity (Glavin & Young, 2017), a lack of supportive supervisors and colleagues (Wallace & Lemaire, 2007), non-standard work hours (Jamal & Badawi, 1995), competing demands (Lowe & Northcott, 1988), and poor relationships with coworkers and managers (Livingston, 2015). Managerial (in)competence has been linked to stress (Shuey, Gordon, & McMullin, 2018). Other work environment contributors to stress include the following: lack of training, lack of appreciation, lack of opportunities, isolation, toxic work environments, and exposure to unsafe working conditions (Canadian Centre for Occupational Health and Safety [CCOHS], 2020).

Workplace stress is important because it contributes to both mental and physical health problems among workers. According to the Mental Health Commission of Canada (Morneau Shepell and the MHCC, 2018), 500,000 Canadian employees are unable to work every week because of mental health issues. Among the most common concerns are depression and anxiety. Stress and mental health challenges can result in illnesses and other physical ailments that also reduce workers' availability to work and negatively affect their well-being. Unfortunately, workers with mental health challenges can rarely access workers' compensation (Lippel & Lanctôt, 2014).

Resistance at Work

Although a lot of workers say they are satisfied, a notable minority (perhaps 20 per cent, or one in five) are not, and research shows that a majority of workers find their work stressful. How do workers cope with unpleasant work? Strategies may be collective or individual and range from avoiding work, to resistance and retaliation, to efforts to bring about positive change.

Unions

Collective forms of resistance include forming unions and occupational associations to fight for workers' shared interests. Unionization was discussed briefly in both Chapters 3 and 4. Workers have traditionally unionized to fight poor working conditions, low wages, and violations of their rights (Walters & Mishel, 2003; Roscigno & Hodson, 2004). Research shows that unions have many positive effects for workers. They raise wages and improve compensation, including benefits. They bring their workers better health care benefits, as well as better pensions and more vacation time. Unions also have an impact on the wages of non-unionized workers; the latter earn more in industries where unions are common (Walters & Mishel, 2003). Moreover, unions fight for safer workplaces and family-friendly work policies (Canada Labour Congress, 2020). Unions tend to be democratic and responsive to the concerns of their members, but generally they fight for fairness and the protection of workers' rights. Unions can contribute to health and well-being not only by fostering safer working environments but by protecting workers' rights. For example, Canadian workers have the right to refuse unsafe work (Canadian Union of Public Employees, 2014), but this right is more often exercised by unionized workers (Smith, 2000). The unionized may be more aware of their rights and feel more confident exercising them, knowing that they have union support behind them.

Nonetheless, there are forces undermining unions' power to defend the rights of their workers, including outsourcing—sending work previously done by unionized workers to other companies that employ non-unionized workers at lower pay (Boivin, 2017)—as well as policy change and market trends conferring greater power and flexibility upon employers (Adanhounme & Lévesque, 2019). While unions continue to fight for workers' rights and support their well-being, their influence appears to have lessened over time. Moreover, as we saw in Chapter 4, the majority of Canadian workers are *not* unionized: only 28 per cent of Canadian workers belong to unions. These trends may encourage workers to organize outside of unions, via social media and other mechanisms, to mobilize for positive workplace change and fair remuneration (see for example, fightfor15.org). Alternatively, workers might pursue individual strategies when faced with unpleasant or stressful work environments (Roscigno & Hodson, 2004).

turnover rate The rate at which people leave work voluntarily or involuntarily

voluntary turnover This occurs when people leave a job because they want to do so

involuntary turnover When people are forced to leave a job when they would rather not

Individual Strategies: Turnover, Absenteeism, Presenteeism

When workers do not like their jobs, they might quit. When jobs are scarce and the economy poor, workers may be reluctant to leave their jobs until they find a replacement. In better times, more workers take their chances and seek more satisfying work (Conference Board of Canada, 2019). Statisticians calculate the turnover rate for various sectors. The **turnover rate** is the percentage of workers in the labour force who annually leave a job. Some distinguish between **voluntary** and **involuntary turnover**: simply stated, the former represents people quitting while the latter reflects those who have been fired. In 2018, the turnover rate in Canada was about 16 per cent (Canadian HR Reporter, 2018), meaning that 16 per cent of Canadian workers left a job either voluntarily or involuntarily that year. Canada's rate was among the highest reported in the world. Turnover rates vary by industry and are typically highest in retail, construction, and professional services and lowest in utilities, transportation, and education (Conference Board of Canada, 2014).

Quitting a job may be a drastic reaction to unpleasant work and one that is potentially costly. Workers experiencing unpleasant or stressful work may also respond through **absenteeism**. There are many reasons why workers do not show up for work, including injury, illness, disability, the need to care for a loved one, or even just taking what some call a "mental health day"—a needed break from work to minimize stress. Although only the latter may seem directly related to unpleasant work, workers experiencing stress are prone to illness. Those with less control over their work have higher rates of absenteeism (Marmot, 1994). Table 8.1 shows absenteeism rates over the past few years in Canada. Here, we can see that absences are higher in the public sector, where policies and unionization typically allow paid sick days.[4] Without such policies, people may drag themselves into work despite illness, potentially spreading their illness to others. Indeed, the lack of paid sick-days was linked to the spread of COVID-19 among Ontario's essential workers in the fall of 2020 and winter 2021: low-paid workers doing essential work had little choice but to come to work, even as symptoms began to manifest, because they could not afford time off (CBC, 2020a).[5]

absenteeism Missing days of work

Presenteeism occurs when people show up for work when they are not at their best—due to injury, illness, chronic stress, or another condition. Although they are present, they are not physically or mentally prepared to function to their best abilities. Business scholars suggest this can be costly for businesses because of lost productivity (Hemp, 2004). Presenteeism is another way in which stress and poor working conditions can negatively affect workers and businesses. Presenteeism may be a coping mechanism for workers: they continue to earn a paycheck but invest less in their jobs to minimize stress and strain.

presenteeism When people show up for work when they are not at their best—due to injury, illness, chronic stress, or another condition—and hence cannot function to their best abilities

Individual Resistance: Ritualism, Theft, and Other Forms of Workplace Misbehaviour

Somewhat similar to presenteeism is **ritualism**, which occurs when workers are disengaged at work to the point that they are largely just going through the motions. Workers who are working ritualistically will do the bare minimum at work, without investing personal

ritualism Going through the motions at work; following the basic rules without any additional effort

TABLE 8.1 Absenteeism: Days Lost per Worker (for Illness, Disability, Personal or Family Reasons) across Time in Canada

	2015	2016	2017	2018	2019
	Number of Days				
Public Sector	12.7	13.5	13.5	14.6	14.6
Private Sector	7.8	8.3	8.4	8.6	9.0

Note: Includes full-time paid workers only.

Source: Statistics Canada 2020c.

[4]The Conference Board of Canada (2014) provides a different calculation that has only full-time workers missing between six and seven days a year on average.

[5]The Ontario government passed legislation allowing workers a few paid sick days, during the pandemic in the spring of 2021.

energy, commitment, or substantial effort. This is a mild form of resistance, adopted by workers who have lost interest in their jobs. Many workers, however, engage in more overt resistance. Like the administrative assistants who refuse to make coffee for their bosses or the service workers who resist sticking closely to assigned scripts, workers may refuse to do tasks they find demeaning, unpleasant, or not in their interests. Such resistance can be risky because workers who do not comply with orders from superiors could be reprimanded or face dismissal. However, deliberately avoiding aspects of work deemed unpleasant may actually increase job satisfaction and reduce stress. It may also allow workers to exercise autonomy, albeit covertly.

workplace misbehaviour Behaviour that intentionally goes against the rules and that is not in the best interests of the employing organization

Workplace misbehaviour is also regarded as a form of resistance (van den Broek & Dundon, 2012; Watts, 2018). The term "misbehaviour" is a sweeping one, usually used to refer to any workers' intentional behaviour that is not in the best interests of their employing organization. It can range from fairly benign behaviours like checking social media, surfing the Internet, and engaging in online shopping while at work, to loafing ("goofing off" at work), employee theft, and even sabotage.

Miltsov's (2018) examination of personal Internet use at work suggests that it is common, especially among younger workers. Workers with less autonomy and those not satisfied with their jobs are more likely to use the Internet for personal reasons at work; however, Miltsov (2018) cautions against seeing "cyberloafing" as an overt act of resistance or sabotage. Indeed, meanings of personal Internet use seem to vary by age, with younger workers regarding it as "everyday behaviour" while older workers see it as a form of misbehaviour.

Although from a managerial viewpoint personal Internet use might be regarded as "time theft" whereby workers misuse paid work time (Snider, 2001), from workers' points of view, such activities are simply breaks from work that may not negatively impact productivity. A cynic might say that such activities do not reflect resistance but rather demonstrate laziness. The fact that there is something more than laziness involved, however, can be seen in studies that show that misbehaviour appears to be more common where workers have less autonomy and when they want to be more involved in decision-making than they are (Watts, 2018). Moreover, critics of the misbehaviour literature question why there is so much focus on what employees do at work, while the behaviour of managers and others in

Source: © Shutterstock/Monkey Business Images

While some companies have attempted to curb workers' use of the Internet for personal reasons during work hours through monitoring software or by blocking social media sites, others have cautioned that regular breaks are essential for maintaining productivity and that creating an untrusting work environment risks increasing employee resistance.

positions of authority is far more likely to have dire consequences at the workplace, environmentally, and in society more broadly (Ackroyd & Thompson, 2016; Watts, 2018).

Employee theft can also be an act of resistance, although at times theft is just a crime of opportunity (Bonet, 2008; Ehrhardt Mustaine & Tewksbury, 2002). In the past, researchers estimated that one-quarter to one-third of employees engaged in theft in the workplace (Hollinger & Clark, 1983; Ehrhardt Mustaine & Tewksbury, 2002). Examples of theft can include getting paid more hours than were worked (here we see the idea of time theft again) but also taking workplace supplies home, undercharging friends and colleagues, and outright stealing. Some workers justify theft of money or supplies as compensation for low wages or bad treatment (Ehrhardt Mustaine & Tewksbury, 2002; Vaz, 1984; Lundberg & Karlsson, 2011). For others it is a game, enlivening otherwise dull and routine work (Lundberg & Karlsson, 2011). Some see supplies and discounts for friends as simply a perk of working certain jobs. That is, workers may not actually regard these activities as theft but rather as part of their compensation for work completed.

Other forms of resistance involve workplace games. Playful exchanges with colleagues and coworkers can make the day pass quickly; however, games can also involve productivity races to maximize output (Burawoy, 1979), or entail strategies to minimize onerous work and take shortcuts (Koski & Järvensivu, 2010). In this manner, games may or may not result in lost productivity. Games provide a way of enlivening sometimes dull work and provide opportunities for social interaction. They also provide an opportunity for workers to take control of production and exercise some autonomy (Koski & Järvensivu, 2010). Even those games that involve taking time away from work do not always undermine productivity if they provide a break for workers and enable them to work effectively in other respects.

A classic study of workplace games comes from researcher Donald Roy (1959). Roy worked a routine job in a manufacturing facility. He found that workers in his small workgroup broke up the day with various rituals and breaks. For instance, "peach time" involved a daily mid-morning snack break when the workers would share peaches. It was followed by "banana time" when one worker would surreptitiously steal a banana from a coworker's lunch box and gobble it down, despite the latter's protests. Roy argues that these strange, daily rituals of sharing and stealing fruit provided workers with opportunities for social interaction and broke up otherwise boring workdays, making it easier for workers to cope with their unpleasant jobs and to continue to work productively. When the games were disrupted because of a vacation or a rift between two workers, the workday was long and miserable. Increased surveillance at work has likely decreased workers' opportunities to play games on the job, so they may have to find other ways to resist unpleasant work.

Sabotage is one of the most dramatic means through which workers resist unpleasant work. **Sabotage** has been defined as working in a manner that slows production or lowers the quality of the product. The term originally applied to workers who broke the machines they worked with in order to disrupt production and protest workplace change. Sabotage may give workers a sense of psychological relief and provide them with opportunities to wrest back control of the labour process. It may be a response to bad leadership, disrespectful treatment, and conflict with managers as well as poor workplace organization (Roscigno & Hodson, 2004). In the early 1990s, Martin Sprouse (1992) collected stories from workers across the US labour market about sabotage on the job: From the retail workers who stole and hid shopping carts and dressed Barbie

sabotage Intentional destruction of employers' property or deliberate hindering of work operations

and Ken in each other's clothes, to the computer programmer who wrote a program to collapse his company's computer network in response to unrealistic deadlines and poor pay. In this light, sabotage can be perceived as efforts by workers to resist unpleasant work, carve out some autonomy, and even take revenge on employers who have taken advantage of them.

Although individual strategies of resistance typically provide workers with some relief from alienating work, they rarely result in any positive change to working conditions. In several instances, they do not even result in lost productivity but may actually increase it by allowing workers to "blow off steam," forge relationships with colleagues, and, at times, keep engaged in what they are doing. Managers have demonstrated concern over employee misbehaviour; however, as Ackroyd and Thompson (2016) suggest, this concern may be misplaced. Several of workers' activities have little negative impact on employing organizations compared to mismanagement by those in positions of influence. Managerial misconduct has received scant attention in the literature.

Work and Health

selection effect In research, when some types of people are more likely to respond than others based on their characteristics

Research has established a relationship between work and health. People who work are healthier on average than people who do not work (Ross & Mirowsky, 1995). Several different explanations have been advanced to explain this relationship. First, this connection between work and health likely reflects what researchers call a "**selection effect.**" That is, workers may report better health than non-workers for the simple reason that healthy people are more likely to work. Nevertheless, researchers have suggested that more is going on here. A second explanation, then, points to the material rewards workers gain from working. Working provides us with income and often benefits that help us to support a healthier lifestyle—including, for example, stable housing, the purchase of healthy food, and medication. A third explanation is that there are intrinsic benefits to working—for instance, satisfaction, stimulation, social interaction, identity, and/or status—that contribute to well-being.

There is some evidence for all three explanations. It is certainly the case that individuals with health problems are less likely to be in the labour force than those who are healthy. At the same time, there are concrete extrinsic and intrinsic benefits associated with working that have been shown to contribute to health (Ross & Mirowsky, 1995; Marmot, 1994).

As we saw in the discussion of work and stress, the character of work can be crucial in shaping outcomes. Work that confers autonomy and lower work demands may improve overall health, while work that entails excessive demands or is precarious has negative implications for health. Recent research has highlighted the negative impact of precarious work on health outcomes (Lippel, Johnstone, & Baril-Gingras, 2017; McGann, Moss, & White, 2012; McGann, White, & Moss, 2016). Job status is also important: those in more subordinate jobs experience worse health outcomes and higher mortality rates (Marmot, 1994). Workplace discrimination also negatively impacts physical and emotional health (Pavalko, Mossakowski, & Hamilton. 2003). Moreover, health status at work varies by gender, race, age, Indigeneity, and immigration status (as we will see later in the chapter) (D'Arcy, 1998). Not everyone has equal opportunities for safe and healthy work.

Research has also documented the negative impact of unemployment on health—on both an individual level and a societal level. Individuals who experience long-term unemployment are prone to depression, stress, and poverty, all of which have deleterious effects on health and well-being (Burman, 1988; Ballantyne, Casey, O'Hagan, & Vienneau, 2016). On a societal level, higher rates of unemployment decrease societal health. For example, one 20th-century American study found that an increase in the national unemployment rate of 1 per cent sustained over six years was associated with 37,000 deaths, including 920 suicides and 650 homicides, not to mention the negative mental health impact (Bluestone & Harrison, 1982).

Occupational Health and Safety

Already in this chapter, we have seen that work enhances health but that work can also be detrimental to health and well-being. Working can cause physical ailments and injuries, and it can expose us to viruses and other illnesses. In an average year, more than 700 Canadian workers—and many more around the world—are hurt badly enough on the job to miss time at work, every single day (AWCBC, 2018). Work can also expose us to toxins that contribute to work-related illnesses. Furthermore, every year almost 1000 Canadians die on the job.

The good news is that the general trend in workplace injury and mortality is downward. However, rates are still high, and there is evidence that official rates underestimate the full extent of workplace injuries and deaths. Still, there is reason to believe that policies implemented to make workplaces safer—including workers' right to refuse unsafe work, WHMIS (Workplace Hazardous Material Information System) training, and prohibitions against smoking in the workplace—have helped to improve workers' physical wellness on the job. For example, anti-smoking legislation not only reduces workers' risks of cancer from second-hand smoke but also lowers secondary health effects such as heart attacks (American Lung Association, 2020).

Workplace Injuries

Workplace injuries are variable in severity and nature. Survey data suggest that as many as 20 per cent of Canadian workers experience a work-related injury annually (Nowrouzi-Kia, Baig, Li, Casole, & Chai, 2019). Workers may experience many types of injuries, including strains from overexertion, injury from contact with objects and equipment, falls, assaults, transportation accidents, exposure to harmful substances, and cuts from working with sharp instruments (AWCBC, 2018). Even sedentary office workers can experience back strains and repetitive strain injuries (RSIs). RSIs are defined as injuries or strains felt in muscles, nerves, and tendons from performing a narrow range of motions repeatedly (NHS, 2020; Ergonomic Trends, 2020). They are usually felt in the wrists, as well as fingers, forearms, and shoulders. Workers on assembly lines, cashiers, and workers on computers all day long (from administrative to information technology workers) are particularly prone to these injuries, which appear to be on the rise (Ergonomic Trends, 2020). Some studies suggest that between one in four and one in two office workers who use computers extensively present RSI symptoms (ibid.). Women are slightly more likely than men to be affected by RSIs (likely because of the nature of their work and their responsibility for domestic tasks, which use some of the same muscles and tendons [ibid.]). Younger workers can also experience RSIs; these injuries are not simply experienced by older workers. RSIs can lead to substantial lost work time and decreased productivity.

workplace injuries
Injuries that occur on the job

On average, men experience more injuries on the job than do women because they are more likely to be employed in jobs requiring physical labour in sectors where injuries are likely to occur, including trades, transport, and primary industries. The Association of Workers' Compensation Boards of Canada (AWCBC, 2018) reports that 60 per cent of workers with lost-time claims are men. Still, a sizeable number of women are injured on the job badly enough to miss time at work. Health care is a female-dominated sector characterized by high injury rates (AWCBC, 2018). Women are also well represented among food counter and kitchen workers, among whom injury claims are also common. Provincial occupational health and safety boards review claims for workplace injury compensation, and they promote workplace safety (Lanoie, 1992). Only some workplace injuries result in a successful compensation claim.

Youth are vulnerable to workplace injuries. Young workers are at risk because they tend to have less experience, training, and preparation, which means they have less knowledge of workplace safety and procedures and are likely unfamiliar with equipment and machinery (WorksafeBC, 2019). The Ontario Ministry of Labour, Training and Skills Development (2016) explains that "workers new to a job are three times more likely to be injured during the first month on a job than more experienced workers." Young workers can also be more likely than some others to work in dangerous jobs (WorksafeBC, 2019). Still, according to the AWCBC (2018), more claims for injury compensation are filed by workers over 50.

Injuries can have negative, long-term implications for workers, leading to disability, which inhibits their ability to work and leads to negative economic and social outcomes, including poverty (Ballantyne et al., 2016). Workers impacted by an injury on the job can find it difficult to access workers' compensation. In fact, many injuries—roughly 50 per cent—are never reported (Thompson, 2007). The system is set up in a manner that discourages reporting by employers and to some extent employees and physicians (ibid.). Workplaces that report more injuries are required to contribute more to fund worker compensation boards. As a result, companies engage in "claims management" to discourage workers from filing claims and fighting claims when filed (Thomason & Pozzebon, 2002).

Occupational Diseases

occupational diseases Illnesses that are acquired while working through on-the-job exposure

Occupational Diseases are health problems caused by exposure to a health hazard in the workplace (WorksafeBC, 2020; World Health Organization, 2020). Such hazards can include, but are not restricted to, the following: viruses, toxins and poisons, dust, gas, noise, radiation, extremes in temperature and air pressure. Among the most common workplace diseases are asthma, COPD (chronic obstructive pulmonary disease), and contact dermatitis (Bepko & Mansalis, 2016); other diseases include cancer, cardiovascular diseases, reproductive diseases, allergies, and cognitive disorders (Prevent Occupational Disease, 2019). Many work-related diseases, such as cancer, have "multiple causes, where factors in the work environment may play a role, together with other risk factors, in the development of such diseases" (World Health Organization, 2020). As a result, some work-related diseases are not recognized as such. For workplace insurance boards to accept a claim for a work-related disease, the illness must first be recognized as an occupational disease, and a worker must demonstrate that their illness is the result of current or past

A CLOSER LOOK

8.2 | Occupational Diseases and WSIB Claims

In a series of articles, *The Toronto Star* exposed the horrendous history of occupational illnesses experienced by workers at a Peterborough General Electric plant. Workers had been exposed to "more than 3,000 toxic chemicals, including at least 40 known or suspected to cause cancer" over a period of decades (Mojtehedzadeh & Monsebraaten, 2017). In fact they "routinely handled toxic substances with their bare hands and were offered little in the way of protective gear" (ibid.). As a result of this exposure, many workers became ill, developing cancers and a range of other illnesses later in life. Hundreds filed claims, but many were denied because of "lack of proof" that their illnesses were work-related, despite decades of reports suggesting that the plant was not upholding safety standards.

This case, also recounted in the documentary *Town of Widows*, not only captures workers' vulnerability to occupational diseases but shows how difficult it is for workers exposed to carcinogens in the workplace to receive compensation.

employment (WorksafeBC, 2020). Since many occupational diseases manifest only years after exposure, proving that the illness you have is the result of your employment, and not any other exposure, can be a challenge. The World Health Organization (2020) has called for improvements in the "diagnosis, reporting and registration of occupational diseases."

Because most of the data on occupational diseases come from accepted claims—and it is difficult to prove claims of occupational illnesses—it is not easy to determine how common such illnesses are. The COVID-19 pandemic provided an extreme example of how viruses can spread within workplaces and negatively affect workers on a large scale. Claims for workplace-contracted COVID-19 had reached 26,000 by fall of 2020. About 20,000 of these claims were granted compensation (CBC, 2020b). However, this

Source: © Aleksandar Malivuk/Shutterstock

The COVID-19 virus became a major factor in occupational health and safety in 2020, with front-line workers like grocery store cashiers becoming particularly vulnerable. Multiple workers at major chains like Loblaws spoke out against workplace practices that seemed designed to protect profits and customers over employees.

TABLE 8.2 Work-Related Fatalities and Lost-Time Injuries, 2017

	Lost-Time Injuries	Injury Fatalities	Illness Fatalities
Alberta	26,328	80	86
British Columbia	52,296	71	87
Manitoba	14,313	3	14
New Brunswick	4,708	7	8
Newfoundland and Labrador	3,368	5	20
Nova Scotia	6,148	2	12
NWT/Nunavut	912	3	1
Ontario	59,529	76	215
PEI	1,061	2	0
Quebec	73,879	62	168
Saskatchewan	8,596	14	13
Yukon	487	1	1
Total (Canada)	251,625	326	625

Source: Tucker & Keefe, 2019.

virus was highly visible. Estimates suggest that perhaps 69 per cent or more of workplace illnesses and injuries are not even reported (Bepko & Mansalis, 2016). Canadian data indicate that there were more than 30,000 lost-time claims for illness in 2018 (AWCBC, 2018); however, these numbers likely represent only a fraction of work-related illnesses. The costs associated with these incidents in terms of health care burden and lost productivity is substantial. In a pandemic year, such as 2020, the costs are staggering.

Work-Related Fatalities

An estimated 2.3 million people globally die from occupational injuries and illnesses every year (Takala et al., 2014). The majority of these deaths result from occupational diseases (Takala et al., 2014; Rushton, 2017). According to Canadian statistics—which come from provincial workplace safety board claims—approximately 1000 Canadian workers die on the job every year. There were 951 workplace deaths in 2017: 625 from occupational diseases and 326 from occupational injuries (Tucker & Keefe, 2019). Table 8.2 shows a breakdown of these workplace deaths by province, as well as figures on workplace injuries that resulted in workers missing work.

The vast majority of workers who die on the job, or because of acknowledged workplace diseases, are men: 97 per cent in 2018 (AWCBC, 2018). Men are overrepresented in construction, manufacturing, transportation, mining, and agriculture where workplace injuries are most common (ibid.). Most of the workers affected were older (in part because it can take a while for occupational diseases to manifest). Still, it is worth noting that women also experience workplace injuries and disease, and they appear to have been particularly vulnerable to exposure to COVID-19 given the kind of work that they do (St Denis, 2020). Women are also vulnerable to violence in the workplace, especially Indigenous and minority women.

The leading causes of injury leading to workplace death include the following (AWCBC, 2018):

- physical reaction to exposure to hazardous substance
- driving, transportation
- contact with objects or equipment
- falls, slips, and trips
- overexertion
- violence at the hands of persons or animals
- fires and explosions

The leading causes of deaths due to illness include cancer, breathing problems, and cardio-vascular illnesses (Bepko and Mansalis, 2016; AWCBC, 2018), to name only a few.

Official statistics are concerning enough, but as noted earlier, there are strong reasons to believe that official statistics underestimate workplace illnesses, injuries, and fatalities. Bittle, Chen, and Hebert (2018) explain that only workers whose deaths have been accepted as deserving of compensation count towards the official statistics. Some deaths do not result in claims, and not all claims are accepted. Self-employed workers and those in the "shadow economy" are not likely to be counted. Workers who are not eligible to file a claim, including agricultural workers in some provinces, are also excluded. Bittle et al.'s (2018) estimate suggests that true calculations of occupational deaths in Canada may be almost 10 times more than official statistics suggest: their calculations find more than 9000 occupational deaths annually. Their numbers include deaths by workers doing illegal work, work-related suicides, and, somewhat controversially, commuter deaths when people die on their way to or from work. Although some might contend their calculations are over-inflated, their analyses are valuable in revealing that work-related fatalities are far more numerous than official statistics suggest. They remind us that even in our modern knowledge economy, work can be dangerous.

To conclude, recent research on work and health raises questions about workplace change and its impact on health and well-being. We would like to think that workers today are healthier than in the past, but that is not necessarily the case. The COVID-19 pandemic reveals how working can expose us to unanticipated hazards and how risks are unevenly distributed. Globalization brings new challenges respecting the spread of illness around the world. Rising precarity, high work demands, and workplace change exacerbate stress and create additional health risks. There is a limit to what workers can do to protect their own health and well-being on the job: unions' power is limited, and individual strategies do not effect broader change. Some health hazards can only be dealt with by broader governmental and intergovernmental agencies or broader community supports (as in Indigenous communities). Scholars have critiqued governments for their failure to regulate work effectively and to provide ample protections for workers (Lippel et al., 2017; Robinson & Smallman, 2006). These are all issues that became clearer during the COVID-19 pandemic and issues that workers, employers, and state actors will continue to grapple with in the years to come.

Global Perspectives

Box 8.3 | Viruses, Illnesses, and Work

The global COVID-19 pandemic drew attention to how viruses can spread through workplaces and work. In an effort to delay and delimit the spread of the virus, many countries around the world closed workplaces, schools, public spaces, and regional and national borders. When possible, workers were asked to work from home (Farrer, 2020; Centers for Disease Control [CDC], 2020). Some essential workers, like health care, grocery store, and delivery workers, worked tirelessly through the crisis, putting their own health at risk and increasing their chances of contracting and even dying from the disease. Evidence suggests that women, immigrants, low-income, Black and other visible minority workers were particularly at risk of being exposed to the virus on the job due to their high participation in health care, and long-term care, manufacturing and distribution, and in low-income, high-touch jobs (such as in the grocery and cleaning sectors) (St Denis, 2020; Choi, Denice, Haan, & Zajacova, 2021).

The spread of the virus through human contact raises concerns about workplaces as incubators and highlights how the lack of protections for vulnerable workers leaves them (and by extension everyone else) at risk. The pandemic also exposed the inability of existing policies to handle virus outbreaks and widespread worker illness. Governments had to intervene and implement extraordinary measures that altered how we live and work. The crisis not only drew attention to the health vulnerabilities for certain groups of workers (such as personal support workers, grocery workers, health care workers) but economic vulnerabilities. Hundreds of thousands of workers lost their jobs; many more had their hours reduced. Many of the most vulnerable workers do not have the option of working from home, and quarantine itself can be economically devastating. Many workers did not have access to paid sick days.

Generally, the pandemic revealed that all workers are potentially at risk for illness spread through contact at work, but it also laid bare the vulnerability of low-paid, precarious workers (including PSWs and migrant workers, among others) and health care workers to illness and disease (Stanford, 2020).

Reviewing the Learning Objectives

Now that you have read this chapter, you should

- Be able to identify the characteristics of work that contribute to job satisfaction.
- Know what characteristics of work contribute to stress.
- Be aware that people respond to unpleasant work through a variety of strategies, both individual and collective in nature.
- Comprehend the complex relationship between work and health: work contributes to well-being but can also undermine health.
- Understand which jobs are among the most dangerous in Canada and have a sense of the incidence of workplace injury, illness, and mortality in Canada.

Questions for Critical Thought

1. Do you think access to work that does not endanger health and offers opportunities for satisfaction is a right or a privilege? If it is a privilege, who deserves the privilege?
2. Workplace stress may be increasing. Do you think it has become more of a concern because of workplace change, broader social change, or both? What factors contribute to workplace stress?

3. How does access to satisfying, healthy work reflect and reproduce broader social inequalities?
4. How do you think the COVID-19 epidemic might influence government policy and workplace practices in the years to come?

Annotated Additional Readings

Marmot M. G. (1994). Social differentials in health within and between populations. *Daedulus, 123,* 197–216.

This article summarizes the findings of some of the classic Whitehall Studies, which revealed the impact of organizational position and status on health outcomes.

Pudrovska, T., & Karraker, A. (2014). Gender, job authority, and depression. *Journal of Health and Social Behavior, 55*(4), 424–441. Retrieved from https://doi.org/10.1177/0022146514555223.

This article reveals that women workers with job authority are more likely to be depressed than are men in similar positions because of gendered workplace structures.

Sprouse, M. (Ed.). (1992). *Sabotage in the American workplace: Anecdotes of dissatisfaction, mischief and revenge*. San Francisco: Pressure Drop Press.

This book provides first-person accounts of sabotage at work.

Ross, C. E., & Mirowsky, J. (1995). Does employment affect health? *Journal of Health and Social Behavior, 36*(3), 230–243.

Classic study documenting the impact of work on health.

Related Websites

Canadian Centre for Occupational Health and Safety webpage devoted to young workers:

https://www.ccohs.ca/youngworkers

Prevent Occupational Disease:

https://www.preventoccdisease.ca/en/index.html

Center for Social Epidemiology: Work Stress:

unhealthywork.org

Canada Life, work strategies for mental health:

https://www.workplacestrategiesformentalhealth.com

9 Occupational Segregation

Learning Objectives

After reading this chapter, readers will:

- Know what occupational segregation is and why it is a significant, enduring characteristic of the labour market.
- Understand that there are different types of occupational segregation.
- Understand that there are multiple causes of occupational segregation.
- Have a sense of the consequences of occupational segregation.

Introduction

There are a plethora of jobs and occupations spread across a variety of industries in the Canadian labour market. However, the distribution of Canadian workers across these jobs is far from random. Rather, there is evidence of clustering across gender, race, and ethnicity, especially. We have seen evidence of this clustering in earlier chapters. For instance, Chapter 3 highlighted that the work done by men and women historically differed and noted variations too by race and Indigeneity. Chapter 5 also mentioned men's and women's concentration in certain occupations. Researchers call this kind of clustering **occupational segregation**: the unequal distribution of people across occupations depending on their social characteristics. Despite changing social attitudes and rising penalties for employment discrimination, occupational segregation is a stubbornly persistent characteristic of the Canadian labour market. It is also common in other countries around the world (Chang, 2004; Jarman, Blackburn, & Racko, 2012).

occupational segregation
This occurs when people who differ by some marker (gender, race, disability status, sexual orientation) work in different occupations

Occupational segregation is important because difference often links to inequality. Occupational segregation by gender (sometimes called sex segregation) is considered one of the primary factors contributing to gender inequality in the labour market and in society more generally (Cohen & Huffman, 2003; England, 2005). Occupational segregation along other dimensions like visible minority status, sexual orientation, and disability has also been associated with income and health inequalities and divergent opportunities. For all these reasons, occupational segregation is a significant characteristic of Canadian society that is deserving of attention. This chapter explores the extent of occupational segregation, its implications, and its causes.

Defining and Measuring Occupational Segregation

Formally defined, occupational segregation is the uneven distribution of workers across and within occupations. Researchers studying this phenomenon have focused on occupational segregation by gender (treating gender as a binary), but studies of segregation along other lines, especially race/ethnicity, are not uncommon. It has become commonplace for researchers to distinguish two components of gender segregation: horizontal and vertical segregation (Charles & Grusky, 2004; Charles, 2005; Jarman et al., 2012; Fortin & Huberman, 2002). **Vertical segregation** is occupational segregation associated with income inequality and occupational status. For example, vertical segregation is evident when men hold positions as corporate executives while women predominate in administrative assistant jobs. Definitions of **horizontal segregation** vary across studies. Some define it as difference that is not linked with inequality; Jarman et al. (2012) use the term in this sense, and for them it is a purely mathematical construct. Others associate horizontal segregation with gender essentialism—beliefs that men and women have different abilities and skills (Charles & Grusky, 2004; Charles, 2005). Gender essentialist ideology suggests that men are best suited for strenuous and physical work and hence likely to predominate in blue-collar occupations, while women's innate natures make them more people-oriented and caring and therefore best suited for service-sector work. Because gender essentialism is also associated with inequalities (in light of the gendering of skill, discussed in Chapter 7), in more recent work Levanon and Grusky (2016) abandon the term "horizontal" and call this dimension of segregation **gender essentialist**. The value of their approach is that both vertical and gender essentialist segregation are not simply theoretical or mathematical constructs, but they map onto observed differences in occupational traits.

vertical segregation Occupational segregation associated with inequalities in income, status, and authority

horizontal segregation Variably defined as either occupational segregation not linked to inequality or occupational segregation consistent with ideologies that men and women are essentially different and have different abilities

gender essentialist segregation Horizontal sex segregation at work that is deemed consistent with stereotypes about the skills and abilities possessed by men and women

It is important to consider multiple dimensions of occupational segregation—especially when exploring segregation by gender—because they appear to be different. Vertical segregation has decreased over time as a result of women's entry into managerial and professional careers such as medicine or law (Levanon & Grusky, 2016; Charles & Grusky, 2004). Gender essentialist segregation, however, has been more persistent. Men still predominate in blue-collar work and are more likely to be in jobs that involve working outside in all conditions. Women still cluster in jobs requiring social skills and services. There appears to be little movement of men into female-dominated jobs and only minimal movement of women into jobs in trades and primary industries (Levanon & Grusky, 2016). The gendering of work and gender essentialist beliefs about the inherent abilities of men and women continue to encourage occupational segregation by gender, even as norms of gender equality undermine vertical segregation. When researchers examine occupational segregation by race/ethnicity or other dimensions, they tend to focus on vertical segregation; however, wherever there are essentialist beliefs about ability and its distribution across social categories, essentialist segregation is possible.

When measuring segregation, scholars have adopted a variety of measures and formulae including the **Index of Dissimilarity** and the Gini coefficient (Fox & Fox, 1987; Jarman et al., 2012; Alonso-Villar, Del Rio, & Gradin, 2012; Levanon & Grusky, 2016). The differences, strengths, and weaknesses of these various methods have been detailed and debated in the literature (see, for example, Charles & Grusky, 2004; Jarman et al., 2012)

Index of Dissimilarity A measure used to calculate the extent of occupational segregation, interpreted as the percentage of people in one group who would have to change jobs to have a distribution identical to a second group and may be of particular interest to specialists. Although some methods appear to offer more accurate calculations of segregation than others, there is a fair degree of consistency across studies in the extent of segregation documented and the nature of trends identified. The appeal of the Index of Dissimilarity or D is its easy interpretation. D compares the occupational distribution of two groups of people (like women and men) and determines what percentage of people in group A (women) would have to change jobs to have the same occupational distribution as people in group B (men). Although it might appear sexist to calculate D in this manner, this is standard in the literature.

Unfortunately, there is a lack of recent data on occupational segregation trends in Canada. Based on previous Canadian estimates and studies of segregation in other countries, it appears that roughly half of women workers in Canada would have to change jobs to have the same occupational distribution as men. Reported rates of occupational segregation by race and/or ethnicity tend to be lower; based on previous research, one can estimate that between one in five and one in four members of ethnic minorities would need to change jobs to have a desegregated labour force. Such statistics, however, obscure considerable complexity and ambiguity.

Trends in Occupational Segregation

By Gender

If men and women in Canada tend to do different types of jobs, what do they do? Table 9.1 provides a list of the most common jobs for Canadian men and women in 2016. As this table shows, many women work in administrative and office jobs. They also work in stores as cashiers and retail salespersons, in teaching, and in health care as nurses, home care

TABLE 9.1 Most Common Jobs: Canadian Women and Men

Women		Men
Retail Sales	1	**Drivers**
Administration (i.e., human resources, purchasing, event planning, and related)	2	**Retail Sales**
Para-professional Occupations in Legal, Social, Community (i.e., paralegals, early childhood educators, social services)	3	**Cleaners**
General Office Work	4	**Computers and Information Systems**
Teaching	5	**Retail and Wholesale Management**
Office Administration Assistants (general, legal, medical)	6	**Trades Helpers and Labourers**
Home Care Providers and Educational Support	7	**Auditors, Accountants, and Investment Professionals**
Cashiers	8	**Machining, Metal Forming, Shaping, and Erecting Trades**
Assisting Occupations in Healthcare	9	**Auto Service Technicians**
Nursing Professionals	10	**Chefs and Cooks**

Source: Statistics Canada, 2016, Census of Population, Catalogue no. 98-400-X2016294.

providers, and in health assistant roles. Many of these jobs are consistent with ideologies of gender essentialism because workers provide service, support, and care to other people. In terms of remuneration, these jobs are variable: some are low-paid, and some pay fairly well; however, none are associated with high incomes. Men's most common jobs are almost entirely different. The only occupation to feature on both "top 10" lists is retail salesperson. Many men's jobs can be classified as blue-collar work: drivers, trades helpers, machinists, auto service technicians. Men are also well represented in white-collar jobs in management, information systems, and investment work. Some of these jobs link with gender essentialist notions of men's abilities, requiring physical strength, manual skill, technical ability, or authority. Incomes for these occupations are variable, but work in trades, management, and professions tends to be well paid.

These 2016 census findings provide a snapshot of common jobs, but they cannot speak to trends or to segregation in the labour force as a whole. Therefore, researchers have turned to statistical analyses.

Research on trends in occupational segregation by gender (or sex segregation) has documented a significant decline since the 1960s. Fox and Fox (1987) calculated an Index of Dissimilarity for Canadian workers in 1961 of 70.7. At that time, then, roughly 71 per cent of Canadian women would have had to change jobs to have the same occupational distribution as men. By 1981, the Index of Dissimilarity was 60.9, indicating only 61 per cent of women would have to change jobs to match men. The decline continued over the next decade: Brooks, Jarman, and Blackburn (2003) found that by 1991, the Index of Dissimilarity was 53. This is a significant decline across a 30-year period. However, evidence of desegregation since 1990 is somewhat mixed. Brooks et al. (2003) actually documented a slight *increase* in segregation by gender between 1991 and 1996 (2 per cent). US studies report a similar trend, with significant decreases in sex segregation from the mid-20th century until the 1990s, followed by relative stasis (Blau, Brummund, & Liu, 2013; Cohen, 2013). For example, Blau et al. (2013) find that gender segregation declined only 2 per cent in the 1990s and 1 per cent during the 2000s. In 2009–10, roughly 51 per cent of American women would have had to change jobs to have the same occupational distribution as men (Blau et al., 2013; Cohen, 2013). Canadian rates of segregation are likely similar to those in the US.

Scholars have raised concerns about these trends, finding in them evidence of a "stalled" gender-equity revolution (England, 2010; Guppy & Luongo, 2015). Some have countered that the revolution has not stalled, but, rather, the pace of change is uneven (Reskin & Maroto, 2011). To understand trends better, it is helpful to disentangle vertical and horizontal/essentialist segregation. As noted, there is evidence that vertical occupational segregation by gender has declined significantly (Blau et al., 2013; Charles & Grusky, 2004; Levanon & Grusky, 2016). However, labour market shifts have combined with lingering gender essentialism to perpetuate gender essentialist segregation (Charles and Grusky, 2004; Blau et al., 2013).

General rates of occupational segregation by gender hide considerable variation. Notably, occupational segregation is lower among men and women with post-secondary education than among those with high school education or less (Cohen, 2013; England, 2005). This trend is not surprising in light of women's entrance into professions and management—occupations that require post-secondary training (Blau et al., 2013; Levanon & Grusky, 2016). Among American men and women, only 40 per cent of women with university degrees would have to change jobs to have the same occupational distribution as men. In contrast, the rate for those with a high school education or less is close to 60 per cent (Blau et al., 2013).

Research has also shown that segregation rates vary depending on whether one looks at the occupational level or the job level. Research suggests segregation is higher at the level of jobs. Analyzing data from the 1960s and 1970s, Bielby and Baron (1986) explored job-level sex segregation within and across several California companies. They found an Index of Dissimilarity of 96 per cent, suggesting almost total segregation. It was rare for men and women to do the same job, with the same job title, at the same institution. There is evidence that job-level segregation has declined over time. Tomaskovic-Devey et al.'s (2006) examination of North Carolina workers in 1989 found that 77 per cent of women would have had to change jobs to eliminate job-level segregation. There is good reason to believe that these numbers have declined even more substantially over the past 30 years.

One of the reasons that job-level segregation is higher than occupation-level segregation is that the latter hides segregation within occupations across workplaces and across specialties. With respect to the workplace level, men and women may share an occupation but work in different firms. For example, retail sales is a common occupation for men and women, but some sales workers are employed in segregated work environments: retail stores catering to women may have an all-female staff, while some catering to men will employ only men. Hence, this seemingly desegregated occupation could be segregated at the workplace level. Within-occupation segregation can also occur by specialization. Women may specialize in some areas of practice while men specialize in others (see Box 9.1).

Source: © JHVEPhoto/Shutterstock

Although retail is one of the top occupations for both men and women, there is some gender segregation within retail. What profile would you expect from the sales team at Aritzia, an upscale women's fashion boutique?

By Race and Ethnicity

A glimpse of occupational segregation by race is shown in Table 9.2, which draws on 2016 census data to list the 10 most common occupations held by visible minority men and women. Comparing Table 9.2 with Table 9.1, one can see that seven of the occupations on visible minority women's "most common" occupations list also appear on the list for all women in Canada. The three distinct occupations on visible minority women's top 10 list are food counter attendant, cleaner, and auditor/accountant. Five occupations appear on both men's lists. New to Table 9.2 are the

A CLOSER LOOK

9.1 | Within-Occupation Segregation in Canadian Medicine

Many occupations and professions are internally sex-segregated. The Canadian Institute for Health Information (CIHI, 2019) provides annual reports on the health workforce, including data on medical specialization. These reports show that women are overrepresented in some medical specialties and under-represented in others. As the following table shows, women make up 42 per cent of all medical doctors and are overrepresented in pediatrics and obstetrics and gynaecology and under-represented in general surgery and ophthalmology, to name a few.

Percentage of Women in Medicine and Selected Medical Specialties, 2017–2018

Medical Profession	42.1%
Pediatrics	60.7%
Ob/Gyn	60.4%
Family Medicine	54.1%
Public Health	50.1%
Psychiatry	45.3%
Internal Medicine	34.6%
Anaesthesiology	31.9%
Radiology	31.6%
Emergency Medicine	30.5%
General Surgery	28.4%
Ophthalmology	26.2%

Do you think that other occupations are internally gender-segregated in a similar way? If so, in what way?

following: food counter attendant, professional engineer, longshore workers, labourers in processing, manufacturing and utilities, and security guards. These findings illustrate what other research has confirmed: there is more variation across ethnicity among men in the labour market than among women. It is also worth noting that there are three occupations that appear on both visible minority men's and women's "most common jobs" lists (while there was only one overlapping occupation in Table 9.1). These occupations are food counter attendant, cleaners, auditors, and accountants. This overlap provides further evidence of occupational segregation by race and reveals the concentration of minority workers in low-wage work and a very few higher-status professions (like accounting, and for men, engineering).

Statistical analyses provide a broader picture. Since the Index of Dissimilarity compares two groups (A&B), some studies limit their focus to a single dichotomy, such as Black and white, or several dichotomies (A&B, C&D, A&C, etc.). Still others compare an individual category to the labour force as a whole (Alonso-Villar et al., 2012). The latter technique was adopted by Lautard and colleagues, who explored ethnic

TABLE 9.2 Most Common Jobs: Canadian Visible Minority Women and Men

Women		Men
Retail Sales	1	**Drivers**
Assisting Occupations in Health Care	2	**Computers and Information Systems**
Home Care Providers and Educational Support	3	**Cleaners**
Food Counter Attendants and Kitchen Help	4	**Chefs and Cooks**
Para-professional Occupations in Legal, Social, Community (i.e., paralegal, early childhood educators, social services)	5	**Auditors, Accountants, and Investment Professionals**
Cashiers	6	**Food Counter Attendants and Kitchen Help**
General Office Work	7	**Civil, Mechanical, Electrical, and Chemical Engineering**
Cleaners	8	**Longshore Workers and Material Handlers**
Auditors, Accountants, and Investment Professionals	9	**Labourers in Processing, Manufacturing, and Utilities**
Administration (i.e., human resources, purchasing, event planning, and related)	10	**Security Guards and Related**

Source: Statistics Canada, 2016, Census of Population, Catalogue no. 98-400-X2016356.

occupational segregation in Canada (Lautard & Loree, 1984; Lautard & Guppy, 1999). For example, considering the year 1971, Lautard and Guppy (1999) identified substantial ethnic segregation in Canada, with the highest levels experienced by men claiming Jewish backgrounds (51), Indigenous men (41), Italian (35), and Asian (36) men. People from a variety of other European ethnic backgrounds had low levels of segregation (British, French, German, Polish, and Ukrainian). In general, men's rates of segregation across ethnicity were higher than women's; gender segregation concentrates women's employment in a narrower range of occupations, allowing less room for variation across ethnicity. The average rate of ethnic occupational segregation in Canada was estimated to be 30 for men and 27 for women in 1971. By 1991, the Index of Dissimilarity had dropped to 25 for men and 20 for women (Lautard & Guppy, 1999). It is not entirely clear whether racial segregation has increased, decreased, or stayed the same in the decades since this research was done.

Since Lautard and Guppy's study, the percentage of Canada's population belonging to visible minorities has increased because of immigration, and immigration status likely complicates the picture. Hou (2009) examined whether immigrants tended to work with others who shared their ethnicity and finds relatively low levels of occupational segregation: only about 10 per cent of immigrants in large Canadian cities worked predominantly with others who shared their ethnicity. However, there were variations across ethnicity, with Chinese and Portuguese immigrants more segregated than others. Further, Hou (2009) finds that segregation by ethnicity varies by immigration status, with the Canadian-born children of immigrants (so-called "second generation immigrants") less likely to work in workplaces in which people who share their ethnicity predominate. Thus, ethnic segregation appears to vary by immigration status. Findings also vary depending on whether the focus is on the occupation or the workplace (Hou, 2009). For example, Hou (2009) finds low levels of segregation at the workplace level for Black Canadians, but Fearon and Wald (2011) show that Black Canadians are under-represented in managerial occupations and overrepresented in lower-level service jobs. More research remains to be done in this area to identify trends in occupation segregation by race and ethnicity and the ways in which such segregation intersects with immigration status and gender.

There is a larger body of research on occupational segregation by race/ethnicity in the United States. For instance, back in the 1990s, studies found that 31 per cent of American workers would have had to change occupations to have a desegregated workforce (Reskin & Cassirer, 1996), while the segregation rate at the level of jobs was about 55 (Tomaskovic-Devey, 1993). Segregation rates vary by racial/ethnic group: Alonso-Villar et al. (2012) report considerable segregation among Hispanic, Asian, Black, and Indigenous workers in the United States. The extent to which racial-ethnic occupational segregation has declined over time is not clear (Tomaskovic-Devey et al., 2006).

Other Dimensions of Segregation

There has been little research on other dimensions of occupational segregation despite their importance. In a pioneering study, Tilcsik, Anteby, and Knight (2015) explore occupational segregation by sexual orientation in the United States. They find that homosexual men are more likely than heterosexual men to be employed in female-dominated occupations and that lesbian women are overrepresented in male-dominated occupations. More important, however, they find that both gay men and lesbians are likely to cluster in jobs that have certain characteristics: "task independence" (they can work independently without depending on others) and "social perceptiveness" (reading and anticipating how others will react). Tilcsik et al. (2015) explain that task independence is appealing because workers can minimize the potential impact of discrimination. Moreover, they suggest, social perceptiveness is a skill learned by many sexual minorities as they navigate interactions with potentially hostile others. In this manner, Tilcsik et al. (2015) not only document sexual orientation segregation, but they also provide insights on the tensions and social contexts that produce that segregation.

Segregation across disability status has also been documented. Maroto and Pettinicchio (2014) find that people with disabilities are overrepresented in lower-skill jobs with lower education and experience requirements. The Index of Dissimilarity indicates that roughly 20 per cent of people with any disability would have to change jobs to have the same distribution as those without disabilities. The extent of segregation varies across disability type, with people with ambulatory disabilities (for example, people who are confined to a wheelchair) and sensory disabilities (for example, people who are deaf or blind) being less segregated (Indices of Dissimilarity at 18.2 and 16.3 respectively) than those with cognitive disabilities (27.1) or those with multiple disabilities (28.3). People with ambulatory disabilities are significantly overrepresented in office and administrative support work, while those with cognitive disabilities are overrepresented in food preparation and serving, cleaning and maintenance, and transportation.[1]

[1]Indigeneity is likely another dimension along which occupational segregation exists; however it has received little attention in the sociological literature. Recently Haan et al. (2020) report that Indigenous workers are under-represented in managerial and professional jobs.

Consequences and Impact of Segregation

Occupational segregation is important because difference often begets inequality. All of the above-mentioned forms of segregation have been linked to income inequality, and some tie to health inequities.

Researchers conducting studies of occupational segregation by race/ethnicity have found significant income penalties for the disadvantaged. For example, Fearon and Wald's (2011) study of segregation between Canadian white and Black workers found a significant earnings gap amounting to $12,400 in yearly income in 2005: four-fifths of this gap could be attributed to occupational segregation and wage discrimination. Gosine (2000) found that Black Canadians were among the most disadvantaged with respect to earnings. More generally, members of visible minorities earn less than white Canadians. UK researchers have also identified an ethnic pay gap favouring white workers, largely accounted for by occupational segregation (Brynin & Güveli, 2012). Research on the US finds that occupational segregation contributes to the racial earnings gap between Black and white workers, especially among men (Mandel & Semyonov, 2016). Occupational segregation explains more of the earnings gap among men than women, who—as we have seen—tend to be less ethnically segregated. Minority workers may also be overrepresented in jobs associated with poor physical and psychological health (Fan & Qian, 2017).

Studies of gender segregation also document income inequalities. Occupational segregation is associated with income inequality favouring men (England, 2005; Cohen, 2013; Gauchat, Kelly, & Wallace, 2012; Levanon & Grusky, 2016). Differences among women can also be at least partially explained by segregation: Fuller (2018) finds that much of the motherhood pay gap—income disadvantage for mothers compared to childless women—is accounted for by mothers clustering in low-wage jobs. With respect to other implications of sex segregation, research finds that women are somewhat advantaged health-wise because their jobs are less often physically hazardous (Levanon & Grusky, 2016; Jarman et al., 2012). In this respect, Levanon and Grusky (2016, p. 601) conclude that "essentialism works to both advantage and disadvantage women." For the situation internationally, see Box 9.2.

Global Perspectives

9.2 | Occupational Segregation by Gender Internationally

Occupational segregation by gender internationally is a subject of interest for many researchers. For example, Jarman et al. (2012) examined sex segregation and gender inequality across 30 different countries. They identified variations in rates of segregation, ranging from a high of 61 in Finland—where about 61 per cent of women would have to change jobs to have the same occupational distribution as men—to a low of 44 in Romania. Among the other countries, Jarman et al. (2012) examined, many had rates hovering around the 50 per cent mark: 15 countries had rates between 48 and 52 (including the US, the UK, Germany, Slovakia, and Brazil). Most surprisingly, Jarman et al. (2012) found that segregation in many regions was not associated with gender inequality as research based on North America would lead us to expect. In fact, in a number of countries, occupational segregation was associated with greater pay equality. Jarman et al.'s (2012) study reminds us of the importance of context, policy regime, and the value of exploring trends internationally.

Why is occupational segregation associated with gender inequality in North America but not in Scandinavia? Do you think that different policy contexts and/or gender norms help to explain these differences?

Maroto and Pettinicchio (2014) document income disparities due to segregation by disability status. These disparities vary by disability type. People with sensory disabilities have earnings that are close to those without such impairments, but the income penalty is larger for people with cognitive and multiple disabilities.

Multiple Causes of Occupational Segregation

What causes occupational segregation? The forces are numerous and complex (Cohen, 2013). This is why occupational segregation persists despite substantial societal and labour market change over the past 50 years. Most scholars distinguish "demand side" and "supply side" contributors. The "supply" side is the workers' side. Supply-side explanations consider what leads workers to gravitate towards certain jobs but not others. The "demand" side is the employers' side. Demand-side explanations consider why employers show a preference for some workers over others. To these explanations we can add contextual factors: labour market trends, social-historical patterns, and social ideologies. To understand segregation, we need to take into account all three types of explanations.

Context: Ideology, Tradition, and Labour Market Trends

Social context—including tradition, ideology, and labour market trends—has important implications for segregation. Remember from Chapter 3 that historically in Canada there has been a gendered division of labour; men and women have done different kinds of work. You may recall that these historical differences were shaped by separate spheres ideology, which held that men and women were intrinsically different (Davidoff & Hall, 1987; Tosh, 1999). While men were thought to be rational, logical, and independent, women were viewed as inherently caring, emotional, and dependent. Although separate spheres ideology was always more ideal than reality, it was important to the extent that it shaped attitudes and behaviour. When employers make decisions about whom to hire, they can be influenced by social norms about what is appropriate. When people seek work, they may similarly think about what is normative. Separate spheres ideology suggests that there is very little that *both* men and women are good at; therefore, the work that they do, and the social roles they fulfill, should be different—complementary, but separate (Davidoff & Hall, 1987). This ideology strongly encourages occupational segregation by gender.

Gender ideologies change over time, and there is less emphasis on gender difference today, although gender essentialist views persist. Cech (2013) has shown how even when young men and women outwardly reject gender essentialism, their career choices are still influenced by those beliefs subconsciously. Historical patterns of working have also been transformed over time. Yet ideology and tradition can have a lasting impact, affecting hiring decisions by shaping our habits, traditions, and expectations. For example, an employer may not actually believe that women are inherently better at childcare but when seeking a childcare employee might look for a woman, without thought, according to custom. On a construction site, employers might look to hire men who are just like those they already employ. Tradition and ideology shape hiring by shaping employees' and employers' understanding of what is possible and the way things should be done.

Ideology and tradition shape other forms of occupational segregation as well. Racist ideologies supported discrimination against racial minorities in years past, closing off opportunities to Black and Asian men and women, for example, and channelling them into a narrow set of occupations—especially subordinate jobs requiring physical strength or providing service. We have already seen how settler-colonial racism undermined Indigenous ways of working and living and channelled Indigenous workers into a narrow range of low-paying jobs. Racial ideologies and racist practices intersect with gender ideologies and practices to structure the work of minority and majority workers, contributing to occupational segregation (Duffy, 2007; Glenn, 2002).

Although ideology and custom can be powerful forces, occupational barriers were also ensconced in formal policies and laws. For instance, British Columbian law forbade Asians from holding professional jobs and working in certain fields (Adams, 2016; Brockman, 1995). Moreover, professional programs implemented quotas to limit the entrance of women, Blacks, and Jews (Levi, 2003). Privileged workers and prominent social institutions have combined to restrict entry of the disadvantaged into high-skill jobs historically. These formal barriers are informed by essentialist ideologies, and they shape social practices. Together, these forces combine to shape hiring patterns beyond the historical time periods and social ideologies from which they originated.

There has been less research focusing on occupational segregation along other dimensions like sexual orientation, gender identity, and (dis)ability. However, each of these dimensions has a social history characterized by discrimination and disadvantage, as well as ideologies of difference. Ideologies that suggest that there are differences in outlook or abilities by sexual orientation also support occupational segregation. The same is true of attitudes towards people with disabilities and transgender people.

At the same time, changing societal attitudes and historical events have led to a decline in occupational segregation. More egalitarian views are associated with egalitarian practices. Legislative changes to prevent discrimination on the basis of gender, race/ethnicity, sexual orientation, and other dimensions have been important as well. Regardless of our personal biases, our laws say hiring should be based on objective grounds. Employers who fail to obey the law could be prosecuted. Laws help to create a culture discouraging discrimination and segregation (Hirsch, 2009). Maternity leave legislation has also been found to have a strong de-segregating influence in some countries (Chang, 2004).

A final contextual factor that is worth noting concerns labour market trends. Occupational desegregation is more likely to occur in times of labour shortages or occupational expansion. A rapidly expanding field desegregates more quickly because the need for workers forces employers to look beyond their traditional labour pool. Chapter 3 noted how during the two world wars, women and minority men were drawn into manufacturing work in larger numbers because of the labour shortages spurred by increased wartime production and men's enlistment. A similar argument has been advanced about women's influx into the profession of law in the 1980s (Chiu & Leicht, 1999) and the medical profession since 1970 (Boulis & Jacobs, 2008). It may be harder for segregation to break down in fields that are contracting (like some blue-collar jobs). In this manner, labour market trends can strongly shape segregation patterns.

Supply-Side Factors

Supply-side explanations for occupational segregation focus on personal choices and the preferences, socialization, education, and abilities that shape job choice. Why do men and women, or racial minority and majority workers, end up in different jobs? The simple answer may be that they choose to do so on the basis of their own preferences and abilities. Certainly, our choices influence our experiences and outcomes, but explanations that end there are seriously lacking. Our choices are structured through social interaction and by our social-historical context, our resources, social structures, ideologies, and so on.

Most often, choice explanations are invoked to explain occupational segregation by gender. One version of these arguments is gender-essentialist: men and women are different, so they gravitate to different kinds of work. Such arguments are reminiscent of separate spheres ideology in that they assume that biological differences link to skill differences, which naturally translate into occupational differences. Men end up in jobs that require their strength, independence, and aggressiveness, while women seek jobs that allow them to care for others. Men's and women's job choices may also be subconsciously influenced by norms of gender essentialism (Cech, 2013). These explanations cannot entirely explain the occupational segregation we see and certainly cannot explain lingering differences at the job level where men and women perform similar tasks under different job titles and/or at different firms (Bielby & Baron, 1986). One variation of this explanation emphasizes **socialization**. According to this argument, observed differences between men and women are the product of how they were raised. If little boys play with trucks while little girls play with dolls, then perhaps we should not be surprised that many men drive and fix trucks while many women teach children. Such explanations are not without value, but socialization cannot explain all the occupational segregation we see (Reskin & Roos, 1990): what we play with as children, or entrenched gender norms, should not affect who becomes a cashier or office worker.

socialization
Processes through which culture and societal norms are transmitted to others

Another related argument is that women prioritize raising a family, so they choose work that is more family-friendly or temporary or has more opportunities for part-time employment. It is true that women still take on primary responsibility for childcare and domestic labour, and their domestic responsibilities can influence their employment (and vice versa). Women may be drawn to careers—like teaching—that are easier to combine with raising kids than some others. Yet it is not always the case that jobs in which women predominate are flexible. Women's work in health and personal care jobs involves long shifts and even on-call work that is not very compatible with family life. Even part-time work in food services and retail is not particularly family-friendly because shifts can be unpredictable, making it difficult for working mothers to obtain daycare on short notice or for evening and weekend work.

Another dimension of the choice argument concerns education. There is considerable evidence that education is gender segregated as well (England & Li, 2006; Charles & Bradley, 2002). That is, women are more likely to undertake post-secondary education than are men; some men then gravitate towards work requiring only a high-school education for entry. Moreover, in post-secondary institutions, what men and women study varies. For example, engineering is male-dominated, as are computer science and physics (England & Li, 2006). In contrast, women are overrepresented in health care, education, and psychology (ibid.). Educational training is a source of segregation to the extent that what we study shapes where we work.

The limitations to this argument are four-fold. First, ultimately, it ends up falling back on the above-mentioned gender essentialist arguments to explain why men and women gravitate to different fields. Second, it assumes that there is a direct link between what we study and where we work. This link is quite evident for professional work. One cannot work as a lawyer or health care professional without advanced field-specific education, so educational segregation in these fields will contribute to occupational segregation. Nevertheless, many students obtain general arts, science, or social science degrees for which there is no clear occupational match. Graduates from these fields can end up in a variety of occupations and industries. Third, education may encourage us to pursue a certain career, but if we find that our opportunities are limited, we will move in a different direction. Research has shown, for instance, that women in some male-dominated fields like project management leave at a higher rate than men because of the structure of work in the field (Legault & Chasserio, 2013). Fourth, you may recall that research has found that people with post-secondary education are *less* occupationally segregated. For all of these reasons, then, education—and especially post-secondary specialization choices—cannot fully explain patterns of occupational segregation.

Choice explanations are less often invoked to explain other types of segregation. It could be argued, though, that ethnic or religious culture instills certain values that might draw some workers to certain fields over others. Moreover, minority groups with lower rates of post-secondary education may be trapped in low-wage jobs compared to groups with higher rates of education. In a similar vein, it could be the case that people with disabilities are drawn to jobs that match their abilities and can accommodate their disabilities. Typically, though, we assume that minority workers will be drawn to the same kinds of jobs to which majority workers are drawn: jobs with good pay, job security, that allow for autonomy or provide work with some meaning and positive social interactions (as discussed in Chapter 8). It is unlikely that members of ethnic minorities or people with disabilities would choose jobs that pay less and are more precarious, regardless of culture or ability. Choice cannot explain the occupational segregation documented. With respect to education, Alonso-Villar et al. (2012) do find that education rates have an impact on occupational segregation among Hispanic men in the United States. However, segregation among Black men, Indigenous men, and all women cannot be explained by education. Overall, the disadvantages experienced by many minority workers cannot be fully explained through choice or education.

To summarize, workers' choices likely do contribute to occupational segregation: socialization, education, culture and religion, concerns for work-life balance, and general interest shape what occupations appeal to us. Our choices, however, are structured by many forces—including ideology, tradition, socio-economic background, labour market and educational opportunities—which delimit what seems possible. No matter what we would like to do, our ability to actually do it often depends on someone hiring us. Employers, then, play a major role.

Demand-Side Factors

Demand-side factors shaping occupational segregation include the availability of jobs and employers' decision-making. Technological, economic, and legislative change are some other factors shaping job availability. Decisions that sort people into jobs are made by employers and their agents, including human resource managers. When they hire, employers may consider several factors: individuals' education and training, their experience, their skills, how hard they work, their "fit" with the company (culture, values or brand, or ability to work with other employees), availability, and so on. However, hiring is not always based on purely objective factors. There will always be some guesswork when hiring. It may be difficult to tell from a résumé and interview whether a job applicant will be a good employee. Hence, hiring involves a leap of faith, and employers may rely on their intuition or "go with their gut." When they do so, they may (re)produce segregated work environments.

A few concepts help to explain how this happens. The first is **statistical discrimination**. Here, employers and managers make calculated decisions about who will be a productive worker for them. When faced with several (or several hundred) qualified applicants, how can an employer reach a hiring decision? To cull the pile, they may draw on gender, race, immigration status, disability status, sexual orientation, or other characteristics as "signals" of productivity. For example, like the employers hiring predominantly low-skill workers in Johanna Shih's (2002) study, they may assume Black women will be more dependable than Black men or that immigrant workers will be more compliant. If they hire on these assumptions, they are engaging in statistical discrimination to the disadvantage of Black, native-born men. Taken to its fullest conclusion, the statistical discrimination argument argues that this behaviour persists because employer beliefs are somewhat accurate. If employers' guesses prove wrong, then they will change their attitudes. The latter contention is questionable. Bielby and Baron (1986) find no evidence that such biases actually result in a more productive labour force. Moreover, they argue that employers appear to make guesses about fit when better screening can determine ability more objectively. In short, there is evidence that employers do engage in statistical discrimination—inferring productivity from personal characteristics—but there is no evidence that doing so is efficient.

statistical discrimination Making hiring decisions based on the belief that certain types of people are more productive than others in specific jobs

The second concept is **homophily**: the tendency of people to be drawn to others like themselves. When employers "go with their gut" about who might be a good employee, they may select people that they really connect with during an interview. Given homophily, it is likely that the person they "click" with is culturally similar to them (Rivera, 2012). Alternatively, managers may anticipate homophily among their workforce and therefore hire individuals who they think will get along with their current employees: people who resemble those they already have on staff. Homophily tendencies, then, can be segregating forces, encouraging hiring practices reproducing existing employment patterns and discouraging the hiring of people whose gender identity, race, class background, or other characteristics differ from prevailing organizational norms.

homophily The tendency of people to be drawn to others like themselves

Gendered and racialized organizational structures also contribute to segregation because they produce cumulative disadvantages that delimit opportunities, as feminist,

glass ceiling
The presence of invisible barriers limiting opportunities to reach the upper echelons of organizational hierarchies

concrete ceiling
Similar to the glass ceiling, the concrete ceiling consists of impenetrable barriers preventing members of minorities from being promoted to organizations' upper echelons

critical race, and intersectional theories have contended (Acker, 1990; Crenshaw, 2011; Carbado & Gulati, 2013; Ferree & Purkayastha, 2000). These structures contribute to a **glass ceiling** for women—invisible barriers limiting women's opportunities to reach the upper echelons. Opportunities for Black Canadians appear to be even more substantial, leading some to use the term **concrete ceiling** to reflect the fact that concrete is much harder to break through than glass. Although there has been very little research on segregation by LGBTQI status, research has shown how heteronormative organizational structures and cultures negatively impact LGBTQI workers' opportunities and careers (Bilimoria & Stewart, 2009; Priola & Lasio, 2018).

While concepts such as statistical discrimination, homophily, and the glass ceiling are important to understand the demand-side forces reproducing occupational segregation, it is important to look beyond them and remember that managers and employers are people. Their decisions are shaped by ideologies, traditions, personal attitudes, and values, just like everyone else's. Employers may hold attitudes that are prejudiced, and they may discriminate on the basis of these prejudices. Moreover, they, like others, are creatures of habit, and they may make hiring decisions based on what worked for them in the past when their applicant pool was not as diverse as it is today. Paying some workers less than others also helps employers to increase their profits and may confirm their own identities by demarcating some marginalized workers as lesser (Harrison & Lloyd, 2013). As previously argued, this is where legislation and policy requiring diversity and employment equity can be valuable. Policies can encourage people to break out of old routines and to take diversity into account when hiring.

The Interplay of Forces and Factors

When we realize that there are so many different factors shaping occupational segregation, its stubborn persistence makes some sense. Desegregating forces, such as changing gender ideologies and legislation discouraging discriminatory hiring, may be counteracted by labour market trends, homophily, and the gendered division of domestic labour. Changing gender ideologies are themselves complex. For instance, the feminist movement and norms of gender equality have encouraged women's entrance into management and formerly male-dominated professions but not blue-collar jobs. Moreover, men have not entered female-dominated occupations to the same extent. Hence, gender essentialist ideals have not entirely disappeared, but they have changed enough that opportunities for women in many attractive careers have increased.

There is also an interplay between employers' decisions, social context, and individual choices, which is important to emphasize. When individuals choose jobs, they may anticipate employers' preferences, read the social context, and make decisions accordingly. Militello's (2017) research exploring the career aspirations of queer university students provides an illustration. Militello found that gay, lesbian, and bisexual young adults anticipated labour market discrimination. In response, some were pursuing careers they believed to be more queer-friendly and welcoming, while others made a decision to conceal their sexual orientation until their careers were established. Here we can see how workers' choices can be structured by social context, and perceptions of employer bias, in a manner than encourages segregation.

One theory of occupational segregation (and desegregation) that encapsulates this interplay of forces is Reskin and Roos's (1990) application of queuing theory. Reskin and Roos argue that employers have "queues" or mental lists of people who would be ideal for a given job. These lists have historically been structured by gender and race such that for some jobs, white men have been preferred; depending on the job, white women or minority men might be seen as the next most attractive. For other jobs, white women might be preferred, with minority women as a secondary preference. When hiring, employers start at the top of their queue and work down. Workers also have "queues" or mental lists about which jobs are most attractive. Reskin and Roos (1990) argue that, historically, white men were at the top of the queue for the most attractive jobs. The best jobs were at the top of these workers' lists as well, and hence a match was made that saw white men dominate the best jobs. Over time, however, these lists have changed, they argue. There are many factors contributing to this change: changing social attitudes, anti-discrimination legislation, more diversity in the labour force, high education levels among women and members of visible minorities, and so on. Employers may no longer place white men at the top of their queues. The result is decreased segregation—especially among jobs requiring post-secondary education. Recent research from Europe, however, finds that such queues have persisted, especially by race: minority men are disadvantaged compared to white men when applying for men's jobs (as are all women), and white women are preferred over minority women (and sometimes men) by employers hiring workers for female-dominated jobs (DiStasio & Larsen, 2020).

Source: © fizkes/Shutterstock

Multiple factors contribute to occupational segregation, including labour market trends, homophily, and Reskin and Roos's queuing theory. Despite government legislation and social pressure to reduce occupation segregation, race remains a major factor in hiring, although gender identity, sexual orientation, and disability are also significant factors.

As Reskin and Roos (1990) make clear, occupational segregation is an enduring characteristic of the labour market, but it is also susceptible to social change. Segregation has decreased over time because social change and shifting laws and policies have altered workers' preferences and employers' decision-making. At the same time, there are many forces contributing to the persistence of occupational segregation by gender, race/ethnicity, and other structured dimensions of inequality. While some of these trends decrease segregation, others encourage its persistence. It could take a concerted effort to reduce occupational segregation further. Making this effort is worthwhile, since occupational segregation contributes to inequalities by gender, race/ethnicity, sexual orientation, gender identity, and disability status.

Reviewing the Learning Objectives

After reading this chapter, you should

- Know what occupational segregation is and understand that its persistence is the result of the confluence of several different processes, actors, and contextual factors.
- Understand that there are different types of occupational segregation.
- Understand that there are multiple causes of occupational segregation.
- Have a sense of the consequences of occupational segregation.

Questions for Critical Thought

1. This chapter has highlighted how employers' and workers' (structured) choices contribute to occupational segregation. How (and when) might a segregated workforce be viewed as beneficial to employers and some workers?
2. How does occupational segregation contribute to social inequality?
3. Occupational segregation has persisted even in the face of substantial social change. What kinds of social change might produce greater reductions in segregation by gender, race, or other factors? Do you think such social change is likely?

Annotated Additional Readings

Fearon, G., & Wald, S. (2011). The earnings gap between white and Black workers in Canada: Evidence from the 2006 Census. *Relations industrielles, 66*(3), 324–348.

This article examines the impact of occupational segregation on the earning gap between Black and white workers.

Maroto, M., & Pettinicchio, D. (2014). Disability, structural inequality, and work: The influence of occupational segregation on earnings for people with different disabilities. *Research in Social Stratification and Mobility, 38*, 76–92.

This article examines occupational segregation by disability and its implications for earnings.

Reskin, B., & Roos, P. (1990). *Job queues, gender queues: Explaining women's inroads into male occupations*. Philadelphia, PA: Temple University Press.

This book provides an insightful theory of segregation and changing patterns over time, followed up by a series of occupational case studies showing how segregation has declined in several fields.

Tilcsik, A., Anteby, M., & Knight, C. R. (2015). Concealable stigma and occupational segregation: Toward a theory of gay and lesbian occupations. *Administrative Science Quarterly, 60*, 446–481.

This article explores segregation along a dimension rarely studied—sexual orientation—providing a nuanced, theoretical look at how and why such segregation emerges.

Related Websites

Washington Center for Equitable Growth, occupational segregation fact sheet:

https://equitablegrowth.org/fact-sheet-occupational-segregation-in-the-united-states/

United Nations Department of Economic and Social Affairs, Social Development Brief 3 on Occupational Opportunities, Race and Ethnicity:

https://www.un.org/development/desa/socialperspectiveondevelopment/wp-content/uploads/sites/27/2017/07/RWSSPolicyBrief3.pdf

Stanford Social Innovation Review, Transforming the workplace to be transgender inclusive:

https://ssir.org/articles/entry/trans_forming_the_workplace_to_be_transgender_inclusive

Canadian Centre for Policy Alternatives, Behind the Numbers. Black women in Canada:

https://behindthenumbers.ca/shorthand/black-women-in-canada/

10 Discrimination and Harassment

Learning Objectives

After reading this chapter, readers will:

- Be able to define discrimination and understand the grounds on which it occurs in Canada.
- Understand the impacts of discrimination on workers.
- Have a sense of key policies in this area.
- Be able to define workplace harassment, sexual harassment, and racial harassment and to recognize other types of harassment at work.
- Understand the impacts of harassment on individuals, organizations, and societies.

Introduction

The #MeToo phenomenon of 2017–18 drew unprecedented attention to the prevalence of workplace sexual harassment. Prior to this, sexual harassment was something many women experienced but rarely discussed. Those who fought against sexual harassment—for instance, by taking their harassers to court—faced serious financial and emotional hardship, and their careers were negatively impacted. The #MeToo movement helped to open up a societal conversation about sexual harassment, bringing awareness to this important issue. Of course, sexual harassment is not the only kind of harassment experienced at work: workers may be harassed on many different grounds. While awareness of other types of harassment is growing, much harassment continues to occur beneath our social radar.

Awareness of discrimination is also on the rise. In Canada, we have outwardly embraced ideals of multiculturalism. One national ideal, succinctly captured in a Canadian Football League (CFL) 2018 campaign is that "Diversity is Strength" (Canadian Football League, 2019). Yet the limited acceptance of this ideal in Canada is all too clear, with the rise of white supremacist groups and hate crimes in recent years. Prejudice is not uncommon, and where there is prejudice, discrimination frequently follows. In fact, increasingly, both minority and majority workers advance claims to discrimination in the workplace.

This chapter explores discrimination and harassment to explain what they are and how the structure of modern workplaces combines with societal values and personal biases to create contexts where they occur. Then, we identify their impacts and describe the policies and practices implemented with the goal of fostering fairer and healthier workplaces.

Discrimination

Defining Discrimination

discrimination The unfair treatment of a person or group on the basis of prejudice

Discrimination consists of the unfair treatment of a person or group on the basis of prejudice. In the workplace, it is most commonly seen in hiring, promotion, the distribution of work assignments, pay, and firing. The Ontario Human Rights Commission (2019a) elaborates that it can include "making stereotypical assumptions based on a person's presumed traits" rather than assessing them on their individual merits. Discrimination is not determined based on intention but on impact. That is, an employer or colleague may not intend to discriminate, but if their actions result in unfair treatment, and the denial of opportunities, the effect is discriminatory. Discrimination is against the law in Canada, with the following grounds being specified (verbatim) in provincial and national legislation (Ontario Human Rights Commission, 2019b):

- Age
- Ancestry, colour, race
- Citizenship
- Ethnic origin
- Place of origin
- Creed (Faith)
- Disability
- Family status
- Marital status (including single status)
- Gender identity, gender expression
- Record of offences (in employment only)
- Sex (including pregnancy and breastfeeding)
- Sexual orientation
- Indigeneity

Note that definitions emphasize that discrimination entails "unfair" treatment and not necessarily "different" treatment. This is because it is recognized that societal institutions may have structural biases—for instance, organizations may be gendered, racialized, and heteronormative, as discussed previously. These biases create structural disadvantages for minority workers. Treating everyone the same when their circumstances and needs are different can result in discrimination. The Ontario Human Rights Commission (2019a) is explicit about this:

> In many cases, discrimination results from a tendency to build society as though everyone is the same as the people in power—all young, one gender, one race,

> one religion or one level of ability. Failing to consider many perspectives, or not planning to include all people, may result in barriers to access for persons identified by the [Human Rights] *Code*. Such barriers, even if unintended, are discrimination.

Although discrimination can occur on many grounds, the sociological literature is most extensive on gender and race but also touches on disability and sexual orientation. The paragraphs that follow highlight these dimensions, not because others are not important but because there have been fewer studies to document them.

Forms of Discrimination

direct discrimination Intentionally denying employment opportunities to individuals based on their characteristics, regardless of their ability, skills, or qualifications

associational discrimination Discrimination against someone based not on their characteristics but of those they are associated with in some way

covert (or subtle) discrimination Denying opportunities through subtle or hidden means

systemic discrimination This occurs when discriminatory processes are embedded in organizational practices and policies

bona fide job requirement Abilities or characteristics absolutely required for performance of a job. When criteria used in hiring are not bona fide, discrimination can occur

Discrimination takes different forms. The most obvious form is **direct discrimination**. When an employer says that they will never hire Indigenous people or Muslims, they are directly discriminating. They are intentionally denying employment opportunities to individuals, regardless of their ability, skills, or qualifications. Such discrimination is often obvious, and because it is illegal, there are potentially significant consequences for employers who engage in direct discrimination. Discrimination may also be **associational**. That is, someone might be discriminated against not because of *their* characteristics but the characteristics of those they associate with. For example, someone who is close to a member of a minority group whom a manager does not like may receive the same treatment as their colleague. Or a mother who takes time off to care for a child with disabilities and is denied a promotion or given an excessive workload as a result may be experiencing associational discrimination (Ontario Human Rights Commission, 2019a).

Discrimination can be **covert or subtle**. Here, discrimination is hidden and hence difficult to identify. It can entail being denied training opportunities or mentorship, being excluded from get-togethers, being subjected to monitoring, being assigned the least desirable tasks, or being blamed for things you did not do (Ontario Human Rights Commission, 2019a). For example, if a supervisor constantly scrutinizes a subordinate's work to look for flaws and metes out discipline for those flaws but does not subject others to the same treatment, the supervisor is covertly discriminating.

Moreover, discrimination can be **systemic**. This form of discrimination is also hard to identify because it is embedded within organizational practices and policies. Hiring criteria that penalize women for taking maternity leaves, and therefore having a "gap" on their résumés, reflect systemic discrimination (Weisshaar, 2018). Networking events that occur after-hours, or at men-only clubs, or venues that are not wheelchair-accessible also systemically discriminate against single parents, women, and people with ambulatory disabilities (respectively). Especially in contexts where these events are important for mentorship, team-building, and winning clients, excluded workers will be highly disadvantaged.

Another type, which intersects with the above-mentioned forms, is discrimination based on criteria that are not "bona fide." When certain criteria must be met to obtain a job but those criteria are not job-relevant, they are not considered **bona fide**. There have been several court cases around bona fide requirements in firefighting, for which physical tests required for entry have been deemed discriminatory. In one influential court case, a BC forest firefighter lost her job because she failed a physical test: When she was asked to run 2.5 km, her time was 49 seconds over the limit. The case found its way to the Supreme Court of Canada. After considering the evidence, the court ruled that the test was discriminatory and not bona fide. Most women would have difficulty running 2.5 km in the time required, but more important, there was no evidence that "these performance standards were in fact necessary to the safe and efficient performance of the job" (Canadian Human Rights Reporter, 1999). Moreover, there was no evidence that women and men needed to have "the same minimum level of aerobic capacity to perform this job safely and efficiently" (ibid.). Whenever job requirements privilege some applicants over others (by gender, age, etc.), employers are required to demonstrate that the stated requirements are indeed bona fide.

Source: THE CANADIAN PRESS/Jonathan Hayward

Morgane Oger, a Vancouver-based trans rights activist, has been vocal about her experiences with workplace discrimination following her transition, when she repeatedly lost out on job opportunities in her chosen field after prospective employers learned that she was trans. Oger has since founded the Morgane Oger Foundation, which seeks to narrow the gap between Canada's anti-discrimination laws and their application.

Some human rights commissions include harassment as a form of discrimination. Harassment will be discussed later in the chapter.

Discrimination in Hiring

Workplace discrimination can manifest during hiring. Discrimination in hiring can be direct (outright refusal to hire someone with certain characteristics), covert (setting aside résumés from people with hard-to-pronounce names), or based on hiring criteria that are not bona fide. Systemic discrimination may also occur in hiring when practices systematically disadvantage certain groups (like parents, people with disabilities, the poor). Researchers have documented biases in hiring. One indication of discrimination in hiring can be found in unemployment rates: As we have seen, Indigenous and Black workers experience high rates of unemployment and underemployment (Lamb et al., 2018). Perhaps the most powerful evidence of discrimination in hiring comes from "audit" studies. Here, researchers send out fictional, paired résumés and applications in response to real posted job advertisements. The résumés are virtually identical in terms of education and experience. What varies across applications is some marker of race, gender, disability status, or sexual orientation. In a world without discrimination, identical résumés (with equal markers of merit) should receive an equal amount of interest from employers.

The classic Canadian audit study was done by Henry and Ginzberg (1985). For this study, the researchers hired Black and white actors, gave them fictional, identical résumés, and sent them out to apply for jobs. Cognizant of sex segregation, the researchers had teams of men (one Black, one white) and women (also Black and white) apply for different jobs. The results were striking. Despite equivalent résumés, white men and women received three times more job offers than comparable Black workers. When Black workers were offered jobs, it was often not the job they applied for but a lower-paying job. On those relatively rare occasions when white and Black workers were both offered a job, the white workers were usually offered more pay. Even when neither Black nor white workers were offered a job, white workers were treated more courteously. This study provided clear evidence of racial discrimination in hiring in Toronto in the 1980s.

The researchers also conducted a telephone test whereby they had confederates call workplaces and inquire about advertised jobs. Callers had a "Canadian" accent, an eastern European accent, a West Indian accent, or an Indo-Pakistani accent. The researchers found that callers with a Canadian accent were told the job was already filled 13 per cent of the time. Others were more likely to find the jobs closed to them: 31 per cent of European-accent callers, 36 per cent of West-Indian-accent callers, and 44 per cent of callers with Indo-Pakistani accents were told the job was already filled. Clearly, the labour market of the 1980s was discriminatory towards minority workers.

What has changed since the 1980s? Several audit studies provide insights into labour market discrimination in the 21st century. Oreopoulos (2011) conducted a large, complex audit study that involved submitting 12,910 résumés to 3225 job advertisements in Toronto and Montreal. The study sought to disentangle effects by racial/ethnic background, foreign/Canadian education and training, and gender. Therefore, résumés varied by the gender of the applicant, their ethnic/racial background signalled by name (Canadian, Chinese, Indian, Pakistani, Greek, British), Canadian or foreign education, and whether their experience was obtained in Canada or abroad. Despite these variations, all fictitious applicants had identical education levels and similar experience; their qualifications were objectively the same. Oreopoulos (2011) found clear evidence of discrimination. Canadian applicants (with English-sounding names, Canadian education, and Canadian experience) received call-backs (requests for interviews or similar follow-ups) from employers 16 per cent of the time. Call-back rates for other applicants were as follows: Greek applicants, 12 per cent; Indian applicants, 11.5 per cent; Chinese applicants, 11.3 per cent; Pakistani applicants, 11.0 per cent. Canadian job experience increased the likelihood of receiving a call-back. Those with foreign experience were disadvantaged. To understand his findings, Oreopoulos (2011) contacted employers and recruiters to see what explanations they could provide. Respondents argued that applicant name (and ethnicity) was taken as a signal of language ability. This seems to suggest that statistical discrimination—wherein employers take ascriptive characteristics as signals of productivity—may be occurring. As discussed in Chapter 9, statistical discrimination is flawed because language ability is not a difficult attribute to test; hence, such arguments are far from convincing.

Other studies provide corroborating evidence of discrimination in the Canadian and American labour markets. For example, an audit study in the United States tested the combined impact of race and university status. Gaddis (2015) sent out 1008 matched résumés for white and Black graduates of elite (Harvard, Stanford, Duke) and respected, mid-tier US universities (University of Massachusetts, University of California-Riverside, and University of North Carolina–Greenboro). To signal race, he varied first names:

Names that signalled "Black applicant" included Jalen, Lamar, Shanice, and Ebony. Names that signalled "white applicant" included Caleb, Charlie, Erica, and Lesly. He found that elite university graduates and white applicants received more call-backs. Black applicants from elite universities received similar call-back rates to white applicants from mid-tier universities; Black applicants from mid-tier universities received the lowest call-back rates. On rare occasions when job offers were made, Black applicants were offered lower starting salaries and lower-prestige jobs than white applicants. Again, this study finds clear evidence of racial discrimination, this time in the US job market.

Oreopoulos's and Gaddis's studies signal race or background through name, but what if applicants alter their names to "Westernize" them? **Résumé whitening** is a term given to the practice whereby applicants alter their names and sometimes their experience and credentials to minimize racial or immigrant signals to employers. Studies vary on the extent to which they find résumé whitening reduces discrimination in hiring. Kang, DeCelles, Tilcsik, and Jun (2016) found that many minority workers whiten their résumés by altering their names to appear more White and/or Western or altering experience to remove racial signals (for instance, by removing records of volunteering with ethnic clubs and organizations). As a follow-up, they conducted an audit study, sending out paired résumés: Would L. James Smith receive more call-backs that Lamar James Smith, or would Lei Zhang receive more call-backs than Luke Zhang if their résumés were otherwise identical? Kang et al. (2016) found that whitened résumés did receive more call-backs, even in organizations that had labelled themselves as "pro-diversity." This study too, then, finds evidence of racial discrimination. In contrast, Oreopoulos (2011) tested the whitened résumé hypothesis and found that the difference in the call-back rates for Tao and Fang Wang and Allen and Michelle Wang were not statistically significant. More research is needed in this area to refine our understanding of résumé whitening; still, existing research provides evidence of labour market discrimination.

résumé whitening
The term given to the practice whereby applicants alter their names, and sometimes their experience and credentials to minimize racial or immigrant signals to employers

Audit studies have been conducted to identify other types of discrimination by gender, sexual orientation, and disability status. With respect to gender, recent research finds mixed results. Some find no overall gender difference (Quadlin, 2018), while others identify an advantage for some women but not others (Oreopoulos, 2011; Waite & Denier, 2020). For example, Quadlin's (2018) US audit study considered gender and college grade point average (GPA). She found that there were no differences in the call-back rates among men and women who graduated with an English degree, but that high-achieving women with a math degree received significantly less interest from employers than men with strong GPAs. In follow-up analyses, Quadlin (2018) found evidence that employers see high-achieving women in non-traditional fields as potentially arrogant. As a result, some not only prefer men but also women with moderate grades, who are viewed as more likeable. In their Canadian audit study exploring gender identity, sexual orientation, and visible minority status, Waite and Denier (2020) found that heterosexual women are particularly advantaged in hiring, while transgender women are particularly disadvantaged. For Oreopoulos (2011), it was Canadian women with English-sounding names who experienced an advantage. Thus, gender intersects with other statuses to shape outcomes.

There have also been audit studies to explore discrimination by sexual orientation. For example, Tilcsik (2011) sent out 3538 résumés to 1769 job posting in seven US states. All applications were from fictitious men who were recent university graduates with similar résumés, differing in their involvement in clubs, one of which signalled homosexuality while the other did not. Tilcsik (2011) found that the résumés with the "gay" signal received fewer call-backs in states with fewer policy protections for LGBTQI workers. Biases and stereotypes encouraged discrimination against gay men but especially in contexts where anti-discrimination policies were lacking (Tilcsik, 2011).

Waite and Denier's (2020) audit study of LGBT discrimination in Canada found no statistically significant differences in call-back rates by sexual orientation: heterosexuals had similar call-back rates to homosexual and bisexual applicants. However, transgender individuals were significantly disadvantaged, especially transgender women. With respect to members of visible minorities, Waite and Denier found that applicants with Chinese last names received fewer job offers, but, again, their sexual orientation did not seem to influence call-back rates. These findings suggest that Canada's anti-discrimination policies are effective for LGB individuals but that transgender individuals are disadvantaged in the labour market and experience discrimination in hiring.

There have been fewer audit studies exploring other dimensions of inequality. With respect to parental status, Weisshaar (2018) finds that parents who take a leave to care for family are disadvantaged on their return to the labour market, receiving fewer offers. Labour market discrimination against people with disabilities has also been identified (Shier et al., 2009; Benoit et al., 2013). Employers may devalue the skills of people with disabilities or refuse to provide needed accommodations (despite legislation supporting accommodation). Women with disabilities are especially disadvantaged in terms of employment (Kim, Skinner, & Parish, 2020). Research has also identified barriers in hiring experienced by recent immigrants to Canada (Beaudry, Gagnon, & Deschênes, 2019) and systemic biases channelling newcomers into low-quality jobs (Malambwe, 2017; Cardona, 2018).

Although audit studies provide some of the strongest available evidence of employment discrimination in the labour market, they have a few limitations, which are important to note. First, they tend to focus on the employment experiences of recent university graduates. The experiences of other workers, including those with work experience and those without university degrees, are not addressed. Hence, the experiences of working-class individuals are less clear; their experiences of discrimination may differ. Veenstra (2013) finds that less-educated men are particularly disadvantaged in the labour market. Second, audit studies typically rely on online job posting services like *Indeed*, but some employers may not use these services, preferring to advertise elsewhere or hire based on referrals. Thus, these studies cannot give us a complete picture of discrimination in employment and hiring. Third, audit studies technically assess which résumés are flagged by employers for follow-up—not usually who gets hired. Employers may have more diversity among those they "short-list" for a job than among those they actually hire. Finally, too few studies explore the significance of intersectionality in shaping job outcomes (with some exceptions, like Waite and Denier, 2020). This is a promising area for future research.

Discrimination in Employment

Discrimination on the job can take many different forms: income inequalities, unfair distribution of assignments, censures for activity others are not censured for, exclusion from opportunities for mentorship and promotion, and even job loss (Das Gupta, 1996).

Issues at Work

10.1 | Workplace Discrimination

Summaries of real-life cases of discrimination and harassment heard by human rights commissions provide striking evidence. Below are some excerpts taken from cases summarized by the Human Rights Legal Support Centre (2019).

Case 1: A woman worked in a restaurant where a coworker "would often criticize her body, tell her she should lose weight, and comment that it was no wonder that her husband left her." Moreover, the worker was told that she could get a raise but she would have to go out with her employer to discuss it. She refused to do so and did not get a raise. When she told her employer about her coworker's discriminatory comments, the employer criticized her for having a bad attitude. She was eventually fired. The tribunal fined the employer and required the coworker to undergo human rights training.

Case 2: A major company originally made an employment offer to an applicant deemed the most qualified but then rescinded that offer on discovering he was an immigrant. The human rights tribunal found this action demonstrated discrimination based on citizenship. In response, the company changed its hiring policies so that proof of eligibility to work in Canada permanently is no longer a required precondition.

Case 3: Three Muslim men were reprimanded by their employer for speaking Bengali. They were "forced to break their religious tenets" and "subjected to racist remarks and threats." When they complained, they were fired. The tribunal found that all three "suffered discrimination during their employment in the workplace on the basis of creed, colour, ancestry, place of origin and ethnic origin."

A few real-life examples of discrimination are summarized in Box 10.1. In scholarly research, most attention has been paid to income inequalities.

There is a persistent wage gap between Canadian men and women, wherein women (age 25–54) earn 87 per cent of what men make (Pelletier, Patterson, & Moyser, 2019). The gap is shrinking over time, with reductions accounted for by decreased occupational segregation by gender (ibid.). The gap is robust across racial-ethnic groupings: for example, Indigenous men earn more than Indigenous women, on average (Haan et al., 2020). Some of the gender wage gap may be attributed to the fact that women experience a so-called "motherhood penalty" while fathers enjoy a wage premium. There is evidence that the motherhood penalty has decreased over time, especially among high-earning women; however, the fatherhood premium remains (Glauber, 2018).

Income inequalities by race and ethnicity have also been identified. University-educated Canadian-born members of visible minorities earn 87 per cent of what their Caucasian peers earn (Conference Board of Canada, 2017a). This racial earnings gap is worse in Ontario and Quebec than in other provinces. It has been attributed to labour market discrimination that sees members of visible minorities more likely to be unemployed and overrepresented in low-wage and temporary jobs, despite high education levels (Block & Galabuzi, 2011).

Moreover, immigrants to Canada earn 20 per cent less than the native-born; the pay gap is higher for immigrant women and for workers in Saskatchewan and Manitoba (Conference Board of Canada, 2017b). Among immigrants, the racialized are particularly disadvantaged. For example, census data reveal that Muslim immigrants, especially women, are disadvantaged in terms of income compared to all other immigrants (Canada Labour Congress, 2019). This disadvantage continues, even for Canadian-born Muslims. Thus, while some of the gap between immigrants and the Canadian-born may be accounted for by language ability, much of it—perhaps especially for Muslim workers—is related to discrimination (Conference Board of Canada, 2017b; Canada Labour Congress, 2019). More generally, immigrants educated in Canada as foreign students tend to do better in the labour market than their foreign-trained counterparts but are still disadvantaged compared to their Canadian-born and educated counterparts (Chen & Skuterud, 2018). Visible minority immigrants are particularly disadvantaged. Perceptions of "language ability" can be biased: Creese and Kambere (2003) show that racialized people with excellent English who happen to talk with an accent are sometimes deemed lacking by employers.

Data on Indigenous workers' income also provide evidence of discrimination (Lamb et al., 2018; Pendakur & Pendakur, 2011; Hu et al., 2019). Indigenous peoples living on reserves and those who identify as First Nations appear to be more disadvantaged than Métis and Inuit workers (Lamb et al., 2018). To account for any gap related to hours and weeks worked, Lamb et al. (2018) look only at full-time, full-year workers, finding that Indigenous-identity men (living off-reserve) earn 13 per cent less than their non-Indigenous counterparts, while the gap between Indigenous and non-Indigenous women workers is roughly 12 per cent. The gap for First Nations men and women living on-reserve is higher. Studies vary in the extent to which they find that observed earnings gaps are explained by education and training (Hu et al., 2019; Lamb et al., 2018).

There is evidence of discrimination impacting sexual and gender minorities as well. For example, homosexual men earn less than heterosexual men (especially when they are in a coupled relationship), but there is evidence that lesbians earn more than heterosexual women (Waite & Denier, 2015; Waite, Pajovic, & Denier, 2020). Bisexual men and women are also disadvantaged in terms of income (Waite et al., 2020). Transgender workers not only have lower incomes than cis-gender workers, but they have lower employment rates too (Carpenter, Eppink, & Gonzales, 2020; Ciprikis, Cassells, & Berrill, 2020).

Incomes and wealth for those with disabilities are negatively impacted by discrimination and unequal labour market opportunities and outcomes (Maroto & Pettinicchio, 2020). University graduates with a disability earn less than their counterparts without disabilities and are more likely to be unemployed as they transition into the labour market (Zarifa et al., 2015).

Discrimination has also been identified in hiring and promotion. Women continue to be under-represented in senior management ranks (Baxter & Wright, 2000). Women have long been said to experience a "glass ceiling" (Ferree & Purkayastha, 2000; Livingstone, Pollock, & Raykov, 2016). Despite recent progress, women comprise only about 20 per cent of all members on corporate boards (Statistics Canada, 2019d; Conference Board of Canada, 2017c). Women are more likely to serve on the boards of government enterprises and those under Canadian control. Women fare better than members of other targeted groups. The Conference Board of Canada (2017c) reports substantial under-representation of some groups: only 1 per cent of board members are Indigenous, 4 per cent are members of visible minorities, 3 per cent are people with disabilities, and only 1.6 per cent identify as LGBTQI. Clearly, minorities do not have the same opportunities as others to rise to the very top and serve on corporate boards (R. A. Smith, 2005). They can be affected by discrimination throughout their careers, and over time, these disadvantages accumulate, reducing opportunities for advancement (Purkayastha, 2005; Ferree & Purkayastha, 2000). Minority women, and especially Black and Muslim women, are particularly disadvantaged in this respect, highly under-represented in top positions, subject to stereotyping, hostilities, and aggressions that limit opportunities (Katshunga, Massaquoi, & Wallace, 2020; Canada Labour Congress, 2019). Indigenous men and women face similar challenges, from lack of mentors to unfriendly work environments that impact promotion opportunities (Henry, 2012) and direct racism (Benoit et al., 2019). The intersection of inequalities can exacerbate disadvantage (R. A. Smith, 2005; Purkayastha, 2005).

Discrimination in work assignments can be harder to identify; it is often covert or subtle discrimination that involves comparisons between similar workers. Some research provides evidence that members of disadvantaged groups receive the least pleasant, most arduous and/or dangerous jobs (Broadway & Stull, 2008). One human rights case involved a young woman on a co-op assignment at a body shop; her employer (co-op supervisor) would not allow her to get any hands-on experience in the shop, assigning her filing and receptionist work (Human Rights Legal Support Centre, 2019). In another case, a minority driver was given routes that were impossible to complete in the time allotted (Jameel & Yerardi, 2019). Covert discrimination in work assignments can also take the form of intense scrutiny, whereby managers closely watch what workers do in order to find fault and initiate disciplinary action (Das Gupta, 1996). Jameel and Yerardi (2019) provide the example of a Black UPS driver fired for "performance problems." His record shows that he was subject to levels of scrutiny that others were not, providing proof of covert discrimination:

> Among the alleged infractions: failure to take lunch, not wearing UPS socks, making an unsafe turn, absences, and tardiness. One time, he said, a manager called him in for breaking a driving rule that didn't exist (Jameel & Yerardi, 2019).

The "absences" were documented sick days for which supporting paperwork was repeatedly "lost."

Failure to accommodate workers who have a disability is another form of workplace discrimination. In fact, complaints of discrimination and failure to accommodate on the grounds of a physical or mental disability are among the most common dealt with by provincial human rights tribunals in recent years (see, for example, Alberta Human Rights Commission, 2020). Failure to accommodate religious practices, including prayer and attire, and religious holidays, is discriminatory as well.

Unfair dismissal is another component of workplace discrimination. Again, human rights complaints are informative here. Examples include women who were fired when their employers found out they were pregnant, men and women fired when their employers discover their sexual orientation, and workers fired because their employer found their disability inconvenient (Human Rights Legal Support Centre, 2019). **Mandatory retirement** is a discriminatory practice that has now been mostly eliminated

Mandatory retirement Policy whereby employees are forced to retire once they reach a certain age

in many jurisdictions (Thornicroft, 2016). Mandatory retirement requires employees to retire once they reach a certain age: 65 was the norm in Canada until 2009. Such policies are blatantly discriminatory because they are not based on merit or ability—solely age. There is no evidence that people cease to be productive after a certain age. Still, laws do allow for exceptions in cases where age is tied with a bona fide occupational requirement. Employers must demonstrate that past a certain age, individuals cannot effectively or safely do a job. Mandatory retirement still exists for some occupations, like firefighting: Ontario firefighters must retire by age 60 because their physical limitations and higher risk for heart attacks have been deemed to pose a substantial risk (Thornicroft, 2016). In some cases, the law may require employers to test employees' abilities to see if they can meet the standard of performance.

Causes of Discrimination

What leads to discrimination? Chapter 9's review of the factors contributing to occupational segregation provides many clues. For instance, ideologies and stereotyping can be influential, leading some employers to view specific types of people as being "unsuitable" for certain work roles (leading to unjustified statistical discrimination). Prejudice and bias are obvious contributors as well. **Homophily** is also relevant, especially in hiring and promotion. Leaders may give preference to people who are like them or people who they think will "fit" with the current workforce and company culture (Elrick, 2016; Rivera, 2012). Given the structures of modern workplaces, these practices disadvantage racial and ethnic minorities, gender and sexual minorities, Indigenous workers, those with disabilities, and other marginalized workers.

homophily The tendency of people to be drawn to others like themselves

There are a few additional mechanisms fostering discrimination that are worth noting. First, employer recruitment methods are important. Do employers have processes for reviewing applications systematically and in a manner that reduces unconscious bias? The term **unconscious bias** is used to recognize the subconscious stereotypes and biases we all hold about members of particular identity groups. To reduce unconscious bias requires conscious effort to challenge assumptions, question stereotypes, and, in hiring, effort to dig beneath taken-for-granted assumptions about who is most likely to be productive, what the ideal worker looks like, and what experience is relevant for a given job. Since hiring often involves some guesswork—employers attempt to infer from a résumé, interviews, and other hiring mechanisms who will be a good, productive worker for a firm—there is space for stereotypes and biases to influence decision-making (Carbado & Gulati, 2013). It is not uncommon for employers to try to reduce the "guesswork" by hiring based on referrals: offering positions to people they know or people referred to them by others they know, including existing employees. Such informal hiring practices can be discriminatory in their impact. Only those known to an employer or his/her contacts have an opportunity to get employment—and because of homophily, people different from employers are less likely to be in their social circle. Minorities may be disadvantaged. More formal recruitment strategies emphasizing merit, with bona fide requirements clearly specified and effort to reduce unconscious bias, are more effective at reducing discrimination.

unconscious bias The subconscious stereotypes and biases we all hold about members of particular identity groups

By their very structure, gendered, racialized, heteronormative, and Westernized organizations also foster discrimination. Minority workers and immigrants may have difficulty meeting "ideal worker" norms and navigating stereotypes to succeed in the workplace (Carbado & Gulati, 2013). In fact, worker training for immigrants often encourages them to dress, talk, and smell just like a "Canadian" worker to secure employment (Ameeriar, 2017). Especially in workplaces historically dominated by men, women have traditionally been at a disadvantage, unable to fit the "masculine" ideal of worker. Workers with family responsibilities may also face challenges meeting ideal worker norms. Those who take time off to care for children—whether on a several-month parental leave or on a case-by-case basis due to illness—may be penalized by employers and disadvantaged in hiring and promotion (Weisshaar, 2018). Years ago, it was common to speak of a "mommy track" at work (Devine, 1992; Noonan & Corcoran, 2004); once women had children, they were no longer considered promotable. Men who take time off to care for children may suffer similar career setbacks (Weisshaar, 2018). Nevertheless, refusing to promote based on gender, minority status, parental status, or the intersection of all three represents employment discrimination.

Social and cultural capital can also contribute to unequal employment outcomes. We discussed Bourdieu's (1986) conceptualization of social and cultural capital in Chapter 2. Social capital consists of your connections and networks—the people that you know. Those who are privileged by class, race, and gender may know more influential people and have contacts that can provide them with an inside track on available jobs. Cultural capital refers to what you know, especially your culturally relevant knowledge that might help you to navigate certain work and social situations more effectively (including modes of speech, dress, and so on). Cultural capital can also help in the labour market, enabling you to ace that interview or get along with your bosses because you share cultural knowledge and interests. As Bourdieu tells us, social and cultural capital are unevenly distributed in society by social class and other dimensions of social inequality. Those disadvantaged by race, class, gender, and other factors often lack social and cultural capital that would enable them to navigate the labour market and employment settings successfully. Regardless of merit, individuals without social or cultural capital, like the economically disadvantaged and/or first- and second-generation immigrants, may find it harder to find work commensurate with their skills (Aslam, 2021; Canada Labour Congress, 2019).

Policy Solutions

Extensive research identifying discrimination at work and elsewhere in society has spurred policy initiatives to counter it. Concern for civil rights in the 1960s and early 1970s led to the establishment of provincial human rights commissions in the mid-1970s and Canada's Charter of Rights and Freedoms in 1982. Human rights commissions promote human rights, while human rights tribunals make decisions respecting alleged violations of human rights policies, including discrimination (Ontario Human Rights Commission, 2019b). Another important piece of legislation was the Federal Employment Equity Act, passed in 1986. This act identifies four disadvantaged groups—members of visible minorities, women, persons with disabilities, and Indigenous peoples—and establishes practices

The Future of Work

10.2 | Discrimination

Researchers have raised concerns about the impact of technological and workplace change on discrimination. One might expect that technological change, and especially the introduction of artificial intelligence, would reduce discrimination, but according to Hirsch (2019), this is not necessarily the case. For example, many companies are turning to technology to monitor their workforce (in line with the electronic panopticon), from tracking their computer activity to monitoring their smartphone usage. Moreover, companies have adopted technology that may not initially appear to have a surveillance function, like badges and card-swipes to enter buildings and rooms. However, all this technology can be used to monitor workers' activity and movements. Some companies are even inserting microchips into their employees' arms—ostensibly to make it easier for them to access certain rooms and their computers. This technology, though, also tracks employees' activities. All of this technology is extremely invasive and could facilitate discriminatory practices. Hirsch talks about one firm that "already uses workers' Internet search histories and medical insurance claims to predict who is at risk of getting diabetes or considering becoming pregnant." Workers with an inconvenient health problem or pregnancy could be terminated without even knowing why. The use of artificial intelligence is also potentially problematic. Hirsch (2019) explains that Amazon invested heavily in developing AI for hiring but had to abandon the project

> because it kept discriminating against women. Apparently, the AI program learned from Amazon's male-dominated workforce that being a man was associated with being a good worker.

Currently, we have few regulations surrounding the use of technology in employee surveillance, leaving the door open for violations of privacy and discrimination to occur.

Do you think that in the future work will be less discriminatory? Or that discrimination will continue but through different mechanisms?

intended to ensure fairness in employment. The need for such legislation was explained by Judge Rosalie Abella in her 1984 Commission on Equality in Employment report:

> It is not that individuals in the designated group are inherently unable to achieve equality on their own. It is that the obstacles in their way are so formidable and self-perpetuating that they cannot be overcome without intervention. It is both intolerable and insensitive if we simply wait and hope that the barriers will disappear with time. Equality in employment will not happen unless we make it happen (Abella, 1984, p. 7).

employment equity Policies aimed at ensuring that the workforce represents the diversity of the Canadian population

The goal of **employment equity** is to ensure that qualifications and merit are carefully evaluated during hiring but also that structural barriers (and unconscious bias) are taken into account. Employers are encouraged to hire qualified people from the designated groups when their qualifications meet the job requirements.

The Employment Equity Act requires employers to be accountable for their hiring practices and to demonstrate that these practices are fair and non-discriminatory (Statutes of Canada, 1995). The legislation requires that organizations study their job categories and workforce to identify employment barriers, remove those barriers, and monitor and report on their progress towards obtaining employment equity. For example, when hiring, firms may be required to report on their applicant pool and to document the number of applicants that fall into each of the designated groups, to the extent possible. They may also have to identify and comment on the nature of the pool from which they are recruiting. Ideally, the characteristics of the applicant pool will reflect the recruitment pool. If 14 per cent of trade apprentices are women, then women should compose at least 14 per cent of applicants for a job in the skilled trades. If this not the case, then the employer should make an effort to reach out to women applicants so that the applicant pool is more representative. Employers also have to report the characteristics of those who won a job and detail why other qualified applicants did not get the job. Having to provide such explanations should prevent companies from turning down eligible minority applicants and thereby minimize discrimination (Abella, 1984). Employment equity policies promote fairness in hiring and remuneration (Leck, 2002).

Nevertheless, employment equity policies have their limitations. For instance, it appears that white women were the main early beneficiaries (Jain & Lawler, 2004). Members of other designated groups have not have benefitted to the same degree, although this may be changing. Second, given the reporting requirements, these programs are expensive. Third, their impact (and application) is more common in larger firms, but many people are employed in smaller firms where the impact of these policies is less. Fourth, employment equity provisions have not formally addressed some dimensions of inequality such as sexual orientation and gender identity. Fortunately, human rights policies have been extended to sexual minority and transgender workers, and policies have been shown to have a positive impact (Lloren & Parini, 2017; Connell, 2012). Nonetheless, there may be policy gaps around transgender workers, who are vulnerable to unemployment and employment in low-quality jobs as a result (Carpenter et al., 2020; Waite & Denier, 2020).

Some confuse Canada's employment equity policies with affirmative action policies that entail quota-based hiring—for instance, requiring that a certain percentage of a firm's workforce be members of designated groups. Employment equity does not involve quotas, although firms are encouraged to set targets for more equitable hiring and work towards those targets. Rather, it aims to enhance fairness and equity in hiring to minimize discrimination.

pay equity The principle of equal pay for work of equal value

Pay equity initiatives have a similar goal—to reduce discriminatory practices. More specifically, pay equity policies aim to reduce the gender gap in pay. Men and women are often not in the same jobs, and it has been the case historically that men's jobs, on average, pay more than women's jobs. Pay equity means that one employee cannot be paid substantially less than another (on the basis of gender) when they are doing similar work (in terms of skill level, effort, and responsibility) (Ontario Pay Equity Commission, 2019). Pay equity legislation requires employers to evaluate jobs to determine levels of skill, effort, and responsibility and to ensure that equivalent workers are paid equitably. The focus is on gender equality in pay, but the exercise of examining job characteristics and ensuring that pay is commensurate should contribute to equality across other dimensions as well.

Harassment

Workplace Harassment and Incivility

workplace harassment "Any negative workplace interpersonal interaction that affects the terms, conditions, or employment decisions related to an individual's job, or creates an intimidating, or offensive workplace environment" (Rospenda & Richman, 2004)

Workplace harassment can be defined as "any negative workplace interpersonal interaction that affects the terms, conditions, or employment decisions related to an individual's job, or creates an intimidating, or offensive workplace environment" (Rospenda & Richman, 2004). General workplace harassment does not necessarily entail an aspect of identity protected under Canada's Charter of Rights and Freedoms, such as gender or race. To clarify what types of behaviours might be classified as manifestations of workplace harassment, Rospenda and Richman (2004) provide a typology with four categories. First is *verbal hostility* wherein colleagues, clients, superiors, or (less often) subordinates yell or swear at, belittle, or constantly criticize a worker or group of workers. Second is *covert hostility* in which someone may be pleasant to your face but behind your back tries to steal your ideas or take credit for your work, ostracizes you, or prevents you from making contacts or accessing information. The third category includes *manipulative behaviour*, such as leaving hostile notes or offensive material for you to find, turning others against you, and issuing bribes or threats. The fourth category is *physical violence*, including being hit, pushed, or having something thrown at you. Richman et al. (1999) find that more than half of all workers at the university they studied reported generalized workplace harassment, with verbal hostility being the most common. Asking only about workplace harassment experienced in the previous year, a 2018 Statistics Canada study found that 19 per cent of Canadian women and 13 per cent of Canadian men reported being harassed (Hango & Moyser, 2018). Here too, the most common form of harassment was verbal abuse, reported by 13 per cent of women and 10 per cent of men. Workers in health care were the most likely to report experiencing workplace harassment—especially women. Fewer Canadians reported threats (3 per cent of men and women) and physical violence (3 per cent of women, 1.5 per cent of men) (Hango & Moyser, 2018). Women were more likely than men to report being abused by a client or customer, while men were more likely to report harassment from a direct supervisor or manager.

Like other forms of harassment, workplace harassment has personal, workforce, and organizational/economic costs. Individuals who are targets of such harassment are negatively impacted psychologically and economically (due to lost time at work as a result of stress and potentially job loss). Those who witness the abuse are also negatively affected; workplace harassment can poison a work environment. Organizations are impacted too because poor working conditions decrease attendance and work effort and increase turnover—all of which have an economic cost.

workplace incivility "Negative relational dimensions of employment with consequences for worker integrity and dignity" (Roscigno et al., 2009, p. 748)

Not all negative workplace behaviour constitutes harassment, but **workplace incivility**—although milder in some respects—can be similarly impactful. Roscigno, Hodson, & Lopez. (2009, p. 748) define workplace incivility as "negative relational dimensions of employment with consequences for worker integrity and dignity." Incivility may overlap with workplace harassment because it encompasses behaviour that includes bullying, infighting, being ignored, demeaned, and condescended to, and having your judgment questioned. Alternative definitions describe workplace incivility as "a form of psychological harassment and emotional aggression" that violates norms of respect (Murrell, 2018). Cortina et al. (2001) indicate that more than 70 per cent of public sector employees reported experiencing workplace incivility in the previous five years. Research by psychologists has found that incivility lowers job satisfaction and increases psychological distress (Cortina, Magley, Williams, & Langhout, 2001). When sociologists study workplace incivility, they focus on the organizational characteristics that encourage or discourage it. For example, Roscigno et al. (2009) find that organizational "chaos"—poor organization and coordination—is associated with infighting, conflict, and bullying. Bullying behaviours have also been tied to job insecurity. Workplace incivility creates a negative work environment, and it is shaped by (and in turn shapes) organizational cultures.

Sexual Harassment

Sexual harassment in the workplace is defined broadly as "any conduct, comment, gesture, or contact of a sexual nature that is likely to cause offence or humiliation to any employee; or that might, on reasonable grounds, be perceived by that employee as placing a condition of a sexual nature on employment or on any opportunity for training or promotion" (Government of Canada, 2018). It encompasses a range of behaviours, from verbal abuse, displaying offensive pictures or other materials, staring or unwelcome comments (for instance, about someone's body), offensive jokes, and inappropriate touching, to sexual requests or suggestions. Sexual harassment can affect people, no matter what their gender is, although women and non-binary individuals appear to experience it more than men. Sexual harassment is an expression of power. Canadian provinces consider harassment a component of discrimination. Certainly, it is discriminatory in its impacts.

sexual harassment "Any conduct, comment, gesture, or contact of a sexual nature that is likely to cause offence or humiliation to any employee; or that might, on reasonable grounds, be perceived by that employee as placing a condition of a sexual nature on employment or on any opportunity for training or promotion" (Government of Canada, 2018)

There are two main types of sexual harassment: (1) sexual coercion or quid pro quo harassment; (2) sexual annoyance or hostile work environment harassment. Sexual coercion involves threats or bribes, as "quid pro quo" implies. Here a perpetrator makes sexual favours a condition for acquiring or keeping a job. Thus, sexual coercion has direct consequences for a worker's employment status or involves a gain or loss of tangible work benefits. The allegations against Harvey Weinstein that sparked #MeToo in 2017 provide a clear example of sexual coercion or quid pro quo harassment. Many actresses and former assistants accused Weinstein of sexually harassing them and sexually assaulting them. Those who refused his advances have accused him of sabotaging their careers. Weinstein is also accused of having preyed on

Source: THE CANADIAN PRESS/Jeff McIntosh

After reflecting on the Black Lives Matter protests of 2020, Service Constable Kim Prodaniuk filed a 132-page affidavit of allegations of police misconduct and sexual harassment experienced during her career with the Calgary police department. Similar complaints have been filed against police services across Canada, indicating widespread issues within these institutions. What kinds of policy changes would be necessary to combat these issues?

the young and vulnerable and appears to have promised employment benefits in return for sexual favours (BBC, 2019).

In contrast, sexual annoyance harassment entails sexually related conduct that is hostile, intimidating, or offensive and contributes to a negative work environment. This behaviour does not involve a direct threat of harm or promise of gain. Harassment is often enacted in-person, but it can be technologically mediated and include cyber harassment. Hostile environment harassment encompasses a range of negative behaviours of a sexual nature. These behaviours can range from sexual touching and propositions to exposure, sexual jokes, cartoons, nicknames, and leering, to name only a few. Many of the activities linked with sexual and gender-based harassment listed in Box 10.3 are typical of this kind of harassment.

Sexual harassment is tied to power. Harassers in influential positions attempt to use their (class, organizational, gender, and/or racial) power to take advantage of others. That power is pertinent to hostile work environment harassment may be less obvious, since the

A CLOSER LOOK

10.3 | Sexual Harassment

The Ontario Human Rights Commission (2019c) provides a list of activities that may fall under sexual and gender-based harassment:

- demanding hugs
- invading personal space
- unnecessary physical contact, including unwanted touching.
- derogatory language and/or comments toward women (or non-binary or men, depending on the circumstances), sex-specific derogatory names
- leering or inappropriate staring
- gender-related comments about a person's physical characteristics or mannerisms
- comments or conduct relating to a person's perceived non-conformity with a sex-role stereotype
- displaying or circulating pornography, sexual pictures or cartoons, sexually explicit graffiti, or other sexual images (including online)
- sexual jokes, including circulating written sexual jokes (*e.g.* by e-mail)
- rough and vulgar humour or language related to gender
- sexual or gender-related comment or conduct used to bully a person
- spreading sexual rumours (including online)
- suggestive or offensive remarks or innuendo about members of a specific gender
- propositions of physical intimacy
- gender-related verbal abuse, threats, or taunting
- bragging about sexual prowess
- demanding dates or sexual favours
- questions or discussions about sexual activities
- requiring an employee to dress in a sexualized or gender-specific way
- paternalistic behaviour based on gender which a person feels undermines their status or position of responsibility
- threats to penalize or otherwise punish a person who refuses to comply with sexual advances (known as reprisal).

harassment is often perpetrated by colleagues or clients. However, it is often an assertion of power because the targets are made to feel as if they are different or that they are not welcome, generating feelings of powerlessness. Moreover, hostile work environment harassment has often been tacitly supported by people in positions of authority who turn a blind eye to it or even support it. Both forms of harassment help to reproduce and reinforce gender inequality in society.

Nevertheless, contra-power harassment does occur. Sometimes the perpetrator is someone in a subordinate organizational position who targets a superior (Rospenda, Richman, & Nawyn, 1998). Harassment can still be devastating in these circumstances; however, the person in a position of authority usually has greater resources to stop the harassment (Rospenda et al., 1998). Successful resistance is shaped not only by organizational position but by the intersection of gender, class, and race. Contra-power harassment is sometimes an attempt by a subordinate to undermine the authority of individuals, especially women and minorities in positions of power, and reassert traditional societal power inequalities (ibid.).

As noted at the beginning of this chapter, most women experience sexual harassment at some point in their lives. The exact incidence is difficult to determine. Sev'er (1999), summarizing previous research, finds that the reported incidence of workplace harassment varies between 40 per cent and 90 per cent depending on who was surveyed and what question they were asked. Studies that ask respondents if they have ever been sexually harassed tend to find lower rates of harassment than studies that ask respondents if they have ever experienced verbal abuse of a sexual nature, inappropriate sexual touching, sexual requests, and so on. In the latter instances, the rates of harassment can jump to 80 per cent or more (Chatterjee, 2018). A recent study that looked at harassment generally found that 81 per cent of women and 43 per cent of men reported experiencing some form of harassment in their lifetimes (Chatterjee, 2018). For most men and women, the harassment was verbal in nature, but 51 per cent of women reported unwelcome sexual touching, and 41 per cent of women and 22 per cent of men reported cyber-sexual harassment. This same study found that about 40 per cent of respondents reported harassment in the workplace. It may be the case that sexual harassment is decreasing. While lifetime percentages of workplace harassment remain high, a Statistics Canada study found that only 4 per cent of Canadian women (and less than 1 per cent of Canadian men) reported experiencing sexual harassment in the previous year (Hango & Moyser, 2018).

More than half (56 per cent) of the Canadian women reporting sexual harassment said that the perpetrators were clients or customers, while 44 per cent indicated that colleagues or peers targeted them. Only 15 per cent of respondents said their supervisors or managers harassed them (Hango & Moyser, 2018). This is not surprising, since hostile work environment harassment is more common than quid pro quo harassment, and it is typically perpetrated by colleagues and clients.

Studies also suggest that some workers are more vulnerable than others to sexual harassment. Younger women, sexual minority women, and Indigenous women report higher rates of harassment than do others (Hango & Moyser, 2018). Moreover, workers who are more vulnerable or isolated tend to be at risk, including those dependent on tips for income, those who work in isolated settings (for example, domestic care workers), and those on temporary work visas (Shaw, Hegewisch, & Hess, 2018). People working in male-dominated fields and those working closely with people who are standouts in their fields (or "stars") are also vulnerable; Shaw et al. (2018) suggest that the latter may feel they are special enough to be above the law. Of course, workers experience harassment and violence outside the workplace in their private lives, and this violence can also follow them into the workplace, creating another set of challenges for workers and organizations; women and members of sexual and other minorities may be particularly vulnerable (Wathen, MacGregor, Tanaka, & MacQuarrie, 2018).

Sexual harassment has a significant negative impact on both those who experience it directly and their employing organizations. Psychological impacts include depression and anxiety and feelings of vulnerability (Hango & Moyser, 2018; Shaw et al., 2018; Sev'er, 1999). Some have symptoms severe enough to classify as PTSD. Studies have also documented negative physiological and physical reactions (Schneider, Tomaka, & Palacios, 2001). Economic impacts include job loss, income loss, and lack of career advancement (Shaw et al., 2018; Sev'er, 1999). In response to harassment, workers may leave their jobs despite negative career and income implications. There is also an organizational cost due to the resulting absenteeism, turnover, and lost productivity. Firms implicated in harassment lawsuits face additional economic losses. The costs of harassment run into the hundreds of millions of dollars (Shaw et al., 2018; Sev'er, 1999).

Racial, Disability, and Sexual Orientation Harassment

racial harassment
A form of harassment based on race, skin colour, ancestry, citizenship, accent, language, or religion

Racial harassment is defined as a form of harassment based on race, skin colour, ancestry, citizenship, accent, language, or religion (Ontario Human Rights Commission, 2012). It resembles other forms of harassment in terms of its variations: verbal abuse, racial slurs, offensive jokes, ridicule and humiliating behaviour, and, in some instances, physical contact and abuse. There has been less research on racial harassment than on sexual harassment, but it can have significant negative effects on workers and poison work environments. Although this is a phenomenon affecting minority workers, even non-visible minority workers harassed for their religion, accent, or language can be affected. In a 2018 case heard in Nova Scotia, a Halifax transit mechanic was found to have experienced racial discrimination and harassment; he was white, but his wife was African-Canadian. Black and Indigenous workers at the same company also experienced harassment from a mechanic at the company who hurled verbal abuse and made offensive comments; the perpetrator also threw objects at the victim and tried to hit him with a bus. The harassed man was terrorized and had been diagnosed with PTSD; he also suffered income loss (Saint-Cyr, 2019).

As with other forms of harassment, it is employers' responsibility to ensure that the work environment is safe and respectful for all workers and to take steps to stop harassment when they become aware of it (Saint-Cyr, 2019). Employers who do not take such steps can be liable for damages. In the above instance, the employer had to pay half a million dollars to the complainant for wage loss and injury to dignity (ibid.). There is evidence from the US, however, that claims of racial harassment are the least likely to be recognized and compensated (Jameel & Yerardi, 2019). They may not be taken seriously, and it is rare that individuals are awarded damages, leading some to question whether existing laws and procedures adequately protect minority workers (Jameel & Yerardi, 2019).

Incidence rates for racial harassment are not widely available, and social awareness of this form of harassment in Canada remains low. Lack of awareness may help to explain recent findings that members of visible minorities report less harassment than do others

(Hango & Moyser, 2018). There is a similar dearth of research respecting **disability harassment**; however there is evidence that intersectionality matters and that older women, perhaps especially those who belong to racial minorities, are more vulnerable to disability harassment (Shaw et al., 2012).

disability harassment Harassment on the basis of disability status

A small body of research has also documented **sexual orientation harassment**—harassment on the basis of sexual orientation. We can distinguish two forms: direct harassment, when an individual is directly targeted for abuse, and hostile work environment, in which the workplace culture is explicitly homophobic (Ryan & Wessel, 2012). We lack precise data about how common sexual orientation harassment is, but Canadian research finds that sexual minorities experience more harassment than do others: approximately 23 per cent of Canadians identifying as homosexual or bisexual report harassment, compared to 15.6 per cent of heterosexual Canadians (Hango & Moyser, 2018). The manifestations of harassment along these grounds are similar to other dimensions of workplace harassment (abuse, humiliation, physical contact, and violence), and the impacts (psychological, economic, physical) are similar as well. More research is needed in this area.

sexual orientation harassment Harassment on the basis of sexual orientation

Policy Context

Under the Canadian Labour Code, employers must provide "a workplace free from harassment" (Canadian Human Rights Commission, 2020). Each employer must establish a sexual harassment policy and "make every reasonable effort to ensure that no employee is subject to sexual harassment" (Government of Canada, 2018). If appropriate action is not taken against an employee who harasses another, employers "can be held responsible for harassment committed by their employees" (Canadian Human Rights Commission, 2020).

The CHRC provides a template to employing organizations, detailing steps and providing advice for establishing anti-harassment policies and procedures. When companies take harassment seriously, they can discourage it and deal with it swiftly and decisively when it occurs. When violations are not effectively dealt with at an organizational level, the case may be heard by a provincial human rights tribunal. Tribunal decisions can include fines and penalties for perpetrators found to have committed discrimination and harassment and especially for those organizations that allowed the abuse to occur. When these mechanisms are effective, they can improve working conditions for people regardless of their race, gender, sexual orientation, Indigeneity, disability, or other factors. Nevertheless, these policies are not universal, leaving many workers vulnerable to harassment at work.

To conclude, harassment and discrimination are often thought of as something that "bad" individuals do. Both, however, are social and organizational phenomena. In the past, organizational cultures not only tolerated harassment, they at times endorsed and encouraged it. Complaints against perpetrators were too often ignored or dismissed. Discrimination often takes place at an organizational level, and it may be intentional or unintentional. Indeed, discrimination is likely to occur unintentionally unless we make a concerted effort to avoid it. Now that our laws and social institutions hold organizations more accountable, we can move towards fairer, less discriminatory, more welcoming workplaces. Given the individual, organizational, and societal costs associated with discrimination and harassment, it is imperative that we do so.

Reviewing the Learning Objectives

Now that you have read this chapter, you should:

- Be able to define discrimination and understand the grounds on which it occurs in Canada.
- Understand the impacts of discrimination on workers.
- Have a sense of key policies in this area.
- Be able to define workplace harassment, sexual harassment, and racial harassment and to recognize other types of harassment at work.
- Understand the impacts of harassment on individuals, organizations, and societies.

Questions for Critical Thought

1. When seeking work, how do you find out about jobs? From online or other job postings? From friends, family members, and acquaintances? Direct inquiries? Which recruitment methods do you think are least discriminatory? Why?
2. Some strategies proposed to help workers navigate discriminatory work environments (such as altering résumés and one's appearance) are themselves discriminatory. Can you think of any non-discriminatory strategies that might help workers to navigate discriminatory workplaces and labour markets?
3. What kinds of policy changes could be made in this area to reduce harassment and discrimination further?
4. Discrimination reproduces social inequalities, but there is little research adopting an explicitly intersectional lens. Based on the research presented in this chapter, how would you expect intersectional inequalities to shape workers experiences of discrimination and harassment?

Annotated Additional Readings

Carpenter, C. S., Eppink, S. T., & Gonzales, G. (2020). Transgender status, gender identity, and socioeconomic outcomes in the United States. *Industrial & Labor Relations Review, 73*(3), 573–599.

A thorough look at the impact of transgender status and gender identity on socio-economic outcomes.

Quadlin, N. (2018). The mark of a woman's record: Gender and academic performance in hiring. *American Sociological Review, 83*, 331–360.

This audit study explores the impact of gender, major, and course average on hiring in the United States.

Waite, S., Pajovic, V., & Denier, N. (2020). Lesbian, gay and bisexual earnings in the Canadian labor market: New evidence from the Canadian community health survey. *Research in Social Stratification and Mobility, 67*. Retrieved from https://doi.org/10.1016/j.rssm.2020.100484.

This paper provides a comprehensive look at sexual orientation and labour market earnings.

Zarifa, D., Walters, D., & Seward, B. (2015). The earnings and employment outcomes of the 2005 cohort of Canadian postsecondary graduates with disabilities. *The Canadian Review of Sociology*, 52, 343.

This article compares the employment and earnings outcomes of post-secondary graduates who have disabilities and those who do not.

Related Websites

Human Rights Legal Support Centre: Cases decided at hearing:

https://www.hrlsc.on.ca/en/human-rights-stories/Cases-decided-at-hearing

British Columbia Human Rights Tribunal:

http://www.bchrt.bc.ca/

Alberta Human Rights Commission:

https://www.albertahumanrights.ab.ca/about/Pages/contact.aspx

Ontario Human Rights Commission, Sexual Harassment Fact Sheet:

http://www.ohrc.on.ca/en/sexual-harassment-employment-fact-sheet

11 Working across the Life Course

Learning Objectives

After reading this chapter, readers will:

- Be familiar with the life course paradigm and the importance of age and life course stage to work experiences.
- Be able to identify some challenges that youth experience as they enter the labour market.
- Know what work-family conflict is and what factors exacerbate or mitigate it.
- Have a sense of older adults' work experiences and transition to retirement.

Introduction

There are moments in our lives that feel profound and life-changing. After this moment, we think, my life will not be the same. Some of these moments are personal in nature, but many are patterned and shared by others at a similar life course stage. In Canadian society, these moments can include graduating high school, entering post-secondary education, getting a first part-time job, landing a first full-time job, having a child, retiring from the workforce, and so on. Not everyone will experience these key life transitions, and those of us who do will likely experience them differently. The age at which we achieve these milestones, our geographic location and social-historical context, our class, gender, race, (dis)ability status, sexual orientation, and other differences are going to shape our experiences in profound ways.

To understand workers' experiences of transitions related to work, it is helpful to draw on an intersectional life course approach and specifically to explore the ways in which age and cohort, social-historical context, and intersectional inequalities combine to shape these experiences. In this chapter, we begin with an overview of the life course paradigm and describe how it can be blended with intersectionality approaches (reviewed in Chapter 2) to understand work-related life transitions. Then we focus on three major transitions experienced by the vast majority of workers: school-to-work transitions, transitions related to work-family conflict, and older workers' transitions to retirement. Throughout, we pay attention to how experiences vary by social location and how these variations are shaped by, and in turn reproduce, social inequalities.

(Intersectional) Life Course Approach

By **life course**, scholars mean the "sequence of roles, opportunities, constraints, and events that shape" our lives from birth to death (Shanahan & Macmillan, 2008, p. 40; Elder, Kirkpatrick, Johnson, & Crosnoe, 2003). These sequences are structured by social institutions and prevailing societal norms. There tends to be a normative sequence of events—an order that seems normal—even though deviations and variations occur all the time. For example, in today's society many people delay child-bearing until after they finish school and are established in the labour market; however, some do have children earlier. Experiencing transitions and major life events "off-time" will be different, and often more difficult, than experiencing such transitions and events when others in your age cohort do.

life course
The "sequence of roles, opportunities, constraints, and events that shape" our lives from birth to death (Shanahan & Macmillan, 2008, p. 40)

A core principle of the life course paradigm is that social-historical and geographic context strongly influences life course patterns and trajectories. Those graduating from university in Canada during the COVID-19 pandemic faced a very different labour market and fewer opportunities than those who graduated during a period of economic growth and labour market expansion. Moreover, the experiences of those looking for work in provinces or regions particularly hard hit by an economic downturn will obviously be different from those seeking work in provinces and regions where there is more economic growth. Context matters a lot, as does age cohort.

An **age cohort**, or generation, consists of people born within the same decade or two. People born into different cohorts will experience major social events at different periods in the life course, and this may lead them to have different life experiences. People in their 70s, for example, experienced the COVID-19 pandemic differently from those in their 20s or 40s. The life events shared by members of a cohort may lead them to have a different outlook, different attitudes and values, and even different styles of working (Mercure, Vulture, & Fleury, 2012). This has the potential to generate conflict in the workplace across cohort (see Box 11.1).

age cohort
A category composed of people born within a decade or two of each other

Another key principle of the life course paradigm concerns **linked lives**. An individual's life course is strongly influenced by their social relationships and social connections. In previous chapters, we have already discussed how our social networks and social capital can shape job opportunities, but this idea of linked lives goes deeper and takes into account our class positions, our family members, and others we interact with. It encourages us to consider how what happens in others' lives impacts our own. If a family member has a serious health problem, for example, we might take some time off of work to care for them, and this may impact our work opportunities, our skill acquisition at work, our relationships with our bosses and colleagues, and so forth.

linked lives
A concept under the life course paradigm that encourages us to consider how what happens in the lives of others connected to us impacts our own lives

Three other life course concepts are relevant for us here: transitions, trajectories, and turning points. **Transitions** are changes in our social roles. One transition that has been of central concern to sociologists is the transition between school and work—our entry into the job market. Here we leave behind the role of student and adopt the role of full-time worker. This transition need not go in only one direction. Once in the labour force, we might continue to take courses or even leave work and embark on a period of more schooling. Each of these changes, however, is a life course transition. These transitions are embedded in (and may partially compose) our life course **trajectory**—patterned pathways we traverse as we live our lives and pursue our goals. For example, we may study certain

transitions
A concept within the life course paradigm used to describe the changes we experience as we move between social roles

trajectories
A concept within the life course paradigm used to capture the patterned pathways we traverse as we live our lives and pursue our goals

The Future of Work

11.1 | Generational Conflict in the Workplace

Management and HR scholars have drawn on generational thinking to argue that organizational and management practices should change to adapt to the needs and demands of new generations of workers, especially Millennials (variously defined but often those born between 1982 and 2000) and Generation Z that follows them. These scholars argue that different generations have distinct characteristics, values, and orientations. Previous work practices may have been suitable for other generations, like Baby Boomers (born between the Second World War and the early 1960s) and, to a lesser extent, Generation X (born between the mid-1960s and 1980). Millennials, however, are said to be different: "tech-savvy," team-oriented workers who expect to be challenged and may be motivated more by intrinsic than extrinsic rewards. They also expect to change employers numerous times in their careers, and they like structure (Williams, 2019). Their different orientation has been seen to generate conflict at work because Millennials' expectations for immediate rewards and early promotions and their need for structure puts them at odds with Gen X and Baby Boomers. Managing Millennial workers has been said to require companies to change and adopt new managerial practices (Williams, 2019).

Influenced by sociological approaches to generations—which recognize generations but do not regard everyone born within a cohort as sharing personality traits—Glynne Williams (2019) challenges these simplistic accounts and sheds light on how they have been constructed. Importantly, he shows how Millennials' so-called traits align with organizational rationalization and prevailing managerial theories, which aim to reduce worker autonomy ("Millennials like structure"), decrease benefits ("Millennials care more about intrinsic than extrinsic benefits"), and minimize company investment in developing workers across their careers ("Millennials expect to have many different employers"). The widespread acceptance of the idea that young workers are different from their predecessors is, then, used to justify and encourage new managerial practices, deteriorating working conditions, and rising precarity. To sum, Williams (2019) encourages us to be skeptical of the generations theories endorsed in managerial publications and their use to structure workplaces, today and in the future, in a manner that is detrimental to workers.

subjects in school and seek out work and volunteer experiences that are consistent with our career goals. Here we are traversing a certain life course trajectory—one that, we hope, will lead to the job we want. Landmark transitions are called **turning points**. Turning points are significant transitions that invoke behavioural changes and alter opportunities. For many of us, the COVID-19 pandemic will be a turning point. It has altered how and where people work, has resulted in substantial job loss, has closed some opportunities, and may bring new job opportunities in previously unanticipated fields. Turning points can alter our life trajectories and shift our life course pathways. A turning point need not be a major societal event but rather can be any significant opportunity, event, or experience that alters our life goals and/or that provides unanticipated opportunities (or blocked opportunities) that send us in a new direction.

turning point
A concept within the life course paradigm used to describe very significant transitions that may alter our opportunities and trajectories

All aspects of our life course are shaped by our social location—not only our physical and social-historical location but our class, gender, race, immigration status, (dis)ability status, sexual orientation, and so on. Those of us making the transition from school to work will experience this differently, depending on our economic means (Are we in a lot of debt due to our schooling? Can our parents support us as we look for a "good" job, or do we need to take whatever is available to make ends meet?). Stereotypes and biases related to our race structure job opportunities, as we have seen in earlier chapters. Thus, it is valuable to combine the life course paradigm with an intersectionality approach to understand barriers and opportunities, transitions and trajectories that we experience at work across our lifetimes (Choroszewicz & Adams, 2019). At the same time, we need to remember the importance of cohort or generation. Your experiences of transitioning into the labour market are likely quite different from your parents' and especially your grandparents' experiences. Combining these two approaches illuminates how age and cohort intersect with gender, class, race, and other structured social inequalities to shape social experiences of key (work-)life transitions and trajectories in certain social-historical contexts and circumstances.

School-to-Work Transitions

The transition between school and full-time work is a significant one. Perhaps more than any other, this transition signals the beginning of independent adulthood. With this transition, we expect that youth will become fully independent from their parents. So many other life changes may hinge on this one—achieving an adult identity, establishing an independent household, forming lasting romantic partnerships, having children, making major purchases, and so on (Yeung & Yang, 2020; Ravanera, Fernando, & Burch, 2003). The fact that this transition today is uncertain and fraught with difficulty is, therefore, a matter of some concern (Yeung & Yang, 2020; Settersten & Ray, 2010). Youth finishing school—whether high school, college, or university—and entering the labour market are met with high youth unemployment rates, underemployment, precarious

Source: © meandering images/Shutterstock

University of Ottawa students beginning the school year in 2020 in the midst of the COVID-19 pandemic. As a student, how has the pandemic affected your experiences of work or your plans to transition into the workplace?

work, and employers who prefer workers to arrive with job-relevant experience and training so that they do not need to bear the costs of training (Pastore, 2018; Hall, 2014). Visible minority and immigrant youth are especially negatively impacted by these trends (Lauer, Wilkinson, Yan, Sin, & Tsang, 2012; Settersten & Ray, 2010; Sun, 2020). Moreover, experiences of these transitions vary by gender, class, and other characteristics (Lehmann, 2005; Wyn, Cuervo, Crofts, & Woodman, 2017; Pullman, 2018). For example, women do not receive the same returns on their education in terms of remuneration or quality of work (Wyn et al., 2017; Pullman, 2018), nor do young people with disabilities (Zarifa et al., 2015; Janus, 2009). Concern has been raised about the impact of difficulty during this transition on subsequent, more long-term trajectories.

Youth employment rates reflect these challenges. Many young people are not employed and are extending the time they spend in school. Indeed, in Canada, youth aged 20–24 are almost equally as likely to be in school as in the labour force. Patterns vary across the country, with youth in Ontario, Quebec, and Newfoundland and Labrador more likely to be in school between the ages of 20 and 24, while in other provinces they are more likely to be employed (Brunet, 2019). More people are completing post-secondary degrees and diplomas, acquiring certifications and taking additional courses, pursuing graduate degrees or other advanced education. With credential inflation, it may take more education to secure good work. Low employment rates, then, partly reflect young people's investments in their education and human capital.

Human capital has been shown to be very important in the school-to-work transition. Having a post-secondary degree improves labour market opportunities. Youth without degrees face dwindling labour market opportunities. Credential inflation (see Chapter 7) has meant that there are fewer jobs available for those without higher education. Such jobs tend to be precarious and low-paid (Kalleberg, 2018). As Figure 11.1 shows, the participation of younger workers (here aged 25–34) in temporary jobs—one form of precarious labour—increased significantly in the 28 years between 1989 and 2017. Rates of temporary employment have more than doubled for young men, while young women were four times more likely to work in temporary jobs in 2017 than in 1989. Such numbers not only reflect the rise in non-standard jobs but show that younger workers—especially women—are particularly affected by these labour market trends. Young workers are also quite likely to be involuntarily employed part-time (Brunet, 2019).

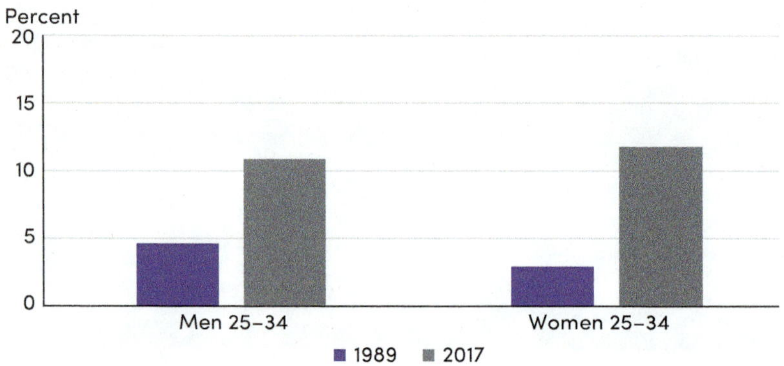

FIGURE 11.1 Temporary employment among full-time employees

Source: Statistics Canada, 2018f.

While temporary and part-time jobs are often not good jobs, they may be better than no job at all. Some young workers—disproportionately those without a post-secondary education (or even a high school diploma)—fall into a category that policy-makers call NEET: Not in Education, Employment or Training. Roughly 12 per cent of Canadian youth aged

20–24 are in this category. Rates, however, vary dramatically across the country, with youth in Nunavut and the Northwest Territories particularly disadvantaged (Brunet, 2019). This phenomenon reflects social exclusion, since youth in this category are not doing what society expects young people to be doing: studying, training, or working. Many different types of people might find themselves in this NEET category for shorter or longer periods of time: People may be between jobs, looking for work, transitioning between school and work, or too ill or disabled to work, or they could be out of the workforce to care for a child or other family member. Statistics Canada estimates that about 40 per cent of Canadian NEET youth are actively looking for employment (Brunet, 2019). Some of those not actively looking could be discouraged: they have had such difficulty finding suitable work that they have given up. Others who might fall into this category include street youth who engage in a variety of informal income-earning activities to survive, such as panhandling, busking, or other creative pursuits (Karabanow, Hughes, & Kidd, 2010), and individuals earning money through illegal activities.

Rates of youth in the NEET category vary internationally, but globally roughly one in five young people are NEET (ILO, 2017); three-quarters of them are women (Yeung & Yang, 2020). Many young women who are NEET are raising children. In Canada, the rates are different, with only about one in 10 youth in the NEET category; just over half of them are men (Brunet, 2019). Among 35 OECD countries, Canada's rate of NEET is the 13th lowest (Brunet, 2019). Yet, as we have seen, regionally and among some groups, NEET remains a problem in Canada. Indigenous youth, especially those in the far north, are particularly vulnerable to NEET, reflecting social exclusion: 23 per cent of Indigenous youth, living off-reserve are NEET (compared to 12 per cent of Canadians 20–24 generally) (Brunet, 2019). Systemic discrimination also means that young Black men are disadvantaged. They are overrepresented in unemployment and NEET (Turcotte, 2020). Differences between Black women and other women are statistically insignificant.

The lack of opportunities for people without human capital is a concern. There is a need for more programs to address youth in this situation and help them to acquire the skills they need to successfully transition into the labour market. Given the fact that trends vary regionally and by social grouping, policy solutions need to be targeted. A one-size-fits-all type of policy will not suffice. Indeed, Canada has implemented programs that specifically target Indigenous youth, like the First Nations and Inuit Youth Employment Strategy (Government of Canada, 2019).

Although labour market conditions for youth with human capital are much better, social trends are still concerning. It can take youth some time to settle into full-time work, and people may spend time in low-paid (or unpaid) internships, temporary and part-time work, and/or jobs in fields outside their expertise before settling into full-time careers. Nevertheless, the vast majority of university graduates do find jobs and earn decent incomes within two years of graduation. Outcomes vary by degree/program of study (as well as other factors like gender, visible minority status, and Indigeneity).

Table 11.1 provides data on university graduate outcomes in Ontario and Alberta (Council of Ontario Universities, 2016; Alberta, Government of, 2018). Ontario's numbers reflect the graduating class in 2013 surveyed in 2015. Alberta's reflect the graduating class of 2016 surveyed in 2018. Survey strategies, years, and program categories are not identical, so caution should be exercised in comparing the two provinces. Patterns are fairly consistent, however, across the two. The vast majority of graduates are employed,

TABLE 11.1 University Graduate Employment Outcomes by Program, Ontario 2015 and Alberta 2018

Ontario, Class of 2013, Surveyed in 2015			Alberta, class of 2016, Surveyed in 2018		
Program	**Employment Rate**	**Average Income (2 years post-grad)**	**Program**	**Employment Rate**	**Income (median)**
Agriculture and Biological Sciences	90.0%	$40,958	Agriculture, Natural Resources, Conservation	93.0%	$47,889
Architecture, Engineering	88.8% 85.0%	$44,874 $64,571	Architecture, Engineering, and Related	90.0%	$64,766
Business and Commerce	88.4%	$53,568	Business, Management, Public Administration	93.0%	$66,642
Education	89.2%	$43,063	Education	98.0%	$66,370
Health Professions	82.5%	$53,202	Health and Related	95.0%	$60,957
Humanities	87.5%	$38,305	Humanities	90.0%	$49,390
Mathematics, Computer Science	84.8% 91.4%	$56,663 $67,100	Mathematics, Computer Science	93.0%	$57,995
Nursing	89.4%	$61,929	Personal, Protective, and Transportation Services	91.0%	$52,185
Physical Sciences	77.8%	$44,091	Physical and Life Sciences	89.0%	$47,599
Social Sciences, Law	85.2% 91.7%	$41,091 $73,108	Social, Behavioural Sciences, and Law	93.0%	$50,656
Arts (Fine and Applied)	86.1%	$35,194	Visual and Performing Arts, Communication Technologies	93.0%	$33,849
Medicine	99.6%	$69,881			

Source: Data from Council of Ontario Universities, 2016; Alberta, Government of, 2018.

and earning decent salaries, two years after graduation. University graduates from professional programs (like medicine, nursing, law, engineering, architecture) tend to have some of the highest employment rates and incomes two years out. Graduates from the physical sciences have worse outcomes, on average, than others, although some arts grads struggle as well. Graduates from social sciences tend to do fairly well: their outcomes are average—higher than some, lower than others.

Overall, while a university degree is a key ingredient in labour market success, the outcomes of university graduates vary. University education is not, in itself, a guarantee of a successful school-to-work transition. Gender, race, and immigration status seem to be particularly influential in shaping outcomes. Gender differences in area of study also impact employment outcomes (Pullman, 2018). Overall, there are not enough good, stable jobs available for all of those ready to fill these jobs, and some employers are reluctant to take a chance on hiring new graduates. People may struggle for a bit before settling into the labour market. There is concern that this initial struggle could have implications for career trajectories.

Research suggests that marginalized youth experience more disadvantages (Settersten & Ray, 2010). Youth with disabilities, for example, are under-represented in full-time employment and overrepresented in unemployment and part-time employment, despite their completion of post-secondary education (Zarifa et al., 2015; Lindsay et al., 2014). Youth with criminal records are also highly disadvantaged (Davies & Tanner, 2003). Rural-urban differences are apparent; youth in rural and remote areas face reduced opportunities and may need to travel to secure work—many to urban centres, although some may move to more remote areas (Hillier, Sano, Zarifa, & Haan, 2020; Power & Norman, 2019). Indigenous youth experience similar barriers (Sun, 2020; Turcotte, 2020; Brunet, 2019).

Several studies have explored the experiences of immigrant youth in Canada. For example, Lauer et al. (2012) found that foreign-trained immigrant youth faced many challenges finding work because employers were often unwilling to recognize their credentials. As a result they were overrepresented in lower-skilled jobs. Wilkinson (2008) found higher rates of unemployment among immigrant, and especially refugee, young workers. Statistics Canada (2018h) data, presented in Figure 11.2, provide additional evidence. This figure displays the proportion of young workers (25–34 years of age) with university degrees who are underemployed—working in jobs requiring only a high school diploma or less. Just under one-fifth of men and women in this age group are underemployed in this manner. Digging deeper and looking at the experiences of immigrant men and women (with foreign degrees) reveals striking disadvantage. Among young foreign-trained immigrants, more than one-third of men and four in 10 women are underemployed. Immigrant youth, then, experience very poor labour market outcomes in Canada. Even second-generation immigrant youth (Canadian-born with immigrant parents) experience barriers because of discrimination and lack of access to social capital; this is particularly true for those who are members of visible minorities (Aslam, 2021).

Labour markets can strongly impact school-to-work transitions too. In times of prosperity, the transition is easier. Over the past 20 years, however, youth labour force participation has dropped almost 10 per cent globally; youth employment has declined, and duration of unemployment spells has risen (ILO, 2017; Yeung & Yang, 2020). The International Labour Organization (ILO, 2017) has also raised concerns about the quality of the jobs that young workers secure.

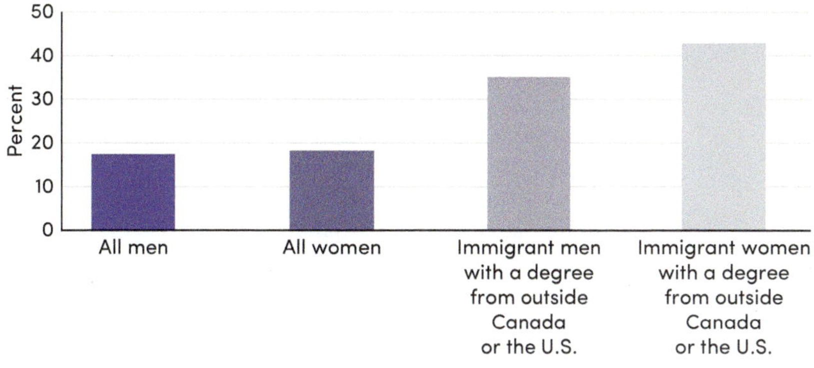

FIGURE 11.2 Proportion of youth aged 25 to 34 with a university degree working in occupations requiring high school education or less

Source: Statistics Canada, National Household Survey, 2011.

As a result of the ongoing labour market difficulties experienced by young workers, the school-to-work transition is now longer in duration. Some may graduate one day and start a new full-time job in their field the next; however, for many it can take years for a graduate to acquire a coveted full-time job in a field of interest, and additional training and education may be required. The transition is also more uneven. Rather than a simple, one-time transition between school and work, people may move back and forth between work and schooling as they try to acquire more credentials, training, and experience that will secure their path along a coveted labour market trajectory. It can be argued that the school-to-work transition is actually now more of a trajectory—requiring several smaller transitions to complete (Witteveen, 2018). During this trajectory, people may rely on their families of origin more and for a longer period of time, creating additional burdens for families (Settersten & Ray, 2010).

In 2020, data indicated that youth were hit harder than others by the COVID-19 pandemic-induced recession. Youth's share of employment dropped by more than 20 per cent in the opening months of the pandemic. The impact was similar regardless of educational attainment. The employment share of those with a post-secondary degree fell by 21 per cent, while the share of those with a high school diploma or less fell by 19 per cent (LMiC, 2020). The youth unemployment rate reached an all-time high of 29.7 per cent in May 2020 before falling slightly in the months following, but remaining high (Trading Economics, 2021). Racialized youth were significantly more likely to be unemployed than white youth during the pandemic (Sharp, 2020). Youth often rely on summer employment, not only to earn a living but to support their post-secondary education. Many students would not have met the minimum conditions for the Canada Emergency Response Benefit (CERB), and while a Canada Emergency Student Benefit (CESB) was established, the latter paid less and was undersubscribed (Lim 2020).[1] In this way, the pandemic brought both labour market and financial difficulty for young adults. These difficulties could have implications for employment and earning outcomes for years to come (Lim, 2021).

The available evidence suggests that more could be done policy-wise to ease youth's transition into the labour force, including, perhaps, incentives for employers to invest in hiring and training youth. Since young workers' experiences are diverse, policy strategies need to be as well (Yeung & Yang, 2020). For example, particular interventions among both youth and employers can make a positive impact on employment opportunities for youth with disabilities (Lindsay et al., 2014). We have already noted the presence of policies targeting Indigenous youth; however, there appear to be few initiatives to support Black youth and other marginalized groups. One might also question the effectiveness of existing policies.

In countries where employers are encouraged to provide opportunities for youth and invest in their training, like Germany, youth outcomes are better (see Box 11.2). While school-to-work transitions have been identified as a growing global concern (ILO, 2017), it is clear that youth in some countries fare better than others. Youth in Canada appear to face a more prolonged transition than those in the US (Fussell, Gauthier, and Evans, 2007); however, they are better off than their counterparts in the Arab states, Africa, and the Caribbean—all of which have higher rates of unemployment (Yeung & Yang, 2020; ILO, 2017).

Addressing these problems is important because challenges in the school-to-work transition (or trajectory) can accumulate across the life course. For instance, Krahn and

---

[1]The Canadian government created relief funding for Canadian workers and student/workers negatively impacted by the COVID-19 pandemic. More information about these programs can be found on government websites (see Government of Canada, 2020b, 2020c).

Global Perspectives

11.2 | Canada, Germany, and International Differences in School-to-Work Transitions

Globally, youth employment has been identified as an area of concern (ILO, 2017; United Nations, 2019). Still, youth outcomes vary geographically depending on education and employment policy environments and labour market conditions, among other factors. Canada shares many similarities with other Anglo-Saxon countries including the United States, United Kingdom, and Australia (Pastore, 2018). In these countries, youth unemployment rates (pre-pandemic) were comparatively low, although often two to three times the adult unemployment rate. Here, as elsewhere, youth unemployment can be strongly impacted by the economic cycle, and youth have difficulty acquiring job-related human capital, since firms prefer to hire people with work experience. In contrast, countries in central Europe like Germany have youth unemployment rates largely in line with adult unemployment rates. German youth benefit from a dual-education system whereby work-related skills are imparted during schooling through apprenticeships and on-the-job training (Pastore, 2018; Lehmann, 2000). This system ensures that youth learn the skills employers want—resulting in lower unemployment and a smoother school-to-work transition. Nevertheless, there are downsides to the German system in terms of its educational tracking: children are streamed into different skilled trades, applied white-collar, and academic paths from a young age (Lehmann, 2000). This streaming reproduces inequalities to the extent that which stream children end up in is shaped by structural inequalities by class, ethnicity, and gender (ibid.). While the German system has many advantages in terms of youth employment outcomes, its inflexibility is a detriment.

After completing an international review of youth school-to-work transitions, Pastore (2018, p. 1) concludes that "education systems that integrate more with the labor market through apprenticeships, job placement services, or direct hiring by firms, seem to set up their youth for success in the labor market."

Chow (2016) find that spells of unemployment experienced by youth (aged 18–32) can accumulate, resulting in lower incomes and lower-quality work for adults in their early 30s. Early labour market difficulty can have a negative impact on career trajectories, mental health, economic autonomy, and identity (Yeung & Yang, 2020).

Work-Family Conflict

Workers, regardless of age or life course stage, may seek to balance their work and personal lives. Such balance can be difficult to achieve, however. Work demands can limit our personal lives and community involvements. Other demands on our time (from family, school, hobbies, volunteering, and other community involvement) can interfere with work. Work-family conflict can be seen as one important dimension of broader **work-life conflicts**: conflicts between work and other aspects of our lives (Kossek & Lee, 2017). Work demands can be extensive, and in our connected world, there is often the expectation that we are constantly available to work, even outside regular work hours (Vallée, 2018). We are just a phone call, text, or email away. Today, work invades our private lives in a manner that was unimaginable a few decades ago. Resulting work-life conflict can reduce job satisfaction and increase job stress (see Chapter 8).

work-life conflicts Conflicts between our work commitments and other aspects of our lives. Work-family conflict is one aspect

work-family conflict When work and family demands conflict or the stress experienced when work and family demands conflict

Work-family conflict occurs when work roles and obligations conflict or interfere with family roles and obligations (Kossek & Lee, 2017). Although anyone can experience work-family conflict, it is especially common among those at a particular life course stage: workers who are parents with (especially small) children living with them. In the literature, work-family conflict is talked about in two different ways. On the one hand, we can think of work-family conflict as a conflict of roles, time, and responsibilities (Kossek & Lee, 2017). You have an important work meeting to attend, but at the same time you need to care for your child who is home sick from school. You cannot be in two places at once and hence are faced with conflicting demands. On the other hand, researchers look at work-family conflict in terms of stress (Fredriksen-Goldsen & Scharlach, 2001; Young, Montazer, & Singh, 2020). If your lack of effective daycare or your heavy eldercare responsibilities impact your ability to meet work demands—or if your work obligations prevent you from being present for your child when needed—you may experience considerable stress. While time and role conflicts often lead to stress, this is not always the case. The presence of a good caregiver, supportive bosses, or family members you can rely on might help you to navigate competing obligations while keeping stress to a minimum. Nevertheless, research suggests that most working parents experience work-family conflict and most find it stressful.

Work-family conflict is endemic in Canadian society because norms and practices related to working are largely incompatible with norms and practices surrounding child-rearing (and providing care for loved ones generally). Remember that organizations are gendered (Acker, 1990): assumptions about gender are embedded in the very structures of our social institutions. One of those assumptions is that workers have no important competing obligations, so they are always available to their employing organizations. This assumption was likely more true back when workers were disproportionately single men or family breadwinners with parents or spouses in the home to ensure that the housework got done and family needs were taken care of. The rise of two-earner and single-parent families since the 1960s means that this assumption no longer holds for most households. Many workers have outside obligations and cannot be constantly available to work. Norms surrounding child-rearing are strikingly similar. Experts suggest that children are in need of constant care and attention from parents if they are to be healthy and well-adjusted (Hays, 1996; Richardson, 1993). Raising kids is a major commitment that involves considerable investment of resources, including time and money. Kids, we believe, should be a priority, and it is important to be there for them when they need us (which could be quite often) (Blair-Loy, 2003; Hays, 1996). Family work can be pressure-filled (Bowen, Elliott, & Brenton, 2014).

In this sense, working and child-rearing are "competing devotions" (Blair-Loy, 2003): both require considerable time, energy, and emotion. Balancing these competing devotions can be very difficult. With rising work expectations and uncertainty—long hours, growing precarity, and constant availability through technology—work demands appear to be on the rise. Family scholars suggest that norms of parenthood have intensified as well. Chapter 6 introduced the concept of intensive mothering: an ideology of parenthood according to which child-rearing should be "child-centred, expert-guided, emotionally absorbing, financially expensive, and labour intensive" (Hays, 1996, p. 8). This ideology is pervasive. Even those who resist it are aware of it. They may feel the need to defend themselves against others' (hypothetical or real) assertions that they are "bad mothers" (Elliott & Bowen, 2018). Norms of fatherhood are changing too, with the "involved father" emerging as a new expectation (Choroszewicz, 2019). Decades ago, rearing children was deemed a one-person job that usually fell to a mother. However, increasingly, all parents (biological, social, adoptive, or otherwise) are expected to be involved in child-rearing.

In light of these conflicting structures and competing devotions, it may not be surprising that work-family conflict is common. According to a Government of Canada (2008) study, 88 per cent of employees experience role overload resulting in work-family conflict: 58 per cent report high levels of overload, with an additional 30 per cent reporting moderate levels. Gender shapes experiences of work-family conflict. Some studies find that fathers report more work-family conflict in terms of time than do women; however, mothers report more stress than do fathers (Tézli & Gauthier, 2009; Kossek & Lee, 2017). While mothers continue to provide more childcare than fathers, they are also more likely to cut back on work hours to do so (potentially reducing time conflict).

Although work-family conflict is a common experience, it may not be experienced by everyone in the same way. For example, Indigenous workers report feeling marginalized and frustrated with work demands that interfere not only with family life but with cultural practices as well (Julien, Somerville, & Brant, 2017). They experience career repercussions when they make time for the latter. For some Indigenous people, balance is not simply a matter of managing working and living but may encompass spiritual, emotional, mental, and physical balance (Walker et al., 2020). Working-class and economically disadvantaged workers may find it more difficult to balance work and family in light of their low incomes. Moreover, LGBTQI workers may have unique challenges, especially those with alternative family structures, including "found family"—deep family-type bonds among people not related by blood or marriage. Responsibilities to found-family members may not be recognized by employers, colleagues, or others in society (Dixon & Dougherty, 2014), adding to stress related to work-family conflict.

While work-family conflict is nearly universal among parents with children in the family home, there are factors that can mitigate (reduce) or exacerbate (worsen) the extent of it and the stress associated with it. Perhaps most important, workplace policies can play a very significant role. Workplaces that allow more flexibility in terms of work hours and location, for example, reduce work-family conflict for their workers. Having the ability to work from home periodically or to leave work in the middle of the day if there is an emergency helps workers to improve their work-family balance; however, this kind of flexibility is not possible in every job. Supervisor and managerial support is important; workers with supportive supervisors appear to experience less conflict and stress (Government of Canada, 2008). Flexibility in these policies is also important. As noted, the alternative family structures of some LGBTQI workers may not be accommodated by workplace policies that rigidly define a family as a heterosexual couple with children (Dixon & Dougherty, 2014). For Indigenous peoples, family leaves that acknowledge a broader conceptualization of family are also important. So too are cultural leaves that allow Indigenous workers to take time off for cultural practices and seasonal activities (Indigenous Corporate Training Inc., 2015).

Work expectations are significant. Workplaces that expect not only long work hours but frequent (and unplanned) overtime will worsen work-family conflict. Jobs without such expectations can be easier to combine with child-rearing. Workplace policies that allow paid sick-days or personal days to care for ill children can also mitigate work-family conflict. The type of work people do can also exacerbate or mitigate work-family stress:

for example, those in emotionally demanding jobs requiring care work may struggle with the care work demands of family members during their "second shift" (Cottingham et al., 2020). Those in stressful, demanding jobs like police-work have reported challenges with shifting between their very different work and family roles (Bikos, 2016).

Personal and family resources and demands are also relevant. Parents with more children or young children as well as single parents face more burdensome obligations. People who have extended family, friends, or community supports to help with childcare and other family responsibilities find it easier to meet work obligations. If you earn a high income, you may be able to afford a bevy of nannies, babysitters, camps, tutors, maids, and other support workers to cover your childcare and domestic duties, leaving you free to work. Those without close friends and family able to help out and those with lower incomes may experience more work-family conflict and hence more stress. The economically and racially marginalized are particularly impacted (Nichols et al., 2018).

Identity and values also shape work-family conflict. If your role as parent is very important to your sense of self and/or you highly value children, you may be particularly stressed when your work obligations force you to be less available to your kids. If your work roles are more important to you and/or you have others you trust who are available to care for your children then pressure to prioritize work is likely experienced as less stressful.

Regardless of identity and values, however, work-family conflict is challenging and a source of stress. Traditionally, many workplaces have regarded work-family conflict as an individual problem rather than a structural one. Although child-rearing is essential for societal functioning, some see family responsibilities as something individuals need to manage on their own (Olakivi & Wrede, 2019). This viewpoint could be changing. The COVID-19 pandemic not only required millions of Canadians to work from home in self-isolation, it closed schools for months on end. Many parents struggled to continue to work while simultaneously caring for (and supervising the online schooling of) their children. Their challenges with work-family conflict became more obvious to all. Early reports were optimistic that the pandemic provided working parents with more opportunities to spend time with children, and that employers would be understanding of workers' intensified burdens. (Doward, 2020). There was hope that more family-friendly workplaces could emerge. However, more recent research has documented hardship for workers, with intensified work-family conflict during the pandemic exacerbating gender inequality (Feng & Savani, 2020). While men increased their participation in child-rearing during quarantine periods (Shafer et al., 2020), women were more negatively affected, taking on more childcare responsibilities, which hindered their ability to work (Topping, 2020; Carlson, Petts, & Pepin, 2020; Feng & Savani, 2020).

Work-family conflict impacts working parents in several ways. This can include stress and burnout, which can lead to absenteeism and sickness—outcomes that have clear, negative implications for employing organizations and workers. Work-family conflict also lowers job satisfaction and increases workplace absenteeism and turnover (Ontario Human Rights Commission, 2020). It may result in negative career repercussions. For instance, work-family conflict can delay promotions and progress along a career ladder. Challenges with work-family conflict can lead people to change jobs, alter their career trajectories, and/or cut back their hours in an effort to achieve some level of work-life balance (Boni-Le Goff, Le Feuvre, Mallard, Lépinard, & Morel, 2019). Alternatively, work-family conflict can reduce involvement in childcare and family life (Choroszewicz, 2019).

Preliminary research on the impact of the pandemic identified similar impacts, with women with young children forced to cut back on work hours (Qian & Fuller, 2020). Some left the labour force, while others experienced blocked opportunities (Desjardins & Freestone, 2020). Pandemic-related work-family conflict may have longer-term career implications as well.

Work-family conflict also has implications for income. Researchers have found, for example, that married men with a stay-at-home partner earn higher incomes than single men and men with working partners (Chun & Lee, 2001). In contrast, women experience **motherhood penalties**: Their incomes and opportunities suffer with the transition to motherhood (Budig & England, 2001). In this manner, work-family conflict is a contributor to gender inequalities (Cloutier, Bernard, & Tremblay, 2011). Furthermore, Weisshaar's (2018) audit study findings (see Chapter 10) suggest that parents who take leaves to care for family members could face labour market disadvantages upon their return. Thus, work-family conflict has significant implications for workers, their well-being, and social inequality. As a result, it is a topic of policy concern and debate.

motherhood penalties Women's incomes and opportunities suffer with the transition to motherhood

Relevant Policies

Since work-family conflict has been regarded by many (especially employers) as a personal problem, workers have been left to strategize solutions on their own. People have sought to reduce work-family conflict by not having children, delaying child-bearing until careers are more established, reducing the number of children they have, or cutting back their work-hours to manage family demands (Vanier Institute, 2009). People may rely on extended family or purchase goods and services (like pre-made meals) to save time on housework. As noted above, working parents might change jobs and seek ones that are more flexible and family-friendly. These solutions can ameliorate time conflicts and stress. Nevertheless, they do nothing to address the structures of parenting and working that produce work-family conflict to begin with. Policy change at the workplace and state level is required if meaningful change is to be achieved. Family-friendly workplace policies include opportunities for flexible work hours, remote work, job sharing, personal days, support for parental leaves, and even workplace daycare provisions.

At the state level, family-friendly policies can include extended parental leaves, paid sick-days, and short-term leaves for caregiving through major illnesses, to name a few. Countries vary widely in terms of their family-friendly policies, with Scandinavia having the most generous and countries like the United States among the least generous. Canada lies between these extremes, falling in the middle of the distribution among wealthy countries (Cision, 2019; UNICEF, 2019). Box 11.3 provides a closer look at leave policies internationally.

Since 1971, Canada has had a maternity leave policy that allows working mothers a paid leave upon the birth of a child. Current leave policies for Canada and the province of Quebec are summarized in Table 11.2. Combining maternity and parental benefits, both the Canadian and Quebec plans grant parents more than a year of benefits, but Quebec provides higher remuneration. Other provinces "top up" the Canadian plan to increase the benefits provided to parents. Some employers also add to the maternity benefits paid out to their workers. Workers employed full-time at large companies with good family-friendly policies may receive their full salaries for at least part of their leaves. Others, however, are not so fortunate.

GLOBAL PERSPECTIVES

11.3 | Family Leave Policies: Canada in International Perspective

UNICEF ranked countries based on their 2016 family leave policies. As the following figure shows, Canada's paid maternity leave policies in 2016 were more generous than those found in the UK, the US, Australia, France, and many other countries. However, Canada lagged well behind many European countries and Japan. In UNICEF's report, Canada was ranked at the bottom in terms of parental leaves for fathers and second parents; however, the 2019 change to Canadian legislation would place Canada around 16th in the ranking (Cision, 2019; UNICEF, 2019).

Although Canada's international ranking is not bad, inequalities and gaps have been identified: "Adopted children, Indigenous children and children in families with low-income or with parents in precarious employment are disproportionately excluded from our policies because of narrow eligibility requirements and a low rate of pay. We must make these policies fully inclusive and equitable" (Pinto, cited in Cision, 2019).

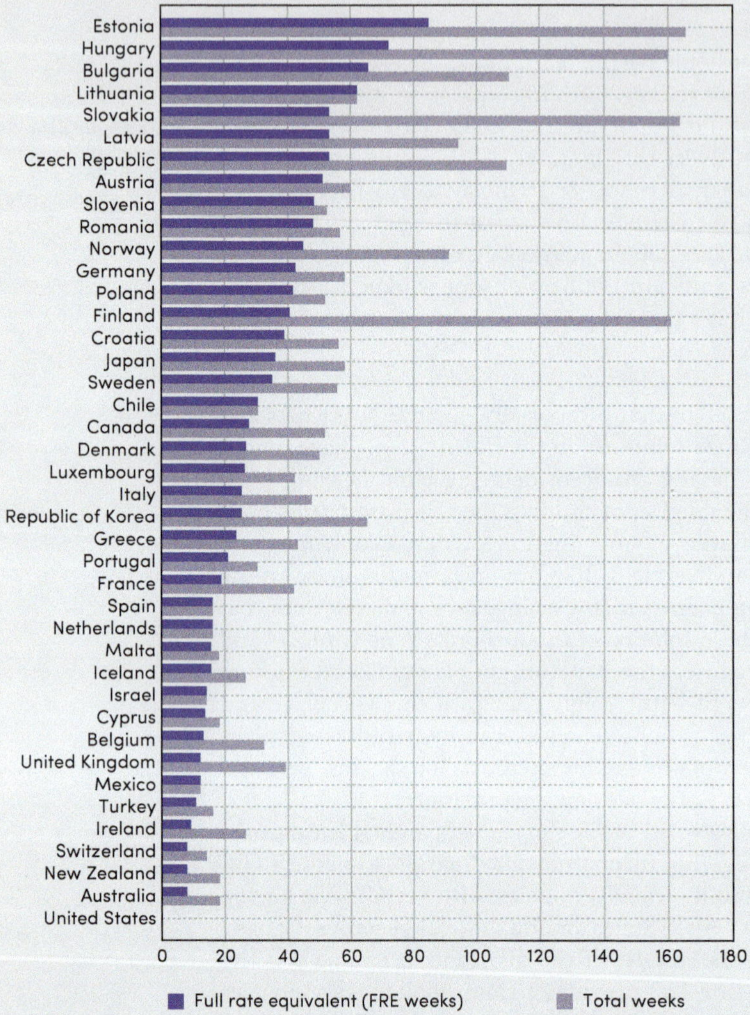

FIGURE 11.3 Paid leave available to mothers, 2016

Source: OECD Family Database, Table PF2.1A.

The 2019 revision to Canada's parental leave plans allows parents to extend their leaves to 18 months (with no additional pay-out of benefits). This extension allows parents to spend more time at home looking after young children and encourages fathers to take parental leaves. Although only mothers can take the 15 weeks of maternity leave (and fathers or second parents the five weeks of paternity leave), parents can split the parental

TABLE 11.2 Parental Leave Policies in Canada and Quebec

	Canada	Quebec
Paid Maternity Leave	15 weeks	18 weeks
Parental Leave	35 weeks (available to either parent)	32 weeks
Fathers/Second Parents	5 weeks (only available to second parent)	5 weeks
Total	55 weeks (remunerated at 55 per cent of average weekly earnings).* Weeks can extend to 61 weeks total (including 8 weeks of paternity), remunerated at lower rate.	55 weeks (remunerated at 70 per cent). Fewer weeks at a higher rate of remuneration is also available.* Work and earnings criteria to qualify are more lenient in Quebec.

Source: UNICEF, 2019.

leave however they want. To take advantage of the leave extension, parents must have worked a minimum of 600 hours in the previous year, or be self-employed, and have contributed to employment insurance for at least a year. Although Canada's leave policies are fairly generous, poorer individuals, those with little work experience in the previous year, and the self-employed are particularly disadvantaged.

These policies help individuals to navigate through this important life course transition, but they are limited in extent and scope. Many challenges remain, especially for those disadvantaged by social class or Indigeneity, those involved in precarious work, and people with alternative family structures (Doucet, Mathieu, & McKay, 2020). These barriers were exacerbated during the pandemic, leading to calls for new policies that move beyond employment-related entitlements towards more universal, citizenship-linked policies (ibid.).

Older Workers and the Transition to Retirement

Another key life course transition workers experience is that between working and retirement. The transition to retirement is a turning point for most workers, signalling a change in identity, status, and lifestyle. However, like the school-to-work transition experienced by those entering the workforce, the work-to-retirement transition is becoming more uneven, stretched out, and interrupted. Many workers do not simply go from working one day to retired the next. Rather, they may retire from one job to embark on another. Or leave the labour force for a time, only to return when financial strains or new opportunities arise. The uneven nature of the work-to-retirement transition is related to several factors, including volatile markets, the economic cycle, longer life expectancies, and trends toward healthy aging. However, challenges with this transition are also related to the changing nature of work and the challenges that older workers face in the labour market.

ageism
Discrimination and stereotyping based on age

One of the significant challenges older workers (age 50 and older) face is **ageism**: discrimination and stereotyping based on age (Harris, Krygsman, Waschenko, & Laliberte Rudman, 2018). Some age-related stereotypes about older workers are positive: for example, older workers are seen as more reliable, experienced, and loyal than

Source: © insta_photos/Shutterstock

Many older workers report encountering employment discrimination because of negative stereotypes about their age. How might this discrimination factor into older workers' transitions into retirement?

younger workers (Harris et al., 2018; Berger, 2009). Many age-related stereotypes are negative. Older workers are believed to be less productive, less innovative, less trainable, slower to learn, and generally out-of-touch (Duerden Comeau & Kemp, 2007; Harris et al., 2018; Berger, 2009). Research has found little to no evidence that any of these negative stereotypes are true (Posthuma & Campion, 2009). In fact, for many jobs, older workers with experience are more productive than younger workers with less experience. Still, these stereotypes persist—especially among younger employees and employers. Older workers battle and contest these stereotypes and strive to keep up-to-date and demonstrate their adaptability, knowledge, and experience (Berger, 2009; Ng & Law, 2014). They are eager to pursue learning opportunities (Fenwick, 2012). When surrounded by negative attitudes, older workers may adopt these negative perceptions of older workers themselves—especially of older women—impacting their identities, their work behaviours, and their retirement decisions (Hurd Clarke & Korotchenko, 2016).

Because of these negative stereotypes, older workers may be turned down for promotions, be denied training opportunities, and face negative treatment from coworkers. The end of mandatory retirement opened up opportunities for older workers to continue working past the age of 65; however, some suggest that this policy change has been accompanied by an extension of performance management and appraisal in which older workers may be found lacking compared to their younger counterparts (in accordance with ageist and managerialist expectations) and encouraged to retire for performance reasons (Beck & Williams, 2015). Older workers may be pushed into retirement and can be vulnerable to downsizing (McMullin & Marshall, 2001; Silver, 2019). This may be particularly true for older workers with disabilities (Denton, Plenderleith, & Chowhan, 2013). Late-career job loss has been found to contribute to poor self-rated health (He & Marshall, 2003) and has clear implications for financial well-being (Denton et al., 2013).

Older workers who lose a job for whatever reason (downsizing, career change, immigration, and so on) may have great difficulty finding a new job (Berger, 2009; Hurd Clarke & Korotchenko, 2016). Older workers experience longer durations of unemployment than younger workers. They also experience labour market discrimination: studies have found that older workers are less likely than younger workers to receive call-backs from potential employers despite identical résumés (Lahey, 2008; Richardson, Webb, Webber, &

Smith, 2013). Older workers on the job market report ageism and discouragement (Berger, 2009). Companies are not willing to invest in older workers in light of stereotypes regarding their inability to learn new things or assumptions that they will retire soon (Berger, 2009).

Unemployed workers in these situations may engage in a variety of strategies to improve their chances on the job market: altering résumés to remove job experience and conceal graduation dates; undertaking training to demonstrate that their skills are up-to-date; learning new buzzwords and lingo to appear current; and altering their physical appearance to appear younger (Berger, 2009). Even with these strategies, however, older workers may struggle to find employment, leading some towards early retirement (Finnie & Gray, 2018) while others settle for part-time, contract, or precarious employment at reduced pay and/or change careers (Berger, 2009; D'Amours, 2009). Existing policies are insufficient to address older workers' difficulties: those too young to draw pensions but deemed too old to work by employers have few supports (LeBlanc & McMullin, 1997; Cooke, 2006; D'Amours, Lesemann, & Crespo, 2001).

Traditionally, retirement was seen as "a time to enjoy life without the burdens of work" (Silver, 2019, p. 22) and as a time for peace and enjoyment after a long work career. However, conceptions of retirement are changing. A newer, emergent ideal is one of **productive aging** (Silver, 2019; Harris et al., 2018; OECD, 2006). Here, workers are encouraged to continue engaging in productive activities later in life, even post-retirement. Some regions have strongly encouraged workers to stay in the labour force longer than in previous decades (Beck & Williams, 2015; OECD, 2006). This ideal may, to some extent, reflect the realities of some retired and semi-retired people who need to continue working (or want to continue working) late in life, whether because they want to keep active and engaged (Silver, 2019; Latulippe et al., 2017) or because of financial need (Berger, 2009; Hazel, 2018; Latulippe, St-Onge, Gagné, Balesteros-Leiva, & Beauchamp-Legault, 2017). The downside of this ideal is that not everyone who wants to continue working has the opportunity to do so. Both formal and informal pressure to retire, combined with ageism, other forms of discrimination, and various labour market barriers may limit opportunities for fulfilling work in later life. The productive aging ideal may cause additional stress for those struggling to find work in older age and work intensification for those who are already in paid employment. Moreover, this ideal may not capture the lived experiences and wishes of all workers; Brooks-Cleator and Giles (2018) explain that this ideal does not take into account the perspectives of Indigenous seniors.

productive aging
A belief that workers should continue to be productive, even post-retirement

Experiences vary by class, race, gender, immigration status, and earlier career work (McMullin & Berger, 2006; D'Amours, 2009). Advantaged workers with economic and social capital often find it easier to continue working post-retirement and engage in more secure work, while those with disabilities, unrecognized foreign credentials, and less economic, social, or cultural capital are particularly disadvantaged. Workers with more precarious and uneven career histories face accumulated disadvantage as they age and experience more fragmented and precarious transitions towards retirement (Fournier, Zimmermann, & Gauthier, 2011; D'Amours, 2009).

Financial limitations, labour market challenges, and ideals of "productive aging" combine to encourage a prolonged work-to-retirement transition. Individuals may retire from their main career—because of burnout, being pushed out, lay-off, or choice—but subsequently pursue other work opportunities, including those linked with their previous career (part-time, consulting, or related work with another company), or pursue new

bridge jobs
Jobs held by older adults as they navigate the transition between their main careers and retirement

career directions. These post-retirement work opportunities have been called **bridge jobs** because older adults use them to navigate between their main careers and retirement. Workers in bridge jobs are disproportionately men who are self-employed or employed in white-collar jobs (D'Amours, Lesemann, & Crespo, 2001). Bridge jobs and related activities lengthen the transition between working and retirement (Latulippe et al., 2017). Indeed, it may be the case—as Witteveen (2018) has argued for youth entering the workforce—that the transition to retirement is increasingly more of a trajectory that involves several transitions (starts and stops, job shifts, paid work, and volunteer work) as older adults navigate the path between working and retirement (Fournier et al., 2011).

For a variety of reasons, labour force participation begins to decline for men and women when they are in their 50s. Although mandatory retirement (at age 65) was eliminated in Canada in 2009, the average age of retirement today is around this age—64 in 2017 (Hazel, 2018). This represents an increase of almost three years since the late 1990s (ibid.). The labour force participation of Canadians in their 60s has also increased over the same period, from 14 to 26 per cent (Hazel, 2018); both Canadian-born and immigrant older workers are more likely to be working than in previous years (Yssaad & Fields, 2018). When workers 60 and over are asked why they are working, roughly half say they have to out of economic necessity, while the rest say this is a choice that improves their lifestyle and well-being. Those working by choice are more likely to be highly educated and/or self-employed, and they are more likely to work in agriculture, professional, science, or research jobs or information, arts, and recreation industries (Hazel, 2018; Fields, Uppal, & LaRochelle-Côté, 2017). These workers may have more fulfilling and satisfying work.

The fact that older adults' labour force participation is increasing while the involvement of young people is decreasing results in a shift in the age distribution of the labour force, shown in Figure 11.4. The figure reveals that Statistics Canada researchers anticipated that these trends would continue into the 2020s. How the COVID-19 pandemic will influence these trends remains to be seen. The pandemic appears to have restricted labour market opportunities for youth but has also impacted older adults. The impact of the recession may encourage older adults to stay in the labour force longer, exacerbating existing trends.

To conclude, workers experience several key life course events and transitions respecting work. These transitions have become more challenging and complex over time. While many workers complete these transitions and trajectories successfully, the economically vulnerable and racially marginalized face particular challenges. The intersection of class, race, and gender with age and life course stage shapes social experience.

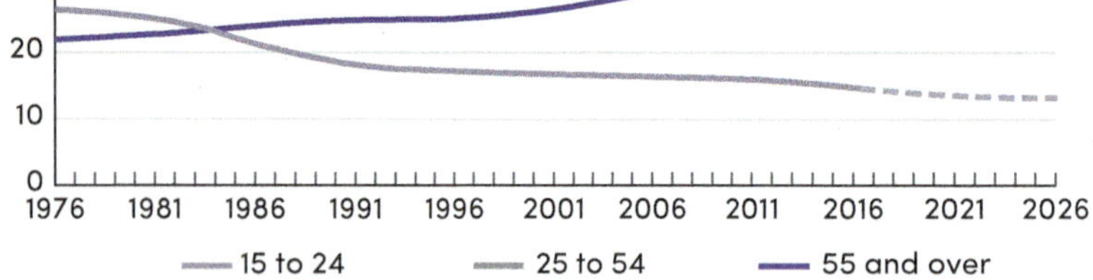

FIGURE 11.4 Distribution of working-age population, by age group, 1976–2026

Source: Statistics Canada, Labour Force Survey, 1976 to 2016; Population Projections for Canada, Provinces and Territories, 2017 to 2026, https://www150.statcan.gc.ca/n1/pub/75-006-x/2017001/article/14826-eng.htm.

Reviewing the Learning Objectives

Now that you have read this chapter, you should:

- Be familiar with the life course paradigm and the importance of age and life course stage to work experiences.
- Be able to identify some of the challenges youth experience as they transition into the labour market.
- Know what work-family conflict is and what factors exacerbate or mitigate it.
- Have a sense of older adults' work experiences and transition to retirement.

Questions for Critical Thought

1. Can you think of examples of "turning points" that might impact one's career trajectory?
2. Many employers are reluctant to hire and train new workers. Why do you think that is the case? What kinds of policies might encourage employers to hire young workers and thereby ease school-to-work transitions?
3. How might race or immigration status shape experiences of work-family conflict?
4. What are the implications of current workforce trends for the transition to retirement? Do you think more workers will continue working into older age? Why or why not?

Annotated Additional Readings

Julien, M., Somerville, K., & Brant, J. (2017). Indigenous perspectives on work-life enrichment and conflict in Canada. *Equality, Diversity and Inclusion, 36*(2), 165–181. https://doi .org/10.1108/EDI-11-2015-0096.

The authors examine work-life balance among Indigenous peoples in Canada.

Mercure, D., Vultur, M., & Fleury, C. (2012). Valeurs et attitudes des jeunes travailleurs à l'égard du travail au Québec: Une analyse intergénérationnelle. *Relations industrielles, 67*(2), 177–198.

This article compares workers' attitudes across generations, finding that age is less important than other factors in shaping attitudes.

Silver, M. P. (2019). The unbearable lightness of being retired. *Canadian Journal on Aging, 38*(1), 21–34.

Silver explores current perspectives on retirement.

Williams, G. (2019). Management millennialism: Designing the new generation of employee. *Work, Employment and Society, 34*(3), 371–387.

This article reveals how stereotypes about millennials are used by firms to worsen working conditions and benefits.

Related Websites

Organisation for Economic Co-operation and Development (OECD). The impact of COVID-19 on youth workers:

http://www.oecd.org/general/focus/youth.htm

Canadian Association for Retired Persons:
https://www.carp.ca/

CBC news article on the impact of COVID-19 pandemic on youth transition to work:
https://www.cbc.ca/news/business/covid-19-jobs-1.5680550

Government of Canada, Indigenous Services, First Nations and Inuit Youth Employment Strategy:
https://www.sac-isc.gc.ca/eng/1100100033607/1533125081187

12 The Future of Work

Learning Objectives

After reading this chapter, readers will:

- Understand that technology shapes work, but how it is implemented and used determines its impact on workers.
- Be able to define terms like "platform economy," "gig economy," "artificial intelligence," and "telework" and have a sense of how these developments impact workers.
- Understand the positive and negative impacts of technological change on workers.

Introduction

The future is always uncertain and unpredictable. The best we can do when trying to predict what will come is to reflect on past events, identify emerging trends, and use this information to anticipate future developments. The future of work is something people have been speculating about for some time. Will we all be replaced by robots or other forms of artificial intelligence? If so, will the result be more leisure time or more precarity? Is the stable job with benefits becoming as endangered as the North Pacific right whale? What kinds of jobs will people be doing in the future? Answers to these questions are subject to debate.

Although there are many potential futures of work, this chapter focuses on what scholars call platform work or gig work, as well as remote work and the impact of artificial intelligence (AI) on work. All of these trends are bound up with technological change. As we have seen, since the Industrial Revolution, theorists and sociologists have endeavoured to understand the impact of technological change on work. What we have learned from previous technological changes is that it is not necessarily the technology itself that transforms work but which stakeholders drive technological change, why they do so, and how technology is implemented (Ritzer, 1996; Spencer, 2017). Is the goal of technological change to rationalize work and facilitate the extraction of surplus value by extending control over workers or reducing the number of workers employed? Or does it empower workers, expand their skills, make their work easier, and increase their autonomy? Does it do both or neither? If we are to understand the impact of AI, platforms, and software on the future of work, we need to consider not just the technologies but the social relations and institutional structures that shape how technologies are used. Only then can we develop a clearer sense of how new forms of work can empower and disempower—sometimes simultaneously.

Platform Work

platform work The use of digital platforms to mediate relationships between workers, employers, and consumers

gig work Work in which individuals do a series of short-term tasks for others as assigned through digital platforms. Often used interchangeably with the term "platform work"

digital platforms Virtual marketplaces where providers of goods and services are connected with buyers

There are many terms that are used to capture aspects of the same overarching trends in work: gig work, digital labour, the sharing economy, and platform work (Berg, 2016; Fleming, Rhodes, & Yu, 2019; Healy et al., 2017; Schor & Attwood-Charles, 2017; Wood et al., 2019a, 2019b). In this chapter, the terms **platform work** and "gig work" are used interchangeably. The first term emphasizes the use of digital platforms to mediate relationships between workers, employers, and consumers. The term **gig work** captures the typically short-term nature of jobs or tasks assigned through digital platforms. Workers in the gig economy may not identify with a single occupation as they jump from one gig to the next to earn a living.

In essence, **digital platforms** are virtual marketplaces where providers of services (and/or goods) are connected with buyers. These platforms are owned by companies who not only maintain the apps and software but also "retain control over the allocation of work, working conditions, and some prices" (Healy et al., 2017, pp. 232–233). These companies, then, seek profit through their software and the connections made between workers and consumers. This profit-seeking aspect is often minimized in rhetoric about the "sharing economy" that highlights the social connections made between buyers and sellers (Schor & Attwood-Charles, 2017; Fleming et al., 2019) and the facility with which platforms connect people who have space to rent with those looking for a short-term rental, such as Airbnb, or connect people who need a ride somewhere with those willing to offer a ride, such as Uber or Lyft. The platform economy extends to the provision of a variety of services, from delivering food to providing care work and from providing professional services to doing odd jobs (Healy et al., 2017; Kessler, 2018; Wood et al., 2019a). Some of these services are provided in person (rides, food delivery, odd jobs), but many others are not. Providers of clerical work, professional services, and other miscellaneous tasks fulfilled virtually can be located almost anywhere in the world—at least anywhere with good, reliable Internet (Wood et al., 2019b; Kessler, 2018; Sutherland, Jarrahi, Dunn, & Nelson, 2019). Advocates suggest that platform work could represent a future of work in which technology enables us to transcend borders and obtain the services and skills we need, when we need them. Or, from workers' point of view, to provide our skills and services to whomever will pay for them and to earn income whenever we want. More negatively, however, the gig economy represents a future of work dominated by precarity and exploitation (Fleming et al., 2019).

Internationally, only a minority of workers engage in gig work. Statistics Canada reports that there were 1.7 million Canadians engaging in gig work in 2016—8 per cent of the labour force (Statistics Canada, 2019e). More than half of these workers combined gig work with other paid employment. Internationally, the figures are similar, with only a small percentage of workers involved in platform work and an even smaller percentage earning most of their living from it. Huws, Spence, Syrdal, and Holts's (2017) survey of gig workers in Europe finds that only 3 per cent of workers in the UK, 5 per cent in Italy, and 2.5 per cent in Germany earned 50 per cent or more of their income through gig work.

Some contend that platform work is ideally suited for younger workers (like Millennials and Gen Z) (Kessler, 2018). You may recall from Chapter 11 that Millennials are often said to differ from older generations of workers because of their comfort with digital technologies, their wish for flexible and fulfilling work, and their desire to connect with others, whether in person or online. While there is reason to question such blanket statements, platform work, at least on the surface, appears to provide what Millennials seek: flexibility, independence, and technologically mediated networking with others. Moreover, workers just entering the labour market, struggling to find full-time stable work, may be able to gain experience through gig work or combine gigs with other jobs to earn a living (Churchill & Craig, 2019). Platform work is one form of digital labour that might appeal to young people who spend long hours online anyway, whether they are engaging in leisure pursuits (gaming, social interaction) or working. There is evidence that youth are highly represented among gig workers (Kessler, 2018; Huws et al., 2017; Sutherland et al., 2019). In Canada, low-income earners and immigrants are also overrepresented among gig workers (Statistics Canada, 2019e).

Supporters of platform work, like platform owners, contend that it can help to overcome the negatives of standard employment relationships: the rigidity and lack of fulfillment or alienation associated with a full-time job (Kessler, 2018; Healy et al., 2017; Schor & Attwood-Charles, 2017). Platform workers are flexible workers. There are no set work hours, but rather people can choose when they want to work and when they do not. Indeed, since service (or goods) providers are independent contractors rather than employees, hypothetically at least they can enjoy the autonomy and fulfillment of self-employment. It has also been argued that platform work makes good use of "idle capacity"—enabling people to profit from that spare room they have or make money from owning a car or riding their bike (Schor & Attwood-Charles, 2017). In this sense, platform work helps people to be productive in their off hours and to profit from goods they already own. Thus, platform work can provide people with opportunities to augment their earnings. Platform work may be flexible enough to combine with schooling, paid work, and unpaid work.

This optimistic picture is belied by sociological research exploring workers' experiences in this sector. While some find this work rewarding and even fun, most engage in it out of economic necessity (Berg et al., 201; Churchill & Craig, 2019; Kessler, 2018; Veen, Barratt, & Goods, 2020). Fleming et al. (2019, p. 497), for example, argue that gig work reflects "an extreme variant of capitalism" that has been "largely stripped of the vestiges of labour protection and regulation and thus rendering employment a rudimentary matter of market-based economic exchange between capital and labour." The result is labour commodification, precarity, and exploitation. Precarity stems from the fact that employment standards, laws, and regulations do not apply to platform workers. Standard employees benefit from minimum wage laws and policies that ensure that their wages are consistent. They earn vacation pay and have paid breaks. They often have steady work hours and an expectation of continued employment (unless they are employed on a temporary contract). Usually, standard employees are provided with the materials and equipment—tools and technology, computers and desks, and so on—required to do their jobs. Platform workers must supply their own equipment and pay their own expenses, and they lack most of the basic rights and privileges that other workers take for granted. Their wages are frequently below minimum wage (Churchill & Craig, 2019; Kessler, 2018).

Platforms' insistence that their workers are independent contractors rather than employees is controversial. These workers have all of the costs associated with self-employment but few of the perks. For example, many cannot choose their own rates, unlike self-employed workers. Pay rates are set by the platform, are variable, and can change with little notice. Platform workers, such as Uber drivers, also have little ability to choose their own clients, since failure to accept clients sent to them by the platform, or app, can limit future assignments and potentially result in loss of future work (Veen et al., 2020; Kessler, 2018). In theory, platform workers can choose their own hours, but the demands of various platforms may curtail that privilege as well.

Moreover, gig workers are closely managed (Veen et al., 2020; Fleming et al., 2019; Sutherland et al., 2019). A variety of managerial control techniques are mobilized; precisely which ones are used varies across platform. Management by algorithm is predominant. Algorithms embedded in the platforms control the flow of jobs to workers; they can be based on amount of jobs taken and customer ratings, as well as other metrics. Those who quickly accept jobs when given to them, complete them effectively, and earn customer appreciation get ranked more highly and hence are more likely to be recommended or chosen for future work (Sutherland et al., 2019; Veen et al., 2020; Wood et al., 2019a). To earn income through the platform, then, workers must be available to accept tasks, and they must provide exemplary service. Even then, however, workers may receive bad reviews as a result of disgruntled clients and sometimes factors beyond their control (Veen et al., 2020; Sutherland et al., 2019). This is not the only form of management. Workers may be placed under surveillance: for instance, apps monitor delivery providers' speed, route, and time to completion (Veen et al., 2020; Mojtehedzadeh, 2020). Those working on computers may have their mouse clicks, keystrokes, and screen displays monitored by clients (Wood et al., 2019a; Sutherland et al., 2019). These so-called independent contractors are subjected to direct labour surveillance and control more extensive than most employees (Fleming et al., 2019). Platform workers, then, "self-discipline" (in Foucauldian terms) to ensure that they keep getting gigs. They also engage in a number of strategies to try to ensure positive ratings, secure their reputations, maintain productivity, manage risk, and build a client-base, when they can (Sutherland et al., 2019; Kessler, 2018). Use of control mechanisms has increased over time (Schor & Attwood-Charles, 2017) as platform owners seek profit.

Worker self-discipline may be enhanced because the competition for jobs can be intense and acquiring gigs a challenge. As Berg et al. (2018, p. 64) explain, "workers cannot just turn on the computer [or open an app] and work whenever they want, as the jobs available are irregular." Moreover, workers may be required to bid on a gig when it is posted on an app. This process may simply require being among the first to sign up to complete a task, but sometimes proposals are required. Because gig workers need to make themselves available when gigs do appear, they are not entirely in control of their work schedules (Berg et al., 2018). Moreover, to get a gig, workers may be required to do considerable unpaid work—maintenance on their cars or bikes, time spent mapping out ideal routes, creating short-cuts to complete work faster and more efficiently, preparing proposals, and so on (Veen et al., 2020; Wood et al., 2019a; Kessler, 2018). When this time and other expenses related to working are accounted for, most gig workers find their net income is very low. Of course, gig workers also typically lack other forms of remuneration, including benefits and vacation pay. Those who do this work on the side, in addition to more standard employment with benefits, may be more satisfied with this work than those who rely on it as their main source of income (Veen et al., 2020; Tassinari & Maccarrone, 2020). Moreover, skilled workers selling professional services appear to be better off (Sutherland et al., 2019; Kessler, 2018).

Research on Amazon Mechanical Turk (or M-Turk) workers reveals unpaid work, self-discipline, and the need to be always available to work. "Turkers" perform **micro-jobs** for micro-pay. For example, they may look at pictures and describe their content, complete short surveys, or complete other small writing tasks on their own computers for pennies (or dollars) a task. Here, anyone contracted through the platform can pick up odd jobs for cash whenever they want. This work may be appealing to those who want to work from home or make some additional money on their own time. However, those seeking to make a living on Mechanical Turk face many difficulties. On average, **crowdworkers** on platforms like Mechanical Turk make between $1 and $5 an hour (Kessler, 2018, pp. 70–71; Berg, 2016). To earn more, they must engage in unpaid work—creating systems to identify the best gigs, bid successfully for them, and complete them quickly. They also make themselves available to work around the clock: Kessler (2018) describes one Mechanical Turk worker sleeping in her office so she could land better-paying jobs, no matter when they appeared. Being constantly available to work, however, takes its toll. Repetitive strain injuries can result from long hours at the computer, and the jobs can be stressful. Moreover, there are hidden dangers in the work—some jobs may involve exposure to graphic images that appear without warning. Also, workers can complete jobs but be denied payment for questionable reasons. Thus, workers are vulnerable in these jobs. Some may find taking on the occasional task enjoyable. Others work around the clock, 24/7, in a high-stress environment for low incomes. Competition for the best jobs can produce an extreme form of self-discipline that is not healthy, or sustainable, for workers.

micro-jobs
Small, odd jobs. For example, Amazon Mechanical Turk (or M-Turk) workers may look at pictures and describe their content, complete short surveys, or complete other small writing tasks on their own computers for pennies (or dollars) a task

crowdworkers
Groups of people who complete crowd-sourced tasks posted through online platforms

Source: © BalkansCat/Shutterstock

While some see the platform economy as an opportunity for greater worker autonomy, it also creates greater precarity both for its workers and the industries with which these platforms interact. While delivery became essential to the survival of restaurants during the COVID-19 pandemic, multiple Toronto restaurants began to boycott Uber Eats in May 2020 because high commission fees resulted in some restaurant owners actually losing money on orders placed through the app.

In fact, some question whether gig work is sustainable for society. Fleming et al. (2019) point out that many platform companies like Uber and Lyft do not earn profits. Evasion of regulations and policies meant to protect workers and consumers likely cannot be sustained over the long term; indeed, there is already evidence of resistance. The long hours required for gig workers to earn a living is also not physically sustainable over the long term. Workers who do not earn enough to live on are terrible consumers, and neither they nor the companies that employ them pay taxes sufficient to sustain societal functioning. For these reasons and others, Fleming et al. (2019) argue that platform work cannot be the future of work; it will never "employ" more than a small minority of the labour force. Nevertheless, gig work is an extreme form of precarious work, and it seems highly likely that precarity will continue to grow in the coming years (Fleming et al., 2019; Statistics Canada 2019e).

The growth of the platform economy can be seen as part of a larger trend towards non-standard work (Healy et al., 2017; Fleming et al., 2019). Several writers draw parallels to the early days of capitalism when labour was commodified and workers faced dangerous and precarious working conditions with little legislation to protect their rights (Healy et al., 2017; Wood et al., 2019b). **Commodification** is the process of turning things that are not inherently commodities—people, forests, the environment, and so on—into commodities to be sold for profit. Worker protections implemented in the 20th century, including workers' compensation, minimum wages, unemployment insurance, the right to unionize, and so on contributed to the de-commodification of labour. While the gig economy is seen as modern and cutting edge, in terms of labour rights and protections it is rolling back the clock, resulting in the "re-commodification" of labour (Huws, 2014; Wood et al., 2019b; Churchill & Craig, 2019). The platform economy evades legislative protections, leaving workers vulnerable to wage decreases, lack of work, competition, and reduced safety and health protections. The fact that the platform economy is perceived as fun, convenient, and technologically innovative, however, partially obscures this commodification and exploitation. Since the focus is on the connections made between workers and consumers, exploitation by platform owners seeking profit may be hidden. Nonetheless, those gig workers who are highly dependent on platform work do challenge management tactics, varying wages, and limited rights, and they fight for positive change (Kessler, 2018; Healy et al., 2017). The numerous court cases against Uber are a case in point (see Box 12.1).

commodification The process of turning things that are not inherently commodities—people, forests, the environment, and so on—into commodities to be sold for profit. Labour commodification is the process of treating workers as commodities, not human beings

The platform economy may not only exacerbate class inequalities but gender and racial inequalities as well. For instance, Schor and Attwood-Charles (2017) show how racial inequalities are reproduced on platforms, with racial minority workers receiving less income, picking up fewer gigs, and being discriminated against as both workers and consumers (also Kessler, 2018). Statistics Canada (2019e) finds that immigrants are more likely than the Canadian-born to engage in gig work, out of economic necessity. Researchers have also argued that the gig economy reproduces intersectional inequalities because marginalized workers with few opportunities in the mainstream economy are forced to rely on the gig economy to earn an income (Gregg & Andrijasevic, 2019; Kessler, 2018). Global inequalities too are reproduced as workers in the Global South perform gig work for consumers in the Global North at very low rates (Wood et al., 2019a, 2019b). In addition, Churchill and Craig (2019) show that the platform economy is somewhat sex-segregated, with men overrepresented in delivery and ride-sharing while women do more creative, clerical, and caring tasks. Moreover, they find that women report more difficulty than men in earning enough through gig work to pay their bills. Intersectional inequalities within the platform economy, however, have received insufficient attention, and this is an important area for future research.

Issues at Work

12.1 | Uber in the Courts

There have been several efforts to unionize gig workers, but these efforts have been met with hostility and firings from platform companies (Mojtehedzadeh, 2020; Kennedy, 2019). For example, Uber has been fighting court battles in various jurisdictions for years. The main issue concerns whether those who work for Uber are contractors or employees. Uber's payment policies have created controversy, especially their practice of cutting rates without warning. Unhappy drivers have launched suits to facilitate their ability to bargain with their employers and earn paid time off, minimum wages, and other rights. If Uber workers are not employees, however, they have no right to unionize and no bargaining power against the platform. Uber has settled some cases through out-of-court agreements to pay drivers. It has appealed and continues to challenge other court rulings that have found against them—like in the UK where it was determined that Uber drivers were in fact employees and should be treated accordingly. Here, the court declared that Uber's insistence that their drivers were independent contractors was "faintly ridiculous" (quoted in Healy et al., 2017, p. 239).

In Canada, Uber drivers have begun to organize and protest their working conditions (see UFCW, 2020; Coiquaud & Martin, 2019). In June 2020, the Supreme Court of Canada opened the door for a class-action lawsuit by drivers against Uber, and potentially for Uber drivers to be considered employees, by declaring that the "company's contract clause, which relies on a costly arbitration process in the Netherlands to settle disputes, was 'unconscionable' and 'unenforceable'" (Stefanovich, 2020). Uber's response has been to advocate for provincial legislation creating a new classification for Uber drivers ("flexible workers"), to avoid treating them like employees (UFCW, 2021). Decisions concerning the classification of gig workers could not only impact their working conditions but could impact the future of the gig economy in the country. Platforms continue to contend that their model is not sustainable if they are required to follow labour laws. This will be an interesting area to watch in years to come.

To understand the impact of the gig economy, it is important to keep in mind that not all platforms are the same (Kessler, 2018; Schor & Attwood-Charles, 2017). Some are more controlling and others less. Workers selling their goods and possessions online do not face the same challenges as those providing direct services—whether in person or online. Skilled workers providing professional and/or technical skills to clients may find themselves well paid, well respected, and with the opportunity to work on a variety of creative projects (Sutherland et al., 2019). They may make enough that the lack of benefits is not a serious issue—at least in the short term (Kessler, 2018). Some skilled workers may use platforms to augment the services they provide. For instance, professional workers may provide in-person services but also establish websites, apps, and software to provide additional information or services to their clients and others. In all of these instances, the workers providing services are skilled and advantaged. These middle-class workers may benefit in ways that more vulnerable workers cannot.

Other platforms may similarly benefit workers, such as those that treat gig workers as permanent employees and provide them with benefits and protections (Kessler, 2018). Co-operative platforms are not numerous, but they may also benefit worker-owners and demonstrate few of the downsides associated with other forms of gig work (Healy et al., 2017). In this sense, platforms can be used to commodify workers, including professional workers; however, they can also be used to assist workers, improve their effectiveness, or expand their service offerings.

Thus, whether a platform exploits or benefits workers depends on how it is implemented and whether workers use those platforms for their own benefit or whether profit-seekers try to use platforms to exploit workers and clients for their own gain. In the latter instances, there is a danger that platform work will contribute to the erosion of workers' rights, "under the guise of technological innovation" (Schor & Attwood-Charles, 2017, p. 7) and that platform workers may be forced to engage in a "race-to-the-bottom" competing with others, globally, for micro-jobs at decreasing wages.

Artificial Intelligence

artificial intelligence "[C]omputer systems that perform tasks that normally require human intelligence" (Pettersen, 2019)

Fears that artificial intelligence (AI) and related technologies will eliminate jobs are long-standing. Optimists posit that AI will free humans from drudgery and provide us with more leisure time; however, the more pessimistic wonder how people will earn a living when they are replaced by machines. **Artificial intelligence** can be defined as "computer systems that perform tasks that normally require human intelligence" (Pettersen, 2019). In its current form, AI is programmed through algorithms to process large amounts of data and looks for patterns in that data to perform certain tasks. AI can "learn": adding new data alters patterns observed and therefore results in better performance in completing tasks. AI's ability to process large amounts of data can make it more efficient than human workers at certain tasks.

Whether AI actually replaces workers, however, depends on a few different things. The first concerns how AI is applied and used. Critical scholars remind us that AI applied in capitalist contexts will be directed to achieving capitalists' goals (surplus value, profit, and so forth) (Spencer, 2017; Pettersen, 2019). The second concerns the nature of the work in which AI is being applied. Pettersen (2019), for example, argues that AI may be best applied in rationalized or McDonaldized environments—those where the work has already been standardized, streamlined, and structured to maximize efficiency, predictability, calculability, and control. Indeed, advocates of the adoption of AI in the workplace insist the first step is to standardize and streamline the labour process and break it down into its component parts (Susskind, 2016) as scientific management advocated more than a century ago (Braverman, 1974). Only once this is done is it possible to determine which tasks formerly done by workers can be taken over by AI to increase efficiency.

Ritzer (1996) argued that McDonaldization could be applied to a wide range of work settings, extending from the fast-food sector into almost every area of public life, including health, education, housing, finances, and so on. AI has similar applications. Susskind (2016), for example, has written on the applications of AI in legal services. He contends that much of what lawyers do is routine—background preparation research for clients, preparing routine contracts and paperwork, dispensing standard legal advice on certain issues. Once this work is standardized and broken down, artificial intelligence can be used to conduct research and generate the required information more quickly, as well as disperse it to clients more effectively and at a lower cost, than trained lawyers ever could. Susskind predicts that the demand for lawyers will decrease over time and that lawyers' roles will evolve in new directions once AI takes hold (see also Armour & Sako, 2020).

Nevertheless, at the time of writing, the use of AI in areas that are not standardized—such as ones where there is a lot of human interaction and unpredictability—is less effective. Thus, if AI replaces some jobs, it cannot replace them all. Susskind (2016) argues that, in law, there will still be jobs for lawyers who deal with specialized cases, as well as lawyers who use the technology to assist them in their work or work with the technology to apply and coordinate the information it provides. Other scholars agree that there are currently limits in the application of AI, so if some routine jobs can be phased out, there will still be jobs that require more complex tasks and especially jobs that require human interaction and situational interpretation. As Pettersen (2019) argues, human knowledge is situational knowledge: it is always embedded not only within a social-historical and cultural context, but meanings may also vary by setting and who we are interacting with. AI requires standardized data and interpretations—the situational nature of meaning, and the variableness of human interaction, therefore, cannot be captured by AI. It requires humans.

The impact of AI on jobs is four-fold. First, AI will be used in the coming years to replace workers—even very skilled workers—by taking over tasks that can be routinized and standardized. Estimates vary about just how many jobs will be lost as a result of AI (Press, 2019). Second, AI will contribute to changes in what workers do. Some will be able to use AI to enhance their work performance, or they will use their skills to inform and improve AI. With respect to lawyers, Susskind (2016) predicts that while there may be fewer lawyers in the future, those who remain will find they exercise slightly different skills. As AI makes routine legal tasks more accessible to the public, those seeking out lawyers may have more complex problems and require more social interaction and care. Additionally, some suggest, jobs will become more interdisciplinary and require more teamwork because AI requires tech specialists and other specialists to work together with complex data (Susskind, 2016). Third, AI will create new jobs—for example, jobs for people to inform and train AI by feeding it new data as it is generated so that output can be improved and jobs for people to interpret AI findings and determine how to apply them (*Wired*, 2018; Susskind, 2016). Old ways of working could break down to be replaced by something new. Finally, AI is likely to change organizational and business models and the ways in which work processes are designed (Armour & Sako, 2020). This could entail, for example, greater use of workers on temporary contracts.

The quality of new jobs is likely to be variable. The task of reviewing and tagging data for processing AI is routine work often performed by platform (crowd)workers, such as those on M-Turk working micro-jobs for below minimum wage. If AI implementation is accompanied by more contracting out, precarious work will increase. At the same time, training and interpreting AI are jobs for skilled specialists and may be rewarding, creative work. Since AI is often implemented by capitalists seeking to increase profit, it is their interests—and not necessarily workers' or society's interests—that will govern job creation (Spencer, 2017).

There is also concern about the quantity of work. Most predict that AI will eliminate many existing jobs—estimates vary from 10 to 30 per cent (Pettersen, 2019; Press, 2019), but futurists differ in their predictions about job creation. Some believe job growth will outpace losses, while others disagree (Press, 2019). What seems certain is that the impact of AI will be felt throughout the labour market, although some fields will be more affected than others.

AI and Social Inequalities

The literature on AI and the future of work tends towards the idealistic. Critical voices express concern over the application of AI to reproduce social inequalities (Spencer, 2017). AI is a tool through which capitalists seek to enhance their profit (Spencer, 2017; Pettersen, 2019), and it is those at the bottom of hierarchies—doing more routine jobs—who might be most negatively affected by job loss. Some predict a polarization of opportunities whereby skilled workers have multiple, global opportunities while other workers are more replaceable (Government of Canada, 2020a); low-wage personal and interactive service work could continue because the application of AI in these fields is less efficient or not cost-effective (Castells, 2000; Dunkerley, 1996). However, AI will affect both skilled and unskilled workers alike, and job loss is expected at all levels. Still, skilled workers may be better able to adapt to the new AI-driven economy than others (Suddaby & Viale, 2011).

There has been little attention in this literature to inequalities by class, gender, gender identity, race-ethnicity, disability status, and other dimensions. Since minority and disadvantaged groups tend to be overrepresented in routine work, we may expect that they would be negatively affected by the implementation of AI more than most. If language and communication skills grow in importance, immigrants could be disadvantaged, since they are often stereotyped to lack language skills regardless of ability (Oreopoulos, 2011). The impact on women could be mixed. On the one hand, women may be disadvantaged: clerical jobs in which women predominate are likely to be substantially reduced with AI implementation (Press, 2019). Moreover, negative stereotyping that calls women's technology skills into question could see them disadvantaged in tech-oriented jobs (Wacjman, 2006). Women's marginalization in the field of technological innovation contributes to the reproduction of gender inequalities (Wacjman, 2006; Spencer, 2017). Yet women's perceived communication skills could be an advantage. Many men will be negatively impacted as well, with variable outcomes by class, skill level, race, and immigration status. Technology could open up new roles for people with disabilities, but stereotypes about ability could limit opportunities as well.

Indigenous workers may be at a heightened risk for job loss due to AI. The Canadian Council for Aboriginal Business (2020) reports that one in three Indigenous workers is employed in an industry vulnerable to automation, especially in the provinces of British Columbia and Alberta. In response, there are calls for more support for education and retraining. Moreover, some programs have been established to encourage Indigenous peoples' involvement in science, technology, engineering, and mathematics (STEM) careers through "culturally responsive" curricula that blend Indigenous knowledge with Western science (Conference Board of Canada, 2020). Other initiatives aim to harness Indigenous knowledges to inform AI development (Indigenous AI, 2020). Such programs not only enhance opportunities for Indigenous learners, they also have the potential to shape AI programming and uses. Indeed, "integrating Indigenous perspectives would allow us to build a different kind of AI" (Kesserwan, 2018), including AI development "from an ethical position that centers Indigenous concerns"

The Future of Work

12.2 | Indigenous AI

The Indigenous AI initiative aims to initiate conversations and encourage the inclusion of Indigenous knowledges in the development of artificial intelligence with the goal of achieving "morally and socially desirable ends" (Lewis et al., 2020, p. 20). Towards these ends, Indigenous peoples from around the world came together to develop a protocol and a set of guidelines. The guidelines emphasize the following seven principles.

1) Locality: "AI systems should be designed in partnership with specific Indigenous communities to ensure the systems are capable of responding to and helping care for that community" (Lewis et al., 2020, p. 21).
2) Relationality and Reciprocity: "AI systems should be designed to understand how humans and non-humans are related to and interdependent on each other" (p. 21).
3) Responsibility, Relevance, and Accountability: "AI systems developed by, with, or for Indigenous communities should be responsible to those communities, provide relevant support, and be accountable to those communities first and foremost" (p. 21).
4) Indigenous-Influenced Governance Guidelines: Governance frameworks guiding the use of AI should be informed by Indigenous protocols (p. 21).
5) Recognize that computational technology is cultural (p. 22).
6) Apply ethical design in all phases (p. 22).
7) Respect and Support Data Sovereignty: Despite principles of open access to data, it is imperative that Indigenous communities control their data, and make decisions on data usage (p. 22).

With the adoption of Indigenous protocols and guidelines in AI development, ethics, relationships, and communities are centred, potentially leading to more socially beneficial uses of AI.

(Indigenous AI, 2020) and AI that considers ramifications and impacts on humanity, our social world, and environment. These positive developments could benefit all workers and consumers (see Box 12.2).

Intersectional inequalities will continue to be important with the impact of AI on workers reflecting the intersection of class, gender, race, and other structured dimensions of social inequality. Minority women and working-class men may be among the most negatively impacted if current trends hold.

Telecommuting/Remote Work

Technology has facilitated the ability of many workers—especially computer-based, white-collar workers—to work from home. A wide variety of terms, with varying definitions, have been applied to this type of work: telework, telecommuting, remote work, and e-work, to name a few (Allen, Golden, & Shockley, 2015; Charalampous, Grant, Tramontano, & Michailidis, 2019). What all of these terms have in common is that they refer to work practices wherein people work outside formal workplace settings, at least some of the time, by relying on computing and related technologies. Where definitions vary is with respect to where workers are working (home or elsewhere), their employment status (distinctions are drawn between the self-employed and paid employees), and to some extent whether the remote work happens occasionally or whether a worker works remotely most of the time. Allen et al. (2015, p. 44) define **telecommuting** as "a work practice that involves members of an organization substituting a portion of their typical work hours . . . to work away from a central workplace—typically principally from home—using technology to interact with others as needed to conduct work tasks" (see also Belzunegui-Eraso & Erro-Garcés, 2020; Charalampous et al., 2019). Self-employed workers can also work remotely, and remote work can be done in a variety of different settings (including cafés, hotels, airports, remote work sites, and others).

telecommuting
A "work practice that involves members of an organization substituting a portion of their typical work hours . . . to work away from a central workplace—typically principally from home—using technology to interact with others as needed to conduct work tasks" (Allen et al., 2015, p. 44)

Many firms offer telework opportunities to at least some of their workers—especially knowledge workers who work autonomously and on their computers most of the time (Abrams, 2019). However, telework has tended to go against company cultures that value being present in the office. Thus, only a minority of workers work remotely, and many of them do it on a part-time basis. Still, the number of workers telecommuting has increased steadily over time (Abrams, 2019).

Telecommuting has been dated to the 1970s and 1980s and has been facilitated by technological developments (Allen et al., 2015). There appear to have been two initial drivers: (1) the environment; (2) work-family balance. Many people commute some distance as they travel to work—Canadians on average spend 50 minutes per day travelling to and from work, with many spending considerably more than that (Statistics Canada, 2019f). Commuting by car generates significant carbon emissions (Belzunegui-Eraso & Erro-Garcés, 2020). Working from home has the potential to benefit the environment. Commute times can also exacerbate work-family conflict. Working outside the home can deny working parents valued flexibility. Parents who work from home may find it easier to balance work and family care because they can time work breaks with childcare duties—dropping the kids off at school and picking them up afterwards, for example.

Source: © Zivica Kerkez/Shutterstock

The COVID-19 pandemic has created a widespread shift to remote work, creating new challenges related to work-life balance, managerial strategies, and privacy. Based on your knowledge of the studies discussed throughout this text, which aspects of remote work would most interest you as a researcher?

Having the flexibility of working from home particularly benefits women with children, minimizing gender wage gaps (Fuller & Hirsh, 2019). Thus, remote working has been seen as a benefit for the environment and for workers with care responsibilities.

Employers have been ambivalent about telecommuting. Some question whether workers at home are *really* working if they are not being supervised. Others may believe that for effective teamwork and collaboration to occur, workers need to be in close physical proximity to each other. There is an extensive literature on telecommuting, however, that identifies positive outcomes. If granted sufficient autonomy, and with a supportive organizational culture, teleworkers can be even more productive than those working in an office (Abrams, 2019). They report less stress, more job satisfaction, and more organizational commitment (Abrams, 2019; Allen et al., 2015). Work-family conflict can be partially alleviated; however, telecommuters do report greater blurring between home life and work (Abrams, 2019; Dimitrova, 2003), which can contribute to stress and burnout. The main negative identified in the literature is that telecommuters report higher levels of social isolation than those who work in an office full-time. This social isolation can be mitigated by combining remote work with in-office work, through leaders' efforts to include remote workers and link them with others, and through workers' concerted efforts to connect with coworkers and others (Abrams, 2019; deVries, Tummers, & Bekkers, 2018; Charalampous et al., 2019). Overall, remote work appears to benefit both workers and their employers (Choudhury, Larson, & Foroughi, 2019).

Some workers may benefit more from telecommuting than others. Studies suggest that young and new workers may be better off working in a workplace setting where they have closer access to colleagues and supervisors. In contrast, older and experienced workers who work autonomously may benefit from working remotely and possibly even at a distance. One study, for example, found that when given the opportunity to work from anywhere, many experienced workers did just that, moving far away to communities where they could live more cheaply and in closer proximity to family, friends, or desired amenities. Their productivity increased when they did so (Choudhury et al., 2019).

The COVID-19 pandemic saw many workers around the globe telecommuting (Belzunegui-Eraso & Erro-Garcés, 2020). Working in the office became impossible, and workers were asked to work remotely if/when they could do so. For the first time, working from home occurred on a mass scale. Technological advances, especially those that allowed work groups to teleconference through online platforms like Zoom and Microsoft Teams, enabled remote workers to collaborate with colleagues and check in with supervisors on a regular basis. Research suggests that about 40 per cent of Canadian jobs can be done remotely (Gallacher & Hossain, 2020). The (short-term) impact on the environment under lockdown was decreased carbon emissions and enhanced air quality (Belzunegui-Eraso & Erro-Garcés, 2020). The impact on working parents was mixed. With schools also closed, parents had to parent, home-school, and work simultaneously. This was a difficult challenge for both women and men; however, women appear to have had a disproportionate burden (Bahn et al., 2020). Some employers contended that remote workers during pandemic lockdowns were not as productive (failing to recognize the challenges generated by massive social change, disruptions to routines, and increased childcare responsibilities) (Frankling, 2020). Yet the balance of evidence shows that remote workers were not only productive, but they extended their work hours during the pandemic (Shi, 2020). From many perspectives, remote working during quarantine periods was a success, keeping workers safe and allowing business to continue (Belzunegui-Eraso & Erro-Garcés, 2020). The problems associated with remote working were less about the act of working from home, than with the difficulty of combining child-rearing, home-schooling, and paid work simultaneously, under stay-at-home orders and conditions of gender inequality (in intersection with other inequalities) (Feng & Savani, 2020; Qian & Fuller, 2020).

Not all workers had the same experience. Online meetings via Zoom or other platforms opened up workers' private lives to the scrutiny of their coworkers, and those whose surroundings did not meet white, middle-class standards felt judged and "othered" (Roberts & McCluney, 2020). Cultural decor and small and/or working-class surroundings were sometimes centred out. Black workers in particular reported feeling uncomfortable, at risk of having their professionalism undermined by coworkers assessing their appearance and surroundings and deeming them lacking (Buchanan, 2020; Roberts & McCluney, 2020). There has been little research on class, race, and gender inequalities in remote working, and these areas are deserving of more attention. People's experiences also differ by age and life course stage (see Chapter 11).

The pandemic may have increased the legitimacy and acceptability of remote working and expanded workers' interest in doing so. One survey, reported in June 2020, found that almost half of office workers surveyed said they would be interested

The Future of Work

12.3 | Trends in Work

In the spring of 2020, the Royal Society of Canada (RSC) conducted a series of member surveys to identify pressing challenges facing Canadian society in light of the pandemic. The RSC is a society that recognizes excellence in research, the arts, and/or scholarship and seeks to draw on this expertise to advance knowledge in Canada. While RSC survey respondents mentioned many issues affecting Canadians (Graham & Manca, 2020; Adams & Tremblay, 2020), the changing nature of work was identified as an area of concern. The following is a sample of some of the key challenges identified:

- The need to re-value labour so that essential workers are properly remunerated and appreciated.
- Unemployment and underemployment of the workforce.
- Workforce precarity.
- Limited labour market opportunities for youth.
- Workplace health and safety.
- Discrimination faced by marginalized groups.
- Challenges with work-family conflict and the need to rethink work so that work and family can be better combined.
- The challenges faced by first-responders and health-care providers in times of crisis.
- The need for a more environmentally sustainable, equitable economy.

These issues (and others raised) reflect key concerns about the future of work and workers' safety and well-being in the years to come.

in continuing to work from home at least some of the time (Doward, 2020). Another found that only about one in 10 working parents in the UK wanted to return to the "old normal"; instead, they wanted more remote work and more time with children. A *Forbes* article agreed, stating: "Workers have gotten a taste of the remote work life—and many won't accept a return to an in-office environment" (Fatemi, 2020). Faced with a possible redesign of office environments to physically distance employees, redesign common areas, and put in place barriers to minimize infection spread, it is expected that some companies will reduce the size of their office space (and its associated costs) and encourage more employees to work from home, at least some of the time (Fatemi, 2020).

Although remote work has been around for some time, it could become a future trend in work, especially in light of the pandemic, which appears to be altering views on work, life, the environment, and work-life balance (Adams & Tremblay, 2020; Belzunegui-Eraso & Erro-Garcés, 2020). This trend is not entirely positive, however, because it is expected that enhanced remote working will be accompanied by greater use of technology to monitor workers remotely and a greater reluctance by firms to rely on full-time permanent employees. There may be a concomitant shift towards precarious, non-standard jobs (Cheremond, 2020). It is also important to note that not everyone has the opportunity to work remotely. Many workers—especially low-wage service workers, among whom members of minorities are overrepresented, and blue-collar workers—must be physically present when working. This leaves them vulnerable to exposure to disease (St Denis, 2020; Bahn et al., 2020).

To summarize, this chapter has emphasized the impact of technology on the future of work, but it is important to remember that it is not technology itself that transforms work but the uses to which it is put. Technology applied to rationalize or to increase profit or surplus value and technology used in a way that exacerbates social inequality will simply worsen working conditions and reproduce prevailing social inequalities. Technology used to enhance work and working may have more positive impacts. With or without technological change, there is every reason to believe that many of the social issues highlighted in this textbook will continue to shape the future of work. Inequalities by class, gender, race, disability status, sexual orientation, Indigeneity, and other dimensions will persist, unless we take action to minimize them. Work will continue to both enhance and undermine health, likely in increasingly complex ways. Workers will still strive to have their work labelled as skilled and to have their skills acknowledged; those deemed skilled will continue to fare better than those socially deemed unskilled. Demands for workers to acquire new and different skills (including skills that are somewhat routine) will likely increase (Government of Canada, 2020a). Occupational segregation, discrimination, and harassment are likely to continue. Experiences of work will continue to vary by age, with younger and older workers experiencing vulnerability but in different ways. Technological change will eliminate some jobs, create others, and alter existing jobs. Technology may provide workers with more flexibility, but that flexibility can also enhance vulnerability. Organizational restructuring will have a similar impact. Workplace precarity seems likely to be exacerbated in the coming years. Still, there is reason for hope, since workers and others can resist negative impacts and strive for meaningful social change that will improve working conditions and contribute to a better society for all.

Reviewing the Learning Objectives

Having read this chapter, you should:

- Understand that technology shapes work, but how it is implemented and used determines its impact on workers.
- Be able to define terms like "platform economy," "gig economy," "artificial intelligence," and "telework" and have a sense of how these developments impact workers.
- Understand the positive and negative impacts of technological change on workers.

Questions for Critical Thought

1. Based on your readings from other chapters and this one, what impact do you anticipate technological change will have on intersectional inequalities in society?
2. Trends including platform work, artificial intelligence, and telecommuting appear to impact workers differently depending on age. How might the experiences of young workers and older workers differ?
3. Which of the sociological theories explored earlier in the textbook do you think are the most useful for understanding recent (and potential future) trends in work?

Annotated Additional Readings

Churchill, B., & Craig, L. (2019). Gender in the gig economy: Men and women using digital platforms to secure work in Australia. *Journal of Sociology, 55*(4), 741–761.

This study provides an overview of who works in the digital economy, who does what, and how they experience it.

Fleming, P., Rhodes, C., & Yu, K.-H. (2019). On why Uber has not taken over the world. *Economy and Society, 48*(4), 488–509.

This article takes a critical look at gig work, exploring why it has not expanded as much as expected, concluding that gig work is not highly sustainable and is unlikely to expand.

Schor, J. B., & Attwood-Charles, W. (2017). The "sharing" economy: Labor, inequality, and social connection on for-profit platforms. *Sociology Compass, 11*(8). Retrieved from https://doi.org/10.1111/soc4.12493.

This article provides an overview of the "sharing economy" and explores inequalities within it.

Wacjman, J. (2006). New connections: Social studies of science and technology and studies of work. *Work, Employment and Society, 20*(4), 773–786.

Wacjman explores the impact of technology on work and workers.

Related Websites

Government of Canada, Beyond 150, The Future of Work:

http://canadabeyond150.ca/reports/future-of-work.html

The Conference Board of Canada—Future of work:

https://www.conferenceboard.ca/insights/future-of-work

Deloitte, Insights, Returning to work in the future of work:

https://www2.deloitte.com/us/en/insights/focus/human-capital-trends/2020/covid-19-and-the-future-of-work.html

Indigenous AI:

https://www.indigenous-ai.net/

Glossary

abject labour Work that is simultaneously repulsive and attractive.

absenteeism Missing days of work.

administrative revolution Period of organizational change in the early 20th century, which saw the expansion of white-collar, managerial, and other administrative jobs.

aesthetic labour Work performed by workers so that their appearance and demeanour reflects their employers' image and brand.

age cohort A category composed of people born within a decade or two of each other.

ageism Discrimination and stereotyping based on age.

alienation Workers' estrangement under capitalism from the products of their labour, the labour process, their true nature/humanity, and others.

attitudes The ways we think or feel about people, places, and things.

artificial intelligence "[C]omputer systems that perform tasks that normally require human intelligence" (Pettersen, 2019).

associational discrimination Discrimination against someone based not on their characteristics but of those they are associated with in some way.

automation The use of labour-saving technology, usually to cut costs and/or speed up production.

autonomy The independence or freedom to utilize one's knowledge and experience.

bad jobs Those that pay little, provide few benefits, are precarious, and/or have unpredictable or undesirable working hours.

bona fide job requirement Abilities or characteristics absolutely required for performance of a job. When criteria used in hiring are not bona fide, discrimination can occur.

blue-collar work Traditionally physical work taking place in the primary or secondary sector.

bridge jobs Jobs held by older adults as they navigate the transition between their main careers and retirement.

bureaucracy Type of organization, discussed by Weber, characterized by advanced divisions of labour, hierarchies, and formal rules, among other characteristics.

bourgeoisie Marx's term for owners who own the means of production.

calculability An emphasis on quantity or quality, often to the point that quantity is taken as a measure of quality.

collective A form of co-operative that operates without hierarchy.

collective bargaining Negotiations between employers and workers' unions concerning the terms and conditions of employment.

colonization A process of settling an area while subordinating Indigenous peoples who already inhabit it.

commodification The process of turning things that are not inherently commodities—people, forests, the environment, and so on—into commodities to be sold for profit. Labour commodification is the process of treating workers as commodities, not human beings.

concrete ceiling Similar to the glass ceiling, the concrete ceiling consists of impenetrable barriers preventing members of minorities from being promoted to organizations' upper echelons.

control The ability to determine one's own, or others' actions.

co-operative A type of organization owned by its members, who govern it democratically

core working age Adults aged 25–64.

covert (or subtle) discrimination Denying opportunities through subtle or hidden means.

credential inflation The tendency of firms to demand higher credentials from workers, even when job requirements do not change.

crisis of expertise Although we are more dependent on science and experts than ever before, we are increasingly skeptical and even dismissive of scientific findings and expert claims.

crowdworkers Groups of people who complete crowd-sourced tasks posted through online platforms.

cultural capital A set of abilities, understandings, and dispositions related to a specific cultural setting that can be used to navigate that setting successfully.

decolonization A set of practices and processes aimed at dismantling colonial power and restoring Indigenous knowledge and ways of life.

deindustrialization The systematic disinvestment in production (manufacturing) within Western countries like Canada and the United States.

deskilling Process of job degradation through which workers are denied the opportunity to use skills (and autonomy) formerly exercised on the job.

digital platforms Virtual marketplaces where providers of goods and services are connected with buyers.

direct discrimination Intentionally denying employment opportunities to individuals based on their characteristics, regardless of their ability, skills, or qualifications.

dirty work Job tasks that are "physically disgusting . . . a symbol of degradation, something that wounds one's dignity" (Hughes, 1958, p. 49).
disability harassment Harassment on the basis of disability status.
discrimination The unfair treatment of a person or group on the basis of prejudice.
domestic labour The tasks involved in running a household, including housework, home maintenance, childcare, and consumption work.
double day A shift of paid work combined with a second shift performing domestic labour.
downsizing Reducing the number of permanent staff members at an organization.

economic cycle The movements between periods of economic growth and recession.
efficiency Finding the best means to achieve a given end. Associated with doing more, faster, at less cost.
emotional labour Work (especially work under the direction of others) requiring the suppression of personal emotions and the manipulation of others' emotions to benefit one's employer.
employment equity Policies aimed at ensuring that the workforce represents the diversity of the Canadian population.
employment rate The ratio of people age 15 and over who are working to the overall population age 15 or over (including those who are not working).
expertise Special skill, knowledge, or judgment; the skill and knowledge claimed by experts (*Oxford English Dictionary*, 2020a).
exploitation For Marxists, exploitation occurs when capitalists extract surplus value from workers during the process of production.
extrinsic rewards Benefits that accompany a job (like income, status) that make it rewarding.

Fordism A manner of organizing production characterized by advanced divisions of labour, automation, mass production, and managerial control.
formal rationality Decisions and goals aligned with formal rules and economic gain. Formal rationality guides instrumentally rational action.

gender essentialist segregation Horizontal sex segregation at work that is deemed consistent with stereotypes about the skills and abilities possessed by men and women.
gendered organizations Expectations about gender—gender ideologies, traditional divisions of labour, gender relations, and so on—have become embedded within organizational structures and practices.
gig work Work in which individuals do a series of short-term tasks for others as assigned through digital platforms. Often used interchangeably with the term platform work.
glass ceiling The presence of invisible barriers limiting opportunities to reach the upper echelons of organizational hierarchies.
globalization A set of processes in which production, capital, labour, communication, and culture are increasingly occurring on a global level.
global economy The world economy.
good jobs Employment that pays well and provides benefits, job security, and reasonable and stable working hours and potentially offers opportunities for promotion.

heteronormativity Assumptions that heterosexuality and the gender binary are normal or preferred.
homophily The tendency of people to be drawn to others like themselves.
horizontal segregation Variably defined as either occupational segregation not linked to inequality or occupational segregation consistent with ideologies that men and women are essentially different and have different abilities.
human capital Investments in skill acquisition, education, and training by individuals, organizations, and societies.

ideal type A description or list of traits to capture the essence of a social phenomenon or institution, while acknowledging that the phenomenon may not actually include all of the traits and the list provided is not exhaustive.
identity Who we think we are and how we believe others perceive us.
independent contractors Workers who contract their services to a company but are not technically employed by them. A form of self-employment.
Index of Dissimilarity A measure used to calculate the extent of occupational segregation, interpreted as the percentage of people in one group who would have to change jobs to have a distribution identical to a second group.
Indigenous knowledges "The understandings, skills and philosophies developed by societies with long histories of interaction with their natural surroundings . . . [and which are] integral to a cultural complex that also encompasses language, systems of classification, resource use practices, social interactions, ritual and spirituality" (UNESCO, 2019).
Industrial Revolution Period of massive economic, technological, and social change occurring in Western countries in the 18th and 19th centuries under capitalism.
institutional isomorphism Processes that encourage an institution or organization to become more like other organizations in the same (or a closely related) field (beyond rationalization processes) (DiMaggio & Powell, 1983).
intensive mothering An ideology that sees appropriate child-rearing as child-centred, expert-guided, emotionally absorbing, financially expensive, and labour-intensive (Hays, 1996, p. 8).

intersectionality Theories advocating that multiple dimensions of inequality (like gender, race, class), and the ways they intersect, should be taken into account simultaneously.
institutional ethnography A methodology that aims to map institutional practices and ruling relations in a given setting. Associated with Dorothy Smith and colleagues.
interactive service work Service work requiring interaction with members of the public (such as retail, food services, and hospitality).
intrinsic rewards Characteristics inherent in a job that make it rewarding or meaningful
instrumentally rational action Action pursued to achieve "calculated ends" (Weber, 1968, p. 24).
Involuntary part-time employment When a worker would prefer full-time hours, but can only secure part-time work.
involuntary turnover When people are forced to leave a job when they would rather not.
iron law of oligarchy The tendency for organizations to be governed by a few, despite efforts towards democracy.

job decision latitude The extent to which workers experience high job demands as well as the autonomy or latitude to solve problems that arise.
job satisfaction An indicator measuring how satisfied workers report they are with their jobs.

knowledge Familiarity with, or understanding of, a particular subject matter, branch of learning, set of experiences, or principles (*Oxford English Dictionary*, 2020c).
knowledge economy Economy dependent on information and educated workers.

labour Paid work done under the direction of a boss or supervisor.
labour force participation rate The ratio of those working for pay and those available and looking for work, divided by the total population.
labour-intensive manufacturing Manufacturing in which labour is a (or the) main cost of production
labour markets Where employers and employees come together and workers are distributed into jobs.
labour market segmentation theory Argument that there are at least two labour markets: a primary one characterized by good jobs and a secondary one characterized by less attractive jobs.
labour process In Marxian theory, the labour process consists of the objects, instruments, and organization of our work as well as what we do.
Labour Process Theory A theoretical approach influenced by Marx that focuses on the labour process and conflicts between managers and workers over the conduct of work.
Labour Theory of Value The belief that labour is the source of all value in goods and services.
lean work environments Environments where staffing is kept to a bare minimum in an effort to cut costs.
life course The "sequence of roles, opportunities, constraints, and events that shape" our lives from birth to death (Shanahan & Macmillan, 2008, p. 40).
linked lives A concept under the life course paradigm that encourages us to consider how what happens in the lives of others connected to us impacts our own lives.
living wage A wage sufficient to sustain a reasonable standard of living.

mandatory retirement Policy whereby employees are forced to retire once they reach a certain age.
Marxist-feminist Theoretical approaches that blend Marxist and feminist theories to explore the intersection of gender and class in shaping work (and life) experiences.
McDonaldization An extreme form of rationalization, characterized by efficiency, predictability, calculability, and control.
mechanization The alteration of work processes through the introduction of machinery.
means of production Tools, instruments, and resources required for production.
means of subsistence The ability to obtain what is needed to ensure human survival.
mechanical solidarity Social bonds generated through similarity of experience, characteristic of pre-capitalist societies.
micro-jobs Small, odd jobs. For example, Amazon Mechanical Turk (or M-Turk) workers may look at pictures and describe their content, complete short surveys, or complete other small writing tasks on their own computers for pennies (or dollars) a task.
mode of production A way of organizing production, which varies across economic systems. The mode of production under capitalism is distinct from other modes of production.
monopoly capitalism Period of capitalist development in which the concentration of capital spurred the rise of larger, more international firms able to restrict the workings of a free competitive market.
motherhood penalties Women's incomes and opportunities suffer with the transition to motherhood.

neoliberalism A theory of governance that holds that "human wellbeing can best be advanced by liberating individual entrepreneurial freedoms" and embracing free market principles (Harvey, 2005, p. 2).
neo-Taylorism A renewed adoption of scientific management, wherein workers are chosen very carefully, with consideration for their work effort and ability to handle intense work pressures, and

subsequently subjected to speed-ups and work intensification (Crowley et al., 2010).
nepotism A practice whereby people in power reserve opportunities for those in their social networks.
non-profit sector This sector includes organizations that are not profit-focused (charities, social services, community organizations).
non-standard work Work that differs from standard work because of its instability, irregular hours, or temporary nature.

occupational diseases Illnesses that are acquired while working through on-the-job exposure.
occupational segregation This occurs when people who differ by some marker (gender, race, disability status, sexual orientation) work in different occupations.
organic solidarity Concept associated with Durkheim: social bonds arise from our interdependency in societies with advanced divisions of labour.
organizational cultures Values, attitudes, meanings, and norms shared by members of an organization.
organizations Collectivities deliberately created to achieve a set of goals or objectives.
outsourcing Organizations contracting other firms and individuals to do work formerly done in-house.
overqualification When workers have more qualifications (for example, academic credentials) than their jobs require, they are overqualified.

pay equity The principle of equal pay for work of equal value.
panopticon An ideal prison design that facilitates surveillance and encourages self-discipline by ensuring that power is both visible and unverifiable.
personal service work Work that entails providing personal services to clients and/or employers.
platform work The use of digital platforms to mediate relationships between workers, employers, and consumers.
pluriactivity The practice of combining two or more economic activities to make a living.
populism A political stance appealing to the "common people" who may feel disenfranchised. Often associated with anti-elite sentiments (especially against political elites and experts, not economic elites).
post-industrial Term used to describe societies in which labour is predominantly found in the services or tertiary sector.
precarious work There is no guarantee that employment will continue, and wages may be uneven and discontinuous.
precarity Situations and work that are precarious.
precarization A set of labour market, organizational, state policy, and social processes increasing insecurity at work across jobs and occupations
predictability A component of McDonaldization and rationalization that aims to ensure that every similar firm functions and looks the same.
presenteeism When people show up for work when they are not at their best—due to injury, illness, chronic stress, or another condition—and hence cannot function to their best abilities.
prestige Respect or admiration. Linked with status.
primary sector The primary sector of the economy is concerned with the extraction and use of raw materials and natural resources (including agriculture, forestry, fishing).
private sector The part of the economy that is under private ownership.
productive aging A belief that workers should continue to be productive, even post-retirement.
productive leisure Engaging in hobbies that involve work (whether paid or unpaid).
professions Occupations traditionally distinguished from others by their advanced education, their expertise, and their social and regulatory status, which grants them a privileged market position (Adams, 2020a).
proletariat Marx's term for workers who do not have access to the means of production.
prosumption The performance of both production and consumption simultaneously (Ritzer, 2015).
protective services Work directed towards protecting people and society (for example, policing and firefighting).
public sector The part of the economy that is under government ownership or is funded by governments (such as public education, public health care)
putting-out system Production system wherein workers are subcontracted to produce goods from their homes or small workshops and then to send completed work back to their employer.

racial harassment A form of harassment based on race, skin colour, ancestry, citizenship, accent, language, or religion
racialized Having experienced a process through which racial markers have been identified as problematic and grounds for subordination.
racialized organizations Assumptions and biases concerning race and ability have become embedded in organizational processes and practices.
rational action Weberian concept referring to social action that is goal-oriented.
rationality "Means-ends calculations that determine how decisions are made" (Geva, 2015, p. 172). Formal and substantive rationality are two types.
rationalization The ongoing search to find the optimum means to achieve a desired end (efficiency).

reserve army of labour A pool of workers who are unemployed or underemployed and ready to fill the jobs of the employed should they be needed. The presence of a reserve army of labour helps to keep wages low.
résumé whitening The term given to the practice whereby applicants alter their names and sometimes their experience and credentials to minimize racial or immigrant signals to employers.
ritualism Going through the motions at work; following the basic rules without any additional effort.
routinization Processes making work more routine and repetitive.

sabotage Intentional destruction of employers' property or deliberate hindering of work operations.
scientific management Management philosophy associated with the writings of F. W. Taylor (also called Taylorism). It is associated with separating conception from execution, management appropriating knowledge about the labour process, and closely directing the work of workers.
second shift Performance of domestic labour after a "first shift" doing paid work.
secondary sector The secondary sector of the economy entails the production and processing of goods as well as construction.
selection effect In research, when some types of people are more likely to respond than others based on their characteristics.
seigneurial system A mode of organization, production, and society common in New France, wherein the French king granted plots of land to elite nobles, or "seigneurs," who in return promised to settle, develop, and oversee the land and its inhabitants.
self-employed Individuals who are not employed by another company but rather earn a living by providing services or products to clients and customers.
self-regulating professions Occupations for which legislation has been passed to allow practitioners (in conjunction with members of the public and the state) to govern their own affairs and regulate aspects of professional practice and discipline.
semi-skilled Requiring some skills and training but not a lot.
settler colonialism A form of colonialism in which the colonists seek land to settle on, establish new communities, and obtain resources.
separate spheres ideology The belief that there are two spheres in society and that men are ideally suited for the public sphere and women for the private sphere because of their "innate" characteristics.
services sector The services or tertiary sector of the economy encompasses the provision of services.
service worker Worker whose job involves providing services to others, especially interactive, personal, or protective service work.
sex work Work that entails selling sexualized services to others.
sexual harassment "Any conduct, comment, gesture, or contact of a sexual nature that is likely to cause offence or humiliation to any employee; or that might, on reasonable grounds, be perceived by that employee as placing a condition of a sexual nature on employment or on any opportunity for training or promotion" (Government of Canada, 2018).
sexual orientation harassment Harassment on the basis of sexual orientation.
skill An ability to do something well, based on one's knowledge, aptitude, and practice (*Oxford English Dictionary*, 2020d).
skill upgrading Sometimes called upskilling. Demand for new, enhanced skills in a workplace or occupation.
social action Behaviour to which an actor attaches meaning that takes into account (and/or is directed towards) the behaviour of others (Weber, 1968).
socialization Processes through which culture and societal norms are transmitted to others.
social relations of production The conflictive relationship between those who own the means of production and those who do not. According to Marx, these relations are a driver of history.
social capital Connections and networks that individuals can use to navigate social fields of power for their own benefit.
social closure Processes through which groups (of workers) seek to maximize their own rewards and opportunities by delimiting others' access to resources, opportunities, and group membership.
social rewards Recognition, appreciation, praise (as opposed to economic rewards like money).
sociological theories Systematic explanations of the social world and people's experiences of their social environments.
standard employment A situation in which workers have full-time, full-year employment with one employer with the expectation that this work will continue to be available to them.
statistical discrimination Making hiring decisions based on the belief that certain types of people are more productive than others in specific jobs
stigma An attribute that at least some members of society associate with disgrace or dishonour
stress "A state of tension produced by pressures or conflicting demands with which the person cannot adequately cope" (Jary & Jary, 2005b, p. 611).
stress of higher status model Higher-status, high-demand jobs may entail resources that increase, rather than decrease, job pressures.
subcultures The cultures shared by a subgroup of members in a broader organization or occupation.
substantive rationality Decisions are based on values, honour, ethical principles, and "doing the

right thing" even if it entails a personal sacrifice. Substantive rationality guides value-rational action.

symbolic capital Resources related to prestige and recognition. Symbolic capital shapes how economic, cultural, and social capital are recognized and rewarded.

symbolic interactionism A set of theoretical approaches focusing on the meanings that people hold about themselves, their experiences, and their social world. These meanings are constructed through social interaction with others.

systemic discrimination This occurs when discriminatory processes are embedded in organizational practices and policies.

tacit skills Often unrecognized skills acquired through close familiarity with technology, work practices, coworkers, or customers/clients.

task orientation An approach to working that focuses on doing what needs to be done, without any substantial concern for time or other factors.

Taylorism See scientific management.

telecommuting A "work practice that involves members of an organization substituting a portion of their typical work hours . . . to work away from a central workplace—typically principally from home—using technology to interact with others as needed to conduct work tasks" (Allen et al., 2015, p. 44).

temporary work Work conducted for a company on a short-term basis; typically, workers are hired by an agency that contracts their work out to other companies.

tertiary sector See services sector.

time discipline Working according to the clock and the schedules of others.

trajectories A concept within the life course paradigm used to capture the patterned pathways we traverse as we live our lives and pursue our goals.

transitions A concept within the life course paradigm used to describe the changes we experience as we move between social roles.

turning point A concept within the life course paradigm used to describe very significant transitions that may alter our opportunities and trajectories.

turnover rate The rate at which people leave work voluntarily or involuntarily.

two-eyed seeing The practice whereby Indigenous peoples learn to see the world through two perspectives: one rooted in their Indigenous ways of knowing and one in Western knowledge systems.

unconscious bias The subconscious stereotypes and biases we all hold about members of particular identity groups.

underemployment Employment that does not utilize the skills and training that workers possess.

underground economy Unrecorded and untaxed economic exchanges; illegal trade in goods or services.

unemployment rate The percentage of workers in the labour force who do not currently have a job but are actively seeking work.

unionization The process of organizing workers into a union.

value-rational action Action that is "determined by a conscious belief in the value for its own sake of some ethical, aesthetic, religious, or other form of behaviour, independent of its prospects of success" (Weber, 1968, pp. 24–25).

vertical segregation Occupational segregation associated with inequalities in income, status, and authority.

voluntary turnover This occurs when people leave a job because they want to do so.

volunteer work Work we do for free that contributes to our neighbourhoods and communities.

welfare management A strategy to encourage worker compliance and commitment by making workplace improvements and providing some work-related perks.

welfare state A system of governance whereby state actors believe they have a responsibility to implement policies that improve the well-being of the population they govern.

white-collar crime Crime committed in employment or other commercial situations for economic gain.

white-collar work Work that typically takes place in office settings and involves administration, the processing of information, and the management of organizational operations, across industries.

work "Human effort adding use value to goods and services" (Tilly & Tilly, 1998, p. 22).

work intensification Processes whereby workers are asked to do more work, to work harder, and to produce more value.

work-family conflict When work and family demands conflict or the stress experienced when work and family demands conflict.

work-life balance A healthy balance between our work commitments and other aspects of our lives.

work-life conflicts Conflicts between our work commitments and other aspects of our lives. Work-family conflict is one aspect.

workplace harassment "Any negative workplace interpersonal interaction that affects the terms, conditions, or employment decisions related to an individual's job, or creates an intimidating, or offensive workplace environment" (Rospenda, Richman, Ehmke, & Zlatoper, 2005, p. 96).

workplace incivility "Negative relational dimensions of employment with consequences for worker integrity and dignity" (Roscigno et al., 2009, p. 748).

workplace injuries Injuries that occur on the job.

workplace misbehaviour Behaviour that intentionally goes against the rules and that is not in the best interests of the employing organization.

References

3M. (2020). *State of Science Index: 2020 global report.* Retrieved from https://multimedia.3m.com/mws/media/1898512O/3m-sosi-2020-pandemic-pulse-global-report-pdf.pdf.

Abada, T., Hou, F., & Lu, Y. (2014). Choice of necessity: Do immigrants and their children choose self-employment for the same reasons? *Work, Employment & Society, 28*(1), 78–94.

Abella, R. S. (1984). *Equality in employment: A royal commission report: General summary.* Toronto, ON: Commission on Equality in Employment.

Abrams, Z. (2019, 1 Oct.). The future of remote work. *Monitor on Psychology, 50*(9). Retrieved from https://www.apa.org/monitor/2019/10/cover-remote-work.

Acker, G. (2017). Transphobia among students majoring in the helping professions. *Journal of Homosexuality, 64*(14), 2011–2029.

Acker, J. (1990). Hierarchies, jobs, bodies: A theory of gendered organizations. *Gender & Society, 4*(2), 139–158. doi:10.1177/089124390004002002.

Acker, J. (2006). Inequality regimes: Gender, class, and race in organizations. *Gender & Society, 20*(4), 441–464. doi:10.1177/0891243206289499.

Ackroyd, S., & Crowdy, P. (1990). Can culture be managed? Working with "raw material." The case of the English slaughtermen. *Personnel Review, 19*(5), 3–13.

Ackroyd, S., & Thompson, P. (2016). Unruly subjects: Misbehaviour in the workplace. In S. Edgell, H. Gottfried, & E. Granter (Eds), *The SAGE Handbook of the Sociology of Work and employment* (pp. 195–204). London: Sage Publications.

Adams, A., Lugsden, E., Chase, J., & Arber, S. (2000). Skill-mix changes and work intensification in nursing. *Work, Employment & Society, 14*(3), 541–555.

Adams, T. L. (2011). Making a living: African Canadian workers in London, Ontario, 1861–1901. *Labour/Le Travail, 67,* 9–43. Retrieved from www.lltjournal.ca/index.php/llt/article/view/5628.

Adams, T. L. (2016). When "citizenship is indispensable to the practice of a profession": Citizenship requirements for entry to practise professions in Canada. *Journal of Historical Sociology, 29*(4), 550–477. doi:10.1111/johs.12112.

Adams, T. L. (2017). Self-regulating professions: Past: present and future. *Journal of Professions and Organization, 4*(1), 70–87. doi:org/10.1093/jpo/jow004.

Adams, T. L. (2018). *Regulating professions: The emergence of professional self-regulation in four Canadian provinces.* Toronto, ON: University of Toronto Press.

Adams, T. L. (2020a). Professions. In C. Rojek & G. Ritzer (Eds), *Wiley Blackwell encyclopedia of sociology* (2nd ed.). Wiley-Blackwell.

Adams, T. L. (2020b). "This happens all the time": Organizations, professionalism, and ethical dilemmas in engineering. *Work, Employment and Society, 34*(6): https://doi.org/10.1177/0950017020902968

Adams, T. L. (2021). Engineers, skills and intra-professional inequalities. In D. W. Livingstone, *Professional power and skill use in the knowledge economy: A class analysis.* Leiden, Netherlands: Brill.

Adams, T. L., & Sawchuk, P. H. (2020). Professional-organizational contradictions and hybridization of knowledge: Insights from the study of engineering and nursing in Canada. *Vocations and Learning.* Retrieved from https://doi.org/10.1007/s12186-020-09253-1.

Adams, T. L., & Tremblay, P. F. (2020). Harsh realities and new opportunities: Royal Society of Canada members on the impact of COVID-19 on Canadian society. *Report for the Royal Society of Canada.* Retrieved from https://rsc-src.ca/en/voices/harsh-realities-and-new-opportunities-royal-society-canada-members-impact-COVID-19-canadian.

Adams, T. L., & Wannamaker, K. (2020). Professional regulation policies and the pandemic response: Comparing Canada, the UK and Australia. Paper presented at the Canadian Health Workforce Virtual Conference, 10 December.

Adanhounme, A. B., & Lévesque, C. (2019). La négociation collective en contexte de flexibilisation de l'emploi dans deux usines au Québec. *Relations industrielles, 74*(1), 14–38.

Akkaymak, G. (2017). A Bourdieuian analysis of job search experiences of immigrants in Canada. *Journal of International Migration and Integration, 18,* 657–674.

Alaska Oil Spill Commission. (1990). Final report. State of Alaska. Retrieved from http://www.evostc.state.ak.us/index.cfm?FA=facts.details.

Alberta, Government of. (2018). Labour market outcomes of graduates of Alberta's post-secondary institutions. Retrieved from https://open.alberta.ca/publications/9871460137185.

Alberta Human Rights Commission. (2020). Decisions. Retrieved from https://www.canlii.org/en/ab/abhrc/nav/date/2020.

Alberti, G., Bessa, I., Hardy, K., Trappmann, V., & Umney, C. (2018). In, against and beyond precarity: Work in insecure times. *Work, Employment and Society, 32*(3), 447–457.

Allen, S. M., Faulconbridge, J. R., & Thomas, P. (2019). The fearful and anxious professional: Partner experiences of working in the financialized professional services firm. *Work, Employment and Society, 33*(1), 112–130.

Allen, T. D., Golden, T. D., & Shockley, K. M. (2015). How effective is telecommuting? Assessing the status of our scientific findings. *Psychological Science in the Public Interest, 16*(2), 40–68. doi .org/10.1177/1529100615593273.

Alonso-Villar, O., Del Rio, C., & Gradin, C. (2012). The extent of occupational segregation in the United States: Differences by race, ethnicity, and gender. *Industrial Relations, 51*(2), 179–212. doi:10.1111/j.1468-232X.2012.00674.x

Ameeriar, L. (2017). *Women, work, and citizenship in the Pakistani diaspora.* Durham, NC: Duke University Press.

American Lung Association. (2020). Health effects of second-hand smoke. Retrieved from https://www.lung .org/stop-smoking/smoking-facts/health-effects-of-secondhand-smoke.html.

Anderson, N., & Hughes, K. D. (2010). The business of caring: Women's self-employment and the marketization of care. *Gender, Work, and Organization, 17*(4), 381–405.

Antunes, P. (2013). A labour market shortage of 1 million by 2020? Where we stand today. Retrieved from https:// www.conferenceboard.ca/newsletter/archive/2014/ feb2014/hot-topics-in-economics-blog/2013/11/11/A_ Labour_Market_Shortage_of_1_Million_by_2020_ Where_We_Stand_Today.aspx

Armour, J., & Sako, M. (2020). AI-enabled business models in legal services: From traditional law firms to next-generation law companies? *Journal of Professions and Organization, 7*(1), 27–46. https://doi.org/10.1093/jpo/ joaa001.

Armstrong, P. (2013). Puzzling skills: Feminist political economy approaches. *Canadian Review of Sociology, 50*(3), 256–283. doi:10.1111/cars.12015.

Armstrong, P., Armstrong H., & Kehoe MacLeod, K. (2015). The threats of privatization to security in long-term residential care. *Ageing International, 41*(1), 99–116.

Armstrong, P., and Day, S. (2017). *Wash, wear, and care: Clothing and laundry in long-term residential care* Montreal and Kingston: McGill-Queen's University Press.

Ashforth, B. E., & Kreiner, G. E. (1999). "How can you do it?" Dirty work and the challenge of constructing a positive identity. *Academy of Management Review, 24*(3), 413–434.

Ashley, L., & Empson, L. (2016). Understanding social exclusion in elite professional service firms: Field level dynamics and the "professional project.'" *Work, Employment and Society, 31*(2), 211–229.

Aslam, A. (2021). The school-to-work transitions of second-generation immigrant youth. *Canadian Review of Sociology,* 58(4).

Aslam, A., & Adams, T. (2021). "The workload is staggering": Changing working conditions of stay-at-home mothers under COVID-19 lockdowns. Working Paper.

AWCBC (Association of Workers' Compensation Boards of Canada). (2018). 2018 lost time claims in Canada. Retrieved from http://awcbc.org/?page_id=14.

Azocar, M. J., & Ferree, M. M. (2016). Engendering the sociology of expertise. *Sociology Compass, 10*(12), 1079–1089. doi:10.1111/cars.12015.

Bahn, K., Cohen, J., and van der Meulen Rodgers, Y. (2020). A feminist perspective on COVID-19 and the value of care work globally. *Gender, Work & Organization, 27,* 695–699.

Baird, C. L. (2012). Going against the flow: A longitudinal study of the effects of cognitive skills and gender beliefs on occupational aspirations and outcomes. *Sociological Forum, 27*(4), 968–1009.

Bakan, J. (2004). *The corporation: The pathological pursuit of profit and power.* Toronto, ON: Penguin Canada.

Bakan, J. (2020). *The new corporation: How "good" corporations are bad for democracy.* Toronto, ON: Penguin Canada. imprint: Allen Lane.

Ballantyne, P., Casey, R., O'Hagan, F., & Vienneau, P. (2016). Poverty status of worker compensation claimants with permanent impairments. *Critical Public Health, 26*(2), 173–90.

Banerjee, A., Daly, T., Armstrong, P., Szebehely, M., Armstrong, H., and Lafrance, S. (2012). Structural violence in long-term residential care for older people: Comparing Canada and Scandinavia. *Social Science and Medicine, 74*(3), 390–398.

Barken, R., Denton, M., Brookman, C., Zeyinoglu, I., & Plenderleith, J. (2015). Home care workers' skills in the context of task shifting: Complexities in care work. *Canadian Review of Sociology, 52*(3), 289–309.

Barley, S. R., & Kunda, G. (2004). *Gurus, hired guns, and warm bodies: Itinerant experts in a knowledge economy.* Princeton, NJ: Princeton University Press.

Bartlett, C., Marshall, M., & Marshall, A. (2012). Two-eyed seeing and other lessons learned within a co-learning journey of bringing together Indigenous and mainstream knowledges and ways of knowing. *Journal of Environmental Studies and Sciences, 2*(4), 331–340. doi:10.1007/s13412-012-0086-8.

Basok, T. (2002). *Tortillas and tomatoes: Transmigrant Mexican harvesters in Canada.* Montreal, QC, and Kingston, ON: McGill-Queen's University Press.

Baxter, J., & Wright, E. O. (2000). The glass ceiling hypothesis: A comparative study of the United States, Sweden, and Australia. *Gender & Society, 14*(2), 275–294. doi:10.1177/089124300014002004.

BBC News. (2019, December 12). Harvey Weinstein timeline: How the scandal unfolded. Retrieved from https://www.bbc.com.

Beagan, B. (2001). Micro inequalities and everyday inequalities: "Race," gender, sexuality and class in medical school. *Canadian Journal of Sociology, 26*(4), 583–610.

Beaudry, C., Gagnon, M., & Deschênes, A-A. (2019). Quand la perception des employeurs à l'égard des personnes immigrantes influence leurs pratiques de gestion de la diversité. *Relations industrielles, 74*(4), 674–696.

Beck, V., & Williams, G. (2015). The (performance) management of retirement and the limits of individual choice. *Work, Employment & Society, 29*(2), 267–277.

Becker, H. S., Geer, B., Hughes, E. C., & Strauss, A. L. (1976). *Boys in white: Student culture in medical school.* New Brunswick, NJ: Transaction Publishers.

Belanger, D., & Candiz, G. (2014). Essential, reliable and invisible: Latin American migrant farm workers in Quebec viewed by the local population. *Canadian Ethnic Studies, 46*(1), 45–66.

Bell, D. (1976). *The coming of post-industrial society: A venture in social forecasting.* New York, NY: Basic Books.

Bell, D. A. (1995). Who's afraid of critical race theory? *University of Illinois Law Review, 893.*

Bell, L.A. (2017). Soft skills, hard rocks: Making diamonds ethical in Canada's Northwest Territories. *Focaal, 79,* 74–88.

Belzunegui-Eraso, A., & Erro-Garcés, A. (2020). Teleworking in the context of the COVID-19 crisis. *Sustainability, 12,* 3662–3680. doi:10.3390/su12093662.

Bennett, J. M. (1987). *Women in the medieval English countryside: Gender and household in Brigstock before the plague.* New York, NY: Oxford University Press.

Benoit, A. C., Cotnam, J., O'Brien-Teengs, D., Greene, S., Beaver, K., Zoccole, A., & Loutfy, M. (2019). Racism experiences of urban Indigenous women in Ontario, Canada: "We all have that story that will break your heart." *The International Indigenous Policy Journal, 10*(2). doi:10.18584/iipj.2019.10.2.1.

Benoit, C., Jansson, M., Jansenberger, M., & Phillips, R. (2013). Disability stigmatization as a barrier to employment equity for legally-blind Canadians. *Disability & Society, 28*(7), 970–983. doi:10.1080/09687599.2012.741518.

Benoit, C., Ouellet, N., Jansson, M., Magnus, S., & Smith, M. (2017). Would you think about doing sex for money? Structure and agency in deciding to sell sex in Canada. *Work, Employment and Society, 31*(5), 731–747.

Benoit, C., Smith, M., Jansson, M., Healey, P. & Magnuson, D. (2021). The relative quality of sex work. *Work, Employment & Society,* 35(2), 239–255.

Bepko, J., & Mansalis, K. (2016). Common occupational disorders: Asthma, COPD, dermatitis, and musculoskeletal disorders. *American Family Physician, 93*(12), 1000–1006.

Berg, J. (2016). *Income security in the on-demand economy: Findings and policy lessons from a survey of crowdworkers.* Geneva, Switzerland: International Labour Office.

Berg, J., Furrer, M., Harmon, E., Rani, U., & Silberman, M.S. (2018). *Digital labour platforms and the future of work: Towards decent work in the online world.* International Labour Organization. Retrieved from https://www.ilo.org/wcmsp5/groups/public/---dgreports/---dcomm/---publ/documents/publication/wcms_645337.pdf

Berge, S. T. (2020). Pedagogical pathways for Indigenous business education: Learning from current Indigenous business practices. *The International Indigenous Policy Journal, 11*(1). doi:https://doi.org/10.18584/iipj.2020.11.1.9374.

Berger, E. D. (2009). Managing age discrimination: An examination of the techniques used when seeking employment. *The Gerontologist, 49*(3), 317–332.

Bernard, A., & Morissette, R. (2018). Employment rates and wages of core-aged workers in Canada and the United States, 2000 to 2017. *Economic Insights* no. 082. Statistics Canada Catalogue no. 11-626-X. Retrieved from https://www150.statcan.gc.ca/n1/pub/11-626-x/11-626-x2018082-eng.htm.

Berntsen, L. (2016). Reworking labour practices: On the agency of unorganized mobile migrant construction workers. *Work, Employment and Society, 30*(3), 472–488. doi:10.1177/0950017015617687.

Bielby, W. T., & Baron, J. N. (1986). Men and women at work: Sex segregation and statistical discrimination. *American Journal of Sociology, 91*(4), 759–799. doi:10.1086/228350.

Bikos, L. J. (2016). "I took the blue pill." The effect of the hegemonic masculine police culture on Canadian policewomen's identities. Masters major research paper. Retrieved from https://ir.lib.uwo.ca/sociology_masrp/7.

Bikos, L. J. (2020). "It's all window dressing": Canadian police officers' perceptions of mental health stigma in their workplace. *Policing: An International Journal, 44*(1) doi:10.1108/PIJPSM-07-2020-0126.

Bilimoria, D., & Stewart, A. (2009). "Don't ask, don't tell": The academic climate for lesbian, gay, bisexual, and transgender faculty in science and engineering. *NWSA Journal, 21*(2), 85–103.

Bittle, S., Chen, A., & Hebert, J. (2018). Work-related deaths in Canada. *Labour/Le Travail, 82*(Fall), 159–187.

Blair-Loy, M. (2003). *Competing devotions: Career and family among women executives.* Cambridge, MA: Harvard University Press.

Blanchard, D. (1983). High steel! The Kahnawake Mohawks and the high construction trade. *Journal of Ethnic Studies, 11*(2).

Blau, F. D., Brummund, P., & Liu, A. Y.-H. (2013). Trends in occupational segregation by gender 1970–2009: Adjusting for the impact of changes in the occupational coding system. *Demography, 50*(2), 471–492. doi:10.1007/s13524-012-0151-7.

Blauner, B. (1964). *Alienation and freedom: The factory worker and his industry.* Chicago, IL: University of Chicago Press.

Bleasdale, R. E. (2018). *Rough work: Labourers on the public works of British North America and Canada, 1841–1882.* Toronto, ON: University of Toronto Press.

Block, S., & Galabuzi, G.-E. (2011). *Canada's colour coded labour market.* Retrieved from Canadian Centre for Policy Alternatives website: https://www.policyalternatives.ca/publications/reports/canadas-colour-coded-labour-market.

Bluestone, B., & Harrison, B. (1982). *The deindustrialization of America: Plant closings, community abandonment, and the dismantling of basic industry.* New York, NY: Basic Books.

Blumer, H. (1969). *Symbolic interactionism: Perspective and method.* Berkeley, CA: University of California Press.

Boivin, L. (2017). La représentation collective au travail en contexte d'externalisation des services publics d'aide à domicile au Québec. *Relations industrielles, 72*(3), 501–523.

Bolton, S. C. (2005). *Emotion management in the workplace.* Red Globe Press.

Bolton, S. C., & Houlihan, M. (2009). Are we having fun yet? A consideration of workplace fun and engagement. *Employee Relations, 31*(6), 556–568.

Bonet, F. (2008). Un crime sans deviance: le vol en interne comme activite routiniere. *Revue francaise de sociologie, 49*(2), 331–350.

Boni-Le Goff, I., Le Feuvre, N., Mallard, G., Lépinard, E., & Morel, S. (2019). Do gender regimes matter? Converging and diverging career prospects among young French and Swiss lawyers. In M. Choroszewicz & T. L. Adams (Eds), *Gender, age, and inequality in the professions* (pp. 114–132). New York, NY: Routledge.

Bonilla-Silva, E. (2015). More than prejudice: Restatement, reflections, and new directions in critical race theory. *Sociology of Race and Ethnicity, 1*(1), 73–87. doi:10.1177/2332649214557042.

Bonilla-Silva, E. (2019). Toward a new political praxis for Trumpamerica: New directions in critical race theory. *American Behavioral Scientist, 63*(13), 1776–1788. doi:10.1177/0002764219842614.

Bonstead Bruns, M. (2007). Work, sociology of. In G. Ritzer (Ed.), *The Blackwell encyclopedia of sociology.* doi:10.1002/9781405165518.wbeosw025.

Booth, A., & Skelton, N. (2011). "There's a conflict right there": Integrating Indigenous community values into commercial forestry in the Tl'azt'en First Nation. *Society and Natural Resources, 24*(4), 368–383.

Bordo, S. (1993). Feminism, Foucault, and the politics of the body. In C. Ramazanoglu (Ed.), *Up against Foucault: Explorations of some tensions between Foucault and feminism* (pp. 179–202). New York, NY: Routledge.

Boulin, J.-Y., Lallement, M., Messenger, J. C., & Michon, F. (Eds). (2006). *Decent working time: New trends, new issues.* Geneva, Switzerland: International Labour Office.

Boulis, A. K., & Jacobs, J. A. (2008). *The changing face of medicine: Women doctors and the evolution of health care in America.* Ithaca, NY: Cornell University Press.

Bourdieu, P. (1986). The forms of capital. In J. G. Richardson (Ed.), *Handbook of theory and research for the sociology of education* (pp. 241–258). New York, NY: Greenwood Press.

Bourdieu, P. (1989). *The state nobility: Elite schools in the field of power* (L. C. Clough, trans.). Stanford, CA: Stanford University Press.

Bourgeault, I. L. (2018). *Healthy professional knowledge workers: Examining the gendered nature of mental health issues, leaves of absence, and return to work experiences from a comparative perspective.* International Sociological Association Congress, Toronto, July.

Bowen, S., Brenton, J. & Elliott, S. (2019). *Pressure cooker: Why home cooking won't solve our problems and what we can do about it.* New York: Oxford University Press.

Bowen, S., Elliott, S., & Brenton, J. (2014). The joy of cooking? *Contexts, 13*(3), 20–25.

Boyd, M. (2003). Sex differences in occupational skill: Canada, 1961–1986. *Canadian Review of Sociology and Anthropology, 27*(3), 285–315. doi:10.1111/j.1755-618X.1990.tb00127.x.

Bradbury, B. (2000). Gender at work at home: Family decisions, the labour market, and girls' contributions to the family economy. In L. S. MacDowell & I. Radforth (Eds), *Canadian working-class history: Selected readings* (2nd ed., pp. 215–234). Toronto, ON: Canadian Scholars' Press.

Braverman, H. (1974). *Labor and monopoly capital: The degradation of work in the twentieth century.* New York, NY: Monthly Review Press.

Brennan Center. (2019). *Proposals for reform volume II: National task force on rule of law & democracy.* Retrieved from https://www.brennancenter.org/our-work/policy-solutions/proposals-reform-volume-ii-national-task-force-rule-law-democracy.

Brewis, J., & Linstead, S. (2000). "The worst thing is the screwing" I: Consumption and the management of identity in sex work. *Gender, Work and Organization, 7*(2), 84–97.

Britton, D. M. (2000). The epistemology of the gendered organization. *Gender & Society, 14*(3), 418–434. doi:10.1177/089124300014003004.

Broadway, M. J., & Stull, D. D. (2008). "I'll do whatever you want, but it hurts": Worker safety and community health in modern meatpacking. *Labor: Studies in Working-Class History of the Americas, 5*(2), 27–37. doi:10.1215/15476715-2007-076.

Brockman, J. (1995). Exclusionary tactics: The history of women and visible minorities in the legal profession in British Columbia. In H. Foster & J. P. S. McLaren (Eds), *Essays in the history of Canadian law* (Vol. VI, pp. 508–561). Toronto, ON: Osgoode Society for Canadian Legal History.

Brooks, B., Jarman, J., & Blackburn, R. M. (2003). Occupational gender segregation in Canada, 1981–1996: Overall, vertical and horizontal segregation. *Canadian Review of Sociology and Anthropology, 40*(2), 197–213. doi:10.1111/j.1755-618X.2003.tb00243.x.

Brooks-Cleator, L., & Giles, A. (2018). Indigenous older adults' perspectives on aging well in an urban community in Canada. *Innovation in Aging, 2*(1), 175.

Browne, I., & Misra, J. (2003). The intersection of gender and race in the labor market. *Annual Review of Sociology, 29*, 487–513. doi:10.1146/annurev.soc.29.010202.100016.

Brownlie, R. J. (2008). "Living the same as the white people": Mohawk and Anishinabe women's labour in southern Ontario, 1920–1940. *Labour/Le Travail, 61*(Spring), 41–68. Retrieved from www.lltjournal.ca/index.php/llt/article/view/5526.

Bruckert, C. (2002). *Taking it off, putting it on.* Toronto, ON: Women's Press.

Brunet, S. (2019). *The transition from school to work: the* NEET *indicator for 20- to 24-year-olds in Canada.* Ottawa, ON: Statistics Canada. https://www150.statcan.gc.ca/n1/pub/81-599-x/81-599-x2019001-eng.htm.

Brynin, M., & Güveli, A. (2012). Understanding the ethnic pay gap in Britain. *Work, Employment & Society, 26*(4), 574–587. doi:10.1177/0950017012445095.

Buchanan, S. (2020, 17 April). Zooming while Black. *Sisters from AARP.* Retrieved from https://www.sistersletter.com/culture/zooming-while-black.

Buddle, M. 2010. *The business of women.* Vancouver, BC: University of British Columbia Press.

Budig, M., & England, P. (2001). The wage penalty for motherhood. *American Sociological Review,* 66(2), 204–225.

Burawoy, M. (1979). *Manufacturing consent: Changes in the labor process under monopoly capitalism.* Chicago, IL: University of Chicago Press.

Burman, P. (1988). *Killing time, losing ground: Experiences of unemployment.* Toronto, ON: Thompson Educational Publishing.

Burstein, M., Tienharra, N., Hewson, P., & Warrander, B. (1975). *Canadian work values: Findings of a work ethic survey and a job satisfaction survey.* Ottawa, ON: Information Canada.

Butler, J. (1990). *Gender trouble.* New York, NY: Routledge.

Buzdugan, R., & Halli, S. S. (2009). Labor market experiences of Canadian immigrants with focus on foreign education and experience. *International Migration Review, 43*(2), 366–386. doi:10.1111/j.1747-7379.2009.00768.x.

Calliste, A. (1987). Sleeping car porters in Canada: An ethnically submerged split labour market. *Canadian Ethnic Studies, 19*(1), 1–20.

Canada Labour Congress (CLC). (2019, March). *Islamophobia at Work: Report.* CLC. Retrieved from http://documents.clc-ctc.ca/human-rights-and-equality/islamophobia/IslamophobiaAtWork-Report-2019-03-20-EN.pdf.

Canada Labour Congress. (2020). *What unions do: Build worker power.* Retrieved from https://canadianlabour.ca/what-unions-do/build-worker-power.

Canada Project. (2019). The seigneurial system. Retrieved from http://www.canadahistoryproject.ca/1663/1663-07-seignurial.html.

Canada. Royal Commission on the Relations of Labor and Capital. (1889). *Report of the Royal Commission on the Relations of Capital and Labor in Canada* (vol. 1). Ottawa, ON: Queen's Printer. Retrieved from http://publications.gc.ca/site/eng/472984/publication.html.

Canadian Centre for Occupational Health and Safety (CCOHS). (2020). What causes stress in the workplace? Retrieved from https://www.ccohs.ca/oshanswers/psychosocial/stress.html.

Canadian Co-operative Association. (2019). https://www.devex.com/organizations/canadian-cooperative-association-cca-16736.

Canadian Council for Aboriginal Business and Future Skills Centre. (2020). Digital differences: The impact of automation on the Indigenous economy in Canada. Retrieved from https://fsc-ccf.ca/wp-content/uploads/2020/07/Digital_Differences_EN-Aug-12.pdf.

Canadian Football League. (2019). Diversity is strength. Retrieved from https://www.cfl.ca/dis.

Canadian HR Reporter. (2018). Canada ranks 4th globally for highest employee turnover. Retrieved from https://www.hrreporter.com/focus-areas/culture-and-engagement/canada-ranks-4th-globally-for-highest-employee-turnover/283061.

Canadian Human Rights Commission (CHRC). (2020). Employer obligations. Retrieved from https://www.chrc-ccdp.gc.ca/eng/content/employer-obligations.

Canadian Human Rights Reporter. 1999. *New test for reasonable accommodation: British Columbia v. B.C.G.E.U.* Retrieved from https://www.cdn-hr-reporter.ca/hr_topics/systemic-discrimination/new-test-reasonable-accommodation.

Canadian Institute of Forestry. (2018). Gender equity in Canada's forest sector initiative. Retrieved from https://www.cif-ifc.org/gender-equity-in-canadas-forest-sector-initiative.

Canadian Union of Public Employees (CUPE). (2014). Refusing unsafe work: A step by step guide. Retrieved from https://cupe.ca/refusing-unsafe-work-step-step-guide.

Capous-Desyllas, M., & Loy, V. (2020). Navigating intersecting identities, self-representation, and relationships: A qualitative study with trans sex workers living and working in Los Angeles, CA. *Sociological Inquiry, 90*(2), 339–370.

Caputo, G. A., & King, A. (2011). Shoplifting: Work, agency, and gender. *Feminist Criminology, 6*, 159–77.

Carbado, D. W., & Gulati, M. (2013). "Working identity" In R. Delgado and J. Stefancic (Eds), *Critical race theory: The cutting edge* (3rd ed., pp. 223–237). Philadelphia, PA: Temple University Press.

Cardona, M. S. (2018). Les agence de placement à Montréal et le travail immigrant: une composante du racism systémique au Québec? *Sociologie et sociétiés, 50*(2), 49.

Carlson, D. L., Petts, R., & Pepin, J. R. (2020). US couples' divisions of housework and childcare during COVID-19 pandemic. *SocArXiv*, 19 May. Retrieved from https://doi.org/10.31235/osf.io/jy8fn.

Carpenter, C. S., Eppink, S. T., & Gonzales, G. (2020). Transgender status, gender identity, and socioeconomic outcomes in the United States. *Industrial and Labor Relations Review, 73*(3), 573–599.

Carroll, W. K. (2017). The changing face(s) of corporate power in Canada. In E. G. Grabb, J. G. Reitz, & M. Hwang (Eds), *Social inequality in Canada: Dimensions of disadvantage* (6th ed., pp. 12–23). Don Mills, ON: Oxford University Press.

Carter, B., Danford, A., Howcroft, D., Richardson, H., Smith, A., & Taylor, P. (2013). "Stressed out of my box": Employee experience of lean working and occupational ill-health in clerical work in the UK public sector. *Work, Employment and Society, 27*(5), 747–767. doi:10.1177/0950017012469064.

Castells, M. (2000). Materials for an exploratory theory of the network society. *The British Journal of Sociology, 51*(1), 5–24. doi:10.1111/j.1468-4446.2000.00005.x.

CBC. (2018). Most Canadian employees are ready to quit their jobs, survey finds. Retrieved from https://www.cbc.ca/news/business/job-satisfaction-employee-retention-canada-1.4945021.

CBC. (2020a, 22 Nov.). Brampton needs "real help" for essential workers: Mayor. Retrieved from https://www.cbc.ca/news/canada/toronto/ontario- COVID19-update-nov22-1.5811782.

CBC. (2020b, 23 Nov.). Workplace compensation claims reflect toll COVID-19 has taken on Canada's workers. Retrieved from https://www.cbc.ca/news/canada/COVID-compensation-wsib-wcb-workers-1.5810305.

Cech, E. A. (2013). The self-expressive edge of occupational sex segregation. *American Journal of Sociology, 119*(3), 747–789. doi:10.1086/673969.

Centers for Disease Control and Prevention (CDC). (2020, Feb.). Interim guidance for businesses and employers to plan and respond to coronavirus disease 2018 (COVID-19). Retrieved from https://www.cdc.gov/coronavirus/2019-ncov/specific-groups/guidance-business-response.html.

Chang, M. L. (2004). Growing pains: Cross-national variation in sex segregation in sixteen developing countries. *American Sociological Review, 69*(1), 114–137. doi:10.1177/000312240406900107.

Chapkis, W. (2000). Power and control in the commercial sex trade. In R. Weitzer (Ed.), *Sex for sale* (pp. 573–599). New York, NY: Routledge.

Charalampous, M., Grant, C. A., Tramontano, C., & Michailidis, E. (2019). Systematically reviewing remote e-workers' well-being at work: A multidimensional approach. *European Journal of Work and Organizational Psychology, 28*(1), 51–73. Retrieved from https://doi.org/10.1080/1359432X.2018.1541886.

Charest, J. (2008). Workforce mobility within the construction industry in Quebec: A dual reality. *Relations industrielles, 63*(2), 290–316.

Charles, M. (2005). National skill regimes, postindustrialism, and sex segregation. *Social Politics: International Studies in Gender, State and Society, 12*(2), 289–316. doi:10.1093/sp/jxi015.

Charles, M., & Bradley, K. (2002). Equal but separate? A cross-national study of sex segregation in higher education. *American Sociological Review, 67*(4), 573–599. doi:10.2307/3088946.

Charles, M., & Grusky, D. B. (2004). *Occupational ghettos: The worldwide segregation of women and men*. Stanford, CA: Stanford University Press.

Chatterjee, R. (2018, 21 Feb.). A new survey finds 81 percent of women have experienced sexual harassment. Retrieved from https://www.npr.org.

Chen, Z. J., & Skuterud, M. (2018). Relative labour market performance of former international students: Evidence from the National Graduates Survey. *Canadian Public Policy, 44*(3), 207–225. Retrieved from https://doi.org/10.3138/cpp.2017-042.

Cheremond, R. J. (2020, 8 June). 9 future of work trends post- COVID-19. Gartner. Retrieved from https://www.gartner.com/smarterwithgartner/9-future-of-work-trends-post- COVID-19.

Chiu, C., & Leicht, K. T. (1999). When does feminization increase equality? The case of lawyers. *Law & Society Review, 33*(3), 557–593. doi:10.2307/3115104.

Choi, K.H., Denice, P., Haan, M., & Zajacova, A. (2021). Studying the social determinants of COVID-19 in a data vacuum. *Canadian Review of Sociology, 58*(2), https://doi.org/10.1111/cars.12336

Choo, H. Y., & Ferree, M. M. (2010). Practicing intersectionality in sociological research: A critical analysis of inclusions, interactions, and institutions in the study of inequalities. *Sociological Theory, 28*(2), 129–149. doi:10.1111/j.1467-9558.2010.01370.x.

Choroszewicz, M. (2019). Fathers in private law practice in Finland: Reconciling work and family life for male lawyers from different generations." In M. Choroszewicz and T. L. Adams (Eds), *Gender, age, and inequality in the professions* (pp. 155–169). New York, NY: Routledge.

Choroszewicz, M., & Adams, T. (Eds). (2019). *Gender, age and inequality in the professions.* New York, NY: Routledge.

Choudhury, P., Larson, B. Z., & Foroughi, C. (2019, 14 Aug.). Is it time to let employees work from anywhere? *Harvard Business Review.* Retrieved from https://hbr.org/2019/08/is-it-time-to-let-employees-work-from-anywhere.

Chun, H., & Lee, I. (2001). Why do married men earn more: Productivity or marriage selection? *Economic Inquiry, 39*(2), 307–319. doi:10.1111/j.1465-7295.2001.tb00068.x.

Churchill, B., & Craig, L. (2019). Gender and the gig economy: Men and women using digital platforms to secure work in Australia. *Journal of Sociology, 55*(4), 741–761.

CIHI (Canadian Institute for Health Information). (2019). *Scott's medical database (SMDB) data tables, 2017–2018.* [Data tables]. Retrieved from https://www.cihi.ca/en/access-data-reports/results?f%5B0%5D=field_primary_theme%3A2047.

Ciprikis, K., Cassells, D., & Berrill, J. (2020). Transgender labour market outcomes: Evidence from the United States. *Gender, Work & Organization, 27*(6), 1378–1401.

Cision. (2019, 13 June). Canada ranks in the middle of the pack for family-friendly policies among wealthy countries. Retrieved from https://www.newswire.ca/news-releases/canada-ranks-in-the-middle-of-the-pack-for-family-friendly-policies-among-wealthy-countries-855617739.html.

Cloutier, G., & Marchand, A. (2020). Identité professionnelle et agressions dans les métiers spécialisés de la construction et du secteur manufacturier au Québec. *Relations industrielles, 75*(1), 52–77.

Cloutier, L., Bernard, P., & Tremblay, D.-G. (2011). Activité professionnelle et responsabilités familiales: les mères sont-elles encore perdantes dans leur qualité d'emploi? *Relations industrielles, 66*(2), 256–278.

Coburn, E., Moreton-Robinson, A., Sefa Dei, G., & Stewart-Harawira, M. (2013). Unspeakable things: Indigenous research and social science. *Socio, 2*(2), 331–348. doi:10.4000/socio.524.

Cockburn, C. (1983). *Brothers: Male dominance and technological change.* London, UK: Pluto Press.

Cohen, M. G. (1988). *Women's work, markets and economic development in nineteenth-century Ontario.* Toronto, ON: University of Toronto Press.

Cohen, P. N. (2013). The persistence of workplace gender segregation in the US. *Sociology Compass, 7*(11), 889–899. doi:10.1111/soc4.12083.

Cohen, P. N., & Huffman, M. L. (2003). Occupational segregation and the devaluation of women's work across U.S. labor markets. *Social Forces, 81*(3), 881–908. doi:10.1353/sof.2003.0027.

Cohn, S. (1985). *The process of occupational sex-typing: The feminization of clerical labor in Great Britain.* Philadelphia, PA: Temple University Press.

Coiquaud, U. (2011). The collective representation of precarious workers: Contemporary evolution and challenges. *Relations industrielles, 66*(4), 631–654.

Coiquaud, U., & Martin, I. (2019). Accès à la justice des travailleurs de plateformes numériques: réponses contrastées des tribunaux canadiens et américains. *Relations industrielles, 74*(3), 577–588.

Collins, P. H. (2010). *Black feminist thought.* Routledge.

Collins, P. H. (2019). *Intersectionality as critical social theory.* Durham, NC: Duke University Press.

Conference Board of Canada. (2014). Compensation planning outlook 2014. Retrieved from https://www.conferenceboard.ca/temp/5e665337-66ff-4728-b2fa-08a7a10a51a2/14-168_CompPlanningOtlk2014.pdf.

Conference Board of Canada (2015). Compassion fatigue: Managing to prevent stress and emotional trauma. Retrieved from https://www.conferenceboard.ca/e-library/abstract.aspx?did=6910.

Conference Board of Canada. (2017a). Racial wage gap. Retrieved from https://www.conferenceboard.ca/hcp/provincial/society/racial-gap.aspx.

Conference Board of Canada. (2017b). Immigrant wage gap. Retrieved from https://www.conferenceboard.ca/hcp/provincial/society/immigrant-gap.aspx.

Conference Board of Canada. (2017c). *Annual report card, 2017: Advancing diverse leadership on Canada's corporate boards.* Retrieved from https://boarddiversity.ca/wp-content/uploads/2018/04/PhaseNyne-ARC-Annual-Report-Card-2017-reduced.pdf.

Conference Board. (2019). Job satisfaction 2019: Satisfaction continues to rapidly increase in a very tight labor market. Retrieved from https://www.conferenceboard.ca/e-library/abstract.aspx?did=10446.

Conference Board of Canada. (2020). Incorporating Indigenous cultures and realities in STEM: Primer. Retrieved from https://www.conferenceboard.ca/e-library/abstract.aspx?did=10697.

Connell, C. (2010). Doing, undoing, or redoing gender? Learning from the workplace experiences of transpeople. *Gender & Society, 24*(1), 31–55.

Connell, C. (2012). Dangerous disclosures. *Sexuality Research & Social Policy, 9*(2), 168–177.

Connell, R. W. (1990). *Masculinities*. Berkeley, CA: University of California Press.

Connelly, M. P. (2006). Women in the labour force. *The Canadian Encyclopedia*. Retrieved from https://www.thecanadianencyclopedia.ca/en/article/women-in-the-labour-force.

Conwell, C., & Sutherland, E. H. (1937). *The professional thief*. Chicago, IL: University of Chicago Press.

Cooke, M. (2006). Policy changes and the labour force participation of older workers: Evidence from six countries. *Canadian Journal on Aging, 25*(4), 387–400.

Cooper, A. (2006). *The hanging of Angélique: The untold story of Canadian slavery and the burning of Old Montréal*. Harper Collins.

Cooperative Development Institute (CDI). (2015). What's the difference between cooperatives and collectives? Retrieved from https://cdi.coop/coop-cathy-coops-and-collectives-difference.

Corman, M. K. (2018). Driving to work: The front seat work of paramedics to and from the scene. *Symbolic Interaction, 41*(3), 291–310.

Cortina, L. M., Magley, V. J., Williams, J. H., & Langhout, R. D. (2001). Incivility in the workplace: Incidence and impact. *Journal of Occupational Health Psychology, 6*(1), 64–80. doi:1037/1076-8998.6.1.64.

Cottingham, M. D., Chapman, J. J., & Erickson, R. J. (2020). The constant caregiver: Work-family spillover among men and women in nursing. *Work, Employment and Society, 34*(2), 281–298.

Coulthard, G. S. (2014). *Red skin, white masks: Rejecting the colonial politics of recognition*. Minneapolis, MN: University of Minnesota Press.

Council of Ontario Universities. (2016). *Grad survey*. Retrieved from https://ontariosuniversities.ca/wp-content/uploads/2016/12/COU-Grad-Survey-2016.pdf.

Cousineau, J.-M., & Boudarbat, B. (2009). The economic performance of new immigrants in Quebec. *Relations industrielles, 64*(2).

Cranford, D., Vosko, L., & Zukewich, N. (2003). The gender of precarious employment in Canada. *Relations industrielles, 58*(3), 454–479.

Creese, G. (1987). Organizing against racism in the workplace: Chinese workers in Vancouver before the Second World War. *Canadian Ethnic Studies, 19*(3), 35–46.

Creese, G. (1999). *Contracting masculinity: Gender, class, and race in a white-collar union, 1944–1994*. Don Mills, ON: Oxford University Press.

Creese, G., & Kambere, E. N. (2003). What colour is your English? *Canadian Review of Sociology and Anthropology, 40*(5), 565–573. doi:10.1111/j.1755-618X.2003.tb00005.x.

Creese, G., & Wiebe, B. (2012). Survival employment: Gender and deskilling among African immigrants in Canada. *International Migration Review, 50*(5), 56–76.

Crenshaw, K. (1989). Demarginalizing the intersection of race and sex: A Black feminist critique of antidiscrimination doctrine, feminist theory and antiracist politics. *The University of Chicago Legal Forum, 140*, 139–167.

Crenshaw, K.W. (2011). Twenty years of critical race theory: Looking back to move forward. *Connecticut Law Review, 43*(5), 1253–1353.

Croall, H. (2001). *Understanding white collar crime*. Open University Press.

Crowley, M., Tope, D., Chamberlain, L. J., & Hodson, R. (2010). Neo-Taylorism at work: Occupational change in the post-Fordist era. *Social Problems, 57*(3), 421–447. Retrieved from https://www.jstor.org/stable/10.1525/sp.2010.57.3.421.

Cruz, E., & Sawchuk, P. H. (2021). Nurses, skills and intra-professional inequalities. In D. W. Livingstone, *Professional power and skill use in the knowledge economy: A class analysis*. Leiden, Netherlands: Brill.

Curl, J. (2009). *For all the people: Uncovering the hidden history of cooperation, cooperative movements, and communalism in America*. Oakland, CA: PM Press.

Currie, G., Richmond, J., Faulconbridge, J., Gabbioneta, C., & Muzio, D. (2019). Professional misconduct in healthcare: Setting out a research agenda for work sociology. *Work, Employment & Society, 33*(1), 149–161.

D'Amours, M. (2009). Non-standard employment after age 50: How precarious is it? *Relations industrielles, 64*(2), 209–229.

D'Amours, M., Lesemann, F., & Crespo, S. (2001). The early exit activity of workers older than 45 years: The impact of firms' practices and of public policies in Canada. *Canadian Journal on Aging, 20*(4), 435–450.

D'Arcy, C. (1998). Health status of Canadians. In D. Coburn, C. D'Arcy, and George Torrance (Eds), *Health and Canadian Society* (pp. 43–68). Toronto, ON: University of Toronto Press.

Das Gupta, T. (1994). Political economy of gender, race, and class: Looking at South Asian immigrant women in Canada. *Canadian Ethnic Studies, 26*(1), 59–74.

Das Gupta, T. (1996). *Racism and paid work*. Toronto, ON: Garamond Press.

Davidoff, L., & Hall, C. (1987). *Family fortunes: Men and women of the English middle class, 1780–1850*. London, UK: Hutchinson.

Davies, S., & Tanner, J. (2003). The long arm of the law: Effects of labeling on employment. *The Sociological Quarterly, 44*(3), 385–404.

Davis, J. D., Miles, G. M., & Quinley, J. H. (2019). "Same same, but different." *The International Journal of Sociology and Social Policy, 39*(7/8), 550–573.

Deery, S., Kolar, D., & Walsh, J. (2019). Can dirty work be satisfying? A mixed method study of workers doing dirty jobs. *Work, Employment and Society, 33*(4), 641–647. doi.org/10.1177/0950017018817307.

Delgado, R., & Stefancic, J. (Eds). (2013). *Critical race theory: The cutting edge* (3rd ed.). Philadelphia, PA: Temple University Press.

Denton, M., Plenderleith, J., & Chowhan, J. (2013). Impact of retirement type on income for people with disabilities. *Disability & Society, 28*(3), 338–352.

Desjardins, D., & Freestone, C. (2020, 19 Nov.). Canadian women continue to exit the labour force. RBC Report. Retrieved from https://thoughtleadership.rbc.com/canadian-women-continue-to-exit-the-labour-force.

Desjardins Group. (2019). Desjardins. Retrieved from https://www.desjardins.com/ca.

Deutsch, F. (2007). Undoing gender. *Gender & Society, 21*(1), 106–127. doi:10.1177/0891243206293577.

DeVault, M. (1991). *Feeding the family: The social organization of caring as gendered work.* Chicago, IL: University of Chicago Press.

Devine, F. (1992). Gender segregation in the engineering and science professions: A case of continuity and change. *Work, Employment and Society, 6*(4), 557–575. doi:10.1177/095001709264002.

deVries, H., Tummers, L., & Bekkers, V. (2018). The benefits of teleworking in the public sector: Reality or rhetoric? *Review of Public Personnel Administration, 39*(4), 570–593. doi.org/10.1177/0734371X18760124.

DiMaggio, P. J., & Powell, W. W. (1983). The iron cage revisited: Institutional isomorphism and collective rationality in organizational fields. *American Sociological Review, 48*(2), 147–160. doi:10.2307/2095101.

Dimitrova, D. (2003). Controlling teleworkers: Supervision and flexibility revisited. *New Technology, Work & Employment, 18*, 181–195.

Dingwall, R. (2001). Theoretical note: Notes toward an intellectual history of symbolic interactionism. *Symbolic Interaction, 24*(2), 237–242. doi:10.1525/si.2001.24.2.237.

Dinovitzer, R., Gunz, H., & Gunz, S. (2014). Unpacking client capture: Evidence from corporate law firms. *Journal of Professions and Organization, 1*(2), 90–117.

DiStasio, V., & Larsen, E. N. (2020). The racialized and gendered workplace: Applying an intersectional lens to a field experiment on hiring discrimination in five European labour markets. *Social Psychology Quarterly, 83*(3), 229–250.

Dixon, J., & Dougherty, D. S. (2014). A language convergence/meaning divergence analysis exploring how LGBTQ and single employees manage traditional family expectations in the workplace. *Journal of Applied Communication Research, 42*(1), 1–19.

Doucet, A., Mathieu, S., & McKay, L. (2020). Reconceptualizing parental leave benefits in COVID-19 Canada: From employment policy to care and social protection. *Canadian Public Policy, 46*(s III), S272–S286.

Doward, J. (2020, 28 June). Only 13% of UK working parents want to go back to "the old normal." *The Guardian*. Retrieved from https://www.theguardian.com/world/2020/jun/28/only-13-of-uk-working-parents-want-to-go-back-to-the-old-normal.

Doyle, S. (2020, 13 July). Migrant workers falling through cracks in health care coverage. *Canadian Medical Association Journal, 192* (28) E819–E820. DOI: https://doi.org/10.1503/cmaj.1095882.

du Preez, M., and Dronfield, J. (2016). *Dr. James Barry: A woman ahead of her time.* Oneworld Publications.

Dubinski, K. (2021, 30 March). Groups representing sex-trade workers launch legal challenge of Canada's prostitution laws. *CBC News*. Retrieved from https://www.cbc.ca/news/canada/london/sex-trade-legal-challenge-canada-1.5969798

Duck, W. (2016). Becoming a drug dealer: Local interaction orders and criminal careers. *Critical Sociology, 42*(7–8), 1069–1085.

Duerden Comeau, T., & Kemp, C. L. (2007). Intersections of age and masculinities in the information technology industry. *Ageing and Society, 27*, 215–232.

Duffy, M. (2007). Doing the dirty work: Gender, race, and reproductive labor in historical perspective. *Gender & Society, 21*(3), 313–336. doi:10.1177/0891243207300764.

Dunkerley, M. (1996). *The jobless economy? Computer technology and the world of work.* Blackwell Publishers.

Dunn, J. C. (2012). "It's not just sex, it's a profession": Reframing prostitution through text and context. *Communication Studies, 63*(3), 345–363. doi:10.1080/10510974.2012.678924.

Durkheim, É. (1933). *The division of labor in society* (G. Simpson, trans.). New York, NY: Free Press. (Original work published 1893)

Edwards, R. (1979). *Contested terrain: The transformation of the workplace in the twentieth century.* New York, NY: Basic Books.

Ehrhardt Mustaine, E., & Tewksbury, R. (2002). Workplace theft: An analysis of student-employee offenders and job attributes. *American Journal of Criminal Justice, 27*, 111–127.

Elder Jr, G. H., Kirkpatrick Johnson, M., & Crosnoe, R. (2003). The emergence and development of life course theory. In J. T. Mortimer and M. J. Shanahan (Eds), *Handbook of the life course.* New York, NY: Kluwer Academic/Plenum Publishers.

Elliott, S., & Bowen, S. (2018). Defending motherhood: Morality, responsibility, and double binds in feeding children. *Journal of Marriage and Family, 80*(2), 499–520.

Elrick, J. (2016). Screening, skills and cultural fit: Theorizing immigrant skill utilization from an organizational perspective. *Journal of International Migration and Integration*, *17*(3), 801–817. doi:10.1007/s12134-015-0433-1.

England, P. (2005). Gender inequality in labor markets: The role of motherhood and segregation. *Social Politics: International Studies in Gender, State and Society*, *12*(Summer), 264–288. doi:10.1093/sp/jxi014.

England, P. (2010). The gender revolution: Uneven and stalled. *Gender & Society*, *24*(2), 149–166. doi:10.1177/0891243210361475.

England, P., & Li, S. (2006). Desegregation stalled: The changing gender composition of college majors, 1971–2002. *Gender & Society*, *20*(5), 657–677. doi:10.1177/0891243206290753.

Englebert, R. 2007. Diverging identities and converging interests: Corporate competition, desertion, and voyageur agency, 1815–1818. *Manitoba History*, 55. Retrieved from http://www.mhs.mb.ca/docs/mb_history/55/divergingidentities.shtml.

Ergonomic Trends. 2020. Repetitive strain injuries. Retrieved from http://ergonomictrends.com/rsi-statistics.

Evetts, J., & Dingwall, R. (2002). Professional occupations in the UK and Europe: Legitimation and governmentality. *International Review of Sociology*, *12*(2), 159–171. doi:10.1080/0390670022000012413.

Eyal, G. (2013). For a sociology of expertise: The social origins of the autism epidemic. *American Journal of Sociology*, *118*(4), 863–907. doi:10.1086/668448.

Eyal, G. (2019). *The crisis of expertise*. Cambridge, UK: Polity Press.

Fagan, J. (1995). Women's careers in drug use and drug selling. *Current Perspectives on Aging and the Life Cycle*, *4*, 155–190.

Fagan, J., and Freeman, R. B. (1999). Crime and work. *Crime and Justice*, *25*, 225–290.

Fan, W., & Qian, Y. (2017). Native-immigrant occupational segregation and worker health in the United States, 2004–2014. *Social Science & Medicine*, *183*, 130–141. doi:10.1016/j.socscimed.2017.04.029.

Fang, T., Lee, B., Timming, A., & Fan, D. (2019). The effects of work-life benefits on employment outcomes in Canada: A multi-variate analysis. *Relations industrielles/Industrial Relations*, *74*(2), 323–351.

Farrer, L. (2020, 5 March). Remote work advocates warn companies about COVID-19 work-from-home strategies. *Forbes*. Retrieved from https://www.forbes.com/sites/laurelfarrer/2020/03/05/ironically-remote-work-advocates-warn-companies-about- COVID-19-work-from-home-strategies/#74d721a42051.

Fast, D., Shoveller, J., Kerr, T. (2017). The material, moral, and affective worlds of dealing and crime among young men entrenched in an inner city drug scene. *International Journal of Drug Policy*, *44*, 1–11.

Fatemi, F. (2020, 3 June). 3 ways COVID-19 will permanently change the future of work. *Forbes*. Retrieved from https://www.forbes.com/sites/falonfatemi/2020/06/03/3-ways-COVID-19-will-permanently-change-the-future-of-work/#cf4991a65b17.

Faulkner, W. (2009). Doing gender in engineering workplace cultures. *I. Observations from the field. Engineering Studies*, *1*(1), 3–18. doi:10.1080/19378620902721322.

Fearon, G., & Wald, S. (2011). The earnings gap between Black and white workers in Canada: Evidence from the 2006 census. *Relations industrielles/Industrial Relations*, *66*(3), 324–348. doi:10.7202/1006342ar.

Feng, Z. & Savani, K. (2020). COVID-19 created a gender gap in perceived work productivity and job satisfaction: implications for dual-career parents working from home. *Gender in Management*, 35(7/8), 719–F736. https://doi.org/10.1108/GM-07-2020-0202

Fenwick, T. (2012). Older professional workers and continuous learning in new capitalism. *Human Relations*, *65*(8), 1001–1020.

Ferraro, K. J., & Moe, A. M. (2003). Mothering, crime, and incarceration. *Journal of Contemporary Ethnography*, *32*(1), 9–40.

Ferree, M. M., & Purkayastha, B. (2000). Equality and cumulative disadvantage: Response to Baxter and Wright. *Gender & Society*, *14*(6), 809–813. doi:10.1177/089124300014006007.

Fields, A., Uppal, S., & LaRochelle-Côté, S. (2017). *The impact of aging on labour market participation rates*. Ottawa, ON: Statistics Canada. Retrieved from https://www150.statcan.gc.ca/n1/pub/75-006-x/2017001/article/14826-eng.htm.

Fingard, J. (1995). From sea to rail: Black transportation workers and their families in Halifax, c. 1870–1916. *Acadiensis*, *24*(2), 49–64.

Finnie, R., & Gray, D. (2018). How do older laid-off workers get by: Reemployment, early retirement, or social insurance benefits? *Canadian Public Policy*, *44*(2), 173–189.

Fleming, P., Rhodes, C., & Yu, K.-H. (2019). On why Uber has not taken over the world. *Economy and Society*, *48*(4), 488–509.

Fleming, S. (1878). Comments made in House of Commons: Debates of the House of Commons, 1878, v. 1, pp. 406–407). Retrieved from http://www.canadiana.ca/view/oocihm.9_07185_4_1/439?r=0&s=1.

Fortin, N. M., & Huberman, M. (2002). Occupational gender segregation and women's wages in Canada: An historical perspective. *Canadian Public Policy*, *28*, S11–S39. doi:10.2307/3552342.

Foster, K., & Birdsell Bauer, L. (2018). *Out of the shadows: Experiences of contract academic staff*. Canadian Association of University Teachers.

Foucault, M. (1977). *Discipline and punish: The birth of the prison*. New York, NY: Vintage.

Fournier, G., Zimmermann, H., & Gauthier, C. (2011). Instable career paths among workers 45 and over: Insight gained from long-term career trajectories. *Journal of Aging Studies, 25*(3), 316–327.

Fournier, V. (1999). The appeal to "professionalism" as a disciplinary mechanism. *The Sociological Review, 47*(2), 280–307. doi:10.1111/1467-954X.00173.

Fox, B. (Ed.). (1980). *Hidden in the household: Women's domestic labour under capitalism*. Toronto, ON: Women's Educational Press.

Fox, B. J., & Fox, J. (1987). Occupational gender segregation of the Canadian labour force, 1931–1981. *Canadian Review of Sociology and Anthropology, 24*(3), 374–397. doi:10.1111/j.1755-618X.1987.tb01102.x.

Frager, R. A., & Patrias, C. (2005). *Discounted labour: Women workers in Canada, 1870–1939*. Toronto, ON: University of Toronto Press.

Frankling, S. (2020, 28 Nov.). Are workers "stealing" time from their companies when working from home? Some employers say yes—but studies say just the opposite. *The Star*. Retrieved from https://www.thestar.com/business/2020/11/28/are-workers-stealing-time-from-their-companies-when-working-from-home-some-employers-say-yes-but-studies-say-just-the-opposite.html.

Fredriksen-Goldsen, K.I., & Scharlach, A.E. (2001). *Families and work: New directions in the twenty-first Century*. Oxford University Press.

Freidson, E. (1970). *Professional dominance: The social structure of medical care*. Atherton Press.

Freidson, E. (2001). *Professionalism: The third logic*. Chicago, IL: University of Chicago Press.

Fudge, J., & MacPhail, F. (2009). The Temporary Foreign Worker Program in Canada: Low-skilled workers as an extreme form of flexible labor. *Comparative Labor Law and Policy Journal, 31*(5), 5–45.

Fulford, M., & Patterson, M. (2019). Multiple jobholders in Canada. *Labour Statistics at a Glance*. Statistics Canada Catalogue no. 71-222-X. Retrieved from https://www150.statcan.gc.ca/n1/pub/71-222-x/71-222-x2019003-eng.htm.

Fuller, L., & Smith, V. (1996). Consumers' reports: Management by customers in a changing economy. In C. L. Macdonald and C. Sirianni (Eds), *Working in the service economy* (pp. 74–90). Philadelphia, PA: Temple University Press.

Fuller, S. (2015). Do pathways matter? Linking early immigrant employment sequences and later economic outcomes: Evidence from Canada. *International Migration Review, 49*(2), 355–405.

Fuller, S. (2018). Segregation across workplaces and the motherhood wage gap: Why do mothers work in low-wage establishments? *Social Forces, 96*(4), 1443–1476.

Fuller, S., & Hirsh, C. E. (2019). "Family-friendly" jobs and motherhood pay penalties: The impact of flexible work arrangements across the educational spectrum. *Work and Occupations, 46*(1), 3–44.

Fuller, S., & Stecy-Hildebrandt, N. (2014). Lasting disadvantage? Comparing career trajectories of matched temporary and permanent workers in Canada. *Canadian Review of Sociology, 51*(4), 293–324.

Fuller, S., & Vosko, L. F. (2008). Temporary employment and social inequality in Canada: Exploring intersections of gender, race, and immigration status. *Social Indicators Research, 88*(1), 31–50.

Fussell, E., Gauthier, A. H., & Evans, A. (2007). Heterogeneity in the transition to adulthood: The cases of Australia, Canada, and the United States. *European Journal of Population, 23*(3–4), 389–414.

Gaddis, S. M. (2015). Discrimination in the credential society: An audit study of race and college selectivity in the labor market. *Social Forces*, 93(4), 1451–1479. doi:10.1093/sf/sou111.

Gale, J. (2012). Government reforms, performance management and the labour process: The case of officers in the UK probation service. *Work, Employment and Society, 26*(5), 822–838. doi:10.1177/0950017012451646.

Gallacher, G. & Hossain, I. (2020). Remote work and employment dynamics under COVID-19. Evidence from Canada. *Canadian Public Policy,* 46 (S1, July), S44.

Garson, B. (1988). *The electronic sweatshop: How computers are transforming the office of the future into the factory of the past*. Simon and Schuster.

Gaskell, J. (1983). Conceptions of skill and the work of women: Some historical and political issues. *Atlantis, 8*(2), 11–25. Retrieved from http://journals.msvu.ca/index.php/atlantis/article/view/4526.

Gatta, M., Boushey, H., & Appelbaum, E. (2009). High-touch and here-to-stay: Future skills demands in US low wage service occupations. *Sociology, 43*(5), 968–989. doi:10.1177/0038038509340735.

Gauchat, G., Kelly, M., & Wallace, M. (2012). Occupational gender segregation, globalization, and gender earnings inequality in U.S. metropolitan areas. *Gender & Society, 26*(5), 718–747. doi:10.1177/0891243212453647.

Geva, D. (2015). Selective service, the gender-ordered family, and the rational informality of the American State. *American Journal of Sociology, 121*(1), 171–204.

Gilchrist, K. (2019, 20 June). LinkedIn says these 5 traits post the biggest skills gap—and it's a global problem. *CNBC Make It*. Retrieved from https://www.cnbc.com/2019/06/21/future-of-work-these-5-traits-pose-the-biggest-skills-gap-linkedin.html.

Glauber, R. (2018). Trends in the motherhood wage penalty and fatherhood wage premium for low, middle, and high earners. *Demography, 55*, 1663–1680.

Glavin, P., and Young, M. (2017). Insecure people in insecure places: The influence of regional unemployment on workers' reactions to the threat of job loss. *Journal of Health and Social Behavior, 58*(2), 232–251.

Glaymann, D., & Grima, F. (2008). Three answers to imposed precariousness: The case of low-skilled contingent workers. *Relations industrielles, 63*(3), 454–478.

Glazebrook, G.P. de T. (1968). *Life in Ontario: A social history.* Toronto, ON: University of Toronto Press.

Glenday, D. (1997). Lost horizons, leisure shock: Good jobs, bad jobs, uncertain future. In A. Duffy, D. Glenday, and N. Pupo (Eds), *Good jobs, bad jobs, no jobs: The transformation of work in the 21st century.* Harcourt Brace Canada.

Glenn, E. N. (2002). *Unequal freedom: How race and gender shaped American citizenship and labor.* Cambridge, MA: Harvard University Press.

Glenn, E. N. (2015). Settler colonialism as structure: A framework for comparative studies of U.S. race and gender formation. *Sociology of Race and Ethnicity, 1*(1), 52–72. doi:10.1177/2332649214560440.

Glenn, E. N., & Feldberg, R. L. (1977). Degraded and deskilled: The proletarianization of clerical work. *Social Problems, 25*(1), 52–64. doi:10.2307/800467.

Goffman, E. (1959), *The presentation of self in everyday life.* Garden City, NY: Doubleday.

Goldstein, A. (2012). Revenge of the managers: Labor cost cutting and the paradoxical resurgence of managerialism in the shareholder value era, 1984 to 2001. *American Sociological Review, 77*(2), 268–294.

Gosine, K. (2000). Revisiting the notion of a "recast" vertical mosaic in Canada: Does a post secondary education make a difference? *Canadian Ethnic Studies, 32*(3), 89–104.

Gould, A. M. (2010). Working at McDonalds: Some redeeming features of McJobs. *Work, Employment and Society, 24*(4), 780–802.

Goutor, D. (2005). Drawing different lines of color: The mainstream English Canadian labour movement's approach to Blacks and the Chinese, 1880–1914. *Labor: Studies in Working Class History of the Americas, 2*(1), 55–76. doi:10.1215/15476715-2-1-55.

Government of Canada. (2008). Reducing work-life conflict: What works? What doesn't? Retrieved from https://www.canada.ca/en/health-canada/services/environmental-workplace-health/reports-publications/occupational-health-safety/reducing-work-life-conflict-what-works-what-doesn.html#a6.

Government of Canada. (2018). Information on labour standards: *Sexual harassment.* Retrieved from https://www.canada.ca/en/employment-social-development/services/labour-standards/reports/sexual-harassment.html.

Government of Canada. (2019). First Nations and Inuit Youth Employment Strategy. Retrieved from https://www.sac-isc.gc.ca/eng/1543242399379/1543242429350.

Government of Canada. (2020a). Beyond 150, the future of work. Retrieved from http://canadabeyond150.ca/reports/future-of-work.html.

Government of Canada (2020b). Canada Emergency Response Benefit (CERB) with CRA. Retrieved from https://www.canada.ca/en/revenue-agency/services/benefits/apply-for-cerb-with-cra/who-apply.html.

Government of Canada. (2020c). Canada Emergency Student Benefit (CESB). Retrieved from https://www.canada.ca/en/revenue-agency/services/benefits/emergency-student-benefit.html.

Graham, J., and Manca, T. (2020, 6 May). Return to a new normal: Royal Society members identify key societal challenges posed by COVID-19. RSC COVID-19 Series, Publication #4. Retrieved from https://rsc-src.ca/en/voices/return-to-new-normal-royal-society-members-identify-key-societal-challenges-posed-by-COVID-19.

Grandea, N., & Kerr, J. (1998). "Frustrated and displaced": Filipina domestic workers in Canada. *Gender and Development, 6*(1), 7–12. https://doi.org/10.1080/741922629.

Grant, P. R., & Nadin, S. (2007). The credentialing problems of foreign-trained personnel from Asia and Africa intending to make their home in Canada: A social psychological perspective. *Journal of International Migration and Integration, 8*(2), 141–162. doi:10.1007/s12134-007-0011-2.

Gregg, M., & Andrijasevic, R. (2019). Virtually absent: Gendered histories and economies of digital labour. *Feminist Review, 123*, 1–7. doi:10/1177/0141778919878929.

Guppy, G., & Luongo, N. (2015). The rise and stall of Canada's gender-equity revolution. *Canadian Review of Sociology, 52*(3), 241–265. doi:10.1111/cars.12076.

Haan, M., Chuatico, G., Cornetet, J. (2020). Aboriginal earnings in Canada: The importance of gender, education, and industry. *Canadian Ethnic Studies, 52*(2), 1–27.

Haas, J. (1974). The stages of the high-steel ironworker apprentice career. *The Sociological Quarterly, 15*, 93–108.

Haas, J. (1977). Learning real feelings: A study of high steel ironworkers' reactions to fear and danger. *Sociology of Work and Occupations, 4*(2), 147–170. doi:10.1177/073088847700400202.

Haight, M. (2021). *Professional gaming and work: Challenges, trajectories, and labour market impacts amongst professional gamers.* PhD dissertation, The University of Western Ontario.

Hall, C. (2014). *Learning development outlook 2014: Strong learning organizations, strong leadership.* Ottawa, ON: Conference Board of Canada. Retrieved from http://www.conferenceboard.ca/e-library/abstract.aspx?did=5734.

Hall, R. H. (1999). *Organizations: Structures, processes, and outcomes* (7th ed.). Upper Saddle River, NJ: Prentice-Hall.

Hallgrímsdóttir, H. K., & Adams, T. L. (2004). The manly working man: Nineteenth-century manhood and the challenge of the Knights of Labor. *Men and Masculinities, 6*(3), 272–290. doi:10.1177/1097184X03257411.

Hallgrímsdóttir, H. K., Phillips, R., & Benoit, C. (2006). Fallen women and rescued girls: Social stigma and media narratives of the sex industry in Victoria, B.C., from 1980 to 2005. *Canadian Review of Sociology & Anthropology, 43*, 265–280.

Ham, J., & Gilmour, F. (2017). "We all have one": Exit plans as professional strategy in sex work. *Work, Employment and Society, 31*(5), 748–763.

Hamilton, L., & McCabe, D. (2016). "It's just a job": Understanding emotion work, de-animalization and the compartmentalization of organized animal slaughter. *Organization, 23*(3), 330–350. doi:10.1177/1350508416629448.

Hampson, I., & Junor, A. (2010). Putting the process back in: Rethinking service sector skill. *Work, Employment and Society, 24*(3), 526–545. doi:10.1177/0950017010371664.

Hanawalt, B. A. (1986). *The ties that bound: Peasant families in medieval England.* New York, NY: Oxford University Press.

Hango, D., & Moyser, M. (2018). Harassment in Canadian workplaces. *Insights on Canadian Society.* Statistics Canada Catalogue no. 75-006-X. Retrieved from https://www150.statcan.gc.ca/n1/pub/75-006-x/2018001/article/54982-eng.htm.

Harris, K., Krygsman, S., Waschenko, J., & Laliberte Rudman, D. (2018). Ageism and the older worker: A scoping review. *The Gerontologist, 58*(2), 1–14.

Harrison, J. L., & Lloyd, S. E. (2013). New jobs, new workers, and new inequalities: Explaining employers' roles in occupational segregation by nativity and race. *Social Problems, 60*(3), 281–301. doi:10.1525/sp.2013.60.3.281.

Harvey, A., & Shepherd, T. (2017). When passion isn't enough: Gender, affect and credibility in digital games design. *International Journal of Cultural Studies, 20*(5), 492–508.

Harvey, D. (2005). *A brief history of neoliberalism.* London: Verso.

Harvey, G., Rhodes, C., Vachhani, S. J., & Williams, K. (2017). Neo-villeiny and the service sector: The case of hyper flexible and precarious work in fitness centres. *Work, Employment and Society, 31*(1), 19–35.

Hays, S. (1996). *The cultural contradictions of motherhood.* New Haven, CT: Yale University Press.

Hazel, M. (2018). *Reasons for working at 60 and beyond.* Labour Statistics at a glance. Statistics Canada. Retrieved from https://www150.statcan.gc.ca/n1/pub/71-222-x/71-222-x2018003-eng.htm.

He, Y., & Marshall, V. (2003). Later-life career disruption and self-rated health: An analysis of General Social Survey data. *Canadian Journal on Aging, 22*(1), 45–57.

Head, B. W. (2010). Reconsidering evidence-based policy: Key issues and challenges. *Policy & Society, 29*(2), 77–94. doi:10.1016/j.polsoc.2010.03.001.

Healy, J., Nicholson, D., & Pekarek, A. (2017). Should we take the gig economy seriously? *Labour and Industry: A Journal of the Social and Economic Relations of Work, 27*(3), 232–248. doi:10.1080/10301763.2017.1377048.

Helliwell, J. F., & Huang, H. (2011). Well-being and trust in the workplace. *Journal of Happiness Studies, 12*(5), 747–767.

Hemp, P. (2004, Oct.). Presenteeism: At work—but out of it. *Harvard Business Review.* Retrieved from https://hbr.org/2004/10/presenteeism-at-work-but-out-of-it.

Hennebry, J. (2006). *Globalization and the seasonal workers agricultural program.* PhD dissertation, The University of Western Ontario.

Henry, F. (2012). Indigenous faculty at Canadian universities: Their stories. *Canadian Ethnic Studies, 44*(2), 101–132.

Henry, F., & Ginzberg, E. (1985). *Who gets the work? A test of racial discrimination in employment.* Toronto, ON: Urban Alliance on Race Relations and Social Planning Council of Metropolitan Toronto.

Henson, K. D., & Rogers, J. K. (2001). "Why Marcia you've changed!": Male clerical temporary workers doing masculinity in a feminized occupation. *Gender & Society, 15*(2), 218–38. doi.org/10.1177/089124301015002004.

Hepburn, S. A. R. (1999). Following the North Star: Canada as a haven for nineteenth-century American Blacks. *The Michigan Historical Review,* 25(2), 91–126. doi:10.2307/20173830.

Heron, C. (1980). The crisis of the craftsman: Hamilton metal workers in the early twentieth century. *Labour / Le Travail,* 6, 7–48.

Heron, C. (1996). *The Canadian labour movement: A short history* (2nd ed.). Toronto, ON: James Lorimer.

Heron, C. (2019a). On the job in Canada. In *Working lives: Essays in Canadian working-class history* (pp. 3–44). Toronto, ON: University of Toronto Press.

Heron, C. (2019b). Ontario's first factory workers. In *Working lives: Essays in Canadian working-class history* (pp. 47–153). Toronto, ON: University of Toronto Press.

Heron, C. (2019c). The Great War, the state, and working-class Canada. In *Working Lives: Essays in Canadian*

Working-Class History (pp. 317–354). Toronto, ON: University of Toronto Press.

High, S. (1996). Native wage labour and independent production during the "era of irrelevance." *Labour/Le Travail, 37*(Spring), 243–264. doi:10.2307/25144044.

Hill, D. G. (1981.) *The freedom-seekers: Blacks in early Canada.* Agincourt, ON: Book Society of Canada.

Hillier, C., Sano, Y., Zarifa, D., & Haan, M. (2020). Will they stay or will they go? Examining the brain drain in Canada's provincial north. *Canadian Review of Sociology, 57*(2), 174–196.

Hirsch, C. E. (2009). The strength of weak enforcement: The impact of discrimination charges, legal environments, and organizational conditions on workplace segregation. *American Sociological Review, 74*(2), 245–271. doi:10.1177/000312240907400205.

Hirsch, J. (2019, 29 Aug.). *Commentary: With AI and automation, workplace laws need updating. Chicago Tribune.* Retrieved from https://www.chicagotribune.com/opinion/commentary/ct-opinion-automation-workplace-labor-laws-20190829-xgcu3ysfp5alnofdiahnfk7h5y-story.html.

Hochschild, A. R. (1997). *The time bind: When work becomes home and home becomes work.* New York, NY: Owl Books.

Hochschild, A. R. (2003). *The managed heart: Commercialization of human feeling.* Berkeley, CA: University of California Press.

Hochschild, A. R., with A. Machung. (1989). *The second shift.* Avon.

Hodson, R. (1989). Gender differences in job satisfaction: Why aren't more women more dissatisfied? *The Sociological Quarterly, 30*(3), 385–399.

Hodson, R., & Sullivan, T. A. (1994). *The social organization of work* (2nd ed.). Wadsworth.

Hollinger, R. C., & Clark, J. (1983). Deterrence in the workplace: Perceived certainty, perceived severity, and employee theft. *Social Forces, 62*(2): 398–418.

Holman, A. C. (2000). *A sense of their duty: Middle-class formation in Victorian Ontario towns.* Montreal, QC: McGill-Queen's University Press.

Holvino, E. (2010). Intersections: The simultaneity of race, gender and class in organization studies. *Gender, Work & Organization, 17*(3), 248–277. doi:10.1111/j.1468-0432.2008.00400.x.

Hou, F. (2009). Immigrants working with co-ethnics: Who are they and how do they fare? *International Migration, 47*(2), 69–100. doi:10.1111/j.1468-2435.2009.00516.x.

Hou, F., Frank, K., & Schimmele, C. 2020. *Economic impact of COVID-19 among visible minority groups. 45280001.* Ottawa, ON: Statistics Canada.

Howatt, B. (2018, 5 July). Workplace stress a main cause of mental health issues, study finds. *Globe and Mail.* Retrieved from https://www.theglobeandmail.com/business/careers/workplace-award/article-workplace-stress-a-main-cause-of-mental-health-issues-study-finds.

Howcroft, I. (2019, 1 August). Leading young people into skilled trades is paying off . . . but more work is needed to curb shortage. *Plant.* Retrieved from https://www.plant.ca/insights/leading-young-people-into-skilled-trades-is-paying-off/#:~:text=Leading%20young%20people%20into%20skilled%20trades%20is%20paying%20off,is%20needed%20to%20curb%20shortage.&text=It's%20estimated%20that%20Ontario%20will,staggering%20560%2C000%20vacancies%20in%202030.

Hoyle, E. (2001). Teaching prestige, status and esteem. *Educational Management and Administration, 29*(2), 139–152.

Hu, M., Daley, A., & Warman, C. (2019). Literacy, numeracy, technology, skill, and labour market outcomes among Indigenous peoples in Canada. *Canadian Public Policy, 45*(1), 48.

Huey, L., & Broll, R. (2015). "I don't find it sexy at all": Criminal investigators views of media glamorization of police "dirty work." *Policing & Society, 25*(2), 236–247. Retrieved from http://dx.doi.org/10.1080/10439463.2013.864654.

Hughes, E. C. (1958). *Men and their work.* London, UK: Collier-Macmillan.

Hughes, K. D. (2003). Pushed or pulled? Women's entry into self-employment and small business ownership. *Gender, Work & Organization, 10*(4), 433–454.

Human Rights Legal Support Centre. (2019). Cases decided at hearing. Retrieved from https://www.hrlsc.on.ca/en/human-rights-stories/Cases-decided-at-hearing.

Hurd Clarke, L., & Korotchenko, A. (2016). "I know it exists . . . but haven't experienced it personally": Older Canadian men's perceptions of ageism as a distant social problem. *Ageing and Society, 36*(8), 1757–1773.

Huws, U. (2001). *The making of a cybertariat: Virtual work in a real world.* New York, NY: Monthly Review Press.

Huws, U. (2014). *Labor in the global digital economy.* New York, NY: Monthly Review Press.

Huws, U., Spence, N., Syrdal, D., & Holts, K. (2017). Work in the European gig economy. Retrieved from https://www.researchgate.net/publication/322234437_Work_in _the_European)Gig_Economy_FEPS_UNI-Europa_and_University of Hertfordshire.

Huzell, H., & Larsson, P. (2012). Aesthetic and athletic employees: The negative outcome of employers assuming responsibility for sickness benefits. *Economic and Industrial Democracy, 33*(1), 103–123.

Iacovetta, F. (2000). From contadina to worker: Southern Italian immigrant working women in Toronto, 1947–1962. In L. S. MacDowall and I. Radforth (Eds), *Canadian working class history* (pp. 620–640). Toronto, ON: Canadian Scholars Press.

Ikeler, P. (2015). Deskilling emotional labour: Evidence from department store retail. *Work, Employment and Society*, 30(6), 966–983. doi:10.1177/0950017015609031

ILO (International Labour Organization). (2017). *Global employment trends for youth, 2017: Paths to a better working future*. Geneva: ILO.

ILO (International Labour Organization). (2019). *Labour market access—a persistent challenge for youth around the world*. Geneva: ILO. Retrieved from https://www.ilo.org/global/statistics-and-databases/publications/WCMS_676196/lang—en/index.htm.

Indigenous AI. (2020). Position paper. Retrieved from https://www.indigenous-ai.net/position-paper.

Indigenous Corporate Training Inc. (2015). Aboriginal retention strategies and cultural leave. Retrieved from https://www.ictinc.ca/blog/aboriginal-retention-strategies.

International Cooperative Alliance (ICA). (2019). Co-operative identity. Retrieved from https://www.ica.coop › cooperatives › cooperative-identity.

Jacobson, J., and Shade, L. R. (2018). Stringtern: Springboarding or stringing along young interns' careers? *Journal of Education and Work*, *31*(3), 320–337. doi:10.1080/13639080.2018.1473559.

Jain, H. C., & Lawler, J. J. (2004). Visible minorities under the Canadian Employment Equity Act, 1987–1999. *Relations industrielles/Industrial Relations*, *59*(3), 585–609. doi:10.7202/010926ar.

Jamal, M., & Badawi, J. (1995). Nonstandard work schedules and work and nonwork experiences of Muslim immigrants: A study of a minority in the majority. *Journal of Social Behavior and Personality*, *10*(2), 395–408.

Jameel, M., & Yerardi, J. (2019, 28 February). Workplace discrimination is illegal. But our data show it's still a huge problem. *Vox*. Retrieved from https://www.vox.com.

Janus, A. L. (2009). Disability and the transition to adulthood. *Social Forces*, *88*(1), 99–120.

Jarman, J., Blackburn, R. M., & Racko, G. (2012). The dimensions of occupational gender segregation in industrial countries. *Sociology*, *46*(6), 1003–1019. doi:10.1177/0038038511435063.

Jary, D., & Jary, J. (2005a). Organization. In *Collins dictionary of sociology* (4th ed., pp. 425–426). Glasgow, Scotland: Harper Collins Publishers.

Jary, D., & Jary, J. (2005b). Stress. In *Collins dictionary of sociology* (4th ed., pp. 425–426). Glasgow, Scotland: Harper Collins Publishers.

Jenkins, S., Delbridge, R., & Roberts, A. (2010). Emotional management in a mass customised call centre; examining skill and knowledgeability in interactive service work. *Work, Employment and Society*, 24(3), 546–564.

Johnston, R., McGregor, D., & Restoule, J.-P. (2018). Introduction. In D. McGregor, J.-P. Restoule, and R. Johnston, R. (Eds), *Indigenous research: Theories, practices, and relationships* (pp. 1–21). Toronto, ON: Canadian Scholars Press.

Jones, A. (2020). Where are the trans men and enbies at? Cissexism, sexual threat and the study of sex work. *Sociology Compass*, *14*(2). https://doi.org/10.1111/soc4.12750.

Jones, E. (2019). *Radical medicine: The international origins of socialized health care in Canada*. ARP Books.

Jones, F. (1984). Reflections on work organization among structural steelworkers. In A. Wipper, (Ed.), *The sociology of work*. Ottawa, ON: Carleton University Press.

Jones, F. E. (1996). *Understanding organizations: A sociological perspective*. Toronto, ON: Copp Clark.

Jones, J. (1998). *American work: Four centuries of Black and white labor*. New York, NY: W.W. Norton.

Julien, M., Somerville, K., & Brant, J. (2017). Indigenous perspectives on work-life enrichment and conflict in Canada. *Equality, Diversity and Inclusion*, *36*(2), 165–181.

Juravich, T. (2017). Artifacts of workers' knowledge: Finding worker skill in the closing and restructuring of a furniture manufacturer. *Ethnography*, *18*(4), 493–514. doi:10.1177/1466138116687590.

Kaida, L., Hou, F., & Stick, M. (2020). The long-term economic integration of resettled refugees in Canada. *Journal of Ethnic and Migration Studies*, *46*(9), 1687–1708.

Kalleberg, A. L. (2000). Nonstandard employment relations: Part-time, temporary and contract work. *Annual Review of Sociology*, *26*, 341–365.

Kalleberg, A. L. (2009.) Precarious work, insecure workers: Employment relations in transition. *American Sociological Review*, *74*(1), 1–22.

Kalleberg, A. L. (2018). *Precarious lives: Job insecurity and well-being in rich democracies*. Cambridge, UK: Polity.

Kalyal, H. (2019). "Well, there's a more scientific way to do it!": Factors influencing receptivity to evidence-based practices in police organizations. *Police Practice and Research: An International Journal*, *20*, 1–15. doi:10.1080/15614263.2019.1608548.

Kang, S. K., DeCelles, K. A., Tilcsik, A., & Jun, S. (2016). Whitened résumés: Race and self-presentation in the labor market. *Administrative Science Quarterly*, *61*(3), 469–502. doi:10.1177/0001839216639577.

Kanter, R. M. (1977). *Men and women of the corporation*. New York, NY: Basic Books.

Karabanow, J., Hughes, J., & Kidd, S. (2010). Work to survive: Exploring the work of street youth. *Criminology*, *43*(1), 7–29.

Karasek, R. (1979). Job demands, job decision latitude, and mental strain: Implications for job redesign. *Administrative Science Quarterly*, *24*(2), 285–308.

Karasek, R., & Theorell, T. (1990). *Healthy work, stress, productivity and the reconstruction of working life*. New York, NY: Basic Books.

Katshunga, J., Massaquoi, N., & Wallace, J. (2020). *Black women in Canada*. Canadian Centre for Policy Alternatives. Retrieved from https://behindthenumbers.ca/shorthand/black-women-in-canada.

Kealey, G. S., & Gagnon, M.-A. (2006). Knights of Labor in Canada. *The Canadian Encyclopedia*. https://www.thecanadianencyclopedia.ca/en/article/knights-of-labor.

Kealey, G. S., & Palmer, B. D. (1982). *Dreaming of what might be: The Knights of Labour in Ontario, 1880–1900*. Cambridge, UK: Cambridge University Press.

Kennedy, B. (2019). I went undercover as an Amazon delivery driver. Here's what I learned about the hidden costs of free shipping. *Toronto Star*, 19 Dec. Retrieved from https://www.thestar.com/news/investigations/2019/12/19/i-went-undercover-as-an-amazon-delivery-driver-heres-what-i-learned-about-the-hidden-costs-of-free-shipping.html.

Kesserwan, K. (2018, Feb.). How can Indigenous knowledge shape our view of AI? *Policy Options*. Retrieved from https://policyoptions.irpp.org/magazines/february-2018/how-can-indigenous-knowledge-shape-our-view-of-ai.

Kessler, S. (2018). *Gigged: The end of the job and the future of work*. New York, NY: St Martin's Press.

Kim, E. J., Skinner, T., & Parish, S. L. 2020. A study on intersectional discrimination in employment against disabled women in the UK. *Disability & Society*, *35*(5), 715–737.

Kmec, J. A. (2013). Why academic STEM mothers feel they have to work harder than others on the job. *International Journal of Gender, Science and Technology*, 5, 79–101.

Knight, R. (1996). *Indians at work: An informal history of native Indian labour in British Columbia, 1858–1930*. Vancouver, BC: New Star Books.

Koebel, K., & Pohler, D. (2020). Labor markets in crisis: The double liability of low-wage work during COVID-19. *Industrial Relations*, 59(4), 503–531.

Kong, S. L. (2020, 3 Feb). Why we need more women in these particular careers than ever before. *Maclean's*. Retrieved from https://www.macleans.ca/work/women-in-skilled-trades.

Konrad, A. M., Kashlak, R., Yoshioka, I., Waryszak, R., & Toren, N. (2001). What do managers like to do? A five-country study. *Group and Organization Management*, *26*(4), 401–433.

Konzelmann, S. J., Wilkinson, F., & Mankelow, R. (2011). *Work intensification and employment insecurity in professional work*. Centre for Business Research, University of Cambridge, Working Paper No. 345. Retrieved from https://papers.ssrn.com/sol3/papers.cfm?abstract_id=1930840.

Koski, P., & Järvensivu, A. (2010). The innovation diffusion paradox in the light of "shop-floor games" and micro-politics. *Economic and Industrial Democracy*, *31*(3), 345–363. doi:10.1177/0143831X09351216.

Kossek, E. E., & Lee, K.-H. (2017). Work-family conflict and work-life conflict. *Oxford research encyclopedia of business and management*. doi:10.1093/acrefore/9780190223851.013.52.

Kovach, M. (2009). *Indigenous methodologies: Characteristics, conversations, and contexts*. Toronto, ON: University of Toronto Press.

Kraft, P. (1977). *Programmers and managers: The routinization of computer programming in the United States*. New York, NY: Springer-Verlag.

Krahn, H., & Chow, A. (2016). Youth unemployment and career scarring: Social-psychological mediating effects? *Canadian Journal of Sociology*, *41*(2), 117–137.

Krüsi,, A. Kerr, T., Taylor, C., Rhodes, T., & Shannon, K. (2016). "They won't change it back in their heads that we're trash": The intersection of sex work-related stigma and evolving policing strategies. *Sociology of Health and Illness*, *38*(7), 1137–1150.

Kücklich, J. (2005). Precarious Playbour: Modders and the digital games industry. *The Fibreculture Journal*, 05. Retrieved from http://five.fibreculturejournal.org.

Kurdek, L. A. (2006). Differences between partners from heterosexual, gay, and lesbian cohabiting couples. *Journal of Marriage and Family*, *68*, 509–528.

Kurdek, L. A. (2007). The allocation of household labor by partners in gay and lesbian couples. *Journal of Family Issues*, *28*, 132–148.

Kwon, E., & Adams, T. L. (2018). Choosing a specialty: Intersections of gender and race among Asian and white women medical students in Ontario. *Canadian Ethnic Studies*, *50*(3), 49–68. doi:10.1353/ces.2018.0022.

Kwon, E. & Adams, T.L. (2021). Feeding the Canadian immigrant family: An intersectional approach to meal preparation among immigrant families in Ontario. *Food, Culture & Society*, 26(2): doi: 10.1080/15528014.2021.1890892.

Lahey, J. N. (2008). Age, women and hiring: An experimental study. *Journal of Human Resources*, *43*, 30–45. doi:10.3368/jhr.43.1.30.

Lahn, J. (2018). Being Indigenous in the bureaucracy: Narratives of work and exit. *The International Indigenous Policy Journal*, *9*(1). doi: https://doi.org/10.18584/iipj.2018.9.1.3.

Lamb, D., Yap, M., & Turk, M. (2018). Aboriginal/non-Aboriginal wage gaps in Canada: Evidence from the 2011 National Household Survey. *Relations industrielles/Industrial Relations, 73*(2), 225–251. doi:10.7202/1048569ar.

Lambert, C. (2015). *Shadow work: The unpaid, unseen jobs that fill your day.* Counterpoint Press.

Lamont, M. (1992). *Money, morals, and manners: The culture of the French and American upper-middle class.* Chicago, IL: University of Chicago Press.

Landrigan, C. P., Rothschild, J. M., Cronin, J. W., Kaushal, R., Burdick, E., Katz, J. T., & Czeisler, C. A. (2004). Effect of reducing interns' work hours on serious medical errors in intensive care units. *The New England Journal of Medicine, 351*(18), 1838–1848. doi:10.1056/NEJMoa041406.

Lanoie, P., (1992). Government intervention in occupational safety: Lessons from the American and Canadian experience. *Canadian Public Policy, 18*(1), 62–75.

Lapointe, P.-A., & Bach, C. (2016). Amélioration ou polarisation? Évolution de la structure et de la qualité des emplois au Québec et au Canada, 1997–2013. *Relations industrielles, 71*(1), 3–32.

Larson, M. S. (1977). *The rise of professionalism: A sociological analysis.* Berkeley, CA: University of California Press.

Larson, M. S. (2018). Professions today: Self-criticism and reflections for the future. *Sociologia, Problemas e Prácticas, 88*, 27–42. doi:10.7458/SPP20188814796.

Latulippe, D., St-Onge, S., Gagné, C., Balesteros-Leiva, F., & Beauchamp-Legault M.-E.. (2017). Extending the working lives of older Quebec workers: A necessity for society, workers and employers? *Retraite et Société, 78*, 45.

Lauer, S., Wilkinson, L., Yan, M. C., Sin, R., & Tsang, A. K. T. (2012). Immigrant youth and employment: Lessons learned from the analysis of LSIC and 82 lived stories. *Journal of International Migration and Integration, 13*(1), 1–19.

Lautard, H., & Guppy, N. (1999). Revisiting the vertical mosaic: Occupational stratification among Canadian ethnic groups. In P. S. Li (Ed.), *Race and ethnic relations in Canada* (2nd ed., pp. 219–252). Don Mills, ON: Oxford University Press.

Lautard, E. H., & Loree, D. J. (1984). Ethnic stratification in Canada, 1931–1971. *Canadian Journal of Sociology, 9*(3), 333–344. doi:10.2307/3340159.

Law, T., & Raguparan, M. (2020). "It's a puzzle you have to do every night": Performing creative problem solving at work in the indoor Canadian sex industry. *Work, Employment and Society, 34*(3), 424–440.

LeBlanc, L. S., & McMullin, J. A. (1997). Falling through the cracks: Addressing the needs of individuals between employment and retirement. *Canadian Public Policy, 23*(3), 289–304.

Leck, J. D. (2002). Making employment equity programs work for women. *Canadian Public Policy, 28*, Supplement: Occupational Gender Segregation: Public Policies and Economic Forces, S85–S100. doi:10.2307/3552345.

Lee, Y.-H., & Lin, H. (2011). "Gaming is my work": Identity work in Internet-hobbyist game workers. *Work, Employment & Society, 25*(3), 451–467.

Legault, M.-J., and Chasserio, S. (2013). The gendered professionalization project among project managers. *Recherches feministes, 26*(1), 89–110.

Lehmann, W. (2000). Is Germany's dual system still a model for Canadian youth apprenticeship initiatives? *Canadian Public Policy, XXVI*(2), 225–240.

Lehmann, W. (2005). Choosing to labour: Structure and agency in school-work transitions. *Canadian Journal of Sociology, 30*(3), 325–350.

Lehmann, W. (2019). Forms of capital in working-class students' transition from university to employment. *Journal of Education and Work, 32*(4), 347–359. doi:10.1080/13639080.2019.1617841.

Letkemann, P. (1973). *Crime as work.* Prentice-Hall.

Levanon, A., & Grusky, D. B. (2016). The persistence of extreme gender segregation in the twenty-first century. *American Journal of Sociology, 122*(2), 573–619. doi:10.1086/688628.

Levi, C. (2003). "There is a definite limitation imposed" (Robin Ross to Claude Bissell, December 4, 1959). The Jewish quota in the Faculty of Medicine, University of Toronto: Generational memory sustained by documentation. *Historical Studies in Education, 15*(1), 131–138. Retrieved from www.historicalstudiesineducation.ca/index.php/edu_hse-rhe/article/view/477/657.

Levy-Garboua, L., & Montmarquette, C. (2004). Reported job satisfaction: What does it mean? *The Journal of Socio-Economics, 33*(2), 135–151.

Lewchuk, W., et al. (2015). The precarity penalty: The impact of employment precarity on individuals, households and communities and what to do about it. Pepso report. Retrieved from https://pepso.ca/documents/precarity-penalty.pdf.

Lewchuk, W., Laflèche, M., Procyk, S., Cook, C., Dyson, D., Goldring, L., . . . Viducis, C. (2016). The precarity penalty: How insecure employment disadvantages workers and their families. *Alternative Routes: A Journal of Critical Social Research, 27*, 87–108. Retrieved from www.alternateroutes.ca/index.php/ar/article/view/22394.

Lewis J. (1998). Learning to strip: The socialization experiences of exotic dancers. *Canadian Journal of Human Sexuality, 7*(1), 51–66.

Lewis, J. E., et al. (Eds). (2020). *Indigenous protocol and artificial intelligence position paper.* Honolulu, Hawaii: The Initiative for Indigenous Futures and the Canadian

Institute for Advanced Research (CIFAR). doi:10.11573/spectrum.library.concordia.ca.00986506.

Li, P. S. (2001). Immigrants' propensity to self-employment: Evidence from Canada. *International Migration Review, 35*(4), 1106–1128.

Lim, J. (2020, 2 Oct.). Emergency benefit for students is finished—with billions left in the pot. *iPolitics*. Retrieved from https://ipolitics.ca/2020/10/02/emergency-benefit-for-students-is-finished-with-billions-left-in-the-pot/#:~:text=The%20CESB%20offered%20eligible%20students,and%20received%202.1%20million%20applications.

Lim, J. (2021, 8 Jan.) Canadian youth may suffer the economic toll of COVID for years to come. *iPolitics*. Retrieved from https://ipolitics.ca/2021/01/08/canadian-youth-may-suffer-the-economic-toll-of-COVID-for-years-to-come/

Lindsay S., Adams T., Sanford R., Mcdougall C., Kingsnorth S., & Menna-Dack, J. (2014). Employers' and employment counselors' perceptions of desirable skills for entry-level positions for adolescents: Does it differ for youth with disabilities? *Disability & Society, 29*(6), 953–967.

Lippel, K., Johnstone, R., & Baril-Gingras, G. (2017). Regulation, change, and the work environment. *Relations industrielles/Industrial Relations, 72*(1), 3–32.

Lippel, K., & Lanctôt, N. (2014). La violence physique au travail et la santé: le droit québécois régissant l'indemnisation et la prevention. *Relations industrielles, 69*(4), 785–812.

Liu, Y., & Grusky, D. B. (2013). The payoff to skill in the third industrial revolution. *American Journal of Sociology, 118*(5), 1330–1374. doi:10.1086/669498.

Livingston, G. (2015, 2 Feb.). Survey says: We're stressed (and not loving it). *Globe and Mail*. Retrieved from https://www.theglobeandmail.com/report-on-business/careers/career-advice/life-at-work/survey-says-were-stressed-and-not-loving-it/article22722102.

Livingstone, D. W. (2019a). Proletarianization of professional employees and underemployment of general intellect in a "knowledge economy": Canada 1982–2016. *Labour/Le Travail, 84*, 141–66. Retrieved from https://doi.org/10.1353/llt.

Livingstone, D. W. (2019b). Underemployment of highly qualified labour in advanced capitalism: Trends and prospects. *Journal of Education and Work, 32*(4), 305–319. doi:10.1080/13639080.2019.1646415.

Livingstone, D.W. (2021). *Professional power and skill use in the "knowledge economy": A class analysis*. Leiden, Netherlands: Brill.

Livingstone, D. W., Pollock, K., & Raykov, M. (2016). Family binds and glass ceilings: Women managers' promotion limits in a "knowledge economy." *Critical Sociology, 42*(1), 145–166. doi:10.1177/0896920514532663.

Livingstone, D. W., & Watts, B. (2018). The changing class structure and pivotal role of professional employees in an advanced capitalist knowledge economy: Canada, 1982–2016. *Studies in Political Economy, 99*(1), 79–96.

Lloren, A., & Parini, L. (2017). How LGBT-supportive workplace policies shape the experience of lesbian, gay men, and bisexual employees. *Sexuality Research and Social Policy, 14*(3), 289–299.

Lloyd, C., & Payne, J. (2009). "Full of sound and fury, signifying nothing": Interrogating new skill concepts in service work—the view from two UK call centres. *Work, Employment and Society, 23*(4), 617–634. doi:10.1177/0950017009344863.

LMiC. (2020, 5 June). Job loss impacts of COVID-19 by education, gender and age. Retrieved from https://lmic-cimt.ca/job-loss-impacts-of- COVID-19-by-education-gender-and-age.

Lo, Y. (2020). The distribution of temporary foreign workers across industries in Canada. Statistics Canada Catalogue no. 11-626-X No. 102. *Economic Insights*. Ottawa, ON: Statistics Canada. Retrieved from https://www150.statcan.gc.ca/n1/pub/45-28-0001/2020001/article/00028-eng.htm.

Lochner, L. (2004). Education, work and crime: A human capital approach. *International Economic Review*, 45, 811–853.

Lowe, G. S. (1987). *Women in the administrative revolution: The feminization of clerical work*. Toronto, ON: University of Toronto Press.

Lowe, G. S. (2000). *The quality of work: A people-centred agenda*. Don Mills, ON: Oxford University Press.

Lowe, G. S., & Northcott, H. C. (1988). The impact of working conditions, social roles, and personal characteristics on gender differences in distress. *Work & Occupations, 15*(1), 55.

LSUC (Law Society of Upper Canada). (2016). Statistical snapshot of lawyers in Ontario. Retrieved from http://annualreport.lsuc.on.ca/2017/common/documents/Snapshot-Lawyers18_English.pdf.

Lu, Y. (2020). The distribution of temporary foreign workers across industries in Canada. *Statistics Canada*. Retrieved from https://www150.statcan.gc.ca/n1/pub/45-28-0001/2020001/article/00028-eng.htm.

Lu, Y., & Hou, F. (2020). Immigration system, labor market structures, and overeducation of high-skilled immigrants in the United States and Canada. *The International Migration Review*, 54(4), 1072–1103.

Lucas, K. (2012). Blue-collar discourses of workplace dignity: Using outgroup comparisons to construct positive identities. *Management Communication Quarterly, 25*(2), 353–374. doi:10.1177/0893318910386445.

Lundberg, H., & Karlsson, J. C. (2011). Under the clean surface: Working as a hotel attendant. *Work, Employment and Society, 25*(1), 141–148. Retrieved from https://doi.org/10.1177/0950017010389246.

Lutz, J. (2000). After the fur trade: The Aboriginal labouring class of British Columbia, 1849–1890. In L. S. MacDowell and I. Radforth (Eds), *Canadian working class history: Selected readings* (pp. 235–59). Toronto, ON: Canadian Scholars Press.

Luxton, M. (1980). *More than a labour of love: Three generations of women's work in the home.* Toronto, ON: The Women's Press.

Luxton, M., & Bezanson, K. (2006). *Social reproduction: Feminist political economy challenges neo-liberalism.* Montreal, QC, and Kingston, ON: McGill-Queen's University Press.

Luxton, M., & Corman, J. (2001). *Getting by in hard times: Gendered labour at home and on the job.* Toronto, ON: University of Toronto Press.

Macdonald, C. L., & Sirianni, C. (1996). The service society and the changing experience of work. In C. L. Macdonald and C. Sirianni (Eds), *Working in the service economy,* (pp. 1–26). Philadelphia, PA: Temple University Press.

Macdonald, D. (2019, July). Unaccommodating: Rental housing wage in Canada. *Canadian Centre for Policy Alternatives.* Retrieved from https://www.policyalternatives.ca/sites/default/files/uploads/publications/National%20Office/2019/07/Unaccommodating%20-%20Rental%20Wage%20in%20Canada.pdf.

MacDonald, Z., & Pyle, D. (Eds). (2000). *Illicit activity: The economics of crime, drugs, and tax fraud.* Ashgate Publishing.

MacKinnon, S. (2015). *Decolonizing employment: Aboriginal inclusion in Canada's labour market.* Winnipeg, MB: University of Manitoba Press.

Madibbo, A. (2020). Reverse Inclusion: Black francophones in the interface between linguicism and anti-Black racism. *Canadian Review of Sociology, 57*(3), 334–355.

Magee, W. (2015). Effects of gender and age on pride in work, and job satisfaction. *Journal of Happiness Studies, 16*(5), 1091–1015. doi:10.1007/s10902-014-9548-x.

Magee, W., & Umamaheswar, J. (2011). Immigrant group differences in job satisfaction. *Race and Social Problems, 3*(4), 252–264.

Makin, K. (2011, 29 April). Farm workers have no right to unionize, top court rules. *Globe and Mail.* Retrieved from https://www.theglobeandmail.com/news/national/farm-workers-have-no-right-to-unionize-top-court-rules/article578141.

Malachowski, C., Boydell, K., Sawchuk, P., & Kirsh, B. (2016). The "work" of workplace mental health. *Society and Mental Health, 6*(3), 207–222.

Malambwe, J.-M. K. (2017). Les Immigrants du Québec: participation au marché du travail et qualité de l'emploi. *Canadian Ethnic Studies, 49*(2), 33–52.

Mandel, H., & Semyonov, M. (2016). Going back in time? Gender differences in trends and sources of the racial pay gap, 1970 to 2010. *American Sociological Review,* 81(5), 1039–1068. doi:10.1177/0003122416662958.

Manning, E., & Bungay, V. (2017). "Business before pleasure": The golden rule of sex work, payment schedules and gendered experiences of violence. *Culture, Health and Sexuality, 19*(3), 338–351.

Marmot, M. G. (1994). Social differentials in health within and between populations. *Daedulus, 123,* 197–216.

Marom, L. (2018). Under the cloak of professionalism: covert racism in teacher education. *Race, Ethnicity and Education,* 22(3), 319-337.

Maroto, M. L., & Pettinicchio, D. (2014). Disability, structural inequality, and work: The influence of occupational segregation on earnings for people with different disabilities. *Research in Social Stratification and Mobility, 38,* 76–92. doi:10.1016/j.rssm.2014.08.002.

Maroto, M. L., & Pettinicchio, D. (2015). Twenty-five years after the ADA: Situating disability in America's system of stratification. *Disability Studies Quarterly, 35*(3), 1–34. doi:10.18061/dsq.v35i3.4927.

Maroto, M. L., & Pettinicchio, D. (2020). Barriers to economic security: Disability, employment, and asset disparities in Canada. *The Canadian Review of Sociology, 57*(1), 53–79.

Marr, B. (2019, 29 April). The 10 vital skills you will need for the future of work. *Forbes.* Retrieved from https://www.forbes.com/sites/bernardmarr/2019/04/29/the-10-vital-skills-you-will-need-for-the-future-of-work/#f815cbf3f5bd.

Martin, M. (Ed.). (1997). *Hard-hatted women: Life on the job.* Seal Press.

Marx, K. (1967). *Capital: A critical analysis of capitalist production* (Vol. 1). New York, NY: International Publishers. (Original work published in 1867)

Marx, K. (1975). The economic and philosophical manuscripts of 1844. In R. Livingstone and G. Benton (trans.), *Early writings* (pp. 279–400). New York, NY: Vintage Books.

Mas-Maschuca, M., Berbegal-Marabent, J., & Alegre, I. (2016). Work-life balance and its relationship with organizational pride and job satisfaction. *Journal of Managerial Psychology, 31*(2), 586–602. doi:10.1108/JMP-09-2014-0272.

Maurial, M. (1999). Indigenous knowledge and schooling: A continuum between conflict and dialogue. In L. Semali, L. M. Semaliand, and J. L. Kincheloe (Eds), *What is Indigenous Knowledge? Voices from the academy* (pp. 59–78). Falmer Press.

Maury, O. (2020). Between a promise and a salary: Student-migrant-workers' experiences of precarious labour markets. *Work, Employment and Society, 34*(5), 809–825.

May, B. (2019). *Precarious work: Understanding the changing nature of work in Canada.* Report of the Standing Committee on Human Resources, Skills, and Social Development and the Status of Persons with Disabilities. Ottawa, ON: Government of Canada.

McCallum, M. J. (2014). *Indigenous women, work, and history, 1940–1980.* Winnipeg, MB: University of Manitoba Press.

McGann, M., Moss, J., & White, K. (2012). Health, freedom and work in rural Victoria: The impact of labour market casualisation on health and wellbeing. *Health Sociology Review, 21*(1), 99–115.

McGann, M., White, K., & Moss, J. (2016). Labour casualization and the psychosocial health of workers in Australia. *Work, Employment and Society, 30*(5), 766–882.

McGivern, G., & Ferlie, E. (2007). Playing tick-box games: Interrelating defences in professional appraisal. *Human Relations, 60*(9), 1361–1385. doi:10.1177/0018726707082851.

McGregor, D., Restoule, J.-P., & Johnston, R. (Eds). (2018). *Indigenous research: Theories, practices, and relationships.* Toronto, ON: Canadian Scholars Press.

McMullin, J. A., & Berger, E. D. (2006). Gendered ageism/age(ed) sexism: The case of unemployed older workers. In T. M. Calasanti and D. F. Slevin (Eds), *Age matters: Re-aligning feminist thinking* (pp. 201–23). New York NY: Routledge.

McMullin, J. A., & Marshall, V. W. (2001). Ageism, age relations and garment industry work in Montreal. *The Gerontologist, 41*(1), 111–122.

Mead, G. H. (1962). *Mind, self, and society from the standpoint of a social behaviorist* (C. W. Morris, Ed.). Chicago, IL: University of Chicago Press.

Melaku, T. M. (2019). *You don't look like a lawyer: Black women and systemic gendered racism.* Lanham, MD: Rowman and Littlefield.

Mercure, D., Vulture, M., & Fleury, C. (2012). Valeurs et attitudes des jeunes travailleurs à l'égard du travail au Québec: une analyse intergénérationnelle. *Relations industrielles, 67*(2), 177–198.

Messenger, J. C. (Ed.) (2004). *Working time and workers' preferences in industrialized countries: Finding the balance.* New York, NY: Routledge.

Michels, R. (1915). *Political parties: A sociological study of the oligarchical tendencies of modern democracy* (E. & C. Paul, trans.). London, UK: Jarrold & Sons.

Militello, K. C. (2017). "I feel like I just need to be more careful, you know?" *Gay and bisexual post-secondary students contemplate the job market.* MA thesis, University of Western Ontario. Retrieved from https://ir.lib.uwo.ca/etd/4942.

Mills, C. W. (1951). *White collar: The American middle classes.* Oxford University Press.

Mills, S. E. (2017). Fractures and alliances: Labour relations and worker experiences in construction. *Labour/Le Travail, 80,* 13–26. Retrieved from www.lltjournal.ca/index.php/llt/article/view/5866.

Milman, O. (2019, 3 October). Trump administration's war on science has hit "crisis point," experts warn. *The Guardian.* Retrieved from https://www.theguardian.com.

Miltsov, A. (2018, Aug.). *Slacking, resisting, withdrawing? A comparative study of personal Internet use at work.* PhD dissertation, McGill University, Montreal.

Minichiello, V., Scott, J., & Callander, D. (2013). New pleasures and old dangers: Reinventing male sex work. *Journal of Sex Research, 50*(3–4), 263–275. doi:10.1080/00224499.2012.760189.

Mojtehedzadeh, S. (2020, 3 Jan.). Foodora couriers subject to "strike log," GPS tracking and misconduct inquiries, labour board documents claim. *Toronto Star.* Retrieved from https://www.thestar.com/news/canada/2020/01/03/foodora-couriers-subject-to-strike-log-gps-tracking-and-misconduct-inquiries-labour-board-documents-claim.html.

Mojtehedzadeh, S., & Monsebraaten, L. (2017, 18 May). GE workers paying price for decades of exposure to toxic chemicals: Report. *Toronto Star.* Retrieved from https://www.thestar.com/news/canada/2017/05/18/ge-workers-paying-price-for-decades-of-exposure-to-toxic-chemicals-report.html.

Molstad, C. (1986). Choosing and coping with boring work. *Urban Life, 15*(2), 215–236.

Moore, M. R. (2008). Gendered power relations among women: A study of household decision making in Black, lesbian stepfamilies. *American Sociological Review, 73,* 335–356.

Moosewood. (2019). Moosewood. Retrieved from https://moosewoodcooks.com.

Morissette, R. (2018). Changing characteristics of Canadian jobs, 1981 to 2018. *Economic Insights,* no. 086. Statistics Canada Catalogue no. 11-626-X. Retrieved from https://www150.statcan.gc.ca/n1/pub/11-626-x/11-626-x2018086-eng.htm.

Morley, J. T. (2006). Co-operative Commonwealth Federation. In *The Canadian encyclopedia.* Retrieved from https://www.thecanadianencyclopedia.ca/en/article/co-operative-commonwealth-federation.

Morneau Shepell & Mental Health Commission of Canada (MHCC). (2018). *Canadian employees report workplace stress as primary cause of mental health concerns.* Mental Health Commission of Canada. Retrieved from https://www.mentalhealthcommission.ca/English/news-article/13522/canadian-employees-report-workplace-stress-primary-cause-mental-health-concerns.

Morton, D. (1998). *Working people: An illustrated history of the Canadian labour movement* (4th ed.). Montreal, QC: McGill-Queen's University Press.

Morton, S. (1993). Separate spheres in a separate world: African–Nova Scotian women in late-19th century Halifax County. *Acadiensis, 22*(2), 61–83.

Moss, P., & Tilly, C. (1996). Soft skills and race: An investigation of Black men's employment problems. *Work and Occupations, 23*(3), 252–276.

Moss, P., & Tilly, C. (2001). *Stories employers tell: Race, skill, and hiring in America*. New York: Russell Sage Foundation.

Moyser, M. (2017). *Labour market experiences of First Nations people living off reserve: Key findings from the 2017 Aboriginal Peoples Survey*. Catalogue no. 89-653-X2018003. Retrieved from https://www150.statcan.gc.ca/n1/pub/89-653-x/89-653-x2018003-eng.htm.

Moyser, M., & Burlock, A. (2018). *Time use: Total work burden, unpaid work, and leisure*. Statistics Canada, Catalogue no. 89-503-X. Ottawa, ON: Statistics Canada.

Müller, J.-W. (2020). Why do rightwing populist leaders oppose experts? *The Guardian*, 26 March. Retrieved from https://www.theguardian.com/commentisfree/2020/mar/26/rightwing-populist-leaders-oppose-experts-not-elites.

Murphy, M. F. (1997). Unmaking and remaking the "one best system": London, Ontario, 1852–1860. *History of Education Quarterly, 37*(3), 291–310. doi:10.2307/369447.

Murrell, A. (2018, 16 July). Stopping the downward spiral of workplace incivility. *Forbes*. Retrieved from https://www.forbes.com.

Muzio, D., & Ackroyd, S. (2005). On the consequences of defensive professionalism: Recent changes in the legal labour process. *Journal of Law and Society, 32*(4), 615–642.

Muzio, D., Faulconbridge, J., Gabbioneta, C., & Greenwood, R. (2016). Bad apples, bad barrels and bad cellars: A boundaries perspective on professional misconduct. In D. Palmer, R. Greenwood, and K. Crowe-Smith (Eds), *Organizational wrongdoing: Key perspectives and new directions* (pp. 141–175). Cambridge, UK: Cambridge University Press.

Myles, J. (1988). The expanding middle: Some Canadian evidence on the deskilling debate. *Canadian Review of Sociology and Anthropology, 25*(3), 335–364. doi:10.1111/j.1755-618X.1988.tb00109.x.

Nakhaie, M. R., & Kazemipur, A. (2013). Social capital, employment and occupational status of the new immigrants in Canada. *Journal of International Migration and Integration, 14*, 419–437.

Nakhaie, R., Lin, X., Guan, J. (2009). Social capital and the myth of minority self-employment: Evidence from Canada. *Journal of Ethnic and Migration Studies, 35*(4), 625–644.

National Indigenous Economic Development Board. (2019). Indigenous economic progress report, 2019. Retrieved from http://www.naedb-cndea.com/wp-content/uploads/2019/06/NIEDB-2019-Indigenous-Economic-Progress-Report.pdf.

Nembhard, J. G. (2014). *Collective courage: A history of African American cooperative economic thought and practice*. Philadelphia, PA: Pennsylvania State University Press.

Nettleton, S. (1992). *Power, pain, and dentistry*. Buckingham, UK: Open University Press.

Neysmith, S., & Reitsma-Street, M. (2000). Valuing unpaid work in the third sector: The case of community resource centres. *Canadian Public Policy, 26*(3), 331–346.

Ng, E. S. W., & Law, A. (2014). Keeping up! Older workers' adaptation in the workplace after age 55. *Canadian Journal on Aging, 33*(1), 1–14.

NHS (National Health Service). (2020). Overview: Repetitive strain injury. Retrieved from https://www.nhs.uk/conditions/repetitive-strain-injury-rsi.

Nichols, L., Etemadi, T., & Tyyskä, V. (2018). Time poverty of Pakistani immigrant women in Toronto. *South Asian Diaspora, 10*(1), 31–44.

Nickson, D., Price, R., Baxter-Reid, H., & Hurrell, S. A. (2017). Skill requirements in retail work: The case of high-end fashion retailing. *Work, Employment and Society, 31*(4), 692–708. doi:10.1177/0950017016672791.

Noonan, M. C., & Corcoran, M. E. (2004). The mommy track and partnership: Temporary delay or dead end? *The Annals of the American Academy of Political and Social Science, 596*(1), 130–50. doi:10.1177/0002716204268773.

NORC (National Opinion Research Center). 2007. Job satisfaction in the United States. Retrieved from https://www-news.uchicago.edu/releases/07/pdf/070417.jobs.pdf.

Nowrouzi-Kia, B., Baig, A., Li, A., Casole, J., & Chai, E. (2019). Occupational injury trends in the Canadian workforce: An examination of the Canadian community health survey. *International Journal of Critical Illness & Injury Science, 9*(1), 29–35.

NSWP. (n.d.). The needs and rights of trans sex workers. Global Network of Sex Work Projects. Retrieved from https://www.nswp.org/sites/nswp.org/files/Trans%20SWs.pdf.

O'Donnell, S., & Perley, D. (2016). Toward a sociology of the reconciliation of conflicting desires. *Canadian Review of Sociology, 53*(4), 474–481.

OECD. (2006). *Live longer, work longer*. Paris, France. soi:10.1787/9789264035881-en.

Oesch, D., & Piccitto, G. (2019). The polarization myth: Occupational upgrading in Germany, Spain, Sweden, and the UK, 1992–2015. *Work and Occupations, 46*(4), 441–469. doi:10.1177/0730888419860880.

Ogbonna, E., & Harris, L.C. (2004). Work intensification and emotional labour among UK university lecturers: An exploratory study. *Organization*

Studies, 25(7), 1185–1203. Retrieved from https://doi.org/10.1177/0170840604046315.

Olakivi, A., & Wrede, S. (2019). Early career doctors and in/justice in work: The invisibility of gender in a "male" profession. In M. Choroszewicz and T. L. Adams (Eds), *Gender, age, and inequality in the professions* (pp. 25–40). New York. NY: Routledge.

Omi, M., & Winant, H. (1994). *Racial formation in the United States: From the 1960s to the 1990s* (2nd ed.). New York, NY: Routledge.

O'Neill, L. (2015). Regulating hospital social workers and nurses: Propping up an "efficient" lean health care system. *Studies in Political Economy, 95*, 115–136.

Ontario Human Rights Commission. (2012). Racial harassment: Know your rights [Brochure]. Retrieved from http://www.ohrc.on.ca/sites/default/files/Racial%20harassment_English_accessible.pdf.

Ontario Human Rights Commission. (2019a). What is "discrimination"? Retrieved from http://www.ohrc.on.ca/en/iii-principles-and-concepts/2-what-discrimination.

Ontario Human Rights Commission. (2019b). Human rights in Ontario. Retrieved from http://www.ohrc.on.ca/en.

Ontario Human Rights Commission. (2019c). Sexual and gender-based harassment. Retrieved from http://www.ohrc.on.ca/en/policy-preventing-sexual-and-gender-based-harassment-0.

Ontario Human Rights Commission. (2020). Employment. Retrieved from http://www.ohrc.on.ca/en/human-rights-and-family-ontario/employment.

Ontario Ministry of Labour, Training, and Skills Development. (2016). New and young workers. Retrieved from https://www.labour.gov.on.ca/english/hs/sawo/pubs/fs_youngworkers.php.

Ontario Pay Equity Commission. (2019). What is pay equity? Retrieved from http://www.payequity.gov.on.ca/en/AboutUs/Pages/the_act.aspx.

Oreopoulos, P. (2011). Why do skilled immigrants struggle in the labor market? A field experiment with thirteen thousand resumes. *American Economic Journal: Economic Policy, 3*(4), 148–171. doi:10.1257/pol.3.4.148.

Overmars, D. (2019). *Wellbeing in the workplace among Indigenous people: An enhanced critical incident study.* PhD dissertation, University of British Columbia.

Oxford English Dictionary. (2020a). *Expertise.* Oxford University Press.

Oxford English Dictionary. (2020b). *Globalization.* Oxford University Press.

Oxford English Dictionary. (2020c). *Knowledge.* Oxford University Press.

Oxford English Dictionary. (2020d). *Skill.* Oxford University Press.

Oxford English Dictionary. (2020e). *Work.* Oxford University Press.

Papp, K. (2003). "Voluntarily put themselves in harm's way": The "bait and switch" of safety training in the construction industry. *Research in the Sociology of Work, 12*, 197–227. doi:10.1016/S0277-2833(03)12008-0.

Park, J. (2018). Overqualification among Aboriginal workers in Canada. *International Indigenous Policy Journal, 9*(1). Retrieved from https://doi.org/10.18584/iipj.2018.9.1.2.

Pastore, F. (2018). Why is youth unemployment so high and different across countries? *I.Z.A. World of Labor.* doi:10.15185/izawol.420.

Patrias, C. (2016). More menial than housemaids? Racialized and gendered labour in the fruit and vegetable industry of Canada's Niagara region, 1880–1945. *Labour/Le Travail, 78*(Fall), 69–104. doi:10.1353/llt.2016.0053.

Pavalko, E. K., Mossakowski, K. N., & Hamilton, V. J. (2003). Does perceived discrimination affect health? Longitudinal relationships between work discrimination and women's physical and emotional health. *Journal of Health and Social Behavior, 44*(1), 18–33.

Pelletier, R., Patterson, M., & Moyser, M. (2019). The gender wage gap in Canada: 1998 to 2018. *Labour Statistics: Research Papers.* Statistics Canada Catalogue no. 75-004-M. Retrieved from https://www150.statcan.gc.ca/n1/pub/75-004-m/75-004-m2019004-eng.htm.

Pendakur, K., & Pendakur, R. (2011). Aboriginal income disparity in Canada. *Canadian Public Policy, 37*(1), 61–83. doi:10.3138/cpp.37.1.61.

Perkel, C. (2020, 21 Feb.). Parts of prostitution law found unconstitutional. *Toronto Star.* Retrieved from https://www.thestar.com/news/canada/2020/02/21/parts-of-prostitution-law-found-unconstitutional-ontario-judge-rules.html.

Peters, S. M., Kessi, S., Boonzaier, F. (2019). Narrative identity: The construction of dignified masculinities in Black male sex workers' narratives. *Social Dynamics, 45*(3), 425–441. doi:10.1080/02533952.2019.1668622.

Pettersen, L. (2019). Why artificial intelligence will not outsmart complex knowledge work. *Work, Employment and Society, 33*(6), 1058–1067.

Pfeffer, C. A. (2010). "Women's Work"? Women partners of transgender men doing housework and emotion work. *Journal of Marriage and the Family, 72*, 165–183.

Pfeffer, J., & Salancik, G. R. (2003). *The external control of organizations: A resource dependence perspective.* Stanford, CA: Stanford Business Books.

Pierce, J. 1995. *Gender trials: Emotional lives in contemporary law firms.* Berkeley, CA: University of California Press.

Pierson, R. R. (1986). *"They're still women after all": The Second World War and Canadian womanhood.* Toronto, ON: McClelland and Stewart.

Pinto, R. (2020, 4 Sept.). Better job protection needed for personal support workers. *New Canadian Media.*

Retrieved from https://newcanadianmedia.ca/better-job-protection-needed-for-personal-support-workers.

Plan International. (2019). Youth unemployment: The facts. Retrieved from https://plan-international.org/eu/youth-unemployment-facts.

Plecher, H. (2019). Distribution of the workforce across economic sectors in Canada 2019. Retrieved from https://www.statista.com/statistics/271244/distribution-of-the-workforce-across-economic-sectors-in-canada.

Podruchny, C. (2006). *Making the voyageur world: Travellers and traders in the North American fur trade.* Toronto, ON: University of Toronto Press.

Posthuma, R., & Campion, M. (2009). Age stereotypes in the workplace: Common stereotypes, moderators, and future research directions. *Journal of Management, 35*, 158–188.

Power, N., & Norman, M. (2019). Re-inscribing gender relations through employment-related geographical mobility: The case of Newfoundland youth in resource extraction. *Canadian Journal of Sociology, 44*(3), 283–308.

Preibisch, K., & Hennebry, J. (2011). Temporary migration, chronic effects: The health of international migrant workers in Canada. *CMA Journal, 183*(9), 1033–1038. Retrieved from https://doi.org/10.1503/cmaj.090736.

Press, G. (2019, 15 July). Is AI going to be a jobs killer? New *Reports about the Future of Work. Forbes.* Retrieved from https://www.forbes.com/sites/gilpress/2019/07/15/is-ai-going-to-be-a-jobs-killer-new-reports-about-the-future-of-work/#4beabe8afb24.

Prevent Occupational Disease. (2019). Diseases. Retrieved from https://www.preventoccdisease.ca/en/diseases.html.

Price, R. (2016), Controlling routine front line service workers: An Australian retail supermarket case. *Work, Employment and Society, 30*(6), 915–931.

Priola, V., & Lasio, D. (2018). The organisation of sexuality and the sexuality of organisation: A genealogical analysis of sexual "inclusive exclusion" at work. *The Interdisciplinary Journal of Organization, Theory and Society, 25*(6), 732–754.

Prus, R. (2003). Ancient forerunners. In L. T. Reynolds & N. J. Herman-Kinney (Eds), *Handbook of symbolic interactionism* (pp. 19–38). Walnut Creek, CA: AltaMira Press.

Pudrovska, T., & Karraker, A. (2014). Gender, job authority, and depression. *Journal of Health and Social Behaviour, 55*(4), 424–441.

Pullman, A. (2018). Gendered pathways from school to work: The association between field of study and non-standard employment outcomes in Canada. *Research in Social Stratification and Mobility, 58*, 44–53.

Purkayastha, B. (2005). Skilled migration and cumulative disadvantage: The case of highly qualified Asian Indian immigrant women in the US. *Geoforum, 36*(2), 181–196. doi:10.1016/j.geoforum.2003.11.006.

Qian, Y., & Fuller, S. (2020). COVID-19 and the gender employment gap among parents of young children. *Canadian Public Policy, 46*(S2), S89-S101.

Quadlin, N. (2018). The mark of a woman's record: Gender and academic performance in hiring. *American Sociological Review, 83*(2), 331–360. doi:10.1177/0003122418762291.

Raguparan, M. (2017). "If I'm gonna hack capitalism": Racialized and Indigenous Canadian sex workers' experiences within the neo-liberal market economy. *Women's Studies International Forum, 60*, 69–76.

Ravanera, Z., Fernando, R., & Burch, T. K. (2003). Early life transitions of Canadian youth: Effects of family transformation and community characteristics. *Canadian Studies in Population, 30*(2), 327–353.

Reitz, J. (2001). Immigrant skill utilization in the Canadian labour market: Implications of human capital research. *Journal of International Migration and Integration, 2*(3), 347–378. doi:10.1007/s12134-001-1004-1.

Reskin, B., & Cassirer, N. (1996). Occupational segregation by gender, race and ethnicity. *Sociological Focus, 29*(3), 231–243. doi:10.1080/00380237.1996.10570642.

Reskin, B. F., & Maroto, M. L. (2011). What trends? Whose choices? Comment on England. *Gender & Society, 25*(1), 81–87. doi:10.1177/0891243210390935.

Reskin, B. F., & Roos, P. A. (1990). *Job queues, gender queues: Explaining women's inroads into male occupations.* Philadelphia, PA: Temple University Press.

Reynolds, L. T. (2003) Intellectual precursors. In L. T. Reynolds & N. J. Herman-Kinney (Eds), *Handbook of symbolic interactionism* (pp. 39–58). Walnut Creek, CA: AltaMira Press.

Rhnima, A., Wils, T., Pousa, C., & Frigon, M. (2014). Work-family conflict and intention to leave in the field of health. *Relations industrielles, 69*(3), 477.

Richardson, B., Webb, J., Webber, L., & Smith, K. (2013). Age discrimination in the evaluation of job applicants. *Journal of Applied Social Psychology, 43*, 35–44.

Richardson, D. (1993). *Women, motherhood and childrearing.* London, UK: St Martin's Press.

Richman, J. A., Rospenda, K. M., Nawyn, S. J., Flaherty, J. A., Fendrich, M., Drum, M. L., & Johnson, T. P. (1999). Sexual harassment and generalized workplace abuse among university employees: Prevalence and mental health correlates. *American Journal of Public Health, 89*(3), 358–363. doi:10.2105/AJPH.89.3.358.

Ridgeway, C. (2001). Gender, status, and leadership. *Journal of Social Issues, 57*, 637–655.

Rinehart, J. W. (2001). *The tyranny of work: Alienation and the labour process* (4th ed.). Toronto, ON: Harcourt Canada.

Rinehart, J., Huxley, C., and Robertson, D. (1997). *Just another car factory? Lean production and its discontents.* Ithaca, NY: ILR Press.

Risman, B. J. (2009). From doing to undoing: Gender as we know it. *Gender & Society, 23*(1), 81–84. doi:10.1177/0891243208326874.

Ritzer, G. (1996). *The McDonaldization of society: An investigation into the changing character of contemporary social life* (rev. ed.). Thousand Oaks, CA: Pine Forge Press.

Ritzer, G. (2015). Prosumer capitalism. *The Sociological Quarterly, 56*, 413–445.

Ritzer, G., & Walczak, D. (1988). Rationalization and the deprofessionalization of physicians. *Social Forces, 67*(1), 1–22. doi:10.2307/2579098.

Rivera, L. (2012). Hiring as cultural matching. *American Sociological Review, 77*(6), 999–1022.

Roberts, L. M., & McCluney, C. L. (2020, 17 June). Working from home while Black. *Harvard Business Review.* Retrieved from https://hbr.org/2020/06/working-from-home-while-black.

Robinson, A. M., & Smallman, C. (2006). The contemporary British workplace: A safer and healthier place? *Work, Employment and Society, 20*(1), 87–107.

Roscigno, V. J., & Hodson, R. (2004). The organization and social foundations of worker resistance. *American Sociological Review, 69*(1), 1–26.

Roscigno, V. J., Hodson, R., & Lopez, S. H. (2009). Workplace incivilities: The role of interest conflicts, social closure and organizational chaos. *Work, Employment and Society, 23*(4), 747–773. doi:10.1177/0950017009344875.

Rospenda, K. M., & Richman, J. A. (2004). The factor structure of generalized workplace harassment. *Violence and Victims, 19*(2), 221–238. doi:10.1891/088667004780927963.

Rospenda, K.M., Richman, J.A., Ehmke, J.L.Z., & Zlatoper, K.W. (2005). Is workplace harassment hazardous to your health? *Journal of Business and Psychology*, 20(1), 95-110. DOI: 10.1007/s10869-005-6992-y.

Rospenda, K. M., Richman, J. A., & Nawyn, S. J. (1998). Doing power: The confluence of gender, race, and class in contrapower sexual harassment. *Gender & Society, 12*(1), 40–60. doi:10.1177/089124398012001003.

Ross, C. E., & Mirowsky, J. (1995). Does employment affect health? *Journal of Health and Social Behavior, 36*(3), 230–243.

Rothman, R. A. (1998). *Working: Sociological perspectives* (2nd ed.). Upper Saddle River, NJ: Prentice-Hall.

Rotolo, T., & Wilson, J. (2007). Sex segregation in volunteer work. *The Sociological Quarterly, 48*(3), 559–585. doi:10.1111/j.1533-8525.2007.00089.x.

Roy, D. F. (1959). "Banana time": Job satisfaction and informal interaction. *Human Organization, 18*(4), 158–168.

Rushton, L. (2017). The global burden of occupational disease. *Current Environmental Health Reports, 4*(3), 340–348. doi:10.1007/s40572-017-0151-2.

Ryan, A. M., & Wessel, J. L. (2012). Sexual orientation harassment in the workplace: When do observers intervene? *Journal of Organizational Behaviour, 33*(4), 488–511. doi:10.1002/job.765.

Ryan, M. (1984). *Cradle of the middle class.* Cambridge, UK: Cambridge University Press.

Saint-Cyr, Y. (2019, 13 June). Workplace culture that includes racism is very costly for employer. *Slaw: Canada's online legal magazine.* Retrieved from http://www.slaw.ca.

Salzinger, L. (2003). *Genders in production: Making workers in Mexico's global factories.* Berkeley, CA: University of California Press.

Sandefur, R. L. (2015). Elements of professional expertise: Understanding relational and substantive expertise through lawyers' impact. *American Sociological Review, 80*(5), 909–933. doi:10.1177/0003122415601157.

Sangster, J. (2010). *Transforming labour: Women and work in post-war Canada.* Toronto, ON: University of Toronto Press.

Sawchuk, P. (2013). *Contested learning in welfare work: A study of mind, political economy and the labour process.* New York, NY: Cambridge University Press.

Sawchuk, P.H. (2006). "Use-value" and the rethinking of skills, learning and the labour process. *Journal of Industrial Relations*, 58(5), 593–617.

Schein, E. H. (1993). *Organizational culture and leadership* (2nd ed.). San Francisco, CA: Jossey-Bass.

Schieman, S. (2013). Job-related resources and the pressures of working life. *Social Science Research, 42*, 271–282.

Schieman, S., Kurashina Whitestone, Y., & Van Gundy, K. (2006). The nature of work and the stress of higher status. *Journal of Health and Social Behavior, 47*(3), 242–257.

Schieman, S., Taylor, C. J., Narisada, A., & Pudrovska, T. (2020). Underpaid boss: Gender, job authority, and the association between under-reward and depression. *Work and Occupations, 47*(1), 44–82.

Schneider, K. T., Tomaka, J., & Palacios, R. (2001). Women's cognitive, affective, and physiological reactions to a male coworker's sexist behaviour. *Journal of Applied Social Psychology, 31*(10), 1995–2018. doi:10.1111/j.1559–1816.2001.tb00161.x.

Schor, J. B., & Attwood-Charles, W. (2017). The "sharing" economy: Labor, inequality, and social connection on for-profit platforms. *Sociology Compass, 11*(8). doi:10.1111/soc4.12493.

Selznick, P. (1948). Foundations of the theory of organization. *American Sociological Review, 13*(1), 25–35. doi:10.2307/2086752.

Semali, L. M., & Kincheloe, J. L. (1999). What is Indigenous knowledge and why should we study it? In L. Semali, L. M. Semaliand, and Kincheloe, K. L. (Eds), *What is Indigenous knowledge? Voices from the academy* (pp. 3–58). Falmer Press.

Seneviratne, P. (2019). Estranged labour on the global assembly line? Sewing-girls of post-colonial garment factories in Sri Lanka. *Journal of International Women's Studies, 20*(2), 151–165.

Sennett, R. (1998). *The corrosion of character.* New York, NY: W.W. Norton.

Sennett, R. (2008). *The craftsman.* New Haven, CT: Yale University Press.

Sethi, B. (2020, 2 Sept). Personal support workers are the backbone of health care but the bottom of the power structure. *The Conversation.* Retrieved from https://theconversation.com/personal-support-workers-are-the-backbone-of-health-care-but-the-bottom-of-the-power-structure-144648.

Settersten, R. A. & Ray, B. (2010). What's going on with young people today? The long and twisting path to adulthood. *The Future of Children, 20*(1), 19–41.

Settersten, R.A., et al. (2020). Understanding the effects of COVID-19 through a life course lens. *Advances in Life Course Research, 45.* Retrieved from https://doi.org/10.1016/j.alcr.2020.100360.

Sev'er, A. (1999). Sexual harassment: Where we were, where we are and prospects for the new millennium. *Canadian Review of Sociology and Anthropology, 36*(4), 469–497. doi:10.1111/j.1755-618X.1999.tb00960.x.

Sewell, G., & Wilkinson, B. (1992). "Someone to watch over me": Surveillance, discipline and the just-in-time labour process. *Sociology, 26*(2), 271–289. doi:10.1177/0038038592026002009.

Shafer, K., Scheibling, C., & Milkie, M. A. (2020). The division of domestic labour before and during the COVID-19 pandemic in Canada: Stagnation versus shifts in fathers' contributions. *Canadian Review of Sociology, 57*(4), 523–549.

Shaffir, W., & Pawluch, D. (2003). Occupations and professions. In L. T. Reynolds and N. J. Herman-Kinney (Eds), *Handbook of symbolic interactionism* (pp. 893–913). Walnut Creek, CA: AltaMira Press.

Shanahan, M.J., & Macmillan, R. (2008). *Biography and the sociological imagination: Contexts and contingencies.* New York, NY: W. W. Norton.

Sharp, A. (2020, 4 Sept.). Canada's youth miss out on much of country's August job gains. *Canada's National Observer.* Retrieved from https://www.nationalobserver.com/2020/09/04/news/canadas-youth-miss-out-much-countrys-august-job-gains.

Shaw, E., Hegewisch, A., & Hess, C. (2018). Sexual harassment and assault at work: Understanding the costs. Retrieved from Institute for Women's Policy Research website: https://iwpr.org/wp-content/uploads/2020/09/IWPR-sexual-harassment-brief_FINAL.pdf.

Shaw, L.R., Chan, F., & McMahon, B.T. (2012). Intersectionality and disability harassment: The interactive effects of disability, race, age, and gender. *Rehabilitation Counselling Bulletin, 55,* 82–91. Doi.10:1177/0034355211431167.

Sheldon, M. (2020, 13 April). "It's really lifesaving": From getting groceries to babysitting, "caremongering" brings communities together. *CBC News.* Retrieved from https://www.cbc.ca/news/canada/toronto/COVID-19-caremongering-1.5518092.

Sherman, R. (2007). *Class acts: Service and inequality in luxury hotels.* Berkeley, CA: University of California Press.

Shi, D. (2020, 28 Aug.). One thing that the pandemic could be changing? Meeting lengths. *Fast Company.* Retrieved from https://www.fastcompany.com/90543500/one-thing-that-the-pandemic-could-be-changing-meeting-lengths?partner=rss&utm_source=rss&utm_medium=feed&utm_campaign=rss+fastcompany&utm_content=rss.

Shier, M., Graham, J. R., & Jones, M. E. (2009). Barriers to employment as experienced by disabled people: A qualitative analysis of Calgary and Regina, Canada. *Disability & Society, 24*(1), 63–75. doi:10.1080/09687590802535485.

Shih, J. (2002). " . . . Yeah, I could hire this one, but I know it's gonna be a problem": How race, nativity, and gender affect employers' perceptions of the manageability of job seekers. *Ethnic and Racial Studies, 25*(1), 99–119. doi:10.1080/01419870120112076.

Shuey, K. M., Gordon, C., & McMullin, J. A. (2018). "It's the lack of structure that's causing the problem": Managerial competence, the treatment of workers, and job stress in precarious firms. *Social Currents, 5*(3), 264–282. Retrieved from https://doi.org/10.1177/2329496517734572.

Shuey, K. M., & Jovic, E. (2013). Disability accommodation in nonstandard and precarious employment arrangements. *Work and Occupations, 40*(2), 174–205.

Shuey, K. M., & Willson, A. E. (2019). Trajectories of work disability and economic insecurity approaching retirement. *The Journals of Gerontology: Series B, 74*(7), 1200–1210. doi:10.1093/geronb/gbx096.

Siebert, S., & Wilson, F. (2013). All work and no play: Consequences of unpaid work in the creative industries. *Work, Employment and Society, 27*(4), 711–721.

Silver, M. P. (2019). The unbearable lightness of being retired. *Canadian Journal on Aging, 38*(1), 21–34.

Smith, A. (2000). *Wealth of nations.* London, UK: Penguin Random House.

Smith, D. (2000). *Consulted to death.* Winnipeg, MB: Arbeiter Ring.

Smith, D. E. (1990). *The conceptual practices of power: A feminist sociology of knowledge*. Toronto, ON: University of Toronto Press.

Smith, D. E. (1996). The relations of ruling: A feminist inquiry. *Studies in Cultures, Organizations and Societies*, *2*(2), 171–190. doi:10.1080/10245289608523475.

Smith, D. E. (2005). *Institutional ethnography: A sociology for people*. Toronto, ON: AltaMira Press.

Smith, R. A. (2005). Do the determinants of promotion differ for white men versus women and minorities? An exploration of intersectionalism through sponsored and contest mobility processes. *The American Behavioral Scientist*, *48*(9), 1157–1181. doi:10.1177/0002764205274814.

Snider, L. (2001). Crimes against capital: Discovering theft of time. *Social Justice*, *28*(3), 105–120.

Sommer, R., Schlanger, D., Hackman, R., & Smith, S. (1984). Consumer cooperatives and worker collectives: A comparison. *Sociological Perspectives*, *27*(2), 139–157. doi:10.2307/1389015.

Spencer, D. (2017). Work in and beyond the Second Machine Age: The politics of production and digital technologies. *Work, Employment & Society*, *31*(1), 142–152.

Spenner, K. I. (1983). Deciphering Prometheus: Temporal change in the skill level of work. *American Sociological Review*, *48*, 824–837.

Sprouse, M. (Ed.). (1992). *Sabotage in the American workplace: Anecdotes of dissatisfaction, mischief and revenge*. San Francisco, CA: Pressure Drop Press.

St Denis, X. (2020). Sociodemographic determinants of occupational risks of exposure to COVID-19 in Canada. *Canadian Review of Sociology*, *57*(3), 399–453.

St-Onge, N. (2016). "He was neither a soldier nor a slave: He was under the control of no man": Kahnawake Mohawks in the northwest fur trade, 1790–1850. *Canadian Journal of History/Annales canadiennes d'histoire*, *51*(1), 1–32. doi:10.3138/cjh.ach.51.1.001.

Stanford, J. (2020, 5 March). Protecting workers is key to protecting public health. *Toronto Star*. Retrieved from https://www.thestar.com/business/2020/03/05/protecting-workers-is-key-to-protecting-public-health.html.

Stasiulis, D., & Bakan, A.B. (1997). Negotiating citizenship: The case of foreign domestic workers in Canada. *Feminist Review*, *57*(1), 112–139.

Statistics Canada. (2015). Unionization rates falling. *Canadian Megatrends*. Statistics Canada Catalogue no. 11-630-X. Retrieved from https://www150.statcan.gc.ca/n1/pub/11-630-x/11-630-x2015005-eng.htm; https://www150.statcan.gc.ca/n1/en/pub/11-630-x/11-630-x2015005-eng.pdf?st=ynp99XO1.

Statistics Canada (2017, 16 March). Aboriginal people and the labour market. *The Daily*. Retrieved from https://www150.statcan.gc.ca/n1/daily-quotidien/170316/dq170316d-eng.htm.

Statistics Canada. (2018a). *Occupation—National Occupational Classification (NOC) 2016 (691), Employment Income Statistics (3), Highest Certificate, Diploma or Degree (7), Visible Minority (15), Work Activity During the Reference Year (4), Age (4D) and Sex (3) for the Population Aged 15 Years and Over Who Worked in 2015 and Reported Employment Income in 2015, in Private Households of Canada, Provinces and Territories and Census Metropolitan Areas, 2016 Census—25% Sample Data*. Catalogue no. 98-400-X2016356, [Table]. Retrieved from https://www12.statcan.gc.ca/census-recensement/2016/dp-pd/dt-td/Rp-eng.cfm?LANG=E&APATH=3&DETAIL=0&DIM=0&FL=A&FREE=0&GC=0&GID=0&GK=0&GRP=1&PID=112125&PRID=10&PTYPE=109445&S=0&SHOWALL=0&SUB=0&Temporal=2017&THEME=124&VID=0&VNAMEE=&VNAMEF=.

Statistics Canada. (2018b). Employment rates and unemployment rates by province. Retrieved from https://www150.statcan.gc.ca/t1/tbl1/en/tv.action?pid=1410028703.

Statistics Canada. (2018c). Employment and unemployment rates by education and gender. Retrieved from https://www150.statcan.gc.ca/t1/tbl1/en/tv.action?pid=1410002001&pickMembers%5B0%5D=1.1&pickMembers%5B1%5D=2.10&pickMembers%5B2%5D=4.1&pickMembers%5B3%5D=5.3.

Statistics Canada. (2018d). Labour force characteristics of immigrants by sex and age group, annual. Retrieved from https://www150.statcan.gc.ca/t1/tbl1/en/tv.action?pid=1410008501.

Statistics Canada. (2018e). The underground economy in Canada, 2016. Retrieved from https://www150.statcan.gc.ca/n1/daily-quotidien/181012/dq181012a-eng.htm.

Statistics Canada. (2018f). Temporary employment among full-time employees. Retrieved from https://www150.statcan.gc.ca/n1/pub/11-631-x/11-631-x2018001-eng.htm.

Statistics Canada. (2018g). Canadian youth and full-time work: A slower transition. Retrieved from https://www150.statcan.gc.ca/n1/pub/11-630-x/11-630-x2017004-eng.htm.

Statistics Canada. (2018h). A portrait of Canadian youth: Chart 22. Retrieved from https://www150.statcan.gc.ca/n1/pub/11-631-x/11-631-x2018001-eng.htm.

Statistics Canada. (2019a). *Occupation—National Occupational Classification (NOC) 2016 (693A), Class of Worker (5A), Labour Force Status (3), Age (13A) and Sex (3) for the Labour Force Aged 15 Years and Over in Private Households of Canada, Provinces and Territories, Census Metropolitan Areas and Census Agglomerations, 2016 Census—25% Sample Data*. Catalogue no. 98-400-X2016294, [Table]. Retrieved from https://www12.statcan.gc.ca/census-recensement/2016/dp-pd/dt-td/Rp-eng.cfm?LANG=E&APATH=

3&DETAIL=0&DIM=0&FL=A&FREE=0&GC=0&GID=0&GK=0&GRP=1&PID=111856&PRID=10&PTYPE=109445&S=0&SHOWALL=0&SUB=0&Temporal=2017&THEME=124&VID=0&VNAMEE=&VNAMEF=.

Statistics Canada. (2019b). Table 14-10-0299-01 Usual hours worked by occupation, annual [Table]. Retrieved from CANSIM database: https://www150.statcan.gc.ca/t1/tbl1/en/tv.action?pid=1410029901.

Statistics Canada. (2019c). Temporary employment in Canada. Retrieved from https://www150.statcan.gc.ca/n1/daily-quotidien/190514/dq190514b-eng.htm.

Statistics Canada. (2019d, 7 May). Study: Representation of women on boards of directors, 2016. *The Daily*. Retrieved from https://www150.statcan.gc.ca/n1/daily-quotidien/190507/dq190507a-eng.htm.

Statistics Canada. (2019e). Measuring the gig economy in Canada using administrative data. *The Daily*. Retrieved from https://www150.statcan.gc.ca/n1/daily-quotidien/191216/dq191216d-eng.htm.

Statistics Canada. (2019f). Long commutes to work by car. Retrieved from https://www150.statcan.gc.ca/n1/daily-quotidien/190225/dq190225a-eng.htm.

Statistics Canada. (2020a). Unemployment rates. Retrieved from www.statcan.ca.

Statistics Canada. (2020b). Table 22-10-0111-01 Job satisfaction by age group and sex, Canada, provinces and regions (x 1,000). Retrieved from https://www150.statcan.gc.ca/t1/tbl1/en/tv.action?pid=2210011101.

Statistics Canada. (2020c). Table 14-10-0196-01 Work absence of full-time employees by public and private sector, annual. doi:https://doi.org/10.25318/1410019601-eng.

Statutes of Canada. (1995). Chapter 44: Employment Equity Act. Retrieved from https://laws-lois.justice.gc.ca/eng/acts/E-5.401.

Stecy-Hildebrandt, N., Fuller, S., & Burns, A. (2019). "Bad" jobs in a "good" sector: Examining the employment outcomes of temporary work in the Canadian public sector. *Work, Employment and Society, 33*(4), 560–579.

Stefanovich, O. (2020, 26 June). Supreme Court sides with Uber drivers, opening door to $400M class-action lawsuit. *CBC News*. Retrieved from https://www.cbc.ca/news/politics/stefanovich-supreme-court-uber-class-action-decision-1.5626853.

Steiger, T. L. (1993). Construction skill and skill construction. *Work, Employment and Society, 7*(4), 535–560.

Steinberg, R. J. (1990) Social construction of skill: Gender, power, and comparable worth. *Work and Occupations, 17*(4), 449–482. doi:10.1177/0730888490017004004.

Stelnicki, A.M., Jamshidi, L., Angehrn, A., Hadjistavropoulos, H.D., &Carleton, R.N. (2020). Associations between burnout and mental disorder symptoms among nurses in Canada. *Canadian Journal of Nursing*. https://doi.org/10.1177/0844562120974194.

Stier, H. (2015). The skill-divide in job quality: A cross-national analysis of 28 countries. *Social Science Research, 49*, 70–80. doi:10.1016/j.ssresearch.2014.07.008.

Stokes, A. (2015). The glass runway: How gender and sexuality shape the spotlight in fashion design. *Gender & Society, 29*(2), 219–243.

Stokes, A. (2017). Fashioning gender: The gendered organization of cultural work. *Social Currents, 4*(6), 518–534.

Storm, P., Braedley, S., & Chivers, S. (2017). Gender regimes in Ontario nursing homes: Organization, daily work, and bodies. *Canadian Journal on Aging, 36*(2), 196–208. doi:10.1017/S0714980817000071.

Strassheim, H., & Kettunen, P. (2014). When does evidence-based policy turn into policy-based evidence? Configurations, contexts and mechanisms. *Evidence & Policy: A Journal of Research, Debate and Practice, 10*(2), 259–277. doi:10.1332/174426514X13990433991320.

Strauss, K., & McGrath, S. (2017). Temporary migration, precarious employment and unfree labour relations: Exploring the "continuum of exploitation" in Canada's Temporary Foreign Worker Program. *Geoforum, 78*, 199–208.

Suddaby, R., & Viale, T. (2011). Professionals and field-level change: Institutional work and the professional project. *Current Sociology, 59*(4), 423–442. doi.org/10.1177/0011392111402586.

Sun, S. (2020). Who can access the "good" jobs? Racial disparities in employment among young men who work in paid care. *The Annals of the American Academy of Political and Social Science, 688*, 55–76. https://doi.org/10.1177/0002716219897249.

Susskind, R. (2016). *Tomorrow's lawyers* (2nd ed.). Oxford, UK: Oxford University Press.

Susskind, R., & Susskind, D. (2015). *The future of the professions: How technology will transform the work of human experts*. Oxford, UK: Oxford University Press.

Sutherland, E. (1940). White collar criminality. *American Sociological Review, 5*(1), 1–12.

Sutherland, W., Jarrahi, M. H., Dunn, M., & Nelson, S. B. (2019). Work precarity and gig literacies in online freelancing. *Work, Employment and Society, 34*(3), 457–475.

Takala, J., et al. (2014). Global estimates of the burden of illness at work in 2012. *Journal of Occupational and Environmental Hygiene, 11*(5), 326–337.

Tannock, S. (2001). *Youth at work: The unionized fast-food and grocery workplace*. Philadelphia, PA: Temple University Press.

Tassinari, A., & Maccarrone, V. (2020). Riders on the storm: Workplace solidarity among gig economy couriers in Italy and the UK. *Work, Employment and Society, 34*(1), 35–54.

Taylor, F. W. (1911). *The principles of scientific management*. New York, NY: Harper and Brothers Publishers.

Taylor, T. L. (2018). *Watch me Play: Twitch and the rise of game live streaming.* Princeton, NJ: Princeton University Press.

Teelucksingh, C., & Galabuzi, C.-E. (2007). Working precariously: The impact of race and immigrant status on employment opportunities and outcomes in Canada. In T. Das Gupta, C. E. James, R. C. A. Maaka, G.-E. Galabuzi, & C. Andersen (Eds.), *Race and racialization: Essential readings* (pp. 202–208). Toronto, ON: Canadian Scholars Press.

Tézli, A., & Gauthier, A. H. (2009). Balancing work and family in Canada: An empirical examination of conceptualizations and measurements. *The Canadian Journal of Sociology, 34*(2), 433–461.

Thiel, D. (2012). Builders, bodies and bifurcations: How London construction workers "learn to labour." *Ethnography, 14*(4), 412–430. doi:10.1177/1466138112463656.

Thoits, P. (1995). Stress, coping, and social support processes: Where are we? What next? *Journal of Health and Social Behavior, Extra issue,* 53–79. doi:10.2307/2626957.

Thomas, W. I., & Thomas, D. S. (1928). *The child in America: Behavior problems and programs.* New York, NY: Alfred A. Knopf.

Thomason, T., & Pozzebon, S. (2002). Determinants of firm workplace health and safety and claims management practices. *Industrial and Labour Relations Review, 55*(2), 286–307.

Thompson, A. (2007). The consequences of underreporting workers' compensation claims. *Canadian Medical Association Journal, 176*(3), 343–344. doi:10.1503/cmaj.060953.

Thompson, A., & Bono, B. A. (1993). Work without wages: The motivation for volunteer firefighters. *American Journal of Economics and Sociology, 52*(3), 323–343.

Thompson, E. P. (1967). Time, work-discipline, and industrial capitalism. *Past and Present, 38*(1), 56–97. doi:10.1093/past/38.1.56.

Thompson, G. (2010). *Working in the shadows.* New York: Nation Books.

Thornicroft, K. W. (2016). The uncertain state of mandatory retirement in Canada. *Labor Law Journal, 67*(2), 397–414.

Thornton, P. H., & Ocasio, W. (1999). Institutional logics and the historical contingency of power in organizations: Executive succession in the higher education publishing industry, 1958–1990. *American Journal of Sociology, 105*(3), 801–43. doi:10.1086/210361.

Tilcsik, A. (2011). Pride and prejudice: Employment discrimination against openly gay men in the United States. *American Journal of Sociology, 117*(2), 586–626. doi:10.1086/661653.

Tilcsik, A., Anteby, M., & Knight, C. R. (2015). Concealable stigma and occupational segregation: Toward a theory of gay and lesbian occupations. *Administrative Science Quarterly, 60*(3), 446–81. doi:10.1177/0001839215576401.

Tilly, C., & Tilly, C. (1998). *Work under capitalism.* Boulder, CO: Westview Press.

Tomaskovic-Devey, D. (1993). *Gender and racial inequality at work.* Ithaca, NY: ILR Press.

Tomaskovic-Devey, D., Stainback, K., Taylor, T., Zimmer, C., Robinson, C., & McTague, T. (2006). Documenting desegregation: Segregation in American workplaces by race, ethnicity, and sex, 1966–2003. *American Sociological Review, 71*(4), 565–588. doi:10.1177/000312240607100403.

Topping, A. (2020, 27 May). Working mothers interrupted more often than fathers in lockdown—study. *The Guardian.* Retrieved from https://www.theguardian.com/world/2020/may/27/workingmothers-interrupted-more-often-than-fathers-in-lockdown-study.

Tosh, J. (1999). *A man's place: Masculinity and the middle-class home in Victorian England.* New Haven, CT: Yale University Press.

Trading Economics. (2019a). Canada employment rate. Retrieved from https://tradingeconomics.com/canada/employment-rate.

Trading Economics. (2019b). Canada unemployment rate. Retrieved from https://tradingeconomics.com/canada/unemployment-rate.

Trading Economics. (2020). Canada employment rate. Retrieved from https://tradingeconomics.com/canada/employment-rate.

Trading Economics. (2021). Canada youth unemployment rate. Retrieved from https://tradingeconomics.com/canada/youth-unemployment-rate#:~:text=Youth%20Unemployment%20Rate%20in%20Canada%20averaged%2014.01%20percent%20from%201976,percent%20in%20May%20of%202019.

Tremblay, M., Chênevert, D., & Hébert, A. (2012). Le rôle des conditions de travail dans la satisfaction et la loyauté des infirmières d'agence au Québec. *Relations industrielles, 67*(3), 477–504.

Trice, H. M., & Beyer, J. M. (1993). *The cultures of work organizations.* Englewood Cliffs, NJ: Prentice-Hall.

Trumpener, B. (2020, 31 January). Accounts of sex assaults in B.C. tree planter camps "deeply disturbing." *CBC News.* Retrieved from https://www.cbc.ca/news/canada/british-columbia/tree-planter-camps-sex-assaults-1.5446211.

TRC (Truth and Reconciliation Commission). (2015). *Honouring the truth, reconciling for the future: Summary of the final report.* Retrieved from http://caid.ca/TRCFinExeSum2015.pdf.

Tuck, E. (2009). Suspending damage: A letter to communities. *Harvard Educational Review, 79*(3):409–428.

Tucker, E. (1988). Making the workplace "safe" in capitalism: The enforcement of factory legislation in nineteenth-century Ontario. *Labour/Le Travail, 21*(Spring), 45–85. doi:10.2307/25142939.

Tucker, S., & Keefe, A. (2019). *2019 Report on Work Fatality and Injury Rates in Canada.* University of Regina. Retrieved from https://www.uregina.ca/business/faculty-staff/faculty/file_download/2019-Report-on-Workplace-Fatalities-and-Injuries.pdf.

Turcotte, M. (2020). Results from the 2016 census: Education and labour market integration of Black youth in Canada. Retrieved from https://www150.statcan.gc.ca/n1/pub/75-006-x/2020001/article/00002-eng.htm.

Tyler, M. (2011). Tainted love: From dirty work to "abject" labour in Soho's sex shops. *Human Relations, 64*(11), 1477–1500.

UFCW (United Food and Commercial Workers). (2020). Justice for Uber drivers. Retrieved from http://www.ufcw.ca/index.php?option=com_mcontent&view=indexlist&layout=blog&searchword=uberd&searchphrase=exact&Itemid=2424&lang=en.

UFCW (United Food and Commercial Workers). (2021, 11 March). Uber Canada's unilateral proposal is 'a dangerous proposition' says Uber workers' union. Retrieved from http://www.globenewswire.com/en/news-release/2021/03/11/2191685/0/en/Uber-Canada-s-unilateral-proposal-is-a-dangerous-proposition-says-Uber-workers-union.html.

UNESCO (United Nations Educational, Scientific and Cultural Organization). (2017). Local and Indigenous knowledge systems. Retrieved from http://www.unesco.org/new/en/natural-sciences/priority-areas/links/related-information/what-is-local-and-indigenous-knowledge.

UNICEF. 2019. *Family-friendly policies in rich countries: How Canada compares.* Toronto: UNICEF Canada. Retrieved from https://oneyouth.unicef.ca/sites/default/files/2019-06/UNICEF_ResearchBrief_CanadianCompanion_EN-FINAL_WEB.pdf.

Union Cab Co-op. (2019). About. Retrieved from https://www.unioncab.com/About.

United Nations Office of the Secretary-General's Envoy on Youth. (2016, 25 August). Global youth unemployment is on the rise again [Blog post]. Retrieved from https://www.un.org/youthenvoy/2016/08/global-youth-unemployment-rise.

United Way. (2011). *It's more than poverty: Employment precarity and household wellbeing.* Toronto: United Way. Retrieved from https://www.unitedwaygt.org/document.doc?id=91.

Usalcas, J. (2014). Hours polarization revisited. *Perspectives on Labour and Income.* Statistics Canada Catalogue no. 75-001-X. Retrieved from https://www150.statcan.gc.ca/n1/pub/75-001-x/2008103/article/10534-eng.htm/

Vachon, A. (1962). *Histoire du notariat canadien, 1621–1960.* Québec: Presses de l'Université Laval.

Vallas, S. P. (1990). The concept of skill: A critical review. *Work and Occupations, 17*(4), 379–398. doi:10.1177/0730888490017004001.

Vallas, S. P. (2003). Rediscovering the color line within work organizations. The "knitting of racial groups" revisited. *Work and Occupations, 30*(4), 379–400.

Vallas, S. P., Finlay, W., & Wharton, A. S. (2009). *The sociology of work.* Oxford University Press.

Vallée, G. (2018). L'obligation de disponibilité du salarié au-delà de son temps et de son lieu de travail. *Relations industrielles, 73*(3), 591.

Vallee, K. E. (2018). *Supporting Indigenous students: A critical analysis of the sociocultural context of nursing education.* PhD dissertation, University of Western Ontario. Retrieved from https://ir.lib.uwo.ca/etd/5233.

Van den Broek, D., & Dundon, T. (2012). (Still) up to no good: Reconfiguring worker resistance and misbehaviour in an increasingly unorganized world. *Relations industrielles/Industrial Relations, 67*(1), 97–121.

Vandenbroucke, G. (2018). Married men sit atop the wage ladder. *Economic Synopses* (No. 24). doi:10.20955/es.2018.24.

Vanier Institute. (2009). Family life and work life: An uneasy balance. *Policy Alternatives.* Spring. Retrieved from https://www.policyalternatives.ca/sites/default/files/uploads/publications/National%20Office/2009/04/Family%20Life%20and%20Work%20Life.pdf.

Vaught, C., & Smith, D. L. (1980). Incorporation and mechanical solidarity in an underground coal mine. *Sociology of Work and Occupations, 7*(2), 159–187.

Vaz, E. W. (1984). Institutionalized stealing among big-city taxi-drivers. In A. Whipper (Ed), *The sociology of work* (pp. 75–91). Ottawa, ON: Carleton University Press.

Veen, A., Barratt, T., & Goods, C. (2020). Platform-capital's "app-etite" for control: A labour process analysis of food-delivery work in Australia. *Work, Employment and Society, 34*(3), 388–406.

Veenstra, G. (2013). The gendered nature of discriminatory experiences by race, class, and sexuality: A comparison of intersectionality theory and the subordinate male target hypothesis. *Sex Roles, 68*(11), 646–659. doi:10.1007/s11199-012-0243-2.

Vézina, M., & Crompton, S. (2012). Volunteering in Canada. Statistics Canada. Retrieved from https://www150.statcan.gc.ca/n1/pub/11-008-x/2012001/article/11638-eng.htm.

Visano, L. A. (1987). *This idle trade.* VitaSana Books.

Vosko, L. (2000). *Temporary work: The gendered rise of a precarious employment relationship.* Toronto, ON: University of Toronto Press.

Vosko, L. (2005). *Precarious employment: Understanding labour market insecurity in Canada.* Montreal, QC, and Kingston, ON: McGill-Queen's University Press.

Vowel, C. (2016). *Indigenous writes: A guide to First Nations, Métis, and Inuit issues in Canada*. Winnipeg, MB: HighWater Press.

Voyageur, C. (2011). Out in the open: Elected female leadership in Canada's First Nations community. *Canadian Review of Sociology, 48*(1), 67–85.

Wacjman, J. (2006). New connections: Social studies of science and technology and studies of work. *Work, Employment and Society, 20*(4), 773–786.

Waite, S., & Denier, N. (2015). Gay pay for straight work: Mechanisms generating disadvantage. *Gender & Society, 29*(4), 561–588. Retrieved from https://doi.org/10.1177/0891243215584761.

Waite, S., & Denier, N. (2016). Self-employment among same-sex and opposite-sex couples in Canada. *Canadian Review of Sociology, 53*(2), 143–175.

Waite, S., & Denier, N. (2020). Somewhere over the rainbow? An LGBT audit study of discrimination in Canada. (Draft paper, used with author's permission).

Waite, S., Pajovic, V., & Denier, N. (2020). Lesbian, gay and bisexual earnings in the Canadian labor market: New evidence from the Canadian community health survey. *Research in Social Stratification and Mobility*, 67. Retrieved from https://doi.org/10.1016/j.rssm.2020.100484.

Walby, K. (2012). *Touching encounters: Sex, work, and male-for-male Internet escorting*. Chicago, IL: University of Chicago Press.

Walby, S. (1986). *Patriarchy at work: Patriarchal and capitalist relations in employment*. Cambridge, UK: Polity Press.

Walker, J., et al. (2020). Ontario First Nations aging study: Overview and report Retrieved from https://laurentian.ca/assets/files/Research/Chairs/First-Nations-Aging-2019.pdf.

Wallace, J. E., & Lemaire, J. (2007). On physician well-being: You'll get by with a little help from your friends. *Social Science & Medicine, 64*(12), 2565–2577.

Walters, M., & Mishel, L. (2003). How unions help all workers. Economic Policy Institute. Retrieved from https://www.epi.org/publication/briefingpapers_bp143.

Wang, Z., & Jing, X. (2018). Job satisfaction among immigrant workers: A review of determinants. *Social Indicators Research, 139*(1), 381–401. doi:10.1007/s11205-017-1708-z.

Waterfield, B., Beagan, B., & Mohamed, T. (2019). "You always remain slightly an outsider": Workplace experiences of academics from working-class or impoverished backgrounds. *Canadian Review of Sociology, 56*(3), 368–388. doi:10.1111/cars.12257.

Wathen, C. N., MacGregor, J. C. D., Tanaka, M., & MacQuarrie, B. J. (2018). The impact of intimate partner violence on the health and work of gender and sexual minorities in Canada. *International Journal of Public Health, 63*(8), 945–955. doi:10.1007/s00038-018-1127-1.

Watts, B. S. J. (2018). *Canadian misbehaving. A quantitative analysis of the factors contributing to perceived frequency of organizational misbehaviour by employees and employers*. PhD dissertation, University of Western Ontario. Retrieved from https://ir.lib.uwo.ca/etd/5879.

Watts, V. (2013). Indigenous place-thought and agency amongst humans and nonhumans (First Woman and Sky Women go on a European World Tour!). *Decolonization: Indigeneity, Education & Society, 2*(1), 20–34.

Weber, M. (1946). Bureaucracy. In H. H. Gerth & C. Wright Mills (Eds. & Trans.), *From Max Weber: Essays in sociology* (pp. 196–44). New York, NY: Oxford University Press.

Weber, M. (1968). *Economy and society: An outline of interpretative sociology* (Vol. 1). New York, NY: Bedminster Press.

Weeden, K. A. (2002). Why do some occupations pay more than others? Social closure and earnings inequality in the United States. *American Journal of Sociology, 108*(1), 55–101.

Weigt, J. (2006). Compromises to carework: The social organization of mothers' experiences in the low-wage labor market after welfare reform. *Social Problems, 53*(3), 332–351.

Weisburd, D., Waring, E., & Chayet, E. F. (2001). *White collar crime and criminal careers*. Cambridge, UK: Cambridge University Press.

Weisshaar, K. (2018). From opt out to blocked out: The challenges for labor market re-entry after family-related employment lapses. *American Sociological Review, 83*(1), 34–60. doi:10.1177/0003122417752355.

West, C., & Zimmerman, D. H. (1987). Doing gender. *Gender & Society, 1*(2), 125–151. doi:10.1177/0891243287001002002.

Wharton, A. S. (1999). The psychosocial consequences of emotional labor. *The Annals of the American Academy of Political and Social Science, 561*(1), 158–176. Retrieved from https://doi.org/10.1177/000271629956100111.

Whitfield, H. A. (2003). Black refugee communities in early nineteenth century Nova Scotia. *Journal of the Royal Nova Scotia Historical Society, 6*, 92–109.

Wilkinson, L. (2008). Labor market transitions of immigrant-born, refugee-born, and Canadian-born youth. *Canadian Review of Sociology/Revue canadienne de sociologie, 45*(2), 151–176.

Williams, C. (2003). "Sky service": The demands of emotional labor in the airline industry. *Gender, Work and Organization, 10*(5), 413–450.

Williams, C. (2006). Disability in the workplace. *Perspectives on Labour and Income, 7*, 16–24.

Williams, C., & Connell, C. (2010). "Looking good and sounding right": Aesthetic labour and social inequality in the retail industry. *Work and Occupations, 37*, 349–377. doi:10.1177/0730888410373744.

Williams, C., & Giuffre, P. (2011). From organizational sexuality to queer organizations: Research on homosexuality and the workplace. *Sociology Compass, 5*(7), 551–563. doi:10.1111/j.1751-9020.2011.00392.x.

Williams, G. (2019). Management millennialism: Designing the new generation of employee. *Work, Employment and Society, 34*(3), 371–387.

Wilson, J., & Musick, M. (1997). Who cares? Toward an integrated theory of volunteer work. *American Sociological Review, 62*, 694–713.

Wilton, R. (2008). Workers with disabilities and the challenges of emotional labour. *Disability and Society, 23*(4), 361–373.

Winder, N. (2020). *Post-secondary education (PSE) Indigenous students' perspectives: Sharing our voices on how we fit into Residential School (RS) history of Canada and the United States using photovoice*. PhD dissertation, University of Western Ontario.

Winks, R. W. (1997). *The Blacks in Canada: A history* (2nd ed.). Montreal, QC: McGill-Queen's University Press.

Wired. (2018, April). AI and the future of work. Retrieved from https://www.wired.com/wiredinsider/2018/04/ai-future-work.

Witteveen, D. (2018). *The trajectory from school to work: A study of life changes of school leavers in the United States, The United Kingdom*, Germany and Sweden. PhD dissertation, City University of New York.

Wong, K. (2020). The improved labour market performance of new immigrants to Canada, 2006–2019. Centre for the Study of Living Standards Research Report. Retrieved from http://www.csls.ca/reports/csls2020-03.pdf.

Wood, A. J., Graham, M., Lehdonvirta, V., & Hjorth, I. (2019a). Good gig, bad gig: Autonomy and algorithmic control in the global gig economy. *Work, Employment and Society, 33*(1), 56–75.

Wood, A. J., Graham, M., Lehdonvirta, V., & Hjorth, I. (2019b). Networked but commodified: The (dis)embeddedness of digital labour in the gig economy. *Sociology, 53*(5), 931–950. doi:10.1177/0038038519828906.

Wood, E. M. (1999). *The origin of capitalism: A longer view*. London, UK: Verso.

WorksafeBC. (2019). Young and new workers. Retrieved from https://www.worksafebc.com/en/health-safety/education-training-certification/young-new-worker.

WorksafeBC. (2020). Occupational diseases. Retrieved from https://www.worksafebc.com/en/claims/report-workplace-injury-illness/types-of-claims/occupational-diseases.

World Economic Forum. (2016). *The future of jobs: Employment, skills and workforce strategy for the fourth industrial revolution*. Global Challenge Insight Report. Retrieved from http://www3.weforum.org/docs/WEF_Future_of_Jobs.pdf.

World Health Organization (WHO). (2020). Occupational and work-related diseases. Retrieved from https://www.who.int/occupational_health/activities/occupational_work_diseases/en.

Wyn, J., Cuervo, H., Crofts, J., & Woodman, D. (2017). Gendered transitions from education to work: The mysterious relationships between the fields of education and work. *Journal of Sociology, 53*(2), 492–506.

Yap, M., Holmes, M., Hannam, C-A., & Cuker, W. (2013). Correlates of career satisfaction in Canada—the immigrants' experience. *International Migration and Integration*. doi:10.1007/s12134-012-0268-y.

Yeung, W-J J., & Yang, Y. (2020). Young adults: An international perspective. *The Annals of the American Academy of Political and Social Science, 688*, 7–19.

Young, M., Montazer, S., & Singh, D. (2020). The consequences of living in childcare deserts: Evidence from Canada. *Canadian Review of Sociology, 57*(4), 550–578.

Yssaad, L., & Ferrao, V. (2019). *Self-employed Canadians: Who and why?* Statistics Canada: Labour Statistics at a Glance. Retrieved from https://www150.statcan.gc.ca/n1/pub/71-222-x/71-222-x2019002-eng.htm.

Yssaad, L., and Fields, A. (2018). The Canadian immigrant labour market: Recent trends from 2006 to 2017. Statistics Canada. Retrieved from https://www150.statcan.gc.ca/n1/pub/71-606-x/71-606-x2018001-eng.htm.

Zarifa, D., Walters, D., & Seward, B. (2015). The earnings and employment outcomes of the 2005 cohort of Canadian postsecondary graduates with disabilities. *The Canadian Review of Sociology, 52*(4), 343–376.

Zeytinoglu, I. U., & Cooke, G. B. (2006). Who is working at weekends? Determinants of regular weekend work in Canada. In J.-Y. Boulin, M. Lallement, J. C. Messenger, & F. Michon (Eds.), *Decent working time: New trends, new issues* (pp. 395–416). Geneva, Switzerland: International Labour Office.

Zeytinoglu, I., Denton, M., Davies, S., Baumann, A., Blythe, J., & Boos, L. (2007). Deteriorated external work environment, heavy workload and nurses' job satisfaction and turnover intention. *Canadian Public Policy, 33*(Supplement), S31-S48.

Zeytinoglu, I. U., Seaton, M. B., Lillevik, W., & Moruz, J. (2005). Working in the margins: Women's experiences of stress and occupational health problems in part-time and casual retail jobs. *Women & Health, 41*(1), 87–107.

Index